# THE SOCIOLOGY OF FAMILY
*An Interdisciplinary Approach*

# The Sociology of Family

*An Interdisciplinary Approach*

Edited by
MAHFOOZ A. KANWAR

LINNET BOOKS • Hamden • Connecticut

Published as a Linnet Book
by The Shoe String Press, Inc.
Hamden, Connecticut 06514
© 1971 by The Shoe String Press, Inc.
ISBN 0–208–01232–X
Library of Congress catalog card number 72–15888
Printed in the United States of America

# Contents

# Preface

This book is intended for use in the Family course offered by
many colleges and universities in their integrative studies, general
education, and interdisciplinary programs, as well as in the departments of sociology and anthropology.

The course dealing with the family and marriage in the departments of sociology and anthropology usually restricts its boundary
to the sociology of family and marriage. In other words, it is organized and taught exclusively by the sociologists or anthropologists
according to the point of view of sociology and anthropology. The
course dealing with the family in the General Education program
is modified and presented inclusively by sociologists and others
according to the diversified approaches to studying the family. This
diversification integrates and harmonizes several disciplines. As part
of the General Education program the course is taught and learned
for its relevance to students' needs and its applicability to their
future life, whether or not they major in sociology or anthropology.
In our view an interdisciplinary view of the family and marriage
shows the most promise of meeting the needs of students. Through
comparative and interdisciplinary methods, students are encouraged
to develop their ability to study critically this area of human behavior. The diversity of family structure and function is also discussed.
Students should be encouraged to relate their own experiences to
others in the seminar or classroom, to the course in general and to
the readings in this book. This should lead to discussions on the
family as a social institution, as a social group, as an agency of social
control, and as an institution for socialization. Knowledge of, and
comparative approaches to, the study of the family itself, and of the
family as a social conservator, as well as a changing phenomenon,
should be expanded in seminar and class discussions.

A few words about the organization of articles in this book are in
order. Because this book is designed for an interdisciplinary course

in the family, we have not limited our selection of articles to sociology; research studies in anthropology and psychology are also represented. This selection is consistent with an interdisciplinary study of the family.

We believe that the book's organization presents a systematic approach to studying the family. The very first and perhaps the most important function of the family is socialization of new members of a society. After a baby is born, fulfillment of his basic needs and his relationship to his mother and his early training with its problems ought to be studied carefully to understand the family. It is said that the family is the very first school for the new member—the baby. Hunger, thirst, comfort, and his attachment to his mother are some of his primary concerns in the early months of his life. Thus, his interaction is mostly limited to his mother. Traditionally, we relate his early interaction with his mother. The chapters on "Breast Feeding" and "Patterns of Attachment Behavior Shown by the Infant in Interaction with his Mother" will develop our understanding of the child and his early upbringing. The child grows and so do his relationships within the family. He extends his "active" membership to his family members beyond his mother. Not only does he take love, care, and attention, but he also returns them. After a certain time, with varying differences in different societies, this extension of his membership is stretched further. He is not only a member of his family now but also of his peer group. His contact with other people is broader than during his early days. With this broader contact problems originate in the field of personality development, the role of learning and playing, and "social and cultural" adjustment. The chapters in the section on *The Family and Early Socialization* enable us to study the process of socialization and the family.

The relationship of the family to other social institutions and other problematic situations, such as the parent-child conflict, changing conceptions in society at large, and their impact on the family and its members, also need special attention. The changing conceptions of love, morality, and obligations (for example) create new circumstances which make it necessary for us to readjust our family relations. The debate whether we should provide sex education for our children at home or at school is a product of our time. Parents still believe that it is their right to have an upper hand in dealing with their children. The younger generation, on the other hand, seems to be in no doubt that our era has created a generation gap that is clearer and more drastic than ever before. The mother still likes to say to her daughter going out on a date, "Have a good time (and) be good." The daughter sometimes takes this advice graciously, sometimes ignores it, and sometimes resents it. She mostly resents the latter part of her mother's advice—"be good." A similar case is the mother's, or both parents' concern for their daughter (or their son for that matter) to come home "before midnight" or "early." Some sons and daughters would resent this. They are now "old enough," "wise enough," and they "know what they are doing" and "what is good or bad for them!" When these things happen, especially with daughters, the parent-youth conflict is usually the result. Chapters on "Love, Morals and the Family," "The Value of Sound Sex Knowledge," "Parent-Child Conflict in Sexual Values," and "The Sociology of Parent-Youth Conflict" provide the reader with an explanation of the conflict between two generations. The explanation is always *a must* for us to understand a situation, and if that situation is a "problem" the explanation helps us to find a solution for it. Part II, *General Family Relations*, introduces the reader to this process.

As we know, human society is not a static group of people; it always undergoes change. The family is still one of the most important institutions and an integral unit of society. It must also experience some change, reformation, and readjustment in its structure and functions. Moreover, scientific advancement and technological development have entailed countless social and other changes. It becomes imperative for us to study the family in relation to social change. "Synopsis and Evaluation of Theories Concerning Family Evolution," "The Family in a Changing Society," "Recent Studies of Change in the Japanese Family," and "Changes in the Colonial and Modern American Family Systems," in the section on *The Family and Social Change*, acquaint the reader with the family system resisting or accepting the social change.

The advanced technology has "blessed" us with a developed and fast means of communication to link us with others. Hence, the family in a society must not be studied without reference to this institution in other societies. We have, therefore, included the family system of as many lands as was possible. The family relations, role expectations, the patterns of courtship and mate selection, marital ceremonies and other customs are quite different in various societies. The countries and areas that are represented in Part IV on *Cross-Cultural Family Systems* are Pakistan, the Philippine Islands, the United States of America (Negro and Hawaiian families), Portugal, Israel (Kibbutz), India, Peru, and Paraguay. The chapter on "Family Stability in Non-European Cultures" presents "the conclusion of special study on the stability of marriage in forty selected Non-

European societies." For research purposes, and for the benefit of readers, we have also included two scales—"A Dating Scale" and "A Familism Scale."

I am grateful to Professor Edmund Vaz of the Sociology Department, University of Waterloo, and Professor Panos Bardis, Department of Sociology, University of Toledo, for their help and encouragement in the organization of this book.

I wish to thank my wife, Shahnaz (a Rajput girl), who helped me set up the chapter on "The Rajput Family System in Pakistan," and for her invaluable help and encouragement throughout this work.

I should like to acknowledge the generous permission of the authors and editors whose articles are included in this book. The articles have been unaltered and unabridged (although they have been completely reset). This means that bibliographical notations and footnotes vary in form: however, I do not believe the variations are such as will interfere with the student's use of such notes. The reader will, of course, note variations too in punctuation and even spelling. But the English language is like the family, full of vitality and changes.

I am grateful to the following for permission to reprint selected articles in this work:

*Psychology Today; Merrill-Palmer Quarterly;* the Journal Press, *The Journal of Genetic Psychology; American Journal of Orthopsychiatry; Journal of Individual Psychology*; The Society for Research in Child Development, Inc., *Child Development*; American Psychological Association, *Journal of Abnormal & Social Psychology; Sexology Magazine*; Society for the Psychological Study of Social Issues, *Journal of Social Issues*; The American Sociological Association; The University of Chicago, *American Journal of Sociology;* Unesco, *International Social Science Journal; Alpha Kappa Deltan; Journal of Negro Education*; Department of Sociology, York University, Ontario; *The Herald Press*, Mennonite Publishing House, Inc.; Department of Anthropology, University of Pittsburgh, *Ethnology*; The American Academy of Political and Social Science, *The Annals*; and the National Council on Family Relations, *Journal of Marriage and the Family*.

Mount Royal College, Calgary, Alberta, must also be included in the list of acknowledgements for its encouragement in this work.

Last, but not least, I acknowledge the typing done by our secretary, Mrs. Joan Frost.

MAHFOOZ A. KANWAR.

# PART I. THE FAMILY AND EARLY SOCIALIZATION

# Breast Feeding

*Niles Newton*

In the 10 years between 1946 and 1956 the number of American mothers who breast fed their newborn babies dropped by almost half. In 1929 in Bristol, England, 77 per cent of three-month-old infants were breast fed; 20 years later, 64 percent of the same age Bristol babies depended upon bottles. It took only five years for the number of breast-fed babies at a French obstetric clinic to drop from nearly 70 per cent to less than 50 per cent.

What has caused this radical change in human behavior? The decrease is far too rapid to be the result of heredity changes. It is too large to be caused by physiological changes short of starvation or widespread, ravaging disease. Instead, the answer seems to lie in psychological factors.

A mother's ability to produce milk for her baby depends upon her own attitude toward breast feeding and toward sex. And her attitude is related to the attitudes of her society. Emotions affect the production of milk through specific psychosomatic mechanisms, several of which have been identified.

The survival of the human race, long before any concept of duty evolved, depended upon the pleasures of two voluntary acts—coitus and breast feeding. Were these acts not so pleasurable that humans sought their repetition, man would have joined the dinosaurs in extinction ages ago.

A woman's body responds similarly to coitus and to lactation. Her uterus contracts, her skin changes measurably and her nipples lengthen and become erect both during suckling and during sexual excitement. Some breast-feeding mothers drip milk more easily than

Reprinted by permission from *Psychology Today* Magazine, June, 1968. Copyright © Communications/Research/Machines/ Inc.

others, possibly due to weaker nipple sphincter muscles. Such women have reported that at times they eject milk during sexual arousal. Breast stimulation alone causes orgasm in some women and during suckling the breast is stimulated extensively. The nipple-erection reflex, which increases nipple length by a centimeter or more, may lead to more efficient nursing.

An aversion to breast feeding appears to be related to a dislike of nudity and of sexuality. E. J. Salber and her associates in Boston worked with American mothers who had never attempted to nurse their babies. The idea of nursing repelled these women, who were embarrassed at the idea of suckling their infants or were too "modest" to nurse. In another study, A. B. Adams, working at Columbia University, interviewed women who were expecting their first child. Both the interviews and tests disclosed that women who said they wished to bottle feed their babies showed significantly more psychosexual disturbances. In a Harvard University Laboratory of Human Development study, R. R. Sears and his colleagues found that mothers who breast fed their infants showed a greater tolerance of masturbation and social sex play in their own children.

Michael Newton and I studied the relation between a woman's own attitude toward breast feeding and her ability to produce milk successfully for her child. I interviewed 91 patients in the maternity wards of the University of Pennsylvania Hospital. Women who refused to suckle their babies, and those who had had premature babies or Caesarean births were excluded from the study. The women were interviewed as soon as possible after delivery, 63 per cent of them within 24 hours and 74 per cent before the baby had been at the breast. Their answers were recorded verbatim and evaluated by two independent judges who knew neither the patient nor her breast-feeding history.

The judges sorted the answers into three categories: positive, doubtful and negative. Positive women expressed a desire or determination to breast feed. Doubtful women expressed mixed feelings, indifference or indecision about breast feeding their children. Judges placed women who talked of giving both breast and bottle from the start in this doubtful category. Negative women preferred bottle feeding, stated they did not like to breast feed, or were noncommittal but mentioned only the negative aspects of breast feeding.

Feeding procedures were the same for all mothers. Nurses brought the babies to their mothers six times each day and left them together for 45 minutes to an hour each time. This permitted the mother to relax with her baby, cuddling him and suckling him as much as four or five hours a day if she so desired.

After their hospital stay the women were divided into successful, unsuccessful and abortive breast feeders. Successful breast feeders produced so much milk that their babies needed no supplementary formula after the fourth day. Unsuccessful breast feeders continued to feed by breast but had to give supplementary formulas after the fourth day. Abortive breast feeders switched their babies entirely to bottles before they left the hospital.

Breast feeding proved to be closely related to what the mother said about her own attitudes toward breast feeding [see table, page 6]. There was also a marked difference in the over-all success of breast feeding and in how the mother's attitude affected her milk production [see table page 8].

In interviewing these mothers I noticed that the desire to breast feed seemed to be associated with other attitudes. I decided to explore these attitudes further in a new group of 123 women in the wards of Jefferson Hospital in Philadelphia. Again what the mother said was written down verbatim. A judge who knew neither the mother nor how she had answered the other questions categorized her comments on each item. Mothers who expressed the most positive attitudes toward breast feeding were found to be quite different from others. They frequently stated that women rather than men have the more satisfying time in life and that labor was easy. Mothers of first babies who strongly wanted to breast feed actually had shorter recorded labors.

Other evidence suggests that maternal behavior and maternal attitude may be related to breast-feeding behavior in women. H. W. Potter of State University of New York College of Medicine at New York City and H. R. Klein of Columbia University College of Medicine studied 25 nursing mothers and babies in a Brooklyn hospital. They scored each mother's "nursing behavior" by observing the way she handled her baby at feeding time. By means of a lengthy interview that centered on questions about doll play in childhood, interest in other people's babies and number of children desired, Potter and Klein also rated each mother on "maternal interest." There was a high correlation between the two measures. Later visits to the homes of 16 mothers showed that all who were rated low on the maternal interest scale had stopped nursing immediately after leaving the hospital. By contrast, all but one of those ranked high on the maternal interest scale continued to nurse their babies.

Michael Newton and I found a similar relation. We recorded the reactions of mothers to the first sight of their babies. Later a different observer, who did not know the first rating, interviewed the mothers and recorded their attitudes toward breast feeding. Mothers who reacted to their babies with visible joy and delight more frequently expressed the desire to breast feed them.

In another study, which I conducted with Dudley Peeler of the University of Mississippi School of Medicine and Carolyn Rawlins, an obstetrician at St. Margaret's Hospital in Hammond, Indiana, an additional difference in the behavior of nursing and non-nursing mothers appeared. An anonymous sheet, requiring only checkmarks to answer, was filled out by 177 mothers whose babies were between one and two months old. It was immediately apparent that college-educated mothers and mothers who had other children practiced breast feeding significantly more than mothers with less education or first-time mothers.

We matched breast-feeding mothers who gave neither formula nor solid food to their babies with mothers of the same educational level and the same number of children but who fed their babies by bottle —with or without solid food. Nursing and non-nursing women did not differ significantly on three measures of maternal behavior, but they did differ, markedly, in their willingness to share a bed with their babies [see illustration, below]. Women who breast feed their children appear willing to disregard current cultural disapproval of

| Maternal behavior | Nursing members of pairs | Non-nursing members of pairs |
|---|---|---|
| Mother sometimes or often sleeps or rests in bed with baby. | 71% | 26% |
| Mother definitely states baby not spanked. | 87% | 95% |
| Mother holds baby ½ hour or more when not eating. | 57% | 62% |
| Mother in different building from baby less than 3 hours daily. | 95% | 86% |

MATERNAL BEHAVIOR. When behaviors of nursing and non-nursing mothers was compared, they differed significantly only in the willingness to share a bed with their babies.

bed-sharing. Close body contact, not merely remaining near enough to watch over the baby, may be the determining factor; nursing mothers did not stay in the same building with their babies significantly more than non-nursing mothers.

Strangely enough, Dudley Peeler and I found a somewhat similar tendency in newly delivered mice. Animal research has interested me in the past few years, since controlled experimentation is the best way of demonstrating cause and effect. Most of my work has concerned mice in labor, but it seemed natural to test mice in the nursing situation.

Surgery was performed on some mice so they could not suckle; these were matched with mice who nursed adoptive young. The nursing and non-nursing mice acted in much the same way on tests but the nursing mice seemed to have a much more intense desire for close contact with the mouse pups. They were willing to cross a charged electric grid time after time to get to the young.

The emotions and behavior of the baby—for example, inefficient sucking—also affect the mother's attempts to breast feed. Mothers sometimes needlessly feel "rejected" by their babies when the cause of the babies' failure to nurse is not emotional in origin. Drugs given to the mother in labor may have a prolonged effect on the baby's ability to suck after birth. The sucking ability of babies, for as long as four days after birth, has been found to vary with the amount of obstetric sedation given the mother. The baby may also refuse the breast because he has been given a supplementary bottle which is easier to suck, or if the mother schedules feedings far apart, thus presenting the child with an overfull breast that temporarily cuts off his air supply.

The responsiveness of the baby may also influence his enjoyment of breast feeding and his cooperation. This responsiveness can be seen clearly in older babies. Their bodies show eagerness and their hands, feet, fingers and toes may move rhythmically, in time with the sucking. Erection of the penis while nursing is common in male babies. After feeding, the baby often relaxes in a manner characteristic of a satisfactorily concluded sexual response. Sensuous enjoyment of breast feeding probably increases the baby's desire to suckle his mother frequently and fully, thus stimulating the secretion of milk.

The individual attitudes of the mother and the baby are not the only influences on breast feeding. Woman's role in life as determined by her culture, education, social class and work, has been repeatedly shown to influence her breast-feeding behavior. In what Toynbee

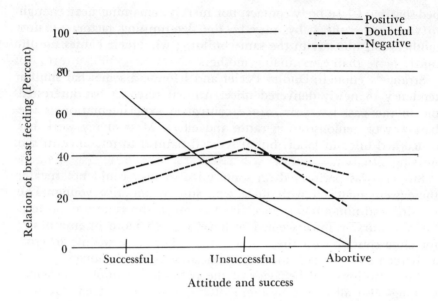

ATTITUDES. The desire to breast feed and successful nursing were closely related.

has called "times of trouble," breast feeding has been popular. Periods of great wealth and luxury in the western world—Imperial Rome, the Athens of Pericles, the era of Louis XIV, early 18th Century England and Colonial America—were characterized by large numbers of women who used artificial feeding or gave their babies to wet nurses. In these eras, upper-class women may have been objects of amusement rather than contributors to the work of society. Because of this, they may have felt somewhat worthless and insecure. Feelings of security may depend in part on the feeling of being needed and essential.

Industrialization breaks up the wider family as the main economic unit of society and deeply affects the role of woman and the value placed on her contributions. When women and children no longer help produce food or manufacture goods at home, they become economic liabilities. The status of women as bearers of children falls. Women who stay at home under these conditions also contribute less economically to society.

Woman's work role certainly influences breast feeding, but the rate of breast feeding depends on how the work is carried out, not on whether the woman works. In cultures that permit the baby to accompany his mother to work, there is little interference. Some nonwestern cultures—both simple and complex—depend heavily on women in the labor force. Yet breast feeding flourishes for two or more years with each baby because the work does not separate the baby from his mother. On the other hand, even simple cultures can become emotionally indifferent to breast feeding when the mother is the chief source of economic support and when her work requires her to be away from her baby for long periods.

Breast-feeding rates differ with even slight variations in region or culture. The number of babies who receive at least some breast milk on discharge from the hospital differs from region to region in the United States. Some states have more than double the breast-feeding rate of others. Studies have shown that the size of the community or the subcultural grouping affects the breast-feeding rate.

Education and social class influence breast feeding in some cultures. College-educated American mothers are more likely to suckle their children than women whose education ends with high school. In England, America, Switzerland and Sweden high breast-feeding rates have been associated with high social status. But in Belgium and France no hint of class difference has been found. In some cultures the lowest as well as the highest social groups breast feed more than does the middle group.

Many people who work with mothers strongly suspect that the attitude of husband, family and friends has a real bearing on breast-feeding behavior. This is difficult to document. No statistical effort appears to have been made to correlate fathers' attitudes toward nursing with its success.

The effect of medical personnel is clearer. The enthusiastic physician can develop a practice in which his patients breast feed far more than the rest of the society. Carolyn Rawlins began a breast-feeding program with her own patients in 1959. In two years, the hospital breast-feeding rate of her patients jumped from 33 to 65 per cent. While previously only 15 per cent of her patients had nursed their babies as long as five months, once the program was established, 52 per cent were still breast feeding at five months. Enthusiasm about breast feeding frequently is considered improper, however, in cultures with declining lactation rates. A physician may lose status if he shows strong enthusiasm under these conditions.

Lack of interest or rejective feelings in any field tend to hinder the dissemination of knowledge in that field. This makes it hard for those who are interested to obtain facts. Rejective feelings in our own culture have made it necessary to hide breast feeding, thus impeding the flow of knowledge by observation. Just 25 years ago in rural Mississippi, breast feeding in church was acceptable. And 80 years ago in Indiana, upper-class women naturally took their babies to afternoon parties to nurse them as needed. Now there is a strong taboo on public nursing in the United States. Even photographs of babies suckling their mothers are frowned upon, yet bottle feeding in public and photographs of bottle-feeding babies are completely acceptable. As a result, a young girl often starts breast feeding without ever once in her life having seen another woman suckle a child. She is ignorant, even if she is interested.

The attitudes of the mother, the baby, the husband, friends, the physician and the culture work together in several ways to determine the success or failure of breast-feeding attempts. Although some psychosomatic mechanisms are probably unknown, three different factors have been identified: the milk-ejection reflex, suckling stimulation and other sensory contact between mother and baby.

The milk-ejection reflex has long been recognized in cattle, where it is called the let-down reflex. As good dairy farmers know, animals who are frightened, placed in unfamiliar surroundings or treated unkindly will not let down their milk. Impulses to the posterior

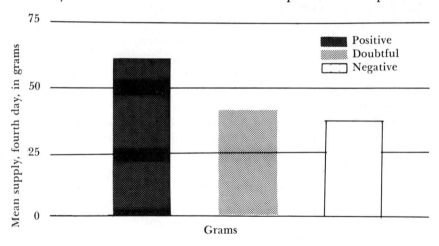

MILK SUPPLY. A mother's attitude toward breast feeding affects her milk production.

pituitary gland release oxytocin, the same hormone used to induce labor. When the oxytocin travels through the bloodstream to the breast, it acts on the cells surrounding the alveoli. These cells contract and force the milk into larger ducts where it is available to the nursing animal or the milking machine.

Assuming the let-down reflex worked similarly in cattle and in people, Michael Newton and I inhibited the reflex experimentally by distracting a mother with techniques that did not appear to disturb her baby. The mother was a 25-year-old woman in good health, who had successfully breast fed her first baby for 11 months. The baby in the experiment, her second, was seven months old and had been entirely breast fed on a demand schedule from birth. At the time of the experiment, the baby was taking orange juice and additional solid food.

Each morning the baby was weighed before and after feeding. On control mornings the mother and baby were not disturbed during the 10-minute nursing period. On the other mornings, the mother was distracted four minutes before the baby was brought to her. Two minutes later, she received an injection of either oxytocin or a sterile saline solution. The mother was not told which solution was used.

The distractions took three different forms. In the first, the mother's feet were immersed alternately in ice water for 10 seconds out of every 30. (This was reported as the worst distraction.) In the second, she was asked a rapid series of mathematical questions. When the mother answered incorrectly or delayed her answer more than 10 seconds, she was given an electric shock of moderate intensity. This shock disturbed the mother emotionally and made her angry, although the effect diminished when the baby was suckling. At these times she tended to have difficulty hearing the question and frequently delayed answering. In the last distraction, surgical gauze was tied around each of the mother's big toes. The bandage was pulled intermittently, causing sharp pain.

On control days, where there was no disturbance, the baby obtained significantly more milk than when the mother was disturbed [see illustration, below]. The amount of milk rose to nearly normal

| Maternal disturbance | Mean amount of milk obtained by baby |
|---|---|
| No distractions–no injection | 168 grams |
| Distraction—saline injection | 99 grams |
| Distraction—oxytocin injection | 153 grams |

EJECTION REFLEX. Interrupted milk flow can be restarted with hormone injection.

levels, however, when the injection of oxytocin set off the milk-ejection reflex artificially.

Another way to demonstrate the relation of the milk-ejection reflex to the success of breast feeding is to study the clinical signs that accompany milk ejection. The signs are easily recognized and can be reported by the mother: milk dripping from the breasts before the baby starts to nurse; uterine cramps during nursing; cessation of nipple discomfort as the baby obtains milk easing the negative pressures on the nipples.

Michael Newton and I compared 53 successful breast feeders, whose babies received no supplementary formula, with 50 unsuccessful breast feeders, whose babies required supplementary bottle feedings. The total average milk-ejection symptoms were significantly higher among the successful mothers: 72 per cent of this group reported symptoms, as compared to 58 per cent of the unsuccessful mothers. The milk-ejection reflex appeared to be sensitive to small differences in the mother's oxytocin level, suggesting that minor psychosomatic changes may influence the amount of milk the baby receives.

When inhibition of the milk-ejection reflex occurs, much milk already in the breast simply cannot be obtained by the baby. To demonstrate this, Michael Newton had mothers nurse their babies. The babies were weighed before and after feeding to determine the amount of milk obtained. Then the mothers' breasts were pumped by machine. Finally, their breasts were repumped after an injection of oxytocin which set off the milk ejection reflex artificially. After the injection of oxytocin, mothers whose attempts at breast feeding were unsuccessful produced almost as much milk as both baby and machine had been able to extract. Before the injection, 47 per cent of their milk had been unavailable to either the baby or milking machine.

Sucking stimulation may be even more important than the ejection reflex to the success of breast feeding. Cultures where breast feeding meets with disapproval seem to permit far less sucking by the baby, and babies in these cultures are weaned earlier. The regulated, restricted, short breast feeding now common in Western industrial countries developed only recently. In 1906, T. S. Southworth, writing in a standard American pediatric textbook, recommended 10 feedings a day for most of the first month, declining gradually to six feedings each day through the 11th month. Southworth approved of night feedings through the fifth month.

There is considerable evidence that the restriction of suckling inhibits milk production. In a study of 1,057 new-born infants, E. J. Salber assigned each baby to one of three groups. Those she placed on a true self-demand schedule gained weight most rapidly. Those on three-hour schedules, although they gained less weight than the babies on self-demand, gained faster than the group on four-hour schedules.

Both the milk-ejection reflex and suckling stimulation depend primarily on sensory stimulation of the nipple, but other sensory contacts—hearing, seeing, smelling and touching the baby—may be important. In cultures where breast feeding is enjoyable enough to continue without restriction, neither the mother nor the baby easily tolerates separation. Mother and baby stay in continuous close sensory contact even when not in the act of nursing.

In contrast to this, Western cultures raise many barriers to sensory contact between mother and baby. Modern Western styles of dress make breast-feeding contact difficult. Families no longer sleep together in one room and the baby is expected to sleep alone. Many hospitals practice separation of mother and child at birth, except for brief feeding periods, and at home the baby frequently has his own room where he spends much of his time. These customs are relatively new—in American hospitals, housing the baby away from the mother started only about 65 years ago.

Here again, the cause for the decline of breast feeding may lie in the changes in attitudes toward family life that accompany full industrialization. A common way in which human beings express mixed feelings or ambivalence is to put distance between themselves and the object in question.

In this country, barriers placed between a mother and her child often begin in the delivery room, when the infant, after brief inspection by the groggy mother, is whisked away to be weighed, cleaned and placed in an aseptic nursery and then presented briefly to the mother every four hours along with a bottle of supplementary formula. If the mother insists on breast feeding, she may be greeted by a skeptical nurse and physician and the raised eyebrows of friends, and be expected to sequester herself at feeding time as if she were enacting a somewhat shameful ritual. Thus the mother who breast feeds her child must go to considerable trouble to do so. Perhaps it is less surprising that the breast-feeding rate continues to decline than that it does not decline faster.

# Patterns of Attachment Behavior Shown by the Infant in Interaction with His Mother[1]

*Mary D. Ainsworth*

Since this paper is concerned with attachment, perhaps I should begin with a definition. According to the Oxford Concise Dictionary, attachment is "the act of fastening oneself to another, binding in friendship, making devoted."

The implications of this definition are as follows: (1) Attachment implies affection. (2) Attachments are specific, and imply discrimination. (3) Attachment is an act; it is behavioral and thus observable. (4) Attachment is an active process; it does not come about merely through being a passive recipient of stimulation. (5) The act of attachment affects the response of the object. Attachment is a two-way process. It implies interaction.

Let us now attempt our own definition of attachment behavior. Attachment behavior is behavior through which a discriminating, differential, affectional relationship is established with a person or object, and which tends to evoke a response from the object, and thus initiates a chain of interaction which serves to consolidate the affectional relationship.

The material that I am going to present is selected from a short-term longitudinal study of 28 babies in interaction with their mothers, visited in their own homes at intervals of approximately two weeks. The age-span best represented in the study is from 2 to 15 months of age.

These babies happened to be all African—all Baganda. But for our purposes here I urge you to consider my sample as merely one of human infants and disregard the fact that they were African (for

From *Merrill-Palmer Quarterly*, 1946, 10(1), pp. 51–58. Reprinted by permission of the editor and author.

I believe the same principles of development apply to infants regardless of specific racial or cultural influences).

These African babies, however, may have been somewhat more accelerated in their development of attachment than babies in our culture. There are three reasons for this opinion. (1) They were generally accelerated in their development, according to Gesell Developmental Schedules. (2) They were breast-fed, with one exception, and this may have facilitated the development of infant-mother attachment. (3) They experienced more interaction with adult figures than many infants in our culture. The modal pattern of infant care among the Baganda was that a baby was never alone when awake. Characteristically, he is held on someone's lap, most frequently his mother's lap, but he is offered to the visitor to hold, as a courteous gesture. As soon as he can sit unsupported he may be placed on the floor, in the midst of the gathering, for everyone sits on mats on the floor. As soon as he can crawl, he is free to move about, and to initiate contacts or to withdraw from them at will.

At the beginning of my study I was interested in the strength and quality of the infant's attachment to his mother, once formed, rather than in the behavior patterns which mediated attachment. This interest led me to attempt to establish criteria of attachment. At first I looked for reactions to separation and to threat of separation—crying when the mother left, following and clinging, especially. But there were some babies, who seemed clearly attached to their mothers, who did not dependably cry, follow or cling when their mothers showed signs of leaving. What, then, gave such a clear impression that they were nevertheless strongly attached to their mothers? In an attempt to answer this question, I examined my field notes exhaustively, and the catalogue of attachment behavior shown in Table 1 is the result.

For each item, the earliest age at which the behavior pattern was observed is shown, as well as the age at which the pattern was commonly observed. Since some of these patterns were identified after the observations were completed, rather than before, and since these observations were therefore unsystematic, it may well be that the earliest and common ages indicated for these items are later than they should be. The data for those patterns are indicated in brackets.

## A Catalogue of Patterns of Attachment Behavior

At the outset may I say that this catalogue of thirteen patterns of attachment behavior omits behavior associated with feeding—the

TABLE 1

Patterns of Attachment Behavior Shown by the Infant
in Interaction with His Mother

| Behavior | Earliest observation | Commonly observed |
|---|---|---|
| Differential crying | 8 weeks | 12 weeks |
| Differential smiling | (9 weeks) | (32 weeks) |
| Differential vocalization | (20 weeks) | ? |
| Visual-motor orientation | (18 weeks) | ? |
| Crying when mother leaves | 15 weeks | 25 weeks |
| Following | 17 weeks | 25 weeks |
| "Scrambling" over mother | (10 weeks) | (30 weeks) |
| Burying face in mother's lap | (22 weeks) | (30 weeks) |
| Exploration from mother as a secure base | 28 weeks | 33 weeks |
| Clinging | 25 weeks | 40 weeks |
| Lifting arms in greeting | (17 weeks) | (22 weeks) |
| Clapping hands in greeting | (28 weeks) | (30 weeks) |
| Approach through locomotion | (26 weeks) | (40 weeks) |

rooting response, sucking and, later, search for the breast—because
I wanted to distinguish attachment to the mother as a person from
mere attachment to the breast as a need-satisfying object. This does
not imply that I consider behavior implicit in the feeding relationship to be irrelevant to attachment, particularly in the case of babies
such as these who were breast-fed for most of the first year or longer.

The first three patterns, listed in Table 1, imply little more than
discrimination of the mother from other people, and differential
responsiveness to her.

*Differential crying.* The baby cries when held by someone other
than the mother, and stops when taken by the mother. Or he cries
and continues to cry when someone else attempts to comfort him,
but stops crying immediately when taken by the mother. It was difficult to judge at first whether the object of attachment was the mother
as a person, or a part-object—the breast—for the first act of many of
these mothers after picking up a crying baby was to offer the breast.

*Differential smiling.* The baby smiles more readily and more frequently in interaction with his mother than in interaction with
another person.

*Differential vocalization.* The baby vocalizes more readily and
more frequently in interaction with his mother than in interaction
with other people.

The next group of patterns have in common a concern on the part of the infant for the whereabouts of his mother—a concern that implies the use of distance receptors, especially vision.

*Visual-motor orientation towards the mother.* The baby, when apart from his mother but able to see her, keeps his eyes more or less continuously oriented towards her. He may look away for a few moments, but he repeatedly glances towards her. When held by someone else, he can be sensed to be maintaining a motor orientation towards his mother, for he is neither ready to interact with the adult holding him, nor to relax in her arms.

*Crying when the mother leaves.* The baby cries when the mother leaves his visual field and cannot be brought back into it through his own visual-motor adjustments. The usual occasion is when the mother leaves the room, in contrast with times when she merely moves to another part of the same room.

*Following.* The baby, once able to crawl, not only cries when his mother leaves the room, but attempts to follow her, by crawling after her, or, when he is older, by walking after her. By about eight or nine months, following tended to occur without crying; the baby follows, but cries only if frustrated by being held back, by a closed door, or by the mother going so fast as to outdistance him hopelessly.

Even before the baby is able to crawl and hence to follow, he can nevertheless take the initiative in makinc contact with his mother when on her lap or when placed on the floor beside her. There are two such patterns, scrambling over the mother, and burying the face in her lap. (I am excluding here behavior that may obviously be interpreted as a search for or a demand for the breast.)

*Scrambling.* This pattern differs from clinging in that there is no apparent effort to preserve a close and continuous physical contact. The baby climbs over his mother, exploring her person, and playing with her face, her hair or her clothes. On occasion, he may explore another person in this way, but since he much more frequently scrambles over his mother, this differential response is included in our catalogue.

*Burying the face.* The baby, whether in the course of scrambling over the mother, or having returned to her after exploring the world at some distance from her, buries his face in her lap. This behavior was observed only in relation to the mother.

As Harlow (1960) has observed with infant monkeys and Arsenian (1943) with pre-school children, the baby, once attached to his mother, can use her as a secure base from which to explore the world, or as a "haven of safety" from which he can face an external threat without panic.

*Exploration from a secure base.* Now that the baby is able to crawl, he does not always keep close to his mother, but rather makes little excursions away from her, exploring other objects and interacting with other people, but he returns to her from time to time. He may even go outside the room altogether if he is permitted to do so. His confidence in leaving the secure base is in remarkable contrast to his distress if the secure base gets up an moves off on *her* own initiative.

*Clinging.* The clinging pattern which is so conspicuous in infant monkeys was not observed in these infants until 25 weeks at the earliest. The most striking instances of clinging in the first year of life were clearly associated with fright. The only clear-cut fear-arousing stimulus which we observed was the stranger. If already in his mother's arms when faced by a stranger, the baby clings to her tightly; if apart from her, he scuttles to her as quickly as possible and then clings. From the safety of his mother's arms he can eye the stranger warily and without crying. If the mother tries to hand him to the stranger, however, the baby screams and clings desperately, resisting all efforts to disengage him. This panicky clinging in response to strangers was not observed in any child younger than 40 weeks of age. A less intense kind of clinging was seen in somewhat younger children. In one six-months old child, for example, the cause seemed to be separation anxiety, for he wanted to be with his mother the whole time, and sometimes clung to her, but in an intermittent way and not so desperately and tightly as did the infants who were frightened by a stranger. Another child clung to his mother in the same intermittent way during a period of illness at about 32 weeks of age. Marked clinging was also manifested by some children for a period immediately following weaning.

Finally, greeting responses are classed as attachment behavior. Some infants, who had become accustomed to being put down by their mothers and left alone to sleep, showed their attachment more by the enthusiastic greeting they gave her when she returned after an absence than by a protest when she departed.

*Lifting arms in greeting.* The baby greets the mother after an absence by lifting his arms towards her, by smiling, and by vocalization that might be described as a crow or delighted shout.

*Clapping hands in greeting.* This response is similar to the previous one except that instead of lifting his arms, the baby, while smiling and vocalizing, claps his hands together in a gesture of obvious delight.

*Approach through locomotion.* After the child is able to crawl, he characteristically terminates his greeting responses by crawling to the loved person as quickly as he is able. Smiling and vocalization usually accompany this response, as they do the other greeting responses. And of course, as described earlier, the infant, if apart from his mother when frightened, crawls to her as quickly as possible and then clings.

These then, together with responses associated with feeding, constitute a catalogue of behavioral components of attachment to the mother as a special person. Let us now consider the development of attachment as a whole.

## Development of Attachment

During the first year of life these infants passed through four main phases in regard to social behavior, one phase leading to another with no sharp boundary between them. First there is a phase of undiscriminating responsiveness to people. Next there is a phase of differential responsiveness to the mother, with continuing responsiveness to other people. Then there is a phase of sharply defined attachment to the mother, with striking waning of undiscriminating friendliness. This is followed quickly by, and overlaps with, a phase of attachment to one or more familiar figures other than the mother.

The second phase, in which discrimination of the mother from other people emerges, began in this sample between 8 and 12 weeks of age, with differential crying as the chief criterion. In this sample, however, it was impossible to determine how much of this earliest attachment was to the mother as a whole person and how much to the breast. During the second quarter-year of life, differential responsiveness to the mother became much more clear-cut, and included differential smiling, differential vocalization, and greeting responses. Crying when the mother left the room was common but inconsistent; infants who were used to being left with other people were more likely to cry if left alone or with a stranger than if left with a familiar figure. As soon as locomotion was attained the following response occurred, in some babies before six months of age, in others shortly afterwards. Following was not invariable or consistent at first; it was most likely to occur when the baby was judged to be hungry, tired, ill, or otherwise unhappy, and if the baby was left alone or with strangers rather than if he was left with a familiar person.

The third phase seemed to begin between six and seven months of age, but without any abrupt transition. Following the mother became more and more consistent, as though the attachment to her were becoming stronger and better consolidated. Protest at the mother's departure became more consistent too—although increasingly protest was not simultaneous with following, and tended to occur only if following was frustrated. Greeting responses became more conspicuous, and babies began to use their mothers as a secure base from which to explore the world.

The fourth phase, as I mentioned earlier, overlapped with the third. Babies who were used to care from adults other than the mother never completely lost tolerance for this care, even though they might initially protest the mother's departure. Very shortly after the baby showed a clear-cut attachment to the mother he began to display attachment to other figures, often the father, chiefly through greeting responses. Sharp preferences were shown; for example, one sibling might be greeted joyously while other siblings were not. After nine months of age the baby, when left with a familiar figure, would follow it about, no longer reserving following solely for the mother. Soon after there was discrimination and attachment to figures other than the mother, fear of strangers, appeared, as early as eight months with some babies.

## Summary and Discussion

I now wish to summarize and discuss these findings, drawing your attention to some considerations that seem important to me. I have identified thirteen patterns of behavior which seem to mediate the attachment of the infant to his mother and soon afterwards to other favorite figures. This catalogue is probably incomplete, although it goes beyond Bowlby's (1958) list, which was limited to sucking, crying, smiling, following and clinging. The behavioral components of these attachment patterns are clearly unlearned—crying, smiling, vocalization, following with the eyes, reaching for an object, locomotion, and so on. These unlearned components become tied into attachment patterns, however, only when they become differentially directed towards different figures, and in the human infant this discrimination does not seem to emerge abruptly.

Although the various patterns of attachment behavior that I have catalogued tend to become organized together with the mother as object, not all of them need be included in a particular attachment. The attachments of some infants seemed chiefly mediated by crying when mother leaves, by following, and later by clinging. The attachment of others seemed more conspicuously mediated by greeting, smiling, vocalization, and visual-motor orientation. Perhaps no one of these components is essential; for example, the behavior associated with the breast-feeding relationship is not essential to attachment in our culture.

I should like to close by emphasizing three features of attachment behavior which I believe to be clearly apparent in the findings of this study.

First, I was struck with the active part the baby himself plays in the development of attachment. All of these behavior patterns, as well as the seeking responses in feeding, show initiative. The striking part played by the infant's own activity in attachment leads me to the hypothesis that it is largely through his own activity that the child becomes attached, rather than through stimulation, or through the passive satisfaction of creature-comfort needs.

I attach a great deal of importance to the active initiative implicit in attachment behavior. I view interaction between the infant and his mother as a chain of behavioral interchange, which may be initiated either by behavior of the mother to which infant responds, or by the infant's behavior—at first his signals and later his actual attachment overtures—which evokes a response in the mother.

Hence, as I have stated elsewhere (Ainsworth, 1962), I believe that maternal deprivation may best be defined as insufficient interaction between the infant and a mother-figure, and not as mere lack of stimulation. In deprivation the infant also lacks response of an adult to the behavior he initiates, including his attachment behavior.

Secondly, attachment behavior is not necessarily terminated by a state of close physical contact between infant and mother. Although some attachment patterns imply physical contact as an end phase, others maintain proximity and interaction without requiring actual contact—vocalization, visual-motor orientation, following, exploring from a secure base, and so on. However important actual physical contact may be to the human infant, it is clear that some of the components of attachment and much important interaction between infant and mother involve distance receptors, rather than tactual and kinaesthetic modalities. Even in infancy, attachment can be sustained through a middle distance in which seeing of expression, movement and gesture, and hearing of vocalization, may form the basis of interaction.

I will not set forth in this present discussion my reasons for believing so, but I believe that it is the anxious infant who requires
close physical contact with his mother, and who is not content to
maintain interaction through a middle distance at least part of the
time.

Third, this study suggests strongly that attachments to other figures
tend to follow attachment to the mother very quickly, provided that
the infant has adequate opportunity to interact with people other
than his mother. Scarcely has the infant passed the phase of undiscriminating social responsiveness and formed a specific attachment
to his mother than he begins to expand his capacity for attachment
to other figures—the father, other adults, or selected older siblings.
At the same time that his attachment to his mother grows in depth
and strength, his general capacity for attachment grows in breadth.
One interesting feature of such attachments is that they can be to
figures who take no part in the routine care of the infant, and who
therefore do not satisfy his creature-comfort needs but merely play
with him and interact with him, smiling and vocalizing.

In final summary, I have made three points. First, the baby is
active and takes initiative in forming attachments. Second attachment does not necessarily imply close physical contact, for it can be
maintained through a middle distance through distance receptors.
Third, the baby becomes attached not only to the mother-figure who
feeds him and satisfies his creature-comfort needs, but also to others
who merely play with him and interact with him.

Taken together, those three points offer support to Bowlby's (1958)
challenge to the so-called secondary-drive theory of attachment which
assumes that the infant becomes attached to a mother-figure solely
because she is instrumental in the satisfaction of his primary visceral
drives.

## References

AINSWORTH, MARY D. The effects of maternal deprivation: a review of findings in the context of research strategy and controversy. *Public Health Papers*,
No. 14. Geneva: World Health Organization, 1962.

ARSENIAN, J. M. Young children in an insecure situation. *J. abnorm. soc.,
Psychol.*, 1943, 38, 225–249.

BOWLBY, J. The nature of the child's tie to his mother. *Internat. J. Psy-
choanal.*, 1958, 39, 1–34.

HARLOW, J. F. Primary affectional patterns in primates. *Amer. J. Orthopsy-
chiat.*, 1960, 30, 676–684.

## Notes

1. This paper was part of a symposium entitled, "Longitudinal studies of mother-infant interaction," presented at the 1963 meeting of the Society for Research in Child Development. The data upon which this paper is based were collected while the author was attached to the East African Institute for Social Research, Makerere College, Kampala, Uganda. During data analysis, support was given by a U.S. Public Health Service grant (M 4644), and support is now received from the Foundations Fund for Research in Psychiatry.

# Adolescent Personal Problems as a Function of Age and Sex[1]

*James F. Adams*

## A. Introduction

The problems of adolescents have been of interest and concern to parents and educators for many years. Although numerous techniques have been used to investigate the problems, the most common procedure has been to use the problem inventory or checklist. Typically a checklist describes a number of specific problem situations and the respondent is asked to check those items that worry him or best describe him. In order of publication date, typical studies are those by Symonds (7), Cheney (1), Elias (2), Morris (5), and Hayden (4). As Symonds has noted, the check-list procedure may require the respondent to indicate what he feels *should be* of importance or of major concern, rather than to indicate *what is* of importance or major concern. Other investigators have used the interview (8), projective techniques (3), and essays (6) to study adolescent problems.

From the studies mentioned, as well as from other studies, it would seem that between one-third and one-half of the school population are anxious about academic work. Health problems are checked frequently on problem lists, but they are seldom mentioned in essays. Girls are more concerned than boys with school problems, family relationships, and social adjustments. Boys, on the other hand, are reported to be more concerned than girls with finances and vocational plans.

From *Journal of Genetic Psychology*, 1964 104 (June), pp. 207–214. Reprinted by permission of the author and the Journal Press.

## B. The Present Study

The author investigated adolescent problems for several reasons. First of all, it seemed that the problem checklist approach, which has been used in many studies, has definite limitations. It does not show whether a respondent checks a problem because he feels that it should be a problem or because it is a problem. Further, the typical procedure does not give satisfactory indication as to whether a problem is a major problem or one that gives the individual little or no difficulty. Second, many studies have combined data on males and females or have reported data on one sex only, so that sex differences have been difficult to ascertain. Third, few studies have a wide age range; hence it has been difficult to observe whether problems change as a function of age. Fourth, as the author is engaged in counselor training, it seemed worthwhile to investigate the types of problems that a counselor reasonably might expect to find of major concern to counselees.

## C. Procedure

What problems are of major concern to adolescents? To get answers to this question, approximately 4,000 boys and girls from over 30 schools were asked to report the biggest personal problem that was causing difficulty. The respondents were predominantly enrolled in the schools of Philadelphia and the surrounding suburban communities. As Table 1 shows, respondents ranged in age from 10 to 19.

TABLE 1

Numbers of Students by Age and Sex

| Age | Males | Females |
| --- | --- | --- |
| 10 | 80 | 88 |
| 11 | 263 | 268 |
| 12 | 328 | 287 |
| 13 | 251 | 213 |
| 14 | 176 | 170 |
| 15 | 190 | 238 |
| 16 | 237 | 207 |
| 17 | 280 | 220 |
| 18 | 196 | 127 |
| 19 | 50 | 60 |
| Total | 2051 | 1878 |

Teachers administered a questionnaire on which four questions were asked. Students were instructed not to sign their names, but were asked to indicate age and sex. Further, in their replies, students were instructed to be as frank and as honest as possible. The questions asked were as follows:

1. What problem do you have right now that you think is a big problem? In other words, what is the biggest personal problem which may be causing you some difficulty?
2. What would be of greatest help to you in solving this problem? Or, to put it another way, if you had the power to solve this problem, how might it be solved?
3. What do you think is the biggest problem for other boys and girls of your age?
4. How do you think this problem might be solved?

The last two questions were asked on the theory that, while students might have some reluctance to list their own personal problems, they might project their problems to members of their peer group.

## D. Results and Discussion

With the exception of a slight tendency for students from suburban communities to list more academic or school problems than other students, there was remarkable agreement among students of the same age and sex, regardless of school. For this reason, data from different schools were combined for tabulation.

It was found that respondents' answers could be categorized into 14 areas. Answers were analyzed by age and sex; however, because presentation of data by age and sex would involve lengthy tables, results by sex alone are reported (Table 2).

Problem areas as listed in Table 2 do not reveal the types of problems that fall within each category. Consequently, there follow some general comments on the types of answers given in each category. In each case, major age and sex differences are noted.

1. *School.* The overwhelming majority were on difficulties in academic work. There were a few unfavorable comments on problems with teachers. Approximately one-third of the boys and one-fourth of the girls reported that their greatest personal problem was some academic difficulty.

From the 11th year on, the academic problem was the major area of concern for boys. It was of less concern for girls. This result is not

TABLE 2

Percentage of Personal Problems Reported by Problem Area for
Self and Peers by Total Male and Female Groups*

|  | Self | | Peer | |
|---|---|---|---|---|
|  | Male | Female | Male | Female |
| School | 35 | 23 | 21 | 14 |
| Interpersonal | 12 | 19 | 23 | 33 |
| Maturity | 2 | 3 | 2 | 7 |
| Emotions | 2 | 4 | 2 | 3 |
| Work | 6 | 5 | 7 | 6 |
| Sports and recreation | 4 | 2 | 5 | 2 |
| Health | 2 | 4 | 2 | 2 |
| Ethical | 1 | 2 | 1 | 2 |
| Family | 10 | 22 | 8 | 17 |
| Habits | 0 | 0 | 1 | 1 |
| Finances | 10 | 4 | 7 | 4 |
| Unclassifiable | 8 | 6 | 8 | 3 |
| No answer | 4 | 3 | 13 | 6 |
| No problem | 4 | 3 | 0 | 0 |

*For the males $N = 2051$; for the females $N = 1878$.

consistent with a consensus derived from earlier studies. In earlier studies, the female consistently had been more concerned than the male with academic problems.

Several explanations for the discrepancy occur to the author. First, it is possible that the discrepancy is due to differences in the population sample or in the techniques used. This does not seem likely; other studies have involved many different procedures with different populations, but consistently indicate that females are more concerned than males with academic work.

Second, it is possible that emphasis upon engineering, science, and the pursuit of a college education has changed or is changing the attitude of the adolescent male toward academic achievement

Third, it is possible that increased emphasis upon college preparation has placed on tenuous ground the individual who is willing to settle for a "gentleman's C." Perhaps there has been an upgrading of standards that has made it more difficult or less acceptable to "get by" with a minimum expenditure of effort. Many educators have observed that there is less peer-group disapproval for an achieving girl than for an achieving boy. The boy's peer-group approval tends to come from areas such as athletics. Consequently, if standards or expectations for academic achievement have been raised, the male may have just cause to be concerned.

Regardless of the reason for their concern, boys viewed academic work as their biggest problem. They also considered it an area of major concern to their peers.

2. *Interpersonal Problems.* Interpersonal problems were with other people in general, with members of the opposite sex, and with the respondent's peer group. In this area, girls were much more concerned than boys, but both boys and girls saw problems in this area as of greater concern to their peers than to themselves.

Problems of adjustment with respect to the opposite sex and with respect to the respondent's peer group received the majority of responses. After age 13 or 14, there was a distinct tendency for problems with one's peers to decrease. This was true for both sexes.

Problems with the opposite sex were reported more frequently by girls than by boys and remained relatively constant for both sexes until the age of 16 or 17. After 16 or 17, problems with the opposite sex decreased markedly.

3. *Maturity.* Recognition of maturity was not a major problem for either sex, but it became a minor problem for girls as early as age 10. It did not occur to any degree for boys until age 13. Lack of parental recognition of maturity caused the greatest number of responses in this area. Less frequently mentioned were lack of recognition of maturity by persons other than parents, and immaturity in one's self.

4. *Emotions.* Problems of moodiness and lack of self-understanding and confidence were minor, but girls reported about twice as many problems as boys; there was some indication that such problems increased in seriousness at 18 or 19 years of age.

5. *Work.* Problems of work were of about equal concern to both sexes. Up to the age of 14 for boys and up to the age of 15 for girls, problems of work were seldom mentioned. From 14 or 15 to 17, problems were the finding of part-time work and the choice of a vocation. After age 17, the choice of a vocation was the major problem for both sexes.

6. *Sports and Recreation.* Twice as many boys as girls reported problems of sports and recreation. Boys listed more problems than girls with respect to leisure time, learning to drive (from age 15), and athletics. Difficulties with hobbies were listed by both sexes at the earlier ages. A few boys listed difficulty in learning to dance.

7. *Health.* Although health is not an area of major concern for either sex, girls list twice as many problems as boys. The difference between the sexes can be accounted for chiefly by the girls' concern

with problems of weight, particularly between the ages of 11 and 14. Problems concerning skin blemishes and general appearance occurred in about equal frequency for the two sexes, usually prior to age 15. Both sexes made minor mention of family mental and physical health problems.

8. *Ethics.* Problems in ethics are of minor concern, but were mentioned more frequently by girls than by boys. At almost all ages, girls mentioned problems of religion and problems in the formulation of moral standards. Boys reported religious problems infrequently.

9. *Family.* Family problems—i.e., relations with either or both parents or with siblings—were of major importance to girls. Girls listed twice as many problems with siblings as did boys. For both sexes, sibling problems were most frequently mentioned prior to age 14.

When the boys mentioned a parental problem, they reported the problem as one that involved both parents. On the other hand, girls, while exceeding boys in mention of problems that involved both parents, frequently mentioned difficulties that involved only one parent (usually the mother).

10. *Habits.* Smoking and drinking were mentioned, but problems in this area seemed practically nonexistent.

11. *Finances.* The problem most frequently mentioned in this area was personal finance. Boys listed the problem twice as frequently as girls did. Other problems concerned family finance and anticipated expenses for college attendance. As might be expected, mention of financial problems increased with age.

12. *Miscellaneous.* One boy reported that he had robbed a store the previous night (and signed his name), but problems of this magnitude were exceedingly rare. Some students did not complete the questionnaire. Some students apologetically said that they had no major problems.

For both sexes, the per cent of students who stated that they had no problems decreased sharply after age 14. On the basis of the literature which has indicated that girls have more problems than boys, it might have been expected that more boys than girls would report that they had no problems or would not answer the questionnaire. Of course, as some studies have implied, it may be that the girls' problems were more severe and more numerous. As the present study asked only for the "biggest" single problem, it sheds no light upon the possibility just mentioned.

13. *Problems of Peers.* Both sexes see their peer groups as having fewer school problems and as having more interpersonal problems

than they report for themselves. Whether or not this perception represents a projection of problems that boys and girls are unwilling to admit for themselves is a matter of conjecture.

14. *Solutions.* Table 3 summarizes the manners in which the subjects suggested they could solve their problems. A solution was *extrinsic* if it involved receiving help from some outside source—

TABLE 3

Percentage of Suggested Solutions Given for Personal Problems of Self and Peers of Total Male and Female Groups*

|  | Self | | Peer | |
|  | Male | Female | Male | Female |
|---|---|---|---|---|
| Extrinsic | 26 | 29 | 34 | 41 |
| Intrinsic | 35 | 33 | 26 | 23 |
| Combination | 8 | 12 | 8 | 14 |
| Fantasy | 5 | 4 | 1 | 0 |
| Flippant | 4 | 1 | 2 | 0 |
| Unclassifiable | 4 | 2 | 2 | 2 |
| No answer | 12 | 10 | 17 | 11 |
| No solution | 6 | 9 | 10 | 9 |

*For the males $N = 2051$; for the females $N = 1878$.

e.g., "getting my parents to help me with my homework." A solution was *intrinsic* if the individual suggested that he, himself, could solve the problem—e.g., "spending more time on my homework." If the solution was extrinsic *and* intrinsic, it was placed in a *combination* category. Unrealistic answers were put in a *fantasy* category—e.g., "if someone would give me 20 million dollars." Answers which were thought to indicate that the respondent was not seriously trying to give a solution were placed in a *flippant* class.

For both sexes, there was a tendency for extrinsic solutions to increase with age (Question 2). Intrinsic solutions tended to decrease with age for girls and tended to remain relatively stable for boys. Both sexes tended to list more extrinsic solutions for problems of their peers than they did for their own problems. For peers, there was also a tendency for extrinsic solutions to increase with age and for intrinsic solutions to decrease with age.

## E. Summary

A questionnaire was given to approximately 4,000 students who ranged in age from 10 to 19. They were asked to list their own biggest personal problem, their peer group's biggest personal problem, and the ways in which these problems could be solved. Most frequently mentioned were school, interpersonal, financial, and family problems. Sex differences were found in that boys reported more problems in school and more financial problems than girls; girls reported more interpersonal and family problems than boys.

Approximately one-third of the boys reported academic difficulty in school as their major problem. Ten per cent mentioned interpersonal, family, and financial problems. School, interpersonal, and family problems accounted for 60 per cent of the problems listed by girls. Both sexes saw their peer group as having fewer school problems and as having more interpersonal problems than they reported for themselves.

There was a tendency for extrinsic solutions to problems to increase with age for both sexes, and for intrinsic solutions to decrease with age for girls but to remain relatively constant for boys. For their peers, both sexes suggested more extrinsic solutions than for themselves and fewer intrinsic solutions.

## References

1. CHENEY, T. A method of identifying problems of high-school students. *Occupations*, 1949, 27, 387–390.

2. ELIAS, L. J. High School Youth Look at Their Problems. Pullman, Wash.: State College of Washington, 1949.

3. FRANK, L. K., *et al.* Personality Development in Adolescent Girls. *Monog. Socie. for Res. in Child Devel.*, 1951, 16, No. 53.

4. HAYDEN, J. R. An Analysis of the Personal-Social Problems Considered Important by the Junior-High-School Adolescent According to Sex, Grade, Age, Intelligence Quotient and Bilingualism. Boston, Mass.: Boston Univ., 1956.

5. MORRIS, G. A. A search for pupil viewpoint: How five schools made plans based on pupil needs. *Clearing House*, 1953, 29, 131–134.

6. POPE, C. Personal problems of high school pupils. *School & Socie.*, 1943, 57, 443–448.

7. SYMONDS, P. M. Life problems and interests of adolescents. *School Rev.*, 1936, 44, 506–518.

8. WITHEY, S. B. What boys see as their problem. *Education*, 1955, 76, 210–213.

## Notes

1. This study was supported by a Bolton Fund Grant from Temple University.

# Development of Autonomy and Parent-Child Interaction in Late Adolescence

*Elizabeth B. Murphy, M.S.W., Earle Silber, M.D.,*
*George V. Coelho, Ph.D., David A. Hamburg, M.D.,*
*and Irwin Greenberg, M.D.*

*This study explores the relationship between the capacity for autonomous behavior among freshman college students and the patterns of interaction between the students and their parents during the transition from high school to college. Autonomous-relatedness, the capacity for integration of both independent behavior and the maintenance of positive family ties, appears related to particular transactional family patterns, which were observed.*

One of the tasks of the late adolescent period involves the integration of a desire for independence from parents with a desire for continuing positive relationships with them. American society places high value upon independent behavior in adult life. Young adults are expected not to rely heavily on their parents or other senior members of an extended family, yet there remains significant emphasis upon close family ties and obligations of parents and children to each other throughout the life span. Consequently, adolescents are faced with the problem of finding ways to develop their own autonomy without, at the same time, heavily sacrificing parental relationships.

Erikson has defined the consolidation of identity as the developmental task of the adolescent period.[4] We would also call attention to the importance of establishing oneself as an autonomous person as re-emerging in salience during this period. While the capacity for

From *American Journal of Orthopsychiatry*, 1963, 33(4), pp. 643–652. Copyright ©, the American Orthopsychiatric Association, Inc. Reproduced by permission of the senior author and American Orthopsychiatric Association, Inc.

establishing autonomy has its antecedents in early childhood, from a psychosocial point of view, the experience of attending college away from home may offer a new and extended opportunity for behavior as an autonomous person.

In April, 1959, the Adult Psychiatry Branch of the National Institute of Mental Health began an exploratory study of the ways in which competent adolescents mobilized their resources to cope with the challenge of a new situation: the transition from high school to college.[5] One phase of the study focused on the development of autonomy in the first year of college and its relation to various patterns of parent-child interaction.

From a large group of volunteers at a suburban Washington, D.C. high school, 20 competent college-bound seniors were chosen on the basis of school records and a screening interview. In assessing competence, we looked for young people who demonstrated academic effectiveness, satisfying and close peer relationships and the ability to participate in social groups. These students had four interviews during the spring of their senior year of high school, three during the summer before they left for college and four during their freshman year—in the early fall, at Christmas vacation, at spring vacation and at the end of the freshman year. The students' parents were interviewed on three occasions: during the summer prior to the student's going to college, after the student had been home for the Christmas vacation, and jointly with the student at the end of the freshman year. One student dropped out of the study after the first college interview. Five of the students originally selected did not meet all of the criteria for competence, but it was felt that the experiences of these students would also be useful to study. Therefore, all 19 of the students who were initially selected and who remained with the project throughout its course are included in this aspect of the study. Our data for this paper are based on the interviews with 19 students and their parents.

A previous study of emotionally healthy adolescents and their family backgrounds, made at McGill University,[6] dealt with identifying patterns of family organization, interaction and social history. In our study we did not attempt to reconstruct early child-rearing practices or to make a comprehensive study of the family dynamics. Instead, we focused on current patterns of parent-child interaction that took place around the immediate task of transition from high school to college.

Separation from parents has generally been described in the psychological literature in terms of its anxiety-arousing component.

Most studies of the separation experience have been made on the young child, and usually under circumstances in which stresses additional to the separation have also been operative.[2,3] The impact of the separation experience is subject to many conditions. The age of the separated subjects, their levels of ego development and the way in which the environment structures the meaning of the separation play a part in the impact of the experience. By late adolescence, separation from parents takes on a different meaning and may be perceived more as an opportunity for mastery of an anticipated and desired experience than as a threat.

Although no student was immobilized by the immediate impact of separation, there were variations in the adequacy and styles with which longer-range aspects of the transition were handled. We felt that the ability to handle separation from home was only one part of a broader developmental issue: a challenge for the exercise of more autonomous functioning. Most of the students in our sample handled this challenge with ease, but some experienced difficulty in functioning at a more autonomous level. This occurred most frequently among the five students who did not meet all of the original criteria for competence. These variations are discussed below.

Such experiences as attending summer camp, independent extended travel and summer jobs away from home contributed to the easy adaptation by most of the students. In addition, while in high school these students had already moved toward an investment in peer relationships in place of parents, thus establishing for themselves a basis for confidence in their ability to live in the world of peers. For these students, then, there was little discontinuity between high school and college in terms of separation from parents.

For most of the students there was a certain anticipated pleasure about separation from parents. There were strong drives to seek separation from parents as a valued opportunity to develop independence. They viewed it as coming into their birthright, rather than as deprivation or abandonment. Family structure that isolates each nuclear family from the families of its origin and the geographical mobility of American families had exposed these young people to separation from parents as a valued and expected experience.

## Definition and Method

We identified various aspects of autonomous behavior as it grew during the transition period, and set up criteria for assessing the observed growth in autonomy in a wide range of life experiences.

All the data on each student was discussed in an assessment conference by five members of the research team, and the students were assessed as high or low in autonomy in comparison with each other. The assessments were made by a consensus in the research group.

"Autonomy" was defined as the ability to make separate, responsible choices. This ability is demonstrated by the feeling of being a separate person rather than an extension of others, an awareness of freedom to make choices in selecting or rejecting outside influences, and assuming responsibility for one's own decisions. We then sought examples of this kind of autonomous behavior in each student's ability to make responsible decisions about his use of time, maintaining academic competency, his choice of major and his vocation, money management, standards of sexual behavior and the commitment to a meaningful heterosexual relationship.

In assessing the degree of autonomy achieved by these students, we differentiated between those students who were able to grow in autonomy while maintaining or increasing a feeling of closeness to their families and the students whose development in autonomy seemed to be achieved at the expense of a feeling of relatedness to their parents.

"Relatedness" was defined as satisfaction for the student in a predominantly positive relationship with his parents—enjoyment in being with his parents based on the student's subjective statements. The criteria for judging relatedness were based on the student's expressed feelings of growing equality with his parents in which there was mutual pleasure, interest in their welfare, desire to communicate with them and his permitting them to be emotionally close to him.

We then combined the two concepts of autonomy and relatedness to parents, and worked out a method of grouping our students. The experiences of each group were studied to determine whether the parent-child interactions showed any consistent patterns within each group.

"Autonomous-relatedness,"[1] a term first suggested to us by Dr. John Bowlby, will be used to describe a capacity for the integration of both independent behavior and maintenance of parental ties.

## Division of Students into Categories

Based on our assessment of autonomy and relatedness, each student was assigned to one of the following four categories.

1. Those high in both autonomy and relatedness (9 students).
2. Those low in both autonomy and relatedness (3 students).

3. Those high in autonomy but low in relatedness (6 students).

4. Those low in autonomy but high in relatedness (1 student).

The 14 students who met all the original competency criteria were classified as follows: Nine were high in both autonomy and relatedness, four were high in autonomy and low in relatedness and one was low in both autonomy and relatedness. Of the five students who did not meet all the original criteria for competency, none was rated high in both autonomy and relatedness, two of them were high in autonomy but low in relatedness, two were low in both autonomy and relatedness and one was low in autonomy but high in relatedness.

Those students rated high in autonomy and relatedness were seen as performing for themselves functions that formerly were carried out by their parents or other adult figures. Having separated themselves from parental care, having compared their family backgrounds with those of new friends at college, most of the students remarked spontaneously that they appreciated their families more now. When they returned home for visits, their increased enjoyment of their parents was based on an awareness of a growing sense of equality between them and their parents. As one boy said:

"I came back with an attitude that I'd like to talk to them more and I know them in a different way. I feel more like an adult and not like a child looking up to his parents. I talk more with them about national affairs and my own future. I have felt closer to them. We spent more time talking together than I would have a year ago."

Another group of students, rated low in both autonomy and relatedness, presented quite a contrast to those described above. They had less a feeling of being separate people and sometimes acted as extensions of their parents. They were less able to assume responsibility for their own decisions. They frequently were unable to perceive where the responsibility for their actions, in fact, resided and looked for others to make decisions for them. They were often unaware that they had freedom to make choices in selecting or rejecting outside influences, and sometimes made their decisions on the basis of slavish negativism. These students found it impossible to budget their time in a way that permitted them to fulfill their academic potential. They complained of a lack of "will power" in withstanding temptations inviting them away from studying. Career choices tended to be made more in terms of their parents' unfulfilled expectations for them. Some of the students in this group avoided involvement in heterosexual relationships and one allowed his peers to define his standards for him without differentiating his ideas from those of his peers.

The experience of being away from home did not result in these students feeling closer to their parents. They came home a minimal number of times during the year and once home did not allow their parents to get close to them. Unlike other students who were also involved outside of the home, they seemed to need actively to avoid warm interaction with their parents. Feelings of distance were maintained through predominantly hostile negativism, detachment or pseudo compliance.

## Parental Interaction with Students of Category 1

The parents of students high in both autonomy and relatedness emerged as distinct people in the interview situation. They were not completely child-centered but were able to meet their own needs as well as the needs of their children. Three mothers holding graduate degrees were combining very successful professional careers with child rearing. Two with fine arts training were using this in group activities. The fathers expressed satisfaction in their vocations. They all demonstrated strong inner direction in their life activities. The parents demonstrated a high degree of clarity in the area of values and standards, and had the ability to communicate these values to the students, particularly noticeable with respect to college. The students were aware of their parents' preferences; the parents did not feel that they had to hide their wishes in order to avoid unduly influencing the students. For example, in discussing this, one mother said:

"We gave her some guidance in terms of dinner table conversation. We'd say such things as the fact that we thought a liberal arts college was what she wanted; that we preferred not such a large place; that we felt because of her academic record she would have to choose a college that had a good academic standing in order to be satisfied with it. We talked of places that we felt would meet what we would like to have for her."

These parents placed a high value on independence and autonomy and their behavior supported this value, giving congruence between belief and action. These were not parents who tended to undermine autonomy, but provided situations for developing it. Even where a family's financial situation made it necessary for a girl to attend college near her home, the parents tried to provide a situation in which she could develop autonomy with a feeling of separation. Her father said, for example:

"I've taken the position that if Sarah were at Northwestern or Purdue or somewhere five or six hundred miles from home, I couldn't be in close touch with her, and I haven't bothered her. I think she can do pretty well to make her own way for a little bit, even though geographically she is close."

These parents could tolerate a wider area of experimentation on the part of the students, but within a framework of family standards. In several instances they tolerated the steady date situation in high school, even though they did not particularly approve of it. This was not in a context of neglect, but was permitted in the interest of growth. They were available to set limits should this have been necessary, and they did not view the world as a dangerous place for their offspring. The parents had set a realistic form of control in letting their children know that if they moved outside of the framework of the family standards they would have to take responsibility for their own action.

The parents of these students had the feeling that they had done their part; they were able to acknowledge that they had made mistakes, but this was viewed as universal and they felt as the student went off to college that he was ready to take responsibility for his own actions. For example, in discussing his daughter's choice of major and vocation, one father said:

"It's a free choice. You've got to make your own mistakes. I fully expect to continue making mistakes myself and feel that children should be allowed to make their own mistakes also."

This, in turn, seemed to give the student a feeling of confidence that he would be able to handle the situation. The parents regarded the separation and the college experience as a normal expectation and a necessary experience for growth. One father said of his daughter:

"I felt she would do well in her studies. I felt she could take care of herself. I knew that, if she had a problem, she would let us know and we would work it out and, above all, she has a good mind, quick and alert and retentive. I know she will succeed in college."

There was a clear definition of boundaries between the parent and child; the child was not used to work out the problems of the parents. One student expressed appreciation for the feeling of freedom she gained from the fact that her parents did not base their living around her. As she said:

"They may be a little stodgy and square, but they don't center their lives around me. Dad is a dedicated scientist; he has his work. He is happy doing his work without getting too much into my things. I'd be fed up with a parent who was a pal."

The parents were aware that the children had internalized some of their values and that these would govern decisions. One mother said:

"After knowing Ruth all these years, I have a feeling that I can say to Ruth 'All right, go ahead and make your decisions.' I have a feeling that we built certain bases for our judgment as far as Ruth is concerned, and she should be able to go out and make any kind of a decision at this point. I do know that I have the feeling that if she comes to a point where a decision is questionable, she will come and ask. But I think she's ready to make her own decisions."

There was a prevalent feeling that the child knew he was free to turn to his parents for help, but that at this point it was the child's responsibility to ask for help, rather than the parents' responsibility to offer it unsolicited. Thus, the child was regarded as having the equipment to make the decision to ask for help. They permitted the student to have areas of privacy and were clear about the legitimate areas of family concern. For instance, in discussing privacy, one mother said:

"I don't feel that that should be the atmosphere of the home—where the children should feel that they have to confide all. If there are certain things she doesn't want to tell, that's fine; they shouldn't be told."

These students were treated with respect by their parents and not shielded from unpleasant facts. When parents were facing serious operations or illnesses, the students were informed of the circumstances. They were regarded by their parents as adult enough to carry this responsibility.

One family in this group of nine differed in several of these characteristics. The fact that their son was also in the highest autonomous-relatedness category seems to point up the fact that children are not completely bound by their family experiences. He was able to maintain a positive feeling for his parents by displacing his negative feelings onto the college authorities. At the same time, he was also able to find positive features in the college that enabled him to expand his intellectual horizons. This provided him with a new basis for relating to his parents, with whom he could then share many of his new interests. In addition, he used supportive people in his environment to strengthen his moves toward autonomy.

## Parental Interaction with Students of Category 2

Parental interaction with students of low autonomy and low relatedness was in marked contrast to the patterns described with the first group. These parents were less clear about who they were and what they stood for. For instance, one father, discussing the change in family social life after his daughter went to college, said:

"We stopped going to affairs. It's ridiculous. Now, when she was home we used to go. Maybe we are escaping from her. I don't know why, really, or what the reason is. Instead of having—you might say—more freedom, in a sense we didn't take advantage; we had less."

In this family, although the parents had strong feelings against sororities, they never discussed this with their daughter when she was thinking of joining one. Her father said:

"We didn't oppose it. If she wanted it, we didn't oppose it, but inwardly we felt that is one way that perhaps she had to drift with the tide, or she was an outsider. As I said, we opposed it in a broad form, not individually."

This girl did not realize her parents' position until she heard it expressed at a joint family interview held at the end of her freshman year.

The parents of these students often did not act in accordance with their stated beliefs. For example, a father who had always been a militant defender of the working classes changed his views when his own son wanted to work in an office during a summer vacation. The student suddenly found the values he had internalized from his father being depreciated; he found himself in conflict, trying to integrate his internalized values and his father's current expectation.

The boundary between the student and his parents appeared less clear in these families. They tended to perceive the student as an extension of themselves and therefore had a less clear perception of what the student's abilities and interests were. One father appeared to be living out his own unfulfilled ambitions through his son, obscuring his perception of the student's own interests. The student was unable to free himself and make use of his own potential in a self-directed manner. The father controlled the son's choice by sug- gestion, rather than by clearly stated preferences. Thus, the student could never be quite sure when he was making his own choices and when he was being manipulated by his father. He said:

"It's always a suggestion you make, but ultimately it's what you want! I don't think I had a choice."

There was a relative lack of communication in these families compared to the first group. Students did not recognize the needs or interests of their parents and the parents were unable to recognize and meet some of the needs of the students. When one girl was asked about changes in family relationships during her freshman year, she said:

"Well, as far as finding out what some of my father's interests are, it sure is a surprise. I wish that I had known about them a long time ago; it might have done me a lot of good. I guess we never talked about it."

### Parental Interaction with Students of Category 3

Six of the students became more autonomous, but their growth seemed accompanied by a sense of distance from their parents. All six reported that they felt more "at home" in college than with their families. One of them did not move from a relationship of closeness to his parents to one of distance during the transition: His attitude of detachment had existed prior to the transition period, indeed seemed to be one of long standing. It can be hypothesized from our limited data that this boy very early began to defend himself from his mother's intrusiveness and his father's criticism by making it impossible for them to be close to him. This attitude had not created strain in the family because the parents tended to substitute the intellectual for the emotional in their interpersonal relationships.

Five of these students broke away from assigned family roles as they moved into the college situation. When they returned home they did not revert to their previous roles, and clashes with parents occurred. In two cases, conflict arose when the students brought back newly acquired values and emerging personal philosophies that ran counter to family standards. These were two girls who had played important care-taking roles in their homes. One girl who had been willing, at least partially, to accept her mother's values and aspirations for her to have a gay social life, found herself completely at home in the strongly intellectual atmosphere of the college she attended. She returned home with new intellectual and religious values and was shocked and hurt that neither parent was able to accept these developments. The other girl, who had felt out of things in high school, plunged happily into the literary life of her college and found many there who shared her interests and enthusiasm. Her commitment to bohemianism as a way of life was a blow to her mother, who had acquired middle-class comforts by dint of hard work and sacrifice.

Another student, whose father had frequently been absent from the family from the time the boy was in junior high school, had moved into the covertly assigned role of father and husband in the family. After being away at college, this student was able to move out of this role and was functioning more autonomously. His mother, however, was unable to accept this shift and considerable friction and distance emerged between them. In another family, a student moved out of the role of baby in the family, and her mother, who had a great deal invested in her maternal role in relationship to this student, found it difficult to accept her daughter's development into young adulthood.

The relationship between each child in a family and his parents is a unique one. Therefore, we did not assume that the characteristic modes of interaction described above necessarily applied to other children in these same families. In some instances we observed that when other children in the family were discussed different patterns of relationship emerged, and we recognized that unique characteristics of particular children evoked different ranges of potential parental responses.

### Summary and Comparison of Interactional Patterns

We could identify a benign pattern of interaction established between the parents and students rated high in autonomy and relatedness—one in which the students were effective in conveying to their parents their ability to handle responsibilities, thus enhancing their parents' confidence in them. This parental confidence enabled the students to reach out and develop in more autonomous ways, and the parents were able to respond in turn with pleasure. There was a gradual loosening of parental reins of control, with more and more responsibility turned over to the students, with a growing feeling of equality emerging between the students and their parents.

These parents tended to have rather stable and consistent values and could communicate these values to the students. In their everyday lives they demonstrated the congruence between their beliefs and actions in such a way as to be models for their children; that is, these parents behaved as autonomous people with inner-directed standards of behavior. Thus, we would assume that the development of autonomy for these students was also facilitated through identification with parents who were available as models of autonomous adults.

The parents of students rated low in autonomy and relatedness lacked confidence in the students' ability to achieve autonomy. They were not sure that the students would be successful in college or that they would be able to get along without them. The students experienced less clarity about their parents' values and there was more often a discrepancy between stated values and parental behavior. Although these students also had experiences with jobs as well as opportunities to live away from home, their parents had not been able to respond to their children's growth by a shift in their own image of the students from dependent children to young adults.

The parents continued to accept major responsibility for the students' own actions and the students reciprocated in this pattern. They did not feel as free to move into a more autonomous position in relation to their parents, and attributed their own difficulty in doing so to their parents' attitudes toward them. As a consequence, the parents and students seemed to be caught in a circle of self-fulfilling prophesies about each other, maintaining the students' difficulty in assuming responsibility for themselves.

Since the boundaries between parents and students seemed less clear, there were more struggles about separation. Often the students needed to fall back on rather extreme forms of negativism as a way of attempting to define themselves as separate from their parents. This negativism manifested itself in students not being able to make full use of their assets, as part of the retaliatory struggle with the parents.

The parents of students rated high in autonomy and low in relatedness were able to provide many of the conditions for the development of autonomy, to see their children as separate individuals, to identify many of their assets, to provide them with opportunities to develop their abilities and interests. However, as a group, these parents differ from the parents of the high autonomy-high relatedness students in this respect: The roles the parents assigned their children were less flexible and adaptable to their growing independence than were the roles of the students in the other category. When these students broke away from these assigned roles and became more autonomous, more conflict with their parents occurred.

Lastly, we feel that the various patterns of autonomous-relatedness observed among the different groups of students do not necessarily denote final solutions of the tasks in this area of development. The arbitrary cutoff date in our project, the end of the freshman year, did not, of course, reflect the total response to the problems imposed by the transition. Perhaps those students who achieved autonomy while maintaining distance in relation to their parents may be in a growth-stimulating situation where continued development of autonomy and further changes in family relationships are possible. For some students development may proceed step-wise, dealing with one side of the issue at a time. Perhaps, unsure of their newly exercised autonomy, it is necessary for them to maintain distance from their parents until a sense of consolidation and mastery is achieved. Similarly, there is a possibility that some of those who show an unusual spurt of autonomy, while maintaining a close relationship with their parents, may be restricted in their further development if they are deeply concerned about maintaining the status quo in relationships with their parents.

## References

1. BOWLBY, J. Personal communication.
2. ———. 1960. Separation anxiety. Int. J. Psychoan. (Parts 2 and 3) 41: 89–113.
3. BURLINGHAM, D. AND A. FREUD. 1944. Infants without Families. Allen & Unwin. London, Eng.
4. ERIKSON, E. 1959. Identity and the life cycle. Psychol. Issues Monogr. 1(1): 88–94.
5. SILBER, E. D., A. HAMBURG, G. V. COELHO, E. B. MURPHEY, M. ROSENBERG AND L. I. PEARLIN. 1961. Adaptive behavior in competent adolescents: coping with the anticipation of college. Arch. Gen. Psychiat. 5: 354–365.
6. WESTLEY, W. A. 1958. Emotionally healthy adolescents and their family backgrounds. *In* The Family in Contemporary Society. I. Gladstone, Ed. International Universities Press, Inc. New York, N.Y.

# Family Constellation as a Basic Personality Determinant

*Walter Toman*

This is an attempt to bring attention to a determinant of personality that has been unduly underestimated in spite of its omnipresence and power, namely, family constellation.

Adler was probably the first to appreciate family constellation as a basic personality determinant, listing it as foremost among the objective factors which afford "trustworthy approaches to the exploration of personality" (2, p. 327). He considered the significance of being a first-born, a second child, or a last-born child; of being an only child, an only girl among boys, or an only boy among girls; or of coming from a family with only boys or only girls (1, pp. 230–241). But he did not take into account that the parents had also been children and siblings, and that their marital union may in varying degrees be similar to their own childhood family constellation. Adler did not take into account the effects this may have on the children. He also did not speak of the effects of losses through death or otherwise. It is in such respects that we are endeavoring to carry the Adlerian observations further.

Freud's Oedipus situation, of course, refers to family constellation, but it does, at least literally, represent no more than the constellation of the only child. There is no mention of any other children in the family (see 8, e.g.). Allport has commented that it is of "little individualizing value" (3, p. 561). And parents of single children tend to keep their child focused on them. Single children, in turn, want to remain children (see p. 49 below). It is perhaps in this sense that Adler stated, "The Oedipus complex characterizes a pampered child" (2, p. 185).

From *Journal of Individual Psychology*, 1959, 15(2), pp. 199–211. Reprinted by permission of the editor, Journal of Individual Psychology.

One thesis is that a person can be characterized relevantly in terms of the people who have been living with him the longest, most intimately, and most regularly, and by incidental losses of such people —i.e., primarily his parents and siblings. The people who have lived with him can, in turn, be characterized relevantly by the people who have been living with *them* the longest, most intimately and most regularly, and by the losses of such people. This will refer primarily to the parents, although the people who have lived with them (their parents and their siblings) are usually no longer present. A person's siblings may need no further attention since their family constellation always overlaps with his own.

As for losses (through death or otherwise) we can deduce the following relationships from several dynamic theories, but also from learning theories and even from common sense: The effects of a loss will ordinarily be severer, (a) the earlier it has occurred in a person's life, (b) the smaller the family, (c) the greater the number of losses that have occurred before, (d) the greater the imbalance of sexes resulting from it, and (e) the longer the responsible survivors took to secure a full-fledged substitute.

Absence of apparent losses in the immediate family does not mean absence of effective losses. Some of the parents' parents or siblings as well as in-laws may have suffered losses, and to the extent that these affect a person's parents, even uncles and aunts, they would have some bearing on the person in question, too. An important aspect of, and guide for, any loss is how the parents take it.

In summary, to characterize a person relevantly one should know the basic givens, or the skeleton, of his family constellation, i.e., the order and the sexes of his siblings, something about the personalities of his parents, and all incidental losses, which he may have suffered. And in order to characterize the parents, one should know the order and sexes of *their* siblings and at least whether their parents "existed" or not, as well as their incidental losses.

In the following we shall examine the effect of family constellation on a person's marital relationship, his friendships, and his vocational choices. This will be followed by the presentation of a clinical case, and a method for quantifying family constellation factors.

## Types of Marriages

In general, it may be assumed that a heterosexual relationship will tend to have better chances of happiness and success, other things being equal, the closer it duplicates for both partners the earliest (intra-familial) patterns set for heterosexual relationships.

Some such hypothesis has been implicit in many of Freud's and Adler's clinical proceedings, but it has been overlooked explicitly as well as implicitly by a number of authors such as Burgess (4, 5, 6, 7), Locke (5, 6, 9), Terman (10), and Wallin (6, 7).

A person can be the first, second, third, etc. child of altogether one, two, three, etc. children, and the sexes may be distributed in many different ways. Varying only position and sex will yield four different constellations with only two children (male-male, male-female, female-female), eight different constellations with three, sixteen with four, or, in short $2^n$ constellations, where $n$ is the number of children in a family. The same holds for each of his parents. Either may come from any one of $2^n$ constellations. Hence their match will be one of $(n\ 2^{n-1})^2$ constellations, if both of them have the same number of siblings, or $nm\ 2^{n+m-2}$, if the numbers of their siblings differ. Consequently, parents who have but one sibling each can theoretically enter no less than sixteen different types of matches with each other. Let us for once pursue all these types of matches with the assumption that no unusual circumstances prevail.

If an older brother of a sister marries the younger sister of a brother [b (g) / (b) g], their chances, other things being equal, would tend to be optimal. They are unlikely to get into conflicts over their seniority rights. He is used to a girl his junior, and she to a boy her senior. And both are used to the other sex.

If an older brother of a sister chooses the older sister of a brother [b (g) / g (b)], things would not be quite so good. Both are used to the other sex, but each would try to be the older one for the spouse, and to transform him or her into a younger sibling. There will be rivalry over seniority rights. Once they have children, preferably of both sexes, they may henceforth be happy with each other, since now they have their "younger siblings."

If an older brother of a sister marries the older sister of a sister [b (g) / g (g)], they would also have conflicts over seniorities. Both were "superior" to their siblings in childhood. But the wife would also have some difficulty in accepting her man. After all, there had been three females in her family (mother, sister, and she, herself) with only one male, father, to share. If they did not want to get into each other's hair, they had to learn how to like each other regardless of the man in the family. They had to become somewhat more "homosexual." Sometimes, of course, especially if they could not work out such a solution, the girl may be only too anxious to get a man of her own; which, by the way, is not the best condition for making such an important decision.

If an older brother of a sister marries the younger sister of a sister [b (g) / (g) g], they may have no problem over seniority. The wife would be used to having a sibling her senior, and her husband to having one his junior. Yet she may not be used to having a man.

Similar arguments could be raised for an older brother of a brother who marries the older sister of a brother [b (b) / g (b)] or of a sister [b (b) / g (g)], or the younger sister of a brother [b (b) / (b) g] or of a sister [b (b) / g (g)]. Now, however, it is he who would tend to have trouble accepting the woman. The match with the least promise of success among these four would be the second. Both partners would have trouble accepting the other sex, and in addition they would tend to be in conflict over their seniority rights. As soon as they have children, however, they have their longed for "juniors" and may be happier, although there will be a tendency for father to gang up with the boys against the girls, and for mother to do so with her daughters.

Similar conditions would also prevail for the younger brother of a sister who marries the younger sister of a brother [(g) b/ (b) g] or of a sister[(g) b / (g) g], or the older sister of a brother [(g) b / g (b)] or of a sister [(g) b / g (g)]. Among these the third combination would come close to an optimal one, although there will be a touch of a reverse authority relationship (dominant wife, dependent husband).

Finally the younger brother of a brother may marry the older sister of a brother [(b) b / g (b)] or of a sister [(b) b / g (g)], or the younger sister of a brother [(b) b / (b) g] or of a sister [(b) b / (g) g]. Other things being equal, the worst of these and, at the same time, the worst of all sixteen combinations would be the last. Both partners would have trouble accepting the other sex, and they would be in conflict over their juniority rights. Both want older siblings. Therefore not even a child of their own would make a difference, as it does with an older brother of a brother who marries the older sister of a sister [b (b) / g (g)]. In fact, they would not want a child in the first place, and if they happen to have one, that may well be all. Since they are so much in need of an older sibling, they will even tend to forge their child into such a role at the earliest possible time, and that means trouble.

Fortunately for life, in general families do not only have two, but also three, four, five, etc., children, and sometimes only one. In cases of $n > 2$ we can claim that the schematic relationships outlined above would tend to hold at least for the oldest and youngest siblings, while those in between would usually learn in their childhoods how to assume double and triple roles. Consequently, they tend to be somewhat better prepared for all eventualities of match-making than the oldest or youngest siblings are, although the latter may well

be more exuberantly happy when they make an optimal of all possible types of choices. Their happiness is somewhat more difficult to
achieve, but it may be "deeper," if there is such a thing. Methods
of treating quantitatively all aspects discussed will be presented
below.

The single child has only his parents to draw on, so to speak. This
does not mean that children from other sibling constellations do *not*
draw on their parents. On the contrary, the parents are the most
important people in any child's life (although compared to sibling
configurations, their existence or "non-existence" is a fairly simple
given). Psychologically speaking, they sometimes manage to change
their children's seniority-juniority relationships and even their sexes.
As a matter of fact, circumstances other than the parents, such as
looks, talents, handicaps, etc. may also interfere, but we have ruled
these out for the time being and would think that they tend to cancel
each other with larger groups of cases. What happens in families with
two, three, four, etc. children, however, is that, among other things,
they turn to each other for what they cannot get from their parents.
If the parents are happy with each other, they will tend psychologically to move into the children's backgrounds. It is easy to come to
terms with such parents. Hence, the siblings will become relatively
stronger determinants. Only parents who are unhappy with each
other may keep their children anxiously focused on them. Normally
the single child is in this position even with happy parents. We might
say that such a family is already a mildly deficient one. The child has
only his parents to turn to. He does not learn what children of larger
families can learn from their parents, namely, how to treat children.
Therefore, singletons may rather look for a father or mother in a
potential spouse than for a sibling, and more often than others be
content without children of their own. They want to remain the
children themselves. Under certain conditions, however, they may
break away from this attitude and have children of their own, occasionally even ambitious numbers of them.

Losses, apart from being effective in their own right, should tend
to aggravate all prevailing conflicts. The most severe losses will be
those of a parent, or both, and/or of one or more siblings when
occurring in early and/or in late childhood.

If our reasoning is correct, it should be expected that any selection
of individuals needing counseling or psychotherapy would show
poorer than average matches among their parents and greater
amounts of loss suffered either by them or their parents than could
be accounted for by chance.

Inspecting the parents of my own clients, as of today some forty

in all, ranging from those who came to see me only for a few hours
to those who saw me for several years, I found not a single instance
of the two most favorable types of matches [b (g) / (b) g and (g) b / g
(b)] or their fair equivalents. By chance alone there should have
been about four. The most unfavorable matches, on the other hand
[b (b) / g (g) and (b) b / (g) g], were represented 7 times. Furthermore, losses suffered by the clients or their parents (losses in early
or late childhood of one parent, or both, and/or of one or more
siblings, through death, separation, or chronic illness) could be
established in 33 cases.

A study of 20 counseling cases of children between 7 and 14 years
of age at a suburban counseling center revealed also that the matches
of their parents were considerably poorer than chance (not a single
optimal match, only one partly optimal match, 13 poorer matches,
and 6 poorest). Besides, in 16 cases severe losses as defined above had
been suffered by the clients or their parents (see also 11).

### Friendships

What holds for heterosexual relationships should hold for like-sex
relationships or friendships as well. They should have better chances,
other things being equal, the closer they duplicate for the partners
involved the earliest (intra-familial) patterns set for like-sex relationships. Hence in a random sample of like-sex friendships the type
represented most frequently should be that between older brothers
of brothers and younger brothers of brothers, and the type represented least frequently should be that between older brothers of
sisters and younger brothers of sisters. Identical sibling positions
should also have little attraction for each other. Such people may
identify with each other, but would not tend really to get along
together.

These, and a few other, more complicated trends were well born
out by a study of bilateral friendships among male non-coeducational
youths, formed during the European equivalent of high school. Fifteen friendships between boys, all from families of two children (the
easiest to handle in this context), were examined. For inclusion in
this sample, a friendship had to have lasted at least a year, and be
remembered as such by at least four of six former classmates who
rated these friendships retrospectively. The results are presented in
Table 1.

The results show that among the 10 possible friendship combinations those between boys of identical sibling positions did not occur

TABLE 1

Distribution of 15 Friendship Combinations Between Boys from
Families of Two Children

|  | | b (b) | (b) b | b (g) | (g) b |
|---|---|---|---|---|---|
| Older brother of a brother: | b (b) | — | 5 | 2 | 2 |
| Younger brother of a brother: | (b) b | | — | 1 | 4 |
| Older brother of a sister: | b (g) | | | — | 1 |
| Younger brother of a sister: | (g) b | | | | — |

at all. Combinations of maximally different sibling positions (difference of rank as well as sex of sibling) were also rare, i.e., b (b) / (g) b and (b) b / b (g) occurred only twice and once, respectively, whereas younger brothers of brothers and younger brothers of sisters did show an affinity for each other (4 cases), possibly because the first has learned better how to be a boy than has the second, even if he was in a junior position to his brother. The greatest affinity was found between b (b) and (b) b, 5 cases.

Only children, incidentally, showed a preference for friendships with other only children, next, for older brothers of brothers. Middle children appeared to be the least particular about their friends, but more often than others they were members of trios, quartets, etc. The latter, in turn, showed a tendency for "complementary diversification." An only child, an older brother of a brother, a younger brother of a brother, and a younger brother of a brother and of a sister would form one such group, while another was composed of an only child, an older brother of a brother, a middle brother of two brothers, and a younger brother of a sister.

Similar trends could be established for all the friendships that the subjects in question had formed during their lifetimes. And as for friendships before marriage with girls, a certain preference for older sister could be found among younger brothers, and one for younger sisters among older brothers. The findings are, however, too complex and too inconclusive yet to be reported.

## Vocational Choices

Regarding vocational choice our data refer to a somewhat unusual kind of vocation. Fourteen unmarried women between 25 and 40 years of age who had become "foster mothers" and each taken on a family of up to nine children in "Children's Villages, Inc.," were compared to eight women who worked for the same institution, but either did not want to take on families of their own or did not meet the requirements (see also 11). "Children's Villages, Inc." is a Central European institution to take over children from broken homes as soon after the break as possible. One of the assumptions investigated was that "foster mothers" would have to have suffered losses of their own in order to develop an interest in doing something for "orphans." Yet these losses would not have been of the most severe type, say loss of both parents in early childhood, for then the women would not be able to carry out the sacrifice involved in their job. And the losses would not have been of the mildest type, say loss of a friend, for then the women would not develop the interest in orphans. It was found that all "foster mothers" investigated, or their parents, had indeed suffered such losses, whereas the control group showed either extremely severe losses, very mild ones, or none at all, even among their parents. Those with extremely severe losses were those who had tried, but failed, to become "foster mothers." Another assumption was that "foster mothers" would come from larger families than the control group in order to wish to take on a family of up to nine children. This was also found to be the case. Finally, it was assumed that in order to be willing to tolerate the general shortage of men that prevails in the Children's Villages, let alone to forego marriage, the "foster mothers" must have been used to such a shortage at home. It was found among their siblings that the girls outnumbered the boys 2 to 1, while in the control group the ratio was approximately 1 to 1.

## A Clinical Case

Although I have collected some anecdotal and systematic clinical evidence of most aspects dealt with above, I should like to focus on the sibling configurations of parents and the prospects of happiness and success in the family life they create by presenting the following case.

Joe, a boy of 15 years, was referred to me by his parents. He had quit high school and enrolled in a school for commercial art. His parents had wanted him to finish high school so that he could go to college, should he decide to, but he had persuaded them that neither high school nor college would be of use to him. The parents let themselves be persuaded. Only when he switched from sculpture and design to photography, did they get worried and insisted on his seeing someone. The boy was among the most precocious and blase-looking youngsters I had ever seen. He talked and behaved as if he knew everything under the sky, and as if whatever he did not know could not possibly matter. Not in general, of course, he explained. No, there was nothing that would not matter to some people. But for him, at this time and under the present circumstances, nothing did matter. Etc.

Our questions in this context were: Why had he been an only child although his parents were well-to-do? And why does he pretend so doggedly to be an adult?

It turned out that his father was the younger brother of a brother, and his mother the younger sister of a sister. Other things being equal, this has been outlined (p. 000)[sic]as the worst of all possible matches of parents coming from families of two children only. Both parents would have conflicts over the acceptance of the other sex and over their juniority rights. Both would want an older sibling. A child would make no difference. They would not even want one, but if they should have one, they would tend to forge it into the role of an older sibling at the earliest possible time.

This is precisely what had happened to Joe. The parents were acutely at a loss as to how to guide him in view of his "poor" educational choice, but unconsciously they had wanted *him* to guide *them* all along, and this is what he had tried to do the best he could. The fact that both parents were the youngest also probably explains why they had no more children. One child was already too much, unless children would come as grown-ups to begin with.

In the course of treatment Joe wanted to quit art school and emigrate to Australia, then to become a pilot, then to join the French Foreign Legion in North Africa, not so much in order to run away from an intolerable home, but to find perhaps what he lacked at home: a leader, a guide, someone, who knew how to distinguish "right" from "wrong," who would not be interested in Joe's elaborate rationalization's for what he was going to do, but would tell him in no uncertain terms what to do.

Our next question was: Why did the parents make such an incompatible choice? It turned out that, at the time of choice, Joe's mother had just been gravely disappointed by a suitor who suddenly married someone else. He was the older brother of two sisters. And Joe's father had just been disappointed, too, although by a girl who had been an only and allegedly very spoiled child. She married a dear friend of his, incidentally an older brother of a brother, whom he had introduced to her with pride. Joe's father and mother found each other while mourning over potential partners they had just lost.

One might say that this was the coincidence that made them find each other "by mistake." But is there such a thing? We are often unable to trace even the most relevant determinants, but that does not mean that they do not exist. In this case, however, some possible determinants were found indeed. The (older) sister of Joe's mother had just been married at that time, conceivably in (imagined) competition with Joe's mother. So when she lost her suitor, she had to get another one quickly. Also her mother had allegedly been an ungiving mother who regretted to this day that she gave up teaching in favor of marriage, and the reasons for this derived, in turn, from her family constellation.

Joe's father, on the other hand, had had a father who entertained women besides his wife as far back as Joe's father could remember. His mother had been a kind of forsaken woman all along, and his older brother had been her chief pride and consolation. Thus Joe's father had been let down by his father, and then by his mother. He had been traumatized by letdowns, both those experienced and identified with. Hence one should expect him to be quite vulnerable in this respect, and either avoid potential letdowns anxiously or, once they had occurred, get out of them as quickly as possible, if necessary by a haphazard marriage.

### Discussion

We have attempted not to prove, but merely to demonstrate, our theses. The examples could be multiplied and pursued in greater detail. Data concerning areas other than skeleton family constellations have been omitted in order not to distract the reader.

Family constellations do not explain everything. Without their consideration, however, explanations will run into dead ends before long, as I have seen in many case conferences including the most sophisticated. What is more, groups of clinical cases, or techniques of treatment, etc. cannot really and reasonably be compared without being matched, among other things, for family constellation. It might well be that some of the contradictory results found in the literature could be clarified in this way.

It could be argued that what matters is how a person perceives his parents. True. But this is inevitably linked to what the parents really are, ultimately even to what they were like as children, and how they, in turn, perceived their parents. Granted, these matters may be difficult to trace, when it comes to grandparents and great-grandparents; but most adults know about their parents' sibling configurations, about the psychological existence or non-existence of the parents' parents, and about deaths or other final losses.

Data that constitute skeleton family constellations surround us everywhere. I recommend to the reader to investigate his own family constellation as well as that of his prospective or actual spouse, but also those of his parents, his friends, and the friendships and antipathies that prevail among them. I promise surprises and interesting insights, and if only a minimum of tact is exercised, nobody will feel offended. On the contrary, everyone usually likes such an inquiry.

And be sure to inspect a person's parents with special care whenever he does not act as expected. Sometimes an oldest brother appears like a youngest, because this is what his father had been. Or, a girl may act like a boy, because her father had come from a family of boys only, expected at least some boys of his own, and had to transform one of his three girls into a son. Or, a younger brother may behave like an oldest, because his older brother happened to be of low intelligence, and his older sister ran away from home when she was fourteen, which left him with two younger sisters.

It has been my experience that data on family constellation are of greater diagnostic and prognostic value than psychological test data that can be secured only in a greater amount of time. Good clinicians, I am sure, have considered these data all along, but did this implicitly or "intuitively" rather than explicitly, which in the long run might not be enough.

## Quantification of Constellation Factors

Generally speaking, the following formulas have been found helpful and valid means of quantifying conflicts and losses for purposes of broader comparison (see also 12).

(a) The degree of sex conflict prevailing in a marriage can be expressed for each spouse by $d_s$, the coefficient of sex distribution, as a function of the number of his same-sex siblings $(n_s)$ over the number of siblings in the family, Formula 1:

$$d_s = \frac{n_s}{n - 1} \qquad (1)$$

Hence the older brother of a sister and brother who married the younger sister of two brothers—expressed symbolically by b(g, b) / ( b, b) g—would have a sex conflict of $d_s = 0.5$, and his wife one of zero. The degree of overall sex conflict $(d_s)$ would be the sum of both.

(b) Similarly, the degree of rank conflict prevailing in a marriage can be expressed for each spouse by $d_r$, the coefficient of rank distribution, as the difference between the number of junior siblings $(n_{jun})$ and the number of senior siblings $(n_{sen})$ over the number of siblings of the person in question, Formula 2:

$$d_r = \frac{n_{jun} - n_{sen}}{n - 1} \qquad (2)$$

A positive value of $d_r$ indicates that the person is more of a senior, a negative value, that he is more of a junior. The absolute value of $d_r$ shows how much. Thus a man who has had an older brother, a young sister and a younger brother—symbolically: (b) b(g, b)—would have a value of $d_r = 0.33$, and the younger sister of a brother and sister—(b, g)g—a value of $d_r = -1$. If these two people were married, the sum of $d_r$ would express their overall rank conflict $(d_{r_m})$. Its value would be $d_{r_m} = -0.67$. The couple would remain somewhat in need of a senior.

(c) Marriage will for many people differ in number from the peer relationships the spouses have had at home. The discrepancy coefficient $d_n = \frac{n - 2}{n}$ would express it for each spouse, and the sum of the absolute values would express it for the couple $(d_{n_m})$.

(d) A last conflict concerns the degree to which the configuration of a couple's children duplicates their own sibling configurations. The coefficient $d_{ch} = 1 - \frac{n_d}{n - 1}$ would express it for each spouse, where $n_d$ is the number of (dual) sibling relationships of a parent that have found (one or more) duplicates in his children, and $n$, as usual, is the number of children that constitute his sibling configuration. There are other ways, too, of considering a couple's children, but they must be foregone in this context.

Pooling all conflicts, we could say that the overall amount of conflict prevailing in a marriage $(d_t)$ is expressed by Formula 3:

$$d_t = \frac{d_{s_m} + d_{r_m} + d_{n_m} + d_{ch_m}}{4} \qquad (3)$$

Losses suffered by spouses could be treated either in their own rights or as aggravators of all prevailing conflicts. The overall amount of loss $(l_t)$ is expressed by Formulas 4 to 8, for each person in question.

In these formulas $l_t$ is the total cumulative loss; $a_p$ the present age (in years) of the person in question; $n_t$ the total number of

$$l_t = \frac{1}{\log a_p} \sum_{i=1}^{n_t} \frac{l_i}{c_i} \qquad (4)$$

$$l = \frac{1}{-\log k} \qquad (5)$$

$$k = \frac{a_l^t}{a_o \, a \, \sqrt{a} \, (n-1)} \qquad (6)$$

$$c = 1 - (s_b - s_a) \qquad (7)$$

$$s = \frac{n_s}{n} \qquad (8)$$

losses the person has suffered; $l$ is the individual loss, and $k$ the measure of its magnitude; $a_l$ the age (in years) of the person lost, $a_o$ the age of the oldest person in the immediate family; $t$ represents the length of time (in years) that the lost person has lived with the person in question; $a$ is the person's own age at the time of loss; $n$ is the number of persons that constitute the family (including parents, siblings, and the person in question); $c$ is the change-of-sex-balance coefficient; $s$ is the sex-balance coefficient, and $n_{s_l}$ the number of persons in the entire family that are of the lost person's sex; $s_b$ is $s$ before the loss, and $s_a$ thereafter. For the sake of simplicity $c$ could be taken as one.

The values of $l_t$ will vary between zero and infinity. The larger they are, the severer the cumulative loss suffered by the person concerned. Values of one and above will indicate severe losses, while values of three and above represent rather hopeless predicaments. The amount of loss prevailing in a marriage $(l_m)$ is the sum of $l_t$ of both spouses.

If a pooled measure of conflict and loss prevailing in a marriage $(P_m)$ is desired, and if we assume that losses aggravate conflicts—an assumption that has withstood a preliminary test of validity—Formula 9 may serve as a first approximation:

$$P_m = (d_t)^{1+l_m} \qquad (9)$$

Conflicts and losses experienced by the spouses' parents could also be included, although they would have to be weighted down (quartered) before summation.

Relationships between people of the same sex can be treated analogously. In Formula 1, however, $n_s$ should be the number of opposite-sex siblings rather than same-sex siblings, and Formula 4 would have to be multiplied rather than divided by $c$.

## Summary

A person can be characterized relevantly and efficiently in terms of the people he has lived with the longest, most intimately and most regularly, and by the losses of such people that he has suffered. A skeleton family constellation can be reconstructed from the order and sexes of a person's siblings, from his parents' positions among their siblings, from the degree of compatibility for each other de-rivedtherefrom, and from the losses that have occurred. The psychological significance for several life problems of these simple and easy-to-obtain data has been illustrated with a number of social psychological studies and a clinical case. A more formal quantitative treatment of the problem has been briefly suggested.

## References

1. ADLER, A. *Social interest*. New York: Putnam, 1939.
2. ADLER, A. *The Individual Psychology of Alfred Adler*. New York: Basic Books, 1956.
3. ALLPORT, G. W. *Personality*. New York: Holt, 1937.
4. BURGESS, E. W., & COTTREEL, L. S. *Predicting success or failure in marriage*. New York: Prentice-Hall, 1939.
5. BURGESS, E. W., & LOCKE, H. J. *The Family from institution to companionship*. (2nd ed.) New York: American Book Co., 1953.
6. BURGESS, E. W., & WALLIN, P. Predicting adjustment in marriage from adjustment in engagement. *Amer. J. Sociol.*, 1944, 49, 524–530.
7. BURGESS, E. W., WALLIN, P., & SCHULTZ, GLADYS D. *Courtship, engagement, and marriage*. Philadelphia: Lippincott, 1954.
8. FREUD, S. *A general introduction to psychoanalysis*. New York: Garden City Publ. Co., 1943.
9. LOCKE, H. J. *Predicting adjustment in marriage*. New York: Holt, 1951.
10. TERMAN, L. M., *Psychological factors in marital happiness*. New York: McGraw-Hill, 1958.
11. TOMAN, W. Die Familienkonstellation und ihre psychologische Bedeutung. *Psychol. Rdsch.*, 1959, 10, 1–15.
12. TOMAN, W. Introduction to psychoanalytic theory. New York: Pergamon Press, in press.

# Sex-Role and Parental Identification

*David B. Lynn*

It is doubtful that psychological theories have fully posed much less resolved the question of the extent of sex differences in personality development. In this connection Sarason *et al.* comment: "No one to our knowledge has denied they [such sex differences] are pervasive, and yet the problem of degree of pervasiveness has not been critically examined despite its implications for theory, methodology, and the direction of future research" (23, p. 260).

A perusal of the journals shows that many studies, which include both male and female Ss in the sample, do not make provisions for sex differences in the hypotheses. Where sex differences are found they are, consequently, rationalized *post facto*. Moreover, often no statistical analysis of sex differences is performed, despite their importance in psychological processes.

This paper presents a theoretical formulation which postulates basic sex differences in the *nature* of sex-role and parental identification, as well as basic differences in the *process of achieving* such identification. The developmental processes described are considered neither inevitable nor universal. If they are appropriate to the U.S. culture today, they may, nevertheless, be inappropriate for many other cultures and for a significantly altered U.S. culture of the future. This formulation refers to the "typical" pattern, although recognizing that a "typical" pattern, if not a myth, is at least an exception. Research findings considered relevant to this formulation are reviewed.

Before developing this formulation, let us briefly define identification as it is used here. *Sex-role identification* refers to the internaliza-

From *Child Development*, 1962, 33, pp. 555–564. Reprinted by permission of the author and The Society for Research in Child Development, Inc. © Society for Research in Child Development, Inc., 1962.

tion of the role considered appropriate to a given sex and to the unconscious reactions characteristic of that role. *Parental identification* refers to the internalization of personality characteristics of one's own parent and to unconscious reactions similar to that parent. Thus, theoretically, an individual might be well identified with the appropriate sex-role generally and yet poorly identified with his same-sex parent specifically. This differentiation also allows for the converse circumstances wherein a person is well identified with his same-sex parent specifically and yet poorly identified with the appropriate sex-role generally. In such an instance the parent with whom the individual is well identified is himself poorly identified with the appropriate sex-role. An example might be a girl who is well identified with her own mother, but the mother is identified with the masculine rather than the feminine role. Such a girl, therefore, through her identification with her mother, is poorly identified with the feminine role.

In a previous paper (17) the author differentiated the concept of *sex-role identification* from *sex-role preference* and *sex-role adoption*. The present formulation is a departure from that previous paper and also shares various features in common with others (2, 3, 11, 24).

This formulation uses a hypothesis from the previous paper as a postulate from which to deduce a number of new hypotheses. Hopefully, this formulation will offer a unified theoretical framework consistent with a number of varied findings concerning sex differences.

The aspects of the previous formulation pertinent to the present one are summarized as follows:

. Both male and female infants were hypothesized to learn to identify with the mother. Boys, but not girls, must shift from this initial identification with the mother to masculine identification. The girl has the same-sex parental model for identification (the mother) with her more than the boy has the same-sex model (the father) with him. Much incidental learning takes place from the girl's contact with her mother which she can apply directly in her life.

However, despite the shortage of male models, a somewhat stereotyped and conventional masculine role is nonetheless spelled out for the boys, e.g., by his mother and women teachers in the absence of his father and male teachers. In this connection a study by Sherriffs and Jarrett (28) indicated that men and women share the same stereotypes about the two sexes. Through the reinforcement of the culture's highly developed system of rewards for indications of masculinity and punishment for signs of femininity, the boy's early learned identification with the mother eventually weakens and becomes more or less replaced by the later learned identification with a culturally defined, somewhat stereotyped masculine role. *"Consequently, males tend to identify with a cultural stereotype of the masculine role, whereas females tend to identify with aspects of their own mothers' role specifically"* (17, p. 130). This hypothesis was generally supported by the research findings reviewed (9, 16).

This hypothesis is not meant to minimize the role of the father in the development of males. Studies of father-absence suggest that the presence of the father in the home is of great importance for boys (1, 18, 25). It is beyond the scope of this paper to elaborate on the role of the father, but it is our position that it has a very different place in the development of the boy's masculine-role identification than does the mother in the girl's mother identification. The father, as a model for the boy, may be thought of as analogous to a map showing the major outline but lacking most details, whereas the mother, as a model for the girl, might be thought of as a detailed map. The father, of course, serves many other functions besides that of model for the boy's masculine-role identification. He may, for example, reinforce the boy's masculine strivings and stimulate his drive to achieve masculine-role identification. Because fathers typically do spend so much time away from home and, even when home, usually do not participate in as many intimate activities with the child as does the mother (e.g., preparation for bed), it is probably true that the time spent with the father takes on much importance in the boy's identification development.

Although recognizing the contribution of the father in the identification of males and the general cultural influences in the identification of females, it nevertheless seems meaningful, for simplicity in developing this formulation, to refer to *masculine-role identification* in males as distinguished from *mother identification* in females.

It is postulated that the task of achieving these separate kinds of identification for each sex requires separate methods of learning. These separate identification tasks seem to parallel the two kinds of learning tasks differentiated by Woodworth and Schlosberg: the *problem* and the *lesson*. "With a problem to master the learner must explore the situation and find the goal before his task is fully presented. In the case of a lesson, the problem-solving phase is omitted or at least minimized, as we see when the human subject is instructed to memorize this poem or that list of nonsense syllables, to examine these pictures with a view to recognizing them later. . . ." (36, p. 529). The task of achieving mother identification for the female is con-

sidered roughly parallel to the learning *lesson,* and the task of achieving masculine-role identification for the male is considered roughly
parallel to the learning *problem.*

It is assumed that finding the goal does not constitute a major
problem for the girl in learning her mother identification lesson.
Since the girl, unlike the boy, need not shift from the initial mother
identification and since she typically has the mother with her a relatively large proportion of the time, it is postulated that the question
of the object of identification (the mother) for the girl seldom arises.
She learns the mother identification lesson in the context of an intimate personal relationship with the mother, partly by imitation,
which as used here includes covert practice of the actions characteristic of the mother (19). She also learns the mother identification
lesson through the mother's selective reinforcement of mother-
similar tendencies in the girl. Hartup (12) did a relevant study
concerning parental imitation in children aged 3 to 5 in which he
correlated sex-role preference in the Brown It Scale (2) with the
degree to which the S's doll play showed the child doll imitating
the same-sex parental doll. The results suggested to Hartup that girls
become feminine partly as a result of a tendency to imitate their
mothers more than their fathers and that the acquisition of masculinity by boys appears to be independent of the tendency to imitate
the father more than the mother.

Similarly, abstracting principles defining mother identification is
not considered concern for the girls. Any bit of behavior on the
mother's part may be of potential importance in learning the mother
identification lesson, and therefore the girl need not abstract principles defining the feminine role. It is not principles defining the
feminine role that the girl need learn, but rather an identification
with her specific mother.

It is assumed, on the other hand, that finding the goal *does* constitute a major problem for the boy in solving that masculine-role
identification problem. There is evidence to indicate that between
two-thirds and three-fourths of children by the age of 3 are able to
make the basic distinction between sexes (6, 7, 26). When the boy
begins to be aware that he does not belong in the same sex-category
as the mother, he must then find the proper sex-role identification
goal. Hartley says, of the identification problem that faces the boy,
". . . the desired behavior is rarely defined positively as something
the child *should* do, but rather negatively as something he should
*not* do or be—anything, that is, that the parent or other people regard

as 'sissy.' Thus, very early in life the boy must either stumble on the right path or bear repeated punishment without warning when he accidentally enters into the wrong ones" (11, p. 458). From these largely negative admonishings, often made by women and often without the benefit of the presence of a male model most of his waking hours, the boy must learn to set the masculine role as his goal. He must also restructure the admonishings, often negatively made and given in many contexts, in order to abstract the principles defining the masculine role.

One of the basic steps in this formulation can now be taken. It is assumed that, in learning the appropriate identification, each sex is thereby acquiring separate methods of learning which are subsequently applied to learning tasks generally. The little girl acquires a learning method which primarily involves: (a) a personal relationship and (b) imitation rather than restructuring the field and abstracting principles. On the other hand, the little boy acquires a different learning method which primarily involves: (a) defining the goal; (b) restructuring the field; and (c) abstracting principles.

## Hypotheses

The following hypotheses are considered to follow from the above formulation:

1. It is in the context of a close personal relationship with the mother that the little girl learns the mother identification lesson. She is reinforced by appropriate rewards for signs that she is learning this lesson. Since the little girl is rewarded in the context of the personal relationship with her mother, maintaining the rewarding relationship with her mother should acquire strong secondary-drive characteristics. By generalization, the need for affiliation in other situations should also have strong secondary-drive characteristics for the girl.

The boy, relative to the girl, has little opportunity to receive rewards for modeling an adult male in a close personal relationship. He receives his rewards for learning the appropriate principles of masculine-role identification as they are abstracted from many contexts. Therefore, the need for affiliation in general should not acquire as much strength as a secondary drive for males as for females. *Consequently, females will tend to demonstrate greater need for affiliation than males.*

2. In learning to identify with the mother, any bit of behavior on the mother's part might be of potential importance in the girl's perception of her. The mother identification lesson does not require that the girl deviate from the given, but rather that she learn the lesson as presented.

For the boys, solving the problem of masculine-role identification must be accomplished without adequate exposure to adult male models. It must be solved by using the admonishings, such as "don't be a sissy," which, occurring in many contexts, serve as guides in defining the masculine role. To solve the masculine-role identification problem the boy must restructure the field. Therefore, the masculine learning method *does* include restructuring the field as a learning principle. *Consequently, females tend to be more dependent than males on the external context of a perceptual situation and hesitate to deviate from the given.*

3. In the process of solving the masculine-role identification problem, the male acquires a method of learning which should be applicable in solving other problems. On the other hand, the feminine learning method, emerging from the process of learning the mother identification lesson, is not well geared to problem-solving. *Consequently, males tend to surpass females in problem-solving skills.*

4. The masculine learning method is postulated to include abstracting principles, whereas the feminine one is not. The tendency to abstract principles should generalize to other problems in addition to the problem of achieving masculine-role identification. It should, for example, generalize to the acquisition of moral standards. If one is very responsive to the moral standards of others, it is relatively unnecessary to internalize standards. If one, on the other hand, tends to learn moral standards by abstracting moral principles rather than being highly responsive to the standards of others, then one *does* need to internalize one's standards. If one is to stick by one's principles, they had better be internalized. It is postulated that males more than females will tend to learn moral standards by abstracting moral principles. *Consequently, males tend to be more concerned with internalized moral standards than females.*

5. Conversely, the feminine learning method indicates that one learns by imitation through a relationship whereas the masculine learning method does not. The little girl, it was assumed, tends to learn the lesson as given, without restructuring. Such a learning method should generalize to the acquisition of standards. *Consequently, females tend to be more receptive to the standards of others than males.*

## Relevant Findings

Let us now see how consistently these hypotheses correspond to previous findings and whether this formulation helps clarify and unify the data.

Hypothesis 1, predicting that females will demonstrate greater need for affiliation than males, is supported by a study by Edwards (4) which showed that women have significantly higher means than men on affiliation on the Edwards Personal Preference Schedule (EPPS).

McClelland, Atkinson, Clark, and Lowell (20) found that college women did not show an increase in achievement motive scores as a result of the arousal instruction, based on reference to leadership and intelligence, effective for male college students. Women did obtain higher scores, however, when the dimension of "achievement" was social acceptability.

Lansky, Crandall, Kagan, and Baker (15), in a study of children aged 13 to 18, used the French Insight Test (5) to measure affiliation. The French test, as used in this study, consisted of 20 items describing a characteristic behavior of a boy (girl), e.g., "Tom never joins clubs or social groups." For each item the S answers these three questions: (a) what is the boy (girl) like? (b) what does he (she) want to have or do? and (c) what are the results of his (her) behavior apt to be? Girls were significantly higher than boys on preoccupation with *affiliation*, which was scored when the goal is to be liked or accepted by others or to be part of a group.

When Harris (10) repeated Symonds' 1935 studies (30, 31) of having adolescents rank interests, he found that girls persist in their greater interest in social relations than boys. When Winkler (34) analyzed the replies of children aged 7 to 16, he found that girls seemed more interested than boys in social relationships, especially face-to-face contacts. The girls' early preoccupation with affiliation was noted by Goodenough (8) who found that nursery school girls drew more pictures of persons and mentioned persons more often than boys.

Thus, these data are consistent with hypothesis 1 that females will demonstrate greater need for affiliation than males.

Evidence concerning hypothesis 2, predicting that females tend to be more dependent than males on the external context of a perceptual situation and will hesitate to deviate from the given, is furnished by Witkin, Lewis, Hertzman, Machover, Meissner, and Wapner (35). They found that female Ss were more readily influenced by misleading cues than were male $S$s and thus were higher in "perceptual-field dependence."

Additional evidence concerning this hypothesis is found in a study by Wallach and Caron (33) with sixth-grade school children. These children were given a concept attainment session in which to establish criteria concerning geometric forms with certain characteristics. A test session followed in which the $S$s judged whether figures of varying deviation from the standard were similar to it. It was found that girls tolerated less deviation than males by every index, thus agreeing with the hypothesis that females more than males hesitate to "move away" from the given. Both studies are in agreement with hypothesis 2.

Studies reported by Sweeney (29) are relevant to hypothesis 3 that males generally surpass females in problem-solving skills. Most of the studies reported by Sweeney support this hypothesis. Moreover, he reported experiments of his own which demonstrate that men solve certain classes of problems with greater facility than do women, even when differences in intellectual aptitude, special knowledge or training, and special abilities are controlled. Sweeney obtained scores on the College Board Scholastic Aptitude test for 130 men and 139 women to whom McNemar (21) had given four tests of logical reasoning: False Premises, Essential Operations, Syllogisms, and Problem Solving. Significant differences favoring the men were found on all four of these tests for 100 pairs who had been matched in verbal aptitude scores. For 90 pairs matched in mathematical aptitude and 69 pairs matched both in verbal and mathematical aptitude, a difference was obtained only for Problem Solving, a test which essentially involves arithmetic reasoning. In Sweeney's most elaborate experiment, large samples of men and women were given a wide variety of problems. Significant sex differences were obtained for groups matched in general intelligence, spatial ability, mechanical comprehension, mathematics achievement, or the amount of training in mathematics. In general, the results confirmed the hypothesis that sex differences favoring men will occur in problems which involve difficulties in restructuring, but not in similar problems which involve no such difficulties.

Milton's study (22) with college students is pertinent to hypothesis 3 concerning sex differences in problem-solving skills. In this study the Terman-Miles M-F test (32) was the primary index of sex-role typing, although other M-F questionnaires were also employed. Two types of problem-solving skill, restructuring and straightforward solution, were employed, half requiring numerical solutions and half nonnumerical. In general, the results indicate that there is a positive relation between the degree of masculine sex-role typing and problem-solving skill both across sexes and within a sex. When this relation is accounted for, the difference between men and women in problem-solving performance is diminished.

Thus, these studies are consistent with hypothesis 3 that males generally surpass females in problem-solving skill. Moreover, Milton's study also suggests that these differences are accounted for in the typical sex-role development of each sex.

Hypothesis 4, suggesting that males tend to be more concerned with internalized moral standards than females, is consistent with findings in the previously mentioned study of children aged 13 to 18 by Lansky, Crandall, Kagan, and Baker (15). The Ss were given a story completion test which was designed to elicit responses regarding severity of moral standards and defenses against guilt following transgression of such standards. *Severity of moral standards* was rated for the degree to which the hero (heroine) punished himself, consciously or unconsciously, for his actions. The boys scored higher than girls on this variable. This finding is considered to support hypothesis 4 in that the *severity of moral standards* was scored when the hero (heroine) punished himself, thus implying that the standards are internalized.

Data from two national sample interview studies of adolescents, reported by Douvan (3), have relevance here. In answer to two questions to detect self-awareness, boys showed greater concern with establishing satisfactory internal standards and personal control than girls.

Findings in Douvan's studies are also in agreement with hypothesis 5 that females will be more receptive to the standards of others than males. Douvan found that girls are more likely to show an unquestioned acceptance of parental regulation. Koch (13, 14), along with Sheehy (27), found girls to be more obedient and amenable to social controls than boys. Thus, these studies seem consistent with hypothesis 5.

In general, the hypotheses that were generated by the theoretical formulation seem consistent with the data. Thus, by postulating that separate learning methods for the two sexes are derived in the process of acquiring appropriate identification, one can formulate hypotheses which are consistent with very diverse findings ranging from the males' superior problem-solving skill to the females' greater need for affiliation. It is not assumed that this formulation, in and of itself, adequately accounts for these diverse findings even though it is generally consistent with them. It is beyond the scope of this paper to attempt to integrate motivation into the formulation, or the psychological implications of anatomical and physiological differences, or adequately to place the role of the father in the development of identification in each sex. These steps, and others, would be necessary adequately to account for these findings. However, it is felt that a formulation along the lines presented here may prove to have a place in more elaborate theories of identification development and may prove helpful in making more sensitive hypotheses concerning psychological sex differences.

## Summary

The purpose of this paper is to present a theoretical formulation which postulates basic sex differences in the *nature* of sex-role and parental identification, as well as basic differences in the *process of achieving* such identification. There was a differentiation made between *sex-role identification and parental identification*.

The theoretical formulation in this paper used a hypothesis from a previous one (17) as a postulate from which to derive a number of new hypotheses. That hypothesis suggested that males tend to identify with a cultural stereotype of the masculine role, whereas females tend to identify with aspects of their own mothers' role specifically. For simplicity this paper refers to *masculine-role identification* in males as distinguished from *mother identification* in females.

This formulation adopted the distinction made by Woodworth and Schlosberg (36) between two kinds of learning tasks, viz., the problem and the lesson. This distinction was used in describing the separate task assigned each sex in learning the appropriate identification. It was further assumed that, in learning the appropriate identification, each sex acquires separate methods of learning which are subsequently applied to learning tasks generally. In learning the mother identification lesson, the little girl acquires a learning method which primarily involves: (a) a personal relationship and (b) imitation rather than restructuring the field and abstracting principles. In solving the masculine-role identification problem, the boy acquires a learning method which primarily involves: (a) finding the goal; (b) restructuring the field; and (c) abstracting principles.

By assuming that these learning methods are applicable to learning tasks generally, the following hypotheses were derived:
1. Females will demonstrate greater need for affiliation than males.

2. Females are more dependent than males on the external context of a perceptual situation and will hesitate to deviate from the given.

3. Males generally surpass females in problem-solving skills.

4. Males tend to be more concerned with internalized moral standards than females.

5. Females tend to be more receptive to the standards of others than males.

These hypotheses were in general agreement with the research findings which were reviewed.

## References

1. BACH, G. R. Father-fantasies and father-typing in father-separated children. *Child Develpm.*, 1946, 17, 63–80.

2. BROWN, D. G. Sex-role preference in young children. *Psychol. Monogr.*, 1956, 70, No. 14 (Whole No. 421).

3. DOUVAN, E., Independence and identity in adolescence. *Children.* 1957, 4, 186–190.

4. EDWARDS, A. L. *Edwards Personal Preference Schedule.* Psychological Corp., 1959.

5. FRENCH, E. G. Development of a measure of complex motivation. In J. W. Atkinson (Ed.), *Motives in fantasy, action, and society: a method of assessment and study.* Van Nostrand, 1958. Pp. 242–248.

6. GESELL, A., *et al. The first five years of life.* Harper, 1940.

7. GESELL, A., ILG, F. L., *et al. Infant and child in the culture of today.* Harper, 1943.

8. GOODENOUGH, E. W. Interest in persons as an aspect of sex differences in the early years. *Genet. Psychol. Monogr.*, 1957, 55, 287–323.

9. GRAY, S. W., & KLAUS, R. The assessment of parental identification. *Genet. Psychol. Monogr.*, 1956, 54, 87–109.

10. HARRIS, D. B. Sex differences in the life problems and interests of adolescents, 1935 and 1957. *Child Develpm.*, 1959, 30, 453–459.

11. HARTLEY, R. E., Sex-role pressures and the socialization of the male child. *Psychol. Rep.*, 1959, 5, 457–468.

12. HARTUP, W. W. Some correlates of parental imitation in young children. *Child Develpm.*, 1962, 33, 85–96.

13. KOCH, H. L. Some personality correlates of sex, sibling position, and sex of sibling among five- and six-year-old children. *Genet. Psychol. Monogr.* 1955, 52, 3–51.

14. KOCH, H. L.The relation of certain family constellation characteristics and attitudes of children toward adults. *Child Develpm.*, 1955, 26, 13–40.

15. LANSKY, L. M., CRANDALL, V. J., KAGAN, J., & BAKER, C. T. Sex differences in aggression and its correlates in middle-class adolescents. *Child Develpm.*, 1961, 32, 45–58.

16. LAZOWICK, L. M. On the nature of identification. *J. abnorm. soc. Psychol.*, 1955. 51, 175–183.

17. LYNN, D. B., A note on sex differences in the development of masculine and feminine identification. *Psychol. Rev.*, 1959, 66, 126–135.

18. LYNN, D. B., & SAWREY, W. L. The effects of father-absence on Norwegian boys and girls. *J. abnorm. soc. Psychol.*, 1959, 59, 258–261.

19. MACCOBY, E. E. Role-taking in childhood and its consequences for social learning. *Child Develpm.*, 1959, 30, 239–252.

20. McCLELLAND, D. C., ATKINSON, J. W., CLARK, R. A., & LOWELL, E. L. *The achievement motive*. Appleton-Century-Crofts, 1953.

21. McNEMAR, O. W. Word association, methods of deduction and induction, and reactions to set in good and poor reasoners. *Stanford Univer. Depart. of Psychol., Tech. Rep.* No. 2, 1954.

22. MILTON, G. A. The effects of sex-role identification upon problem-solving skill. *J. abnorm. soc. Psychol.*, 1957, 55, 208–212.

23. SARASON, S. B. DAVIDSON, K. S., LIGHTHALL, F. F., WÁITE, R. R., & RUEBUSH, B. K. *Anxiety in elementary school children*. Wiley, 1960.

24. SEARS, R. R., MACCOBY, E. E., & LEVIN, H. *Patterns of child rearing*. Row, Peterson, 1957.

25. SEARS, R. R., PINTLER, M. H., & SEARS, P. S. Effect of father separation on pre-school children's doll play aggression. *Child Develpm.*, 1946, 17, 219–243.

26. SEWARD, G. H. *Sex and the social order*. McGraw-Hill, 1946.

27. SHEEHY, L. M., *A study of preadolescents by means of a personality inventory*. Catholic Univer. of America, 1938.

28. SHERRIFFS, A. C., & JARRETT, R. F. Sex differences in attitudes about sex differences. *J. Psychol.*, 1953, 35, 161–168.

29. SWEENEY, E. J. Sex differences in problem solving. *Stanford Univer. Depart. of Psychol., Tech. Rep.* No. 1, 1953.

30. SYMONDS, P. M. Life interests and problems of adolescence. *Sch. Rev.*, 1936, 44, 506–518.

31. SYMONDS, P. M. Sex differences in the life problems and interests of adolescents. *Sch. & Soc.*, 1936, 43, 751–752.

32. TERMAN, L. M., & MILES, C. C. *Sex and personality*. McGraw-Hill, 1936.

33. WALLACH, M. A., & CARON, A. J., Attribute criteriality and sex-linked conservatism as determinants of psychological similarity. *J. abnorm. soc. Psychol.*, 1959, 59, 43–50.

34. WINKLER, J. B. Age trends and sex differences in the wishes, identifications, activities and fears of children. *Child Develpm.*, 1949, 20, 191–200.

35. WITKIN, H. A., LEWIS, H. B., HERTZMAN, M., MACHOVER, K., MEISSNER, P. B., & WAPNER, S. *ePrsonality through perception*. Harper, 1954,

36. WOODWORTH, R. S., & SCHLOSBERG, H. *Experimental psychology*. Holt, 1954.

# A Cross-Cultural Survey
# of Some Sex Differences in Socialization

*Herbert Barry III, Margaret K. Bacon, and Irvin L. Child*

In our society certain differences may be observed between the typical personality characteristics of the two sexes. These sex differences in personality are generally believed to result in part from differences in the way boys and girls are reared. To the extent that personality differences between the sexes are thus of cultural rather than biological origin, they seem potentially susceptible to change. But how readily susceptible to change? In the differential rearing of the sexes does our society make an arbitrary imposition on an infinitely plastic biological base, or is this cultural imposition found uniformly in all societies as an adjustment to the real biological differences between the sexes? This paper reports one attempt to deal with this problem.

## Data and Procedures

The data used were ethnographic reports, available in the anthropological literature, about socialization practices of various cultures. One hundred and ten cultures, mostly nonliterate, were studied. They were selected primarily in terms of the existence of adequate ethnographic reports of socialization practices and secondarily so as to obtain a wide and reasonably balanced geographical distribution. Various aspects of socialization of infants and children were rated on a 7-point scale by two judges (Mrs. Bacon and Mr. Barry). Where the ethnographic reports permitted, separate ratings were made for the socialization of boys and girls. Each rating was indicated as either

From *Journal of Abnormal and Social Psychology*, 1957, 55(3), pp. 327–332. Reprinted by permission of the senior author and American Psychological Association.

confident or doubtful; with still greater uncertainty, or with complete lack of evidence, the particular rating was of course not made at all. We shall restrict the report of sex difference ratings to cases in which both judges made a confident rating. Also omitted is the one instance where the two judges reported a sex difference in opposite directions, as it demonstrates only unreliability of judgment. The number of cultures that meet these criteria is much smaller than the total of 110; for the several variables to be considered, the number varies from 31 to 84.

The aspects of socialization on which ratings were made included:

1. Several criteria of attention and indulgence toward infants.
2. Strength of socialization from age 4 or 5 years until shortly before puberty, with respect to five systems of behavior; strength of socialization was defined as the combination of positive pressure (rewards for the behavior) plus negative pressure (punishments for lack of the behavior). The variables were:

(a) Responsibility or dutifulness training. (The data were such that training in the performance of chores in the productive or domestic economy was necessarily the principal source of information here; however, training in the performance of other duties was also taken into account when information was available.)

(b) Nurturance training, i.e., training the child to be nurturant or helpful toward younger siblings and other dependent people.

(c) Obedience training.

(d) Self-reliance training.

(e) Achievement training, i.e., training the child to orient his behavior toward standards of excellence in performance, and to seek to achieve as excellent a performance as possible.

Where the term "no sex difference" is used here, it may mean any of three things: (a) the judge found separate evidence about the training of boys and girls on this particular variable, and judged it to be identical; (b) the judge found a difference between the training of boys and girls, but not great enough for the sexes to be rated a whole point apart on a 7-point scale; (c) the judge found evidence only about the training of "children" on this variable, the ethnographer not reporting separately about boys and girls.

## Sex Differences in Socialization

On the various aspects of attention and indulgence toward infants, the judges almost always agreed in finding no sex difference. Out of

96 cultures for which the ratings included the infancy period, 88 (92%) were rated with no sex difference by either judge for any of those variables. This result is consistent with the point sometimes made by anthropologists that "baby" generally is a single status undifferentiated by six, even though "boy" and "girl" are distinct statuses.

TABLE 1

Ratings of Cultures for Sex Differences on Five Variables of
Childhood Socialization Pressure

| Variable | Number of Cultures | Both Judges Agree in Rating the Variable Higher in | | One Judge Rates No Difference, One Rates the Variable Higher in | | Percentage of Cultures with Evidence of Sex Difference in Direction of | | |
|---|---|---|---|---|---|---|---|---|
| | | Girls | Boys | Girls | Boys | Girls | Boys | Neither |
| Nurturance | 33 | 17 | 0 | 10 | 0 | 82% | 0% | 18% |
| Obedience | 69 | 6 | 0 | 18 | 2 | 35% | 3% | 62% |
| Responsibility | 84 | 25 | 2 | 26 | 7 | 61% | 11% | 28% |
| Achievement | 31 | 0 | 17 | 1 | 10 | 3% | 87% | 10% |
| Self-reliance | 82 | 0 | 64 | 0 | 6 | 0% | 85% | 15% |

On the variables of childhood socialization, on the other hand, a rating of no sex difference by both judges was much less common. This finding of no sex difference varied in frequency from 10% of the cultures for the achievement variable up to 62% of the cultures for the obedience variable, as shown in the last column of Table 1. Where a sex difference is reported, by either one or both judges, the difference tends strongly to be in a particular direction, as shown in the earlier columns of the same table. Pressure toward nurturance, obedience, and responsibility is most often stronger for girls, whereas pressure toward achievement and self-reliance is most often stronger for boys.

For nurturance and for self-reliance, all the sex differences are in the same direction. For achievement there is only one exception to the usual direction of difference, and for obedience only two; but for responsibility there are nine. What do these exceptions mean? We have reexamined all these cases. In most of them, only one judge had rated the sexes as differently treated (sometimes one judge, sometimes the other), and in the majority of these cases both judges were now inclined to agree that there was no convincing evidence of a real difference. There were exceptions, however, especially in cases where a more formal or systematic training of boys seemed to imply greater pressure on them toward responsibility. The most convincing cases were the Masai and Swazi, where both judges had originally agreed in rating responsibility pressures greater in boys than in girls. In comparing the five aspects of socialization we may conclude that responsibility shows by far the strongest evidence of real variation in the direction of sex difference, and obedience much the most frequently shows evidence of no sex difference at all.

In subsequent discussion we shall be assuming that the obtained sex differences in the socialization ratings reflect true sex differences in the cultural practices. We should consider here two other possible sources of these rated differences.

1. The ethnographers could have been biased in favor of seeing the same pattern of sex differences as in our culture. However, most anthropologists readily perceive and eagerly report novel and startling cultural features, so we may expect them to have reported unusual sex differences where they existed. The distinction between matrilineal and patrilineal, and between matrilocal and patrilocal cultures, given prominence in many ethnographic reports, shows an awareness of possible variations in the significance of sex differences from culture to culture.

2. The two judges could have expected to find in other cultures the sex roles which are familiar in our culture and inferred them from the material on the cultures. However, we have reported only confident ratings, and such a bias seems less likely here than for doubtful ratings. It might be argued, moreover, that bias has more opportunity in the cases ambiguous enough so that only one judge reported a sex difference, and less opportunity in the cases where the evidence is so clear that both judges agree. Yet in general, as may be seen in Table 1, the deviant cases are somewhat more frequent among the cultures where only one judge reported a sex difference.

The observed differences in the socialization of boys and girls are consistent with certain universal tendencies in the differentiation of adult sex role. In the economic sphere, men are more frequently allotted tasks that involve leaving home and engaging in activities where a high level of skill yields important returns; hunting is a prime example. Emphasis on training in self-reliance and achievement for boys would function as preparation for such an economic role. Women, on the other hand, are more frequently allotted tasks at or near home that minister most immediately to the needs of others (such as cooking and water carrying); these activities have a nurturant character, and in their pursuit a responsible carrying out of established routines is likely to be more important than the development of an especially high order of skill. Thus training in nurturance, responsibility, and, less clearly, obedience, may contribute to preparation for this economic role. These consistencies with adult role go beyond the economic sphere, of course. Participation in warfare, as a male prerogative, calls for self-reliance and a high order of skill where survival or death is the immediate issue. The childbearing which is biologically assigned to women, and the child care which is socially assigned primarily to them, lead to nurturant behavior and often call for a more continuous responsibility than do the tasks carried out by men. Most of these distinctions in adult role are not inevitable, but the biological differences between the sexes strongly predispose the distinction of role, if made, to be in a uniform direction.[2]

The relevant biological sex differences are conspicuous in adulthood but generally not in childhood. If each generation were left entirely to its own devices, therefore, without even an older generation to copy, sex differences in role would presumably be almost absent in childhood and would have to be developed after puberty at the expense of considerable relearning on the part of one or both sexes. Hence, a pattern of child training which foreshadows adult differences can serve the useful function of minimizing what Benedict termed "discontinuities in cultural conditioning" (1).

The differences in socialization between the sexes in our society, then, are no arbitrary custom of our society, but a very widespread adaptation of culture to the biological substratum of human life.

## Variations in Degree of Sex Differentiation

While demonstrating near-universal tendencies in direction of difference between the socialization of boys and girls, our data do not show perfect uniformity. A study of the variations in our data may allow us to see some of the conditions which are associated with, and perhaps give rise to, a greater or smaller degree of this difference. For this purpose, we classified cultures as having relatively large or small sex difference by two different methods, one more inclusive and the other more selective. In both methods the ratings were at first considered separately for each of the five variables. A sex difference rating was made only if both judges made a rating on this variable and at least one judge's rating was confident.

In the more inclusive method the ratings were dichotomized,

separately for each variable, as close as possible to the median into those showing a large and those showing a small sex difference. Thus, for each society a large or a small sex difference was recorded for each of the five variables on which a sex difference rating was available. A society was given an over-all classification of large or small sex difference if it had a sex difference rating on at least three variables and if a majority of these ratings agreed in being large, or agreed in being small. This method permitted classification of a large number of cultures, but the grounds for classification were capricious in many cases, as a difference of only one point in the rating of a single variable might change the over-all classification of sex difference for a culture from large to small.

In the more selective method, we again began by dichotomizing each variable as close as possible to the median; but a society was now classified as having a large or small sex difference on the variable only if it was at least one step away from the scores immediately adjacent to the median. Thus only the more decisive ratings of sex difference were used. A culture was classified as having an over-all large or small sex difference only if it was given a sex difference rating which met this criterion on at least two variables, and only if all such ratings agreed in being large, or agreed in being small.

We then tested the relation of each of these dichotomies to 24 aspects of culture on which Murdock has categorized the customs of most of these societies[3] and which seemed of possible significance for sex differentiation. The aspects of culture covered include type of economy, residence pattern, marriage and incest rules, political integration, and social organization. For each aspect of culture, we grouped Murdock's categories to make a dichotomous contrast (sometimes omitting certain categories as irrelevant to the contrast). In the case of some aspects of culture, two or more separate contrasts were made (e.g., under form of marriage we contrasted monogamy with polygyny, and also contrasted sororal with nonsororal polygyny). For each of 40 comparisons thus formed, we prepared a 2 x 2 frequency table to determine relation to each of our sex-difference dichotomies. A significant relation was found for six of these 40 aspects of culture with the more selective dichotomization of over-all sex difference. In four of these comparisons, the relation to the more inclusive dichotomization was also significant. These relationships are all given in Table 2, in the form of phi coefficients, along with the outcome of testing significance by the use of $\chi^2$ or Fisher's exact test. In trying to interpret these findings, we have also considered the nonsignificant correlations with other variables, looking for consistency and inconsistency with the general implications of the significant findings. We have arrived at the following formulation of results:

1. Large sex difference in socialization is associated with an economy that places a high premium on the superior strength, and superior development of motor skills requiring strength, which characterize the male. Four of the correlations reported in Table 2

TABLE 2

Culture Variables Correlated with Large Sex Difference in Socialization, Separately for Two Types of Sample

| Variable | More Selective Sample | | More Inclusive Sample | |
|---|---|---|---|---|
| | $\phi$ | N | $\phi$ | N |
| Large animals are hunted | .48* | (34) | .28* | (72) |
| Grain rather than root crops are grown | .82** | (20) | .62** | (43) |
| Large or milking animals rather than small animals are kept | .65* | (19) | .43 * | (35) |
| Fishing unimportant or absent | .42* | (31) | .19 | (69) |
| Nomadic rather than sedentary residence | .61** | (34) | .15 | (71) |
| Polygyny rather than monogamy | .51* | (28) | .38** | (64) |

$*p < .05.$
$**p < .01.$
Note.—The variables have been so phrased that all correlations are positive. The phi coefficient is shown, and in parentheses, the number of cases on which the comparison was based. Significance level was determined by $\chi^2$, or Fisher's exact test where applicable, using in all cases a two-tailed test.

clearly point to this generalization: the correlations of large sex difference with the hunting of large animals, with grain rather than root crops, with the keeping of large rather than small domestic animals, and with nomadic rather than sedentary residence. The correlation with the unimportance of fishing may also be consistent with this generalization, but the argument is not clear.[4] Other correlations consistent with the generalization, though not statistically significant, are with large game hunting rather than gathering, with the hunting of large game rather than small game, and with the general importance of all hunting and gathering.

2. Large sex difference in socialization appears to be correlated with customs that make for a large family group with high cooperative interaction. The only statistically significant correlation relevant here is that with polygyny rather than monogamy. This generaliza-

tion is, however, supported by several substantial correlations that fall only a little short of being statistically significant. One of these is a correlation with sororal rather than nonsororal polygyny; Murdock and Whiting (4) have presented indirect evidence that co-wives generally show smoother cooperative interaction if they are sisters. Correlations are also found with the presence of either an extended or a polygynous family rather than the nuclear family only; with the presence of an extended family; and with the extreme contrast between maximal extension and no extension of the family. The generalization is also to some extent supported by small correlations with wide extension of incest taboos, if we may presume that an incest taboo makes for effective unthreatening cooperation within the extended family. The only possible exception to this generalization, among substantial correlations, is a near-significant correlation with an extended or polygynous family's occupying a cluster of dwellings rather than a single dwelling.[5]

In seeking to understand this second generalization, we feel that the degree of social isolation of the nuclear family may perhaps be the crucial underlying variable. To the extent that the nuclear family must stand alone, the man must be prepared to take the woman's role when she is absent or incapacitated, and vice versa. Thus the sex differentiation cannot afford to be too great. But to the extent that the nuclear family is steadily interdependent with other nuclear families, the female role in the household economy can be temporarily taken over by another woman, or the male role by another man, so that sharp differentiation of sex role is no handicap.

The first generalization, which concerns the economy, cannot be viewed as dealing with material completely independent of the ratings of socialization. The training of children in their economic role was often an important part of the data used in rating socialization variables, and would naturally vary according to the general economy of the society. We would stress, however, that we were by no means using the identical data on the two sides of our comparison; we were on the one hand judging data on the socialization of children and on the other hand using Murdock's judgments on the economy of the adult culture. In the case of the second generalization, it seems to us that there was little opportunity for information on family and social structure to have influenced the judges in making the socialization ratings.

Both of these generalizations contribute to understanding the social background of the relatively small difference in socialization of boys and girls which we believe characterizes our society at the present time. Our mechanized economy is perhaps less dependent than any previous economy upon the superior average strength of the male. The nuclear family in our society is often so isolated that husband and wife must each be prepared at times to take over or help in the household tasks normally assigned to the other. It is also significant that the conditions favoring low sex differentiation appear to be more characteristic of the upper segments of our society, in socioeconomic and educational status, than of lower segments. This observation may be relevant to the tendency toward smaller sex differences in personality in high status groups (cf. Terman and Miles, 8).

The increase in our society of conditions favoring small sex differences has led some people to advocate a virtual elimination of sex differences in socialization. This course seems likely to be dysfunctional even in our society. Parsons, Bales, *et al.* (5) argue that a differentiation of role similar to the universal pattern of sex difference is an important and perhaps inevitable development in any social group, such as the nuclear family. If we add to their argument the point that biological differences between the sexes make most appropriate the usual division of those roles between the sexes, we have compelling reasons to expect that the decrease in differentiation of adult sex role will not continue to the vanishing point. In our training of children, there may now be less differentiation in sex role than characterizes adult life—so little, indeed, as to provide inadequate preparation for adulthood. This state of affairs is likely to be especially true of formal education, which is more subject to conscious influence by an ideology than is informal socialization at home. With child training being more oriented toward the male than the female role in adulthood, many of the adjustment problems of women in our society today may be partly traced to conflicts growing out of inadequate childhood preparation for their adult role. This argument is nicely supported in extreme form by Spiro's analysis of sex roles in an Israeli kibbutz (7). The ideology of the founders of the kibbutz included the objective of greatly reducing differences in sex role. But the economy of the kibbutz is a largely nonmechanized one in which the superior average strength of men is badly needed in many jobs. The result is that, despite the ideology and many attempts to implement it, women continue to be assigned primarily to traditional "women's work," and the incompatibility between upbringing or ideology and adult role is an important source of conflict for women.

*Note on regional distribution.* There is marked variation among regions of the world in typical size of sex difference in socialization. In our sample, societies in North America and Africa tend to have large sex difference, and societies in Oceania to have small sex difference. Less confidently, because of the smaller number of cases, we can report a tendency toward small sex differences in Asia and South America as well. Since most of the variables with which we find the sex difference to be significantly correlated have a similar regional distribution, the question arises whether the correlations might better be ascribed to some quite different source having to do with large regional similarities, rather than to the functional dependence we have suggested. As a partial check, we have tried to determine whether the correlations we report in Table 2 tend also to be found strictly within regions. For each of the three regions for which we have sizable samples (North America, Africa, and Oceania) we have separately plotted 2 x 2 tables corresponding to each of the 6 relationships reported in Table 2. (We did this only for the more inclusive sample, since for the more selective sample the number of cases within a region would have been extremely small.) Out of the 18 correlations thus determined, 11 are positive and only 3 are negative (the other 4 being exactly zero). This result clearly suggests a general tendency for these correlations to hold true within regions as well as between regions and may lend further support to our functional interpretation.

## Summary

A survey of certain aspects of socialization in 110 cultures shows that differentiation of the sexes is unimportant in infancy, but that in childhood there is, as in our society, a widespread pattern of greater pressure toward nurturance, obedience, and responsibility in girls, and toward self-reliance and achievement striving in boys. There are a few reversals of sex difference, and many instances of no detectable sex difference; these facts tend to confirm the cultural rather than directly biological nature of the differences. Cultures vary in the degree to which these differentiations are made; correlational analysis suggests some of the social conditions influencing these variations, and helps in understanding why our society has relatively small sex differentiation.

# References

1. BENEDICT, RUTH. Continuities and discontinuities in cultural conditioning. *Psychiatry*, 1938, 1, 161–167.
2. MEAD, MARGARET. *Male and Female*. New York: Morrow, 1949.
3. MURDOCK, G. P. Comparative data on the division of labor by sex. *Social Forces*, 1937, 15, 551–553.
4. MURDOCK, G. P., & WHITING, J. W. M. Cultural determination of parental attitudes: The relationship between the social structure, particularly family structure and parental behavior. In M. J. E. Senn (Ed.), *Problems of infancy and childhood: Transactions of the Fourth Conference*, March 6–7, 1950. New York: Josiah Macy, Jr. Foundation, 1951. Pp. 13–34.
5. PARSONS, T., BALES, R. F., et al. *Family, socialization and interaction process*. Glencoe, Ill.: Free Press, 1955.
6. SCHEINFELD, A. *Women and men*. New York: Harcourt, Brace, 1944.
7. SPIRO, M. E. *Kibbutz: Venture in Utopia*. Cambridge: Harvard Univer. Press, 1956.
8. TERMAN, L. M., & MILES, CATHERINE C. *Sex and personality*. New York: McGraw-Hill, 1936.

# Notes

1. This research is part of a project for which financial support was provided by the Social Science Research Council and the Ford Foundation. We are greatly indebted to G. P. Murdock for supplying us with certain data, as indicated below, and to him and Thomas W. Maretzki for suggestions that have been used in this paper.
2. For data and interpretations supporting various arguments of this paragraph, see Mead (2), Murdock (3), and Scheinfeld (6).
3. These data were supplied to us directly by Professor Murdock.
4. Looking (with the more inclusive sample) into the possibility that this correlation might result from the correlation between fishing and sedentary residence, a complicated interaction between these variables was found. The correlation of sex differentiation with absence of fishing is found only in nomadic societies, where fishing is likely to involve cooperative activity of the two sexes, and its absence is likely to mean dependence upon the male for large game hunting or herding large animals (whereas in sedentary societies the alternatives to fishing do not so uniformly require special emphasis on male strength). The correlation of sex differentiation with nomadism is found only in nonfishing societies; here nomadism is likely to imply large game hunting or herding large animals, whereas in fishing societies nomadism evidently implies no such special dependence upon male strength. Maximum sex differentiation is found in nomadic nonfishing societies (15 with large difference and only 2 with small) and minimum sex differentiation in nomadic fishing societies (2 with large difference and 1 with small difference). These findings further strengthen the argument for a conspicuous influence of the economy upon sex differentiation.

5. We think the reverse of this correlation would be more consistent with our generalization here. But perhaps it may reasonably be argued that the various nuclear families composing an extended or polygynous family are less likely to develop antagonisms which hinder cooperation if they are able to maintain some physical separation. On the other hand, this variable may be more relevant to the first generalization than to the second. Occupation of a cluster of dwellings is highly correlated with presence of herding and with herding of large rather than small animals, and these economic variables in turn are correlated with large sex difference in socialization. Occupation of a cluster of dwellings is also correlated with polygyny rather than monogamy and shows no correlation with sororal vs. nonsororal polygyny.

PART II. GENERAL FAMILY RELATIONS

# The Value of Sound Sex Knowledge

*Panos D. Bardis, Ph.D.*

One of the main reasons, if not the main one, why countless teen-agers and adults have myriad problems related to sex is a lack of scientific knowledge in this area. Indeed, the people whom I have taught or counseled have frequently reminded me of Alexander Pope's famous verse: "So by false learning is good sense defac'd."

## Stomach Babies and Other Tales

Such false learning is especially revealed on the first day of each semester, when I ask my *college* students—many of whom are *seniors* —various questions about the anatomy and physiology of the human reproductive system. Here are some of these questions, together with a few of the answers given by teen-age and adult persons:

1. "How often do men menstruate?" "Usually when they have a dream about sex."

2. "What is the meaning of prepuce?" "An Indian baby." (The woman who gave this reply obviously confused "prepuce" with "papoose.")

3. "Where is the hymen located?" "In the mouth of the womb; between the womb and the vagina." (The reason for this incorrect answer was the belief that menstrual blood comes from the vagina and not originally from the womb, and that if the maidenhead stretched across the opening of the vagina—as it actually does—then it would prevent the flow of menstrual blood. At any rate, such a problem does not exist, since this membrane ordinarily has one or more holes.)

Reprinted from *Sexology* Magazine Dec. 1966 by permission. © 1966 by Sexology Corporation.

4. "Identify vulva." "This is a car model."

5. "What does cesarean section mean?" "A baby's delivery by cutting through the mother's stomach."

## Crocodile's Testes, Quinces, and Wife-Beating

Such unfamiliarity with one's own organs is both inexcusable and dangerous. It is inexcusable, simply because science is now so advanced, and reliable information so easy to secure that almost everyone can acquire scientific sex knowledge. It is further inexcusable because beliefs such as those presented above, which are held by people of the space age, are actually no sounder than those prevalent in ancient civilizations. Here are some old beliefs, for example:

1. The ancient Egyptians asserted that eating a crocodile's testicles reinforces a man's virility. In addition, according to the *Ebers Papyrus* (1550 B.C.), magic incantations can cure many female diseases.

2. The Hebrews considered the left testis smaller and weaker. As a result, they added, males, who are created by the right testicle, are superior to the fair sex.

3. In classical Greece ritualistic wife-beating was regarded as one of the best methods of increasing fertility. Plutarch also tells us that, to achieve the same goal, the bride was required to eat a quince before being shut up in a chamber with the groom.

4. The Romans placed the betrothal ring on the fourth finger of the bride's left hand, due to their conviction that a special nerve connects it with the heart.

## How to Kill Doderlein's Brave Soldiers

Ignorance is also dangerous because it generates innumerable physical, psychological, and social problems.

One of my students, for instance, developed a serious vaginal infection by frequently washing her *internal* organs with antiseptic douches. Quite obviously, this persnickety coed ignored the following facts: first, it is the *external* genitalia that need frequent washing. Second, the odors of the vagina are seldom sufficiently concentrated to be offensive. Third, the normal vagina ordinarily contains Döderlein's bacilli, which attack and destroy the harmful bacteria that invade a woman's organs. Fourth, these beneficial bacilli are easily exterminated by frequent antiseptic or even highly concentrated cleansing douches (for example, bichloride of mercury). And fifth, strong antiseptics irritate the vagina, thus making it susceptible to infection.

In conclusion, the prevailing lack of sound sex knowledge results in many serious problems. Scientific information, on the other hand. may readily lead to health, happiness, and creativity. Today, luckily, as Oliver Wendell Holmes wrote:

> "The tree of knowledge in your garden grows,
> Not single, but at every humble door."

# Love, Morals, and the Family

*Panos D. Bardis*

But it is essential to . . . keep before our eyes how far superior man is by nature to cattle and other beasts: they have no thought except for sensual pleasure and this they are impelled by every instinct to seek; but man's mind is nurtured by study and meditation.

CICERO

The polemical outbursts of the defenders of morality and of those advocating uninhibited erotic experimentation are probably as old as mankind. Today, however, this controversy seems to be getting more hysterical and more irrational than ever. It would be interesting, therefore, to examine certain aspects of this issue.

## Ancient Censors

According to Plato, one of the main duties of the guardians in the ideal State would be to ban Homer and Hesiod, since both of these epic poets often portrayed the gods as libidinal creatures. The sentimental Lydian melodies, the soft Ionian harmonies, and especially flute music were also considered positively immoral. On the other hand, the harp, the lyre, and the shepherd's pipe, being quite innocent and ethical, should not be banned!

His most famous pupil, Aristotle, was about equally conservative in regard to morality. "The law," he advised, "ought to forbid young people the seeing of comedies, such permission not being safe till age and discipline had confirmed them in sobriety, fortified their virtue, and made them, as it were, proof against debauchery."

In the *Tagenistae*, a lost play by Aristophanes, the great comedian

From *Social Science*, June, 1960. Reprinted by permission.

averred that a certain young man's immorality was due to "a book, to Prodicus, or to bad company." A few centuries later, Plutarch, the brilliant biographer, complained violently that Aristophanes' comedies were obscene and pornographic!

The Romans were not less concerned about the problem of immorality. Augustus, for example, banished Publius Ovidius Naso to the Euxine, perhaps because the poet had persistently attempted to practice his amatorial art on the Emperor's daughter, or perhaps because his *Ars Amatoria* had shocked too many conservative Romans. For Ovidius was an honest fellow who did not hesitate to write about love quite frankly. In fact, without wasting any time, he revealed the purpose of his work in its very first lines:

> It is by art ships sail the sea,
>     It is by art that chariots move;
> If then unskilled in love you be,
>     Come to my school and learn to love.
> In all the process of seduction
> This handbook gives you full instruction.

Then, boldly and intrepidly, he bragged that he knew what he was talking about, since his "instruction" was based on a great deal of training which he had received in the school of Cupid's mother.

> I speak of facts with ripened knowledge,
> A graduate of Venus' college.

Nevertheless, Rome's censors were not completely successful. Indeed, when the Parthians defeated the Romans, the conquerors found many copies of Aristides' *Milesian Tales* in the enemy camp. Surena, the Parthian chieftain, then knew why the Romans had lost the battle! "Even in the wars," he explained to his soldiers, "they could not refrain from doing evil, and the reading of such vile books."

### Dura Lex, Sed Lex

In modern times, legal authorities, vigilant and Argus-eyed, have frequently attempted to suppress whatever appears immoral. In *Regina vs. Bedborough,* for instance, the grand jury discussed the famous case of Havelock Ellis, "the sage of sex," as follows:

> The jurors for our Sovereign Lady the Queen upon their oath present that George Bedborough, being a person of a wicked

and depraved mind and disposition, and unlawfully and wickedly devising, contriving, and intending to vitiate and corrupt
the morals of the liege subjects of our said Lady the Queen, and
to raise and create in them lustful desires, and to bring the said
liege subjects into a state of wickedness, lewdness, and debauchery, on the 27th day of May, in the year of our Lord, one thousand eight hundred and ninety eight, at a certain shop, to wit,
Number 16 John Street, Bedford Row, in the County of London, and within the jurisdiction of the said Court, unlawfully,
wickedly, maliciously, scandalously and wilfully did publish,
sell and utter, and cause and procure to be published, sold and
uttered, a certain lewd, wicked, bawdy, scandalous, and obscene
libel, in the form of a book entitled *Studies in the Psychology
of Sex: Vol. I. Sexual Inversion*, by Havelock Ellis, in which
said book are contained among other things, divers wicked,
lewd, impure, scandalous and obscene libels and matters, . . .

Of course, the efforts of the law in this area are not always unjustifiable. Inconsistency, however, seems to be one of the main
weaknesses of the legal campaign against immorality. For while
"divers wicked, lewd, impure, scandalous and obscene libels" are
condemned, many classics that are about equally "lewd" are permitted to circulate quite freely. In Shakespeare's *Romeo and Juliet*, for
example, the loquacious Nurse says to Lady Capulet:

> And then my husband—God be with his soul!
> A' was a merry man—took up the child:
> 'Yea,' quoth he, 'dost thou fall upon thy face?
> Thou wilt fall backward when thou hast more wit;
> Wilt thou not, Jule?' and, by my holidame,
> The pretty wretch left crying, and said 'Ay.'
> To see, now, how a jest shall come about!
> I warrant, and I should live a thousand years,
> I never should forget it: 'Wilt thou not, Jule?' quoth he;
> And, pretty fool, it stinted, and said 'Ay.' (I, 3)

In the same bard's *Measure for Measure*, Elbow exclaims:

> He, sir! a tapster, sir; parcel-bawd; one that serves a bad
> woman; whose house, sir, was, as they say, pluck'd down in the
> suburbs; and now she professes a hot-house, which, I think, is a
> very ill house too. (II, I)

### The Errant Scientists

Unfortunately, inconsistencies and other weaknesses, shortcomings,
and foibles are also typical of many social scientists, who often sacri-

fice scientific principles on the altar of their personal prejudices. This may be illustrated by means of a randomly selected article, Mr. Robert A. Harper's "Marriage Counseling and the Mores: A Critique."[1]

In this paper the author introduces his subject by asserting that "the time would seem to have come, . . . for we [sic] marriage counselors and family life educators to lift ourselves from our conventional moralistic thinking about marriage and family life." (P. 13) Rather peremptorily, he then suggests that we place greater emphasis on the scientific approach, which, undoubtedly, every serious scholar would consider much more effectual than many principles and practices based on traditionalism. He also declares that "So-called God-fearing people in our various social groups are often thought-fearing, science-fearing, love-fearing, and life-fearing people." (P. 19) This, too, cannot be disputed, as there *are* social scientists, ministers, doctors, and other counselors, whose counseling is often dominated by tartuffism, incompetence, charlatanism, unprofessional meddlesomeness, unwholesome curiosity, and downright unethicalness.

Nevertheless, Mr. Harper's statements regarding the value of the scientific approach in the field under consideration today sound rather commonplace, insipid, and trite when they appear in a professional periodical like *Marriage and Family Living*, and especially when they are presented as an address "at American Association of Marriage Counselors Meeting" (p. 13), since many of these counselors have already made analogous statements—perhaps more adequately—in their own writings. Most of his more specific assertions and recommendations, being rather utopian, unscientific, and nonsensical, are also unsatisfactory, as the following passages indicate.

1. "We need also to give up traditional moral judgments about all aspects of life." For "Moral judgments, . . . are childish judgments." (P. 13) Such sweeping generalizations (*all* aspects of life) are at least amusing, in view of the fact that the author has often boasted of his "compulsively professional" attitudes! The unqualified assertion concerning moral judgments in the area of deontology, judgments in the area of axiology, or Kant's moral judgment, which enjoins a categorical imperative, are not *all* "childish judgments." It is especially unprofessional, naive, and emotional to speak of "our completely unnecessary, utterly idiotic premarital sexual morality" (p. 17), for many of the precepts of man's great, religious systems have often proved quite valuable, *some of them even coinciding with the dictates of modern psychology, medicine, and other sciences.* On the other hand, most of Mr. Harper's exhortations are based on

*untested hypotheses* dealing with a libidinous universe governed by impulses, lust, animalism, sensualism, and promiscuity, and inhabited by Guiscardo and Ghismonda, Lorenzo and Isabetta, Strignario and Peronella, and other lewd, wanton, lecherous, and lascivious characters.

2. "If we try to do away with moral judgments, what then shall we substitute? . . . Anarchy? Not at all. . . . We substitute . . . realistic appraisal. . . . We stop thinking . . . adultery is wrong; premarital sexual intercourse is wicked"; (p. 13). Apparently, the writer was somewhat disturbed by the obvious incertitude regarding the consequences of doing away with morality and desperately attempted to combat it. But a successful analysis and better understanding of a subject such as this presupposes extensive historical knowledge, which he does not appear to possess; for as Dr. Pitirim A. Sorokin[2] and Carle C. Zimmerman[3] have shown—although not always quite convincingly—overindulgence of the sex drive has often led to the downfall of great civilizations.

3. Mr. Harper also advises us to stop teaching young people "that premarital sexual intercourse is bad, but to teach them how to exercise their own critical faculties about deciding under what sorts of circumstances and with what sorts of partners it is likely to be functionally desirable for all parties concerned." (P. 17) And "The writer would trust young people, thus educated, to have considerably superior judgment in such matters than the second-hand judgments that come to them from the ready-made codes of moralists." (Pp. 17–18) If this is not a wildly utopian pedagogical dream, then Raphael Hythloday's description of Amaurote's ideal commonwealth is an unadulterated empirical statistical treatise!

4. "Probably more consistently enjoyable sensations proceed from the unhampered erotic relationship of a man and a woman than from any other life activity." (P. 18) This again is anything but science, as it constitutes a sweeping generalization based on definitely inadequate information and ignoring man's multitude of sensations and the nature and extent of enjoyment accompanying each of them. Such statements are too impressionistic not to be considered analogous to superstitious beliefs and old wives' tales. Indeed, a *very old tale* recalled by similar comparisons is that found in the third fragment of Hesiod's *Melampodeia*, according to which, when Zeus and Hera asked Teiresias to decide the question whether the male or the female has more pleasure in coition, the famous seer answered:

> Out of ten degrees of pleasure,
> Only one a man enjoys;
> But a woman, at her leisure,
> All ten eagerly employs.

5. Finally, Mr. Harper reveals that many of his conclusions are derived from his antifamily prejudice. "The proper view of a marriage counselor," he writes, "is not as a savior of marriage." "A marriage counselor can much more accurately be compared to a garage mechanic than to anything more glorious, romantic, or moral." (P. 14) In other words, human beings, marriage, and the family are not among the most complex and unfathomable phenomena. On the contrary, they are as simple as an automobile! Furthermore, despite what studies like Dr. Hornell Hart's[5] indicate, namely, that the highest degree of happiness is usually created by the family, this institution is not really more important than a modern vehicle! In addition—but it is futile and unavailing to persist in opposing "compulsively UNprofessional" attitudes. Suffice it to say, the family, which, for thousands of years, has been able to survive wars, revolutions, and other social catastrophes, as well as the hysterical attacks of history's Harpers, must be characterized not only by weaknesses, but also by many noble and valuable qualities of which mankind is not anxious to get rid. Instead of opposing it blindly and emotionally, therefore, it seems wiser to combat only its negative aspects and reinforce its positive ones by adopting policies and practices dictated by scientific objectivity, respect for certain truths, maturity, wisdom, and *genuinely* professional attitudes.

## Notes

1. *Marriage and Family Living*, 21 (February 1959), pp. 13–19.
2. *The American Sex Revolution*, Boston: Porter Sargent, 1956, *passim*.
3. *Family and Civilization*, New York: Harper and Brothers, 1947, pp. 578, 798, *et passim*; and *idem*, "The Developing Family Crisis," *Rural Sociology*, 11 (December 1946), pp. 319–330. Concerning Dr. Zimmerman's thesis, see also Panos D. Bardis, "A Comparative Study of Familism," *ibid.*, 24 (December 1959), pp. 362–371.
4. Translated by Panos D. Bardis.
5. *Chart for Happiness*, New York: The Macmillan Company, 1940, p. 33.

# Parent-Child Conflict in Sexual Values

*Robert R. Bell*

The old cliché that as one grows older he becomes more conservative may be true, if premarital sexual values held by parents are
compared with the values they held when they were younger. In
this paper, the interest is in the nature of sex value conflict between
parents and their unmarried late adolescent and young adult children. Our discussion will focus on values held by parents and by
their unmarried children toward premarital sexual intimacy.

Conceptually, our approach focuses upon values related to a specific area of sexual behavior held by individuals from two very
different role perspectives. The perspectives differ because. parents
and children are always at different stages in the life cycle, and while
parents are highly significant in the socialization of their children,
other social forces increasingly come to influence the child as he
grows older. The various social values that influence the child's
sexual behavior are often complementary, but they may also be
contradictory. Furthermore, various types of influences on the acceptance of a given set of values may operate on the child only during
a given age period. For example, the youngster at age fifteen may
be influenced by his age peers to a much greater extent than he will
be at age twenty.

Given their different stages in the life cycle, parents and children
will almost always show differences in how they define appropriate behavior for a given role. Values as to "proper" premarital sexual role
behavior from the perspective of the parents are greatly influenced
by the strong emotional involvement of the parent with his child.
Youth, on the other hand, are going through a life cycle stage in

From *Journal of Social Issues*, 1966, Volume XXII, No. 2, pp. 34–44. Reprinted
by permission of Society for the Psychological Study of Social Issues.

which the actual behavior occurs, and they must relate the parent values to what they are doing or may do. There is a significant difference between defining appropriate role conduct for others to follow and defining proper role conduct to be followed by oneself. Even more important for actual behavior, there is often more than one significant group of role definers to which the young person can turn to as guides for his sex role behavior. Therefore, our discussion will focus more specifically on parent values related to premarital sexual intimacy, the peer group values of youth, and how these two different age groups, as role definers, influence the sexual values and behavior of unmarried youth.

*Limits of Discussion.* For several reasons, our discussion will center primarily on the middle class. First, this class level has been highly significant in influencing changes in general sexual values and behavior. Second, and on a more pragmatic level, what little research has been done on parent-child conflict over sexual values has been done with middle-class groups. Third, the general values of the middle class are coming to include an increasing proportion of the American population. This also suggests that the values and behavior of college youth are of increasing importance as this group continues to expand in size and influence within the middle class.

A further limit is that our main focus is on the generational conflict between mother and daughter. The history of change in sexual values in the United States has been completely interwoven with the attainment of greater sex equality and freedom by the female (2). Also, the relationship between the mother and daughter tends to be the closest of the possible parent-child relationships in the family socializing of the child to future adult sex roles. Furthermore, whatever the value system verbalized and/or applied by the girl, she often has more to gain or lose personally than the boy by whatever premarital sexual decision she makes.

We also believe that any analysis of conflict over premarital sex between generations should center on *value* changes rather than *behavioral* changes. On the basis of available evidence, it appears that there have been no significant changes in the *frequency* of premarital sexual petting or coitus since the 1920's. Kinsey has pointed out that "there has been little recognition that the premarital petting and coital patterns which were established then (1920's) are still with us" (15, p. 300). Therefore, it is important to recognize that the parents and even some of the grandparents of today were the youth who introduced the new patterns of premarital sexual behavior about forty years ago.

## Parent Values About Premarital Sex

The transmission of sexual values by parents to their children is only a small part of parent values passed on during the family socialization process. Most parents do a more deliberate and comprehensive job of transmitting values to their children in such areas as educational attainment, career choice, religious beliefs, and so forth than they do with reference to any aspect of sexual values. Often when parents do discuss sex with their children it may be from a "clinical, physiological" perspective with overtones of parental embarrassment and a desire to get a distasteful task over with.

But perhaps more important than the formal confrontation between the parent and child in sexual matters are the informal values transmitted by the parent. In the past girls were often taught that premarital sexual deviancy was dirty and shameful, and that nonconformity to premarital sexual chastity values would mean suffering great personal and social shame. This highly negative view of premarital sex is undoubtedly less common today, but the newer, more "positive" values may also have some negative consequences. Very often today the mother continues to place great value on the daughter's virginity, and stresses to the daughter the great virtues of maintaining her virginity until marriage. But the "romantic" view of the rewards for the girl who waits for coitus until after marriage are often highly unrealistic and may sometimes create problems by leading the girl to expectations that cannot be realistically met in marital sex. Morton Hunt writes with regard to this approach that "if the woman has been assured that she will, that she ought, and she *must* see colored lights, feel like a breaking wave, or helplessly utter inarticulate cries, she is apt to consider herself or her husband at fault when these promised wonders do not appear" (13, 114). Whether or not the "romantic" view of marital sex is presented by her mother the girl often encounters it in the "approved" reading list suggested by the adult world, which tells her about the positive delights of waiting for sex until after marriage. So, though premarital sexual control may be "positive" in that it is based on rewards for waiting. it can be "negative" if the rewards are unrealistic and unobtainable.

For many parents, a major problem as their child moves through adolescence and into early adult years centers around how much independence to allow the child. Because they often recall the child's younger dependency, it may be difficult to assess the independency of the same child who is now older. Also, over the years the growing child has increasingly become involved with reference groups outside—and sometimes competing with—the family. In other words, the self-role definitions by the child and the parents' definitions of the child's role undergo constant change as the child grows older. For example, "The daughter in her younger years has her role as daughter defined to a great degree by her mother. But as she grows older she is influenced by other definitions which she internalizes and applies to herself in her movement toward self-determination. The mother frequently continues to visualize the daughter's role as it was defined in the past and also attaches the same importance to her function as mother in defining her daughter's role. But given the rapid social change associated with family roles the definer, as well as the definitions, may no longer be institutionally appropriate" (5, 388).

Parents may also be biased in their definitions of their child as less mature than they, the parents, were when they were the child's age. One cannot recall experiences earlier in the life cycle free from influence by the events that have occurred since. This may result in many parents' thinking of their younger selves as being more mature than they actually were. At the same time the parents' view of their child's degree of maturity may be biased by their recall of him when he was younger and less mature. Thus, from the parents' perspective they may recall themselves as youngsters within the context of what has occurred since (more mature) and may see their offspring within the context of their earlier childhood (less mature).

There also may be some symbolic significance for parents who must define their children as having reached the age when something as "adult" as sexual behavior is of relevance. In part, viewing one's children as too young for sexual involvement may contribute to the parents' feeling young, while seeing their children as old enough to be involved in sexual activity may lead to some parents feeling forced to view themselves as aging. For example, the comment about a man seen out with a young woman that "she is young enough to be his daughter" may have implications for his self-role image if the young woman is his daughter. We have little research data on how the aging process of parents influences their definitions of appropriate behavior for their young adult children.

In general, it is probable that most parents assume that their children, especially their daughters, accept the traditional restrictive values about premarital sexual behavior unless they are forced to do otherwise. Also, because of the great emotional involvement of parents with their own children, there is a common parental tendency to attribute sexual "immorality" to other youngsters. For many parents to face the possibility that their children do not conform to their values is to suggest some failure on the part of the parents. Often, rather than admit failure, the parents may define their children as having been forced to reject the parent values by other social influences or that their children have willfully let them down.

## Youth Views About Premarital Sex

The importance of age peer group influence on the values and behavior of young people has been shown by a number of social scientists (see: 6, 9, 10, 11, 12, 14, 19, 20, 21, 22). Because youth subcultures are to some degree self-developing, they often have conflict points in relation to some dominant adult values. However, the inconsistency and lack of effective adult definitions for adolescent behavior have also contributed to the emergence of youth subcultural values. That adults often view the adolescent with indicision as to appropriate behavior means that sometimes given adolescent behavior is treated one way at one time and in a different way at another time. Since the young person desires some decisiveness and precision in his role definitions, he often develops his own role prescriptions. Often when he creates his own role expectations, he demands a high degree of conformity by other adolescents as "proof" of the rightness of his definitions. It is ironical that the adolescent often thinks of himself as a social deviant. What he fails to realize is that his adolescent group deviates from the adult world, but that the requirements for conformity within his youth subculture are very strong (1, 369–74).

Youth subcultures have developed great influence over many aspects of premarital male-female interaction. The patterns of dating and courtship, appropriate behavior, success and failure are for the most part patterns defined by the youth group and not by the adult world. Yet, heterosexual relationships of youth are often based on adult role patterns, and they are therefore an important part of the youth world because they are seen by the youth as symbolizing adult status. To many young people, who are no longer defined by the adult world as children, but are not yet given full status as adults, their involvement in what they see as adult roles is important to them in seeking for adult status and recognition.

A part of the American youth subculture has been the development of new values related to premarital sexual intimacy. Reiss suggests that "It might well be that, since the 1920's, what has been occurring is a change in attitudes to match the change in behavior of that era" [premarital sexual behavior] (16, 233). The evidence suggests that for at least some college students new sex norms are emerging at the various stages of dating and courtship. One study found that "on the dating level necking is the norm for females and petting for males. During going steady and engagement, petting seems to be acceptable for both sexes. This would suggest that the young people both act and accept a higher level of intimacy than has generally been suggested by courtship norms." (3, 63).

In the past, emphasis was placed on the girl's virginity at the time of marriage, but today, many young people may only emphasize her being a virgin until she is in love, which may mean at the stage of going steady or engagement (8, Ch. 5 and 16, Ch. 6). If the girl is in love, some premarital sexual relations may be acceptable by peer group standards, although the dominant adult values—that love *and* marriage are basic prerequisites for coitus—continue. In the United States love as a prerequisite for sexual relations has long been a necessary condition for most middle-class females. The condition has not changed; rather, the point in the courtship-marriage process where it may be applied to sexual involvement has shifted. Hence, the major point of parent-child conflict over permarital sex centers around the parent value that one should be in love *and* married before entering coitus and the modified value system of youth that an emotional and interpersonal commitment is important, but that this may occur before marriage.

There are two recent studies that provide some evidence on the nature of generational conflict; one study is of youth and adults in general and the other study is specifically concerned with mothers and their daughters. Reiss, in his extensive study of premarital sexual permissiveness, provides data on values held by adults as contrasted with values in a sample of high school and college students. The respondents were asked to express their beliefs about different combinations of intimacy and degree of interpersonal commitment for both unmarried males and females. Respondents were asked if they believed petting to be acceptable when the male or female is engaged. In the adult sample the belief that petting during engagement was acceptable for the engaged male was the response of 61 per cent, and for the engaged female the response was 56 per cent. Of the student responses 85 per cent approved for the engaged male and 82 per cent for the engaged female (17, 190–91); thus adult attitudes about petting during engagement were more conservative than those of the student population. It may also be noted that for both the adult and student groups there was a single standard—that is, the acceptance rates were essentially the same for both males and females.

Reiss also asked his respondents if they believed full sexual relations to be acceptable if the male or female were engaged. Approval was the response given by 20 per cent of the adult group for males and 17 per cent for females. In the student group acceptance was given by 52 per cent for the male and 44 per cent for the female (17, 190–91). Here, as with petting, there are significant differences between the adult and the student samples, and once again both respondent groups suggest a single standard of acceptance or rejection for both males and females.

A study by Bell and Buerkle compared the attitudes of 217 coeds with those of their mothers. Both mothers and daughters were asked to respond to the question, "How important do you think it is that a girl be a virgin when she marries?" Of the mothers, 88 per cent answered "very important," 12 per cent "generally important," and 0 per cent "not important"; compared to 55 per cent, 34 per cent and 13 per cent of the daughters (4, 391). Both the mothers and daughters were also asked: "Do you think sexual intercourse during engagement is: very wrong; generally wrong; right in many situations?" The percentages for each response category were 83 per cent, 15 per cent and 2 per cent for the mothers; and 35 per cent, 48 per cent, and 17 per cent for the daughters (4, 391).

Both of the above questions show sharp differences between the value responses of the mothers and daughters with reference to premarital chastity. Many mothers were undoubtedly influenced in their responses by having a daughter in the age setting where the questions had an immediate and highly emotional application. Nevertheless, the differences in mother and daughter responses indicate that the area of premarital sexual behavior is one of potentially great conflict. One means of minimizing conflict is for the daughter not to discuss her sexual values or behavior with her mother. In the Bell and Buerkle study it was found that only 37 per cent of the daughters, in contrast with 83 per cent of the mothers, felt daughters should freely answer questions from their mothers in regard to attitudes toward sexual intimacy (4, 392).

The area of sexual values appears to be highly influenced by emotion, especially for the mother with reference to her daughter. Generational conflict with regard to premarital sexual intimacy has a variety of implications. First, the conflict in values clearly suggests that the traditional morality is often not socially effective as a meaningful determinant of behavior. Social values have behavioral influence when they emerge as social norms with significant rewards and punishments. In the case of sexual norms, however, there are rarely clearly-articulated rewards, or positive consequences, for the conforming individual. In almost all situations the effectiveness of sexual norms is dependent upon their negative sanctions, or punishments. For example, the traditional norm of female premarital chastity bases its behavioral influence primarily on negative consequences for the girl who fails to conform. This negative means of control is most commonly found as a part of the adult value system. In effect, the major sanctions over premarital chastity are based upon punishments for the girl and for her family if she deviates. Yet, in most cases the girl who has premarital coitus is not discovered by her parents or by the community. The real danger for the girl often centers around pre-marital pregnancy, because if that occurs and becomes known there can be no denying premarital coitus. Vincent has suggested that an important part of the negative sanction toward premarital pregnancy is not the pregnancy itself, but rather that it symbolizes premarital coitus *and* getting caught (23, Ch. 1).

The available studies indicate that fear of pregnancy is not the major deterrent for most girls (7, 344 and 15, 315). The personal values of the girl appear far more important in restricting her from engaging in premarital coitus. Yet, within the privacy of the youth world, there may operate for some girls certain values positive toward premarital coitus. For example, there may be a strong emotional desire and commitment to the boy and a positive feeling by the girl of wanting to engage in greater sexual intimacy.

There is a tendency by parents, as well as by many who give professional advice, to overlook the pleasurable aspects of sex at all ages, especially for the young who are experiencing sexual pleasure for the first time. Undoubtedly many girls engage in premarital sexual intimacy to "compensate" for some need and many may suffer some negative consequences. But it is foolish to state categorically that the "artificial" setting of premarital sex always makes it negative and unpleasant for the girl. We would be much more honest if we recognized that for many girls premarital coitus is enjoyable and the participants suffer no negative consequences. This was illustrated in the Kinsey research; it was found that "69 per cent of the still unmarried females in the sample who had premarital coitus insisted they did not regret their experiences. Another 13 per cent recorded some minor regrets" (15, 316). Kinsey also found that "77 per cent of the married females, looking back from the vantage point of their more mature experience, saw no reason to regret their premarital coitus" (15, 316).

## The Extent of Generational Conflict

With the evidence suggesting strong conflict between generations with regard to premarital sexual values, our final consideration is: how permanent is this generational conflict? We can provide some evidence on this question by examining the values of college-educated females of different ages. This appears justified because higher educated females are generally the most liberal in their views about sexual rights and expectations for women.

The evidence suggests that the premarital sexual liberalism of the college girl may be a temporary phenomenon. The coed's sexual liberalism must be seen as related to the interactional context of her being emotionally involved, and to a future commitment to an on-going paired relationship. The Bell and Buerkle study (4) found that the values of daughters toward the importance of premarital virginity were very similar to those of their mothers, until they had spent some time in college. However, at "around 20 there emerge sharp differences between mothers and daughters in regard to pre-marital sexual attitudes. Behavioral studies indicate that it is at this point that sexual activity is greatly intensified, perhaps because it is at this age that college girls are entering engagement. A suggested pattern is that the college girl of 20 or 21 years of age, in her junior or senior year and engaged, has a strong 'liberal' pattern toward premarital sexual behavior and attitudes" (4, 392 and 18, 696).

We can get some indication of the persistence of premarital sexual liberalism by comparing the values of mothers by education. In the mothers' views as to the importance of premarital virginity it was found that the college educated mothers were actually as "conserva-tive" as those mothers with lower levels of education (4, 392). It is quite possible that in the future the coeds will become as conserva-tive as the college educated mothers. This may occur when the coed's attitudinal rationales are not related to herself, but as a mother to her own daughter. It is therefore possible that the "sexual emanci-pation" of the college girl exists only for a short period of time, centering mainly around the engagement years.

Yet, even if the girl becomes more conservative as she grows older, and especially with reference to her own daughter, her temporary "liberalism" probably is contributing to some shift in adult values about premarital sexual intimacy. Certainly, today's parental generation accepts greater sexual intimacy as a part of the premarital heterosexual relationship. Probably most parents assume that their adolescent and young adult children are engaging in necking and even some petting. Most parents, as long as they don't actually see the sexual intimacy, don't concern themselves about it. However, to suggest that parents may be more liberal (or tolerant) of premarital sexual intimacy does not necessarily suggest that parents are liberal if the intimacy reaches coitus.

It also appears that there has been some reduction in the severity of negative sanctions by parents if the daughter deviates and is caught. Among middle-class parents today it may be less common to reject the unwed daughter if she becomes pregnant than in the past, and more common for the parents to help her. This is not to suggest that today's parents offer any positive sanctions for premarital pregnancy, but that they may be able to adapt (often painfully) to it, rather than respond with high rejection and anger.

If our suggestion is correct (that parents take a less totally negative view of "discovered" premarital coitus), then this further suggests that traditional sexual values are being altered, since, as we have suggested, in the past the values of premarital chastity were primarily based on the negative consequences for those who deviated and were caught. If these negative consequences have been reduced, then the social force of the traditional values has been reduced as a means utilized by parents to control premarital sexual deviancy.

## Conclusions

Based on the available evidence, there are several general speculations that may be made about future generational conflict over premarital sex. In general we would suggest that conflict between parents and their adolescent-young adult children with regard to premarital sexual intimacy may decrease in the future, because of several trends.

1. The trend in the United States is toward a more liberal view of sexual behavior in general. This is reflected in the generally accepted professional opinion that the woman has a right to sexual satisfaction, and that sexual satisfaction is a desirable end in itself. The trend toward a belief in a single sexual standard for both men and women, even though within the setting of marriage, is bound to influence the beliefs and behavior of the unmarried. For the unmarried, there may be an increasing tendency to attach less im-

portance to the marriage act as the arbitrary dividing line between socially approved and socially disapproved sexual intimacy.

2. Since the evidence suggests that over the past three or four generations the rates of female premarital coital experience have not changed, and since the younger generation has developed some value frameworks for its behavior, modification of traditional values and behavior may increasingly influence the values of parents to be more liberal. That is, it may become increasingly difficult for many parents to hold their children to a set of conservative values which they, the parents, did not hold to when they were younger.

3. Parents seem increasingly unwilling to strongly punish their daughters who sexually deviate and are caught. This parental reduction of punishment may be influenced by the increasing public attention directed at such social problems as illegal abortion. For example, many parents may be more willing to accept and help an unmarried pregnant daughter than take the risk of her seeking out an illegal abortion. The possible negative consequences of abortion may appear more undesirable than the premarital pregnancy.

4. Less generational conflict will occur if parents know less about the sexual activities of their children. A great part of the social activity of young people is carried out in the privacy of their age peer setting; what they do in the way of sexual intimacy is increasingly less apt to be noted by their parents. With the development and marketing of oral contraceptives, the risks of premarital pregnancy will be greatly reduced. In the future the rates of premarital coitus may remain the same, but with the chances of pregnancy reduced parents may be less aware of their children's premarital coitus.

Over time, then, the values of parents and the adult community in general may become more liberal and the conflict between generations reduced. (There seems little possibility that the opposite will occur; i.e., the younger generation's reducing the conflict by becoming more conservative.) But in the meantime, and certainly in the near future, it appears that parents and their children will continue to live with somewhat different value systems with regard to premarital sexual values. Parents will probably continue to hold to traditional values, and assume that *their* child is conforming to those values unless his actions force them to see otherwise. The youth generation will probably continue to develop their own modified value systems and keep those values to themselves, and implicitly allow their parents to believe they are behaving according to the traditional values of premarital sexual morality. For many parents and their children, the conflict about premarital sex will continue to be characterized by the parent's playing ostrich and burying his head in the sand, and the youth's efforts to keep the sand from blowing away.

# References

1. BELL, ROBERT R. *Marriage and Family Interaction*, Homewood Ill.: The Dorsey Press, 1963.
2. BELL, ROBERT R. *Premarital Sex In A Changing Society*, Englewood Cliffs, N.J.: Prentice Hall, (in press).
3. BELL, ROBERT R. AND LEONARD BLUMBERG. "Courtship Stages and Intimacy Attitudes," *Family Life Coordinator*, 1960, 8, 60–63.
4. BELL, ROBERT R. AND JACK V. BUERKLE. "Mother and Daughter Attitudes to Premarital Sexual Behavior," *Marriage and Family Living*, 1961, 23, 390–92.
5. BELL, ROBERT R. AND JACK V. BUERKLE. "Mother-Daughter Conflict During The 'Launching Stage,'" *Marriage and Family Living*, 1962, 24, 384–88.
6. BERNARD, JESSIE (Editor). "Teen-Age Culture," *Annals of the American Academy of Political and Social Science*, November, 1961, 338.
7. BURGESS, ERNEST AND PAUL WALLIN. *Engagement and Marriage*, Chicago: J. B. Lippincott, 1953.
8. EHRMANN, WINSTON. *Premarital Dating Behavior*, New York: Henry Holt, 1959.
9. GINSBERG, ELI. *Values and Ideals of American Youth*, New York: Columbia University Press, 1962.
10. GOTTLIEB, DAVID AND CHARLES RAMSEY. *The American Adolescent*, Homewood, Ill.: The Dorsey Press, 1964.
11. GRINDER, ROBERT. *Studies in Adolescence*, New York: Macmillan, 1963.
12. HECHINGER, GRACE AND FRED. *Teen-Age Tyranny*, New York: Crest, 1962.
13. HUNT, NORTON M. *The Natural History of Love*, New York: Alfred A. Knopf, 1959.
14. KELLEY, EARL C. *In Defense of Youth*, Englewood Cliffs, N.J.: Prentice-Hall, 1962.
15. KINSEY, ALFRED C., WARDELL B. POMEROY, CLYDE E. MARTIN AND PAUL H. GEBHARD. *Sexual Behavior in the Human Female*, Philadelphia: W. B. Saunders, 1953.
16. REISS, IRA L. *Premarital Sexual Behavior in America*, Glencoe, Ill.: The Free Press, 1960.
17. REISS, IRA L. "The Scaling of Premarital Sexual Permissiveness," *Journal of Marriage and the Family*, 1964, 26, 188–98.
18. REISS, IRA L. "Premarital Sexual Permissiveness Among Negroes and Whites," *American Sociological Review*, 1964, 29, 688–98.
19. REMMERS, H. H. AND D. H. RADLER. *The American Teenager*, New York: Charter, 1957.
20. SEIDMAN, JEROME. *The Adolescent*, New York: Holt, 1960.
21. SMITH, ERNEST A. *American Youth Culture*, New York: The Free Press, 1963.
22. SYMONDS, P. M. *From Adolescent to Adult*, New York: Columbia University Press, 1961.
23. VINCENT, CLARK. *Unmarried Mothers*, Glencoe, Ill.: The Free Press, 1961.

# The Sociology of Parent-Youth Conflict

*Kingsley Davis*

It is in sociological terms that this paper attempts to frame and solve the sole question with which it deals, namely: Why does contemporary western civilization manifest an extraordinary amount of parent-adolescent conflict?[1] In other cultures, the outstanding fact is generally not the rebelliousness of youth, but its docility. There is practically no custom, no matter how tedious or painful, to which youth in primitive tribes or archaic civilizations will not willingly submit.[2] What, then, are the peculiar features of our society which give us one of the extremest examples of endemic filial friction in human history?

Our answer to this question makes use of constants and variables, the constants being the universal factors in the parent-youth relation, the variables being the factors which differ from one society to another. Though one's attention, in explaining the parent-youth relations of a given milieu, is focused on the variables, one cannot comprehend the action of the variables without also understanding the constants, for the latter constitute the structural and functional basis of the family as a part of society.

*The Rate of Social Change.* The first important variable is the rate of social change. Extremely rapid change in modern civilization, in contrast to most societies, tends to increase parent-youth conflict, for within a fast-changing social order the time-interval between generations, ordinarily but a mere moment in the life of a social system, become historically significant, thereby creating a hiatus between one generation and the next. Inevitably, under such a condition, youth is reared in a milieu different from that of the

From *American Sociological Review*, 1940, 5 (4), pp. 523–534. Reprinted by permission of American Sociological Association.

parents; hence the parents become old-fashioned, youth rebellious, and clashes occur which, in the closely confined circle of the immediate family, generate sharp emotion.

That rapidity of change is a significant variable can be demonstrated by three lines of evidence: a comparison of stable and nonstable societies;[3] a consideration of immigrant families; and an analysis of revolutionary epochs. If, for example, the conflict is sharper in the immigrant household, this can be due to one thing only, that the immigrant family generally undergoes the most rapid social change of any type of family in a given society. Similarly, a revolution (an abrupt form of societal alteration), by concentrating great change in a short span, catapults the younger generation into power—a generation which has absorbed and pushed the new ideas, acquired the habit of force, and which, accordingly, dominates those hangovers from the old regime, its parents.[4]

*The Birth-Cycle, Decelerating Socialization, and Parent-Child Differences.* Note, however, that rapid social change would have no power to produce conflict were it not for two universal factors: first, the family's duration; and second, the decelerating rate of socialization in the development of personality. "A family" is not a static entity but a process in time, a process ordinarily so brief compared with historical time that it is unimportant, but which, when history is "full" (i.e., marked by rapid social change), strongly influences the mutual adjustment of the generations. This "span" is basically the birth-cycle—the length of time between the birth of one person and his procreation of another. It is biological and inescapable. It would, however, have no effect in producing parent-youth conflict, even with social change, if it were not for the additional fact, intimately related and equally universal, that the sequential development of personality involves a constantly decelerating rate of socialization. This deceleration is due both to organic factors (age—which ties it to the birth-cycle) and to social factors (the cumulative character of social experience). Its effect is to make the birth-cycle interval, which is the period of youth, the time of major socialization, subsequent periods of socialization being subsidiary.

Given these constant features, rapid social change creates conflict because *to* the intrinsic (universal, inescapable) differences between parents and children it adds an extrinsic (variable) difference derived from the acquisition, at the same stage of life, of differential cultural content by each successive generation. Not only are parent and child, at any given moment, in different stages of development, but the content which the parent acquired at the stage where the child now is, was a different content from that which the child is now acquiring. Since the parent is supposed to socialize the child, he tends to apply the erstwhile but now inappropriate content (see Diagram). He makes this mistake, and cannot remedy it, because, due to the logic of personality growth, his basic orientation was formed by the experiences of his own childhood. He cannot "modernize" his point of view, because *he* is the product of those experiences. He can change in superficial ways, such as learning a new tune, but he cannot change (or *want* to change) the initial modes of thinking upon which his subsequent social experience has been built. To change the basic conceptions by which he has learned to judge the rightness and reality of all specific situations would be to

FIGURE 1. The Birth-Cycle, Social Change, and Parent-Child
Relations at Different Stages of Life*

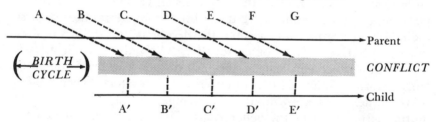

*Old* Cultural Content Acquired at Each Stage of Life

*New* Cultural Content at Each Stage

*Because the birth-cycle interval persists throughout their conjoint life, parent and child are always at a different stage of development and their relations are always therefore potentially subject to conflict. E.g., when the parent is at stage *D*, the child is at stage *B*. But social change adds another source of conflict, for it means that the parent, when at the stage where the child now is, acquired a different cultural content from that which the child must now acquire at that stage. This places the parent in the predicament of trying to transmit old content no longer suited to the offspring's needs in a changed world. In a stable society, *B* and *B'* would have the same cultural content. In a changing society, they do not, yet the parent tries to apply the content of *A*, *B*, *C*, etc., to the corresponding stages in the child's development, *A'*, *B'*, *C'*, etc., which supposedly and actually have a different content. Thus, a constant (the birth-cycle) and a variable (social change) combine to produce parent-youth conflict.

Though the birth-cycle remains absolutely the same, it does not remain relatively the same, because it occupies, as time goes on, a successively smaller percentage of the total time lived. Furthermore, because of the decelerating rate of socialization, the difference in the total amount of cultural content as between parent and child becomes less pronounced. After the period of adolescence, for example, the margin is reduced to a minimum, which explains why a minimum of conflict is achieved after that stage.

render subsequent experience meaningless, to make an empty cari-
cature of what had been his life.

Although, in the birth-cycle gap between parent and offspring,
astronomical time constitutes the basic point of disparity, the actual
sequences, and hence the actual differences significant for us, are
physiological, psychosocial, and sociological—each with an accelera-
tion of its own within, but to some degree independent of, sidereal
time, and each containing a divergence between parent and child
which must be taken into account in explaining parent-youth conflict.

*Physiological Differences.* Though the disparity in chronological
age remains constant through life, the precise physiological differences between parent and offspring vary radically from one period
to another. The organic contrasts between parent and *infant*, for
example, are far different from those between parent and adolescent.
Yet whatever the period, the organic differences produce contrasts
(as between young and old) in those desires which, at least in part,
are organically determined. Thus, at the time of adolescence the
contrast is between an organism which is just reaching its full powers
and one which is just losing them. The physiological need of the
latter is for security and conservation, because as the superabundance
of energy diminishes, the organism seems to hoard what remains.

Such differences, often alleged (under the heading of "disturbing
physiological changes accompanying adolescence") as the primary
cause of parent-adolescent strife, are undoubtedly a factor in such
conflict, but, like other universal differences to be discussed, they
form a constant factor present in every community, and therefore
cannot in themselves explain the peculiar heightening of parent-
youth conflict in our culture.

The fact is that most societies avoid the potential clash of old and
young by using sociological position as a neutralizing agent. They
assign definite and separate positions to persons of different ages,
thereby eliminating competition between them for the same position
and avoiding the competitive emotions of jealousy and envy. Also,
since the expected behavior of old and young is thus made complementary rather than identical, the performance of cooperative functions is accomplished by different but mutually related activities
suited to the disparate organic needs of each, with no coercion to
behave in a manner unsuited to one's organic age. In our culture,
where most positions are *theoretically* based on accomplishment
rather than age, interage competition arises, superior organic pro-
pensities lead to a high evaluation of youth (the so-called "accent on

youth"), a disproportionate lack of opportunity for youth manifests itself, and consequently, arrogance and frustration appear in the young, fear and envy, in the old.

*Psychosocial Differences: Adult Realism versus Youthful Idealism.* The decelerating rate of socialization (an outgrowth both of the human being's organic development, from infant plasticity to senile rigidity, and of his cumulative cultural and social development), when taken with rapid social change and other conditions of our society, tends to produce certain differences of orientation between parent and youth. Though lack of space makes it impossible to discuss all of these ramifications, we shall attempt to delineate at least one sector of difference in terms of the conflict between adult realism (or pragmatism) and youthful idealism.

Though both youth and age claim to see the truth, the old are more conservatively realistic than the young, because on the one hand they take Utopian ideals less seriously and on the other hand take what may be called operating ideals, if not more seriously, at least more for granted. Thus, middle-aged people notoriously forget the poetic ideals of a new social order which they cherished when young. In their place, they put simply the working ideals current in the society. There is, in short, a persistent tendency for the ideology of a person as he grows older to gravitate more and more toward the status quo ideology, unless other facts (such as a social crisis or hypnotic suggestion) intervene.[5] With advancing age, he becomes less and less bothered by inconsistencies in ideals. He tends to judge ideals according to whether they are widespread and hence effective in thinking about practical life, not according to whether they are logically consistent. Furthermore, he gradually ceases to bother about the *untruth* of his ideals, in the sense of their failure to correspond to reality. He assumes through long habit that, though they do not correspond perfectly, the discrepancy is not significant. The reality of an ideal is defined for him in terms of how many people accept it rather than how completely it is mirrored in actual behavior.[6] Thus, we call him, as he approaches middle age, a realist.

The young, however, are idealists, partly because they take working ideals literally and partly because they acquire ideals not fully operative in the social organization. Those in authority over children are obligated as a requirement of their status to inculcate ideals as a part of the official culture given the new generation.[7] The children are receptive because they have little social experience—experience being systematically kept from them (by such means as censorship, for example, a large part of which is to "protect" children). Consequently, young people possess little ballast for their acquired ideals, which therefore soar to the sky, whereas the middle-aged, by contrast, have plenty of ballast.

This relatively unchecked idealism in youth is eventually complicated by the fact that young people possess keen reasoning ability. The mind, simply as a logical machine, works as well at sixteen as at thirty-six.[8] Such logical capacity, combined with high ideals and an initial lack of experience, means that youth soon discovers with increasing age that the ideals it has been taught are true and consistent are not so in fact. Mental conflict thereupon ensues, for the young person has not learned that ideals may be useful without being true and consistent. As a solution, youth is likely to take action designed to remove inconsistencies or force actual conduct into line with ideals, such action assuming one of several typical adolescent forms—from religious withdrawal to the militant support of some Utopian scheme—but in any case consisting essentially in serious allegiance to one or more of the ideal moral systems present in the culture.[9]

A different, usually later reaction to disillusionment is the cynical or sophomoric attitude; for, if the ideals one has imbibed cannot be reconciled and do not fit reality, then why not dismiss them as worthless? Cynicism has the advantage of giving justification for behavior that young organisms crave anyway. It might be mistaken for genuine realism if it were not for two things. The first is the emotional strain behind the "don't care" attitude. The cynic, in his judgment that the world is bad because of inconsistency and untruth of ideals, clearly implies that he still values the ideals. The true realist sees the inconsistency and untruth, but without emotion; he uses either ideals or reality whenever it suits his purpose. The second is the early disappearance of the cynical attitude. Increased experience usually teaches the adolescent that overt cynicism is unpopular and unworkable, that to deny and deride all beliefs which fail to cohere or to correspond to facts, and to act in opposition to them, is to alienate oneself from any group,[10] because these beliefs, however unreal, are precisely what makes group unity possible. Soon, therefore, the youthful cynic finds himself bound up with some group having a system of working ideals, and becomes merely another conformist, cynical only about beliefs of other groups.[11]

While the germ of this contrast between youthful idealism and adult realism may spring from the universal logic of personality development, it receives in our culture a peculiar exaggeration. Social change, complexity, and specialization (by compartmentalizing different aspects of life) segregate ideals from fact and throw together incompatible ideologies while at the same time providing the intellectual tools for discerning logical inconsistencies and empirical errors. Our highly elaborated burden of culture, correlated with a variegated system of achieved vertical mobility, necessitates long years of formal education which separate youth from adulthood, theory from practice, school from life. Insofar, then, as youth's reformist zeal or cynical negativism produces conflict with parents, the peculiar conditions of our culture are responsible.

*Sociological Differences: Parental Authority.* Since social status and office are everywhere partly distributed on the basis of age, personality development is intimately linked with the network of social positions successively occupied during life. Western society, in spite of an unusual amount of interage competition, maintains differences of social position between parent and child, the developmental gap between them being too clearcut, the symbiotic needs too fundamental, to escape being made a basis of social organization. Hence, parent and child, in a variety of ways, find themselves enmeshed in different social contexts and possessed of different outlooks. The much publicized critical attitude of youth toward established ways, for example, is partly a matter of being on the outside looking in. The "established ways" under criticism are usually institutions (such as property, marriage, profession) which the adolescent has not yet entered. He looks at them from the point of view of the outsider (especially since they affect him in a restrictive manner), either failing to imagine himself finding satisfaction in such patterns or else feeling resentful that the old have in them a vested interest from which he is excluded.

Not only is there differential position, but also *mutually* differential position, status being in many ways specific for and reciprocal between parent and child. Some of these differences, relating to the birth-cycle and constituting part of the family structure, are universal. This is particularly true of the super- and subordination summed up in the term *parental authority.*

Since sociological differences between parent and child are inherent in family organization, they constitute a universal factor potentially capable of producing conflict. Like the biological differences, however, they do not in themselves produce such conflict. In fact, they may help to avoid it. To understand how our society brings to expression the potentiality for conflict, indeed to deal realistically with the relation between the generations, we must do so not in generalized terms but in terms of the specific "power situation."

Therefore, the remainder of our discussion will center upon the nature of parental authority and its vicissitudes in our society.

Because of his strategic position with reference to the new-born child (at least in the familial type of reproductive institution), the parent is given considerable authority. Charged by his social group with the responsibility of controlling and training the child in conformity with the mores and thereby insuring the maintenance of the cultural structure, the parent, to fulfill his duties, must have the privileges as well as the obligations of authority, and the surrounding community ordinarily guarantees both.

The first thing to note about parental authority, in addition to its function in socialization, is that it is a case of authority within a primary group. Simmel has pointed out that authority is bearable for the subordinate because it touches only one aspect of life. Impersonal and objective, it permits all other aspects to be free from its particularistic dominance. This escape, however, is lacking in parental authority, for since the family includes most aspects of life, its authority is not limited, specific, or impersonal. What, then, can make this authority bearable? Three factors associated with the familial primary group help to give the answer: (1) the child is socialized within the family, and therefore knowing nothing else and being utterly dependent, the authority of the parent is internalized, accepted; (2) the family, like other primary groups, implies identification, in such sense that one person understands and responds emphatically to the sentiments of the other, so that the harshness of authority is ameliorated;[12] (3) in the intimate interaction of the primary group control can never be purely one-sided; there are too many ways in which the subordinated can exert the pressure of his will. When, therefore, the family system is a going concern, parental authority, however inclusive, is not felt as despotic.

A second thing to note about parental authority is that while its duration is variable (lasting in some societies a few years and in others a lifetime), it inevitably involves a change, a progressive readjustment, in the respective positions of parent and child—in some cases an almost complete reversal of roles, in others at least a cumulative allowance for the fact of maturity in the subordinated offspring. Age is a unique basis for social stratification. Unlike birth, sex, wealth, or occupation, it implies that the stratification is temporary, that the person, if he lives a full life, will eventually traverse all of the strata having it as a basis. Therefore, there is a peculiar ambivalence attached to this kind of differentiation, as well as a constant directional movement. On the one hand, the young person, in the stage of maximum socialization, is, so to speak, *moving into* the social organization. His social personality is expanding, i.e., acquiring an increased amount of the cultural heritage, filling more powerful and numerous positions. His future is before him, in what the older person is leaving behind. The latter, on the other hand, has a future before him only in the sense that the offspring represents it. Therefore, there is a disparity of interest, the young person placing his thoughts upon a future which, once the first stages of dependence are passed, does not include the parent, the old person placing his hopes vicariously upon the young. This situation, representing a *tendency* in every society, is avoided in many places by a system of respect for the aged and an imaginary projection of life beyond the grave. In the absence of such a religio-ancestral system, the role of the aged is a tragic one.[13]

Let us now take up, point by point, the manner in which western civilization has affected this *gemeinschaftliche* and processual form of authority.

*1. Conflicting Norms.* To begin with, rapid change has, as we saw, given old and young a different social content, so that they possess conflicting norms. There is a loss of mutual identification, and the parent will not "catch up" with the child's point of view, because he is supposed to dominate rather than follow. More than this, social complexity has confused the standards *within* the generations. Faced with conflicting goals, parents become inconsistent and confused in their own minds in rearing their children. The children, for example, acquire an argument against discipline by being able to point to some family wherein discipline is less severe, while the parent can retaliate by pointing to still other families wherein it is firmer. The acceptance of parental attitudes is less complete than formerly.

*2. Competing Authorities.* We took it for granted, when discussing rapid social change, that youth acquires new ideas, but we did not ask how. The truth is that, in a specialized and complex culture, they learn from competing authorities. Today, for example, education is largely in the hands of professional specialists, some of whom, as college professors, resemble the sophists of ancient Athens by virtue of their work of accumulating and purveying knowledge, and who consequently have ideas in advance of the populace at large (i.e., the parents). By giving the younger generation these advanced ideas, they (and many other extrafamilial agencies, including youth's contemporaries) widen the intellectual gap between parent and child.[14]

*3. Little Explicit Institutionalization of Steps in Parental Au-*

*thority.* Our society provides little explicit institutionalization of the progressive readjustments of authority as between parent and child. We are intermediate between the extreme of virtually permanent parental authority and the extreme of very early emancipation, because we encourage release in late adolescence. Unfortunately, this is a time of enhanced sexual desire, so that the problem of sex and the problem of emancipation occur simultaneously and complicate each other. Yet even this would doubtless be satisfactory if it were not for the fact that among us the exact time when authority is relinquished, the exact amount, and the proper ceremonial behavior are not clearly defined. Not only do different groups and families have conflicting patterns, and new situations arise to which old definitions will not apply, but the different spheres of life (legal, economic, religious, intellectual) do not synchronize, maturity in one sphere and immaturity in another often coexisting. The readjustment of authority between individuals is always a ticklish process, and when it is a matter of such close authority as that between parent and child it is apt to be still more ticklish. The failure of our culture to institutionalize this readjustment by a series of well-defined, well-publicized steps is undoubtedly a cause of much parent-youth dissension. The adolescent's sociological exit from his family, via education, work, marriage, and change of residence, is fraught with potential conflicts of interest which only a definite system of institutional controls can neutralize. The parents have a vital stake in what the offspring will do. Because his acquisition of independence will free the parents of many obligations, they are willing to relinquish their authority; yet, precisely because their own status is socially identified with that of their offspring, they wish to insure satisfactory conduct on the latter's part and are tempted to prolong their authority by making the decisions themselves. In the absence of institutional prescriptions, the conflict of interest may lead to a struggle for power, the parents fighting to keep control in matters of importance to themselves, the son or daughter clinging to personally indispensable family services while seeking to evade the concomitant control.

4. *Concentration within the Small Family.* Our family system is peculiar in that it manifests a paradoxical combination of concentration and dispersion. On the one hand, the unusual smallness of the family unit makes for a strange intensity of family feeling, while on the other, the fact that most pursuits take place outside the home makes for a dispersion of activities. Though apparently contradictory, the two phenomena are really interrelated and traceable ulti-

mately to the same factors in our social structure. Since the first refers to that type of affection and antagonism found between relatives, and the second to activities, it can be seen that the second (dispersion) isolates and increases the intensity of the affectional element by sheering away common activities and the extended kin. Whereas ordinarily the sentiments of kinship are organically related to a number of common activities and spread over a wide circle of relatives, in our mobile society they are associated with only a few common activities and concentrated within only the immediate family. This makes them at once more instable (because ungrounded) and more intense. With the diminishing birth rate, our family is the world's smallest kinship unit, a tiny closed circle. Consequently, a great deal of family sentiment is directed toward a few individuals, who are so important to the emotional life that complexes easily develop. This emotional intensity and situational instability increase both the probability and severity of conflict.

In a familistic society, where there are several adult male and female relatives within the effective kinship group to whom the child turns for affection and aid, and many members of the younger generation in whom the parents have a paternal interest, there appears to be less intensity of emotion for any particular kinsman and consequently less chance for severe conflict." Also, if conflict between any two relatives does arise, it may be handled by shifting mutual rights and obligations to another relative.[16]

5. *Open Competition for Socioeconomic Position.* Our emphasis upon individual initiative and vertical mobility, in contrast to rural-stable regimes, means that one's future occupation and destiny are determined more at adolescence than at birth, the adolescent himself (as well as the parents) having some part in the decision. Before him spread a panorama of possible occupations and avenues of advancement, all of them fraught with the uncertainties of competitive vicissitude. The youth is ignorant of most of the facts. So is the parent, but less so. Both attempt to collaborate on the future, but because of previously mentioned sources of friction, the collaboration is frequently stormy. They evaluate future possibilities differently, and since the decision is uncertain yet important, a clash of wills results. The necessity of choice at adolescence extends beyond the occupational field to practically every phase of life, the parents having an interest in each decision. A culture in which more of the choices of life were settled beforehand by ascription, where the possibilities were fewer and the responsibilities of choice less urgent, would have much less parent-youth conflict.[17]

*6. Sex Tension.* If until now we have ignored sex taboos, the omission has represented a deliberate attempt to place them in their proper context with other factors, rather than in the unduly prominent place usually given them.[18] Undoubtedly, because of a constellation of cultural conditions, sex looms as an important bone of parent-youth contention. Our morality, for instance, demands both premarital chastity and postponement of marriage, thus creating a long period of desperate eagerness when young persons practically at the peak of their sexual capacity are forbidden to enjoy it. Naturally, tensions arise—tensions which adolescents try to relieve, and adults hope they will relieve, in some socially acceptable form. Such tensions not only make the adolescent intractable and capricious, but create a genuine conflict of interest between the two generations. The parent, with respect to the child's behavior, represents morality, while the offspring reflects morality *plus* his organic cravings. The stage is thereby set for conflict, evasion, and deceit. For the mass of parents, toleration is never possible. For the mass of adolescents, sublimation is never sufficient. Given our system of morality, conflict seems well nigh inevitable.

Yet it is not sex itself but the way it is handled that causes conflict. If sex patterns were carefully, definitely, and uniformly geared with nonsexual patterns in the social structure, there would be no parent-youth conflict over sex. As it is, rapid change has opposed the sex standards of different groups and generations, leaving impulse only chaotically controlled.

The extraordinary preoccupation of modern parents with the sex life of their adolescent offspring is easily understandable. First, our morality is sex-centered. The strength of the impulse which it seeks to control, the consequent stringency of its rules, and the importance of reproductive institutions for society, make sex so morally important that being moral and being sexually discreet are synonymous. Small wonder, then, that parents, charged with responsibility for their children and fearful of their own status in the eyes of the moral community, are preoccupied with what their offspring will do in this matter. Moreover, sex is intrinsically involved in the family structure and is therefore of unusual significance to family members *qua* family members. Offspring and parent are not simply two persons who happen to live together; they are two persons who happen to live together because of past sex relations between the parents. Also, between parent and child there stand strong incest taboos, and doubtless the unvoiced possibility of violating these unconsciously intensifies the interest of each in the other's sexual conduct. In addi-

tion, since sexual behavior is connected with the offspring's formation of a new family of his own, it is naturally of concern to the
parent. Finally, these factors taken in combination with the delicacy
of the authoritarian relation, the emotional intensity within the
small family, and the confusion of sex standards, make it easy to
explain the parental interest in adolescent sexuality. Yet because
sex is a tabooed topic between parent and child,[19] parental control
must be indirect and devious, which creates additional possibilities
of conflict.

*Summary and Conclusion.* Our parent-youth conflict thus results
from the interaction of certain universals of the parent-child relation
and certain variables the values of which are peculiar to modern
culture. The universals are (1) the basic age or birth-cycle differential between parent and child, (2) the decelerating rate of socialization with advancing age, and (3) the resulting intrinsic differences
between old and young on the physiological, psychosocial, and sociological planes.

Though these universal factors *tend* to produce conflict between
parent and child, whether or not they do so depends upon the
variables. We have seen that the distinctive general features of our
society are responsible for our excessive parent-adolescent friction.
Indeed, they are the same features which are affecting *all* family
relations. The delineation of these variables has not been systematic,
because the scientific classification of whole societies has not yet been
accomplished; and it has been difficult, in view of the interrelated
character of societal traits, to seize upon certain features and ignore
others. Yet certainly the following four complex variables are important: (1) the rate of social change; (2) the extent of complexity in the
social structure; (3) the degree of integration in the culture; and
(4) the velocity of movement (e.g., vertical mobility) within the
structure and its relation to the cultural values.

Our rapid social change, for example, has crowded historical
meaning into the family time-span, has thereby given the offspring
a different social content from that which the parent acquired, and
consequently has added to the already existent intrinsic differences
between parent and youth, a set of extrinsic ones which double the
chance of alienation. Moreover, our great societal complexity, our
evident cultural conflict, and our emphasis upon open competition
for socioeconomic status have all added to this initial effect. We have
seen, for instance, that they have disorganized the important relation
of parental authority by confusing the goals of child control, setting
up competing authorities, creating a small family system, making

necessary certain significant choices at the time of adolescence, and leading to an absence of definite institutional mechanisms to symbolize and enforce the progressively changing stages of parental power.

If ours were a simple rural-stable society, mainly familistic, the emancipation from parental authority being gradual and marked by definite institutionalized steps, with no great postponement of marriage, sex taboo, or open competition for status, parents and youth would not be in conflict. Hence, the presence of parent-youth conflict in our civilization is one more specific manifestation of the incompatibility between an urban-industrial-mobile social system and the familial type of reproductive institutions.[20]

## Notes

1. In the absence of statistical evidence, exaggeration of the conflict is easily possible, and two able students have warned against it. E. B. Reuter, "The Sociology of Adolescence," and Jessie R. Runner, "Social Distance in Adolescent Relationships," both in *Amer. J. Sociol.*, November 1937, 43: 415–16, 437. Yet sufficient nonquantitative evidence lies at hand in the form of personal experience, the outpour of literature on adolescent problems, and the historical and anthropological accounts of contrasting societies to justify the conclusion that in comparison with other cultures ours exhibits an exceptional amount of such conflict. If this paper seems to stress conflict, it is simply because we are concerned with this problem rather than with parent-youth harmony.
2. Cf. Nathan Miller, *The Child in Primitive Society*, New York, 1928; Miriam Van Waters, "The Adolescent Girl Among Primitive Peoples," *J. Relig. Psychol.*, 1913, 6: 375–421 (1913) and 7: 75–120 (1914); Margaret Mead, *Coming of Age in Samoa*, New York, 1928 and "Adolescence in Primitive and Modern Society," 169–188, in *The New Generation* (ed. by V. F. Calverton and S. Schmalhausen, New York, 1930; A. M. Bacon, *Japanese Girls and Women*, New York and Boston, 1891 and 1902.
3. Partially done by Mead and Van Waters in the works cited above.
4. Soviet Russia and Nazi Germany are examples. See Sigmund Neumann, "The Conflict of Generations in Contemporary Europe from Versailles to Munich," *Vital Speeches of the Day*, August 1, 1939, 5: 623–28. Parents in these countries are to be obeyed only so long as they profess the "correct" (i.e., youthful, revolutionary) ideas.
5. See Footnote 11 for necessary qualifications.
6. When discussing a youthful ideal, however, the older person is quick to take a dialectical advantage by pointing out not only that this ideal affronts the aspirations of the multitude, but that it also fails to correspond to human behavior either now or (by the lessons of history) probably in the future.
7. See amusing but accurate article, "Fathers Are Liars," *Scribner's Magazine*, March, 1934.
8. Evidence from mental growth data which point to a leveling off of the growth curve at about age 16. For charts and brief explanations, together with references, see F. K. Shuttleworth, *The Adolescent Period*, Monographs

of the Society for Research in Child Development, III, Serial No. 16 (Washington, D.C., 1938), Figs. 16, 230, 232, 276, 285, 308.

Maturity of judgment is of course another matter. We are speaking only of logical capacity. Judgment is based on experience as well as capacity; hence, adolescents are apt to lack it.

9. An illustration of youthful reformism was afforded by the Laval University students who decided to "do something about" prostitution in the city of Quebec. They broke into eight houses in succession one night, "whacked naked inmates upon the buttocks, upset beds and otherwise proved their collegiate virtue. . . ." They ended by "shoving the few remaining girls out of doors into the cold autumn night." *Time*, October 19, 1936.

10. This holds only for expressed cynicism, but so close is the relation of thought to action that the possibility of an entirely covert cynic seems remote.

11. This tentative analysis holds only insofar as the logic of personality development in a complex culture is the sole factor. Because of other factors, concrete situations may be quite different. When, for example, a person is specifically trained in certain rigid, other-worldly, or impractical ideals, he may grow increasingly fanatical with the years rather than realistc, while his offspring, because of association with less fanatical persons, may be more pragmatic than he. The variation in group norms within a society produces persons who, whatever their orientation inside the group, remain more idealistic than the average outsider, while their children may, with outside contacts, become more pragmatic. Even within a group, however, a person's situation may be such as to drive him beyond the everyday realities of that group, while his children remain undisturbed. Such situations largely explain the personal crises that may alter one's orientation. The analysis, overly brief and mainly illustrative, therefore represents a certain degree of abstraction. The reader should realize, moreover, that the terms "realistic" and "idealistic" are chosen merely for convenience in trying to convey the idea, not for any evaluative judgments which they may happen to connote. The terms are not used in any technical epistemological sense, but simply in the way made plain by the context. Above all, it is not implied that ideals are "unreal." The ways in which they are "real" and "unreal" to observer and actor are complex indeed. See T. Parsons, *The Structure of Social Action*, 396, New York, 1937, and V. Pareto, *The Mind and Society*, III: 1300–1304, New York, 1935.

12. House slaves, for example, are generally treated much better than field slaves. Authority over the former is of a personal type, while that over the latter (often in the form of a foreman-gang organization) is of a more impersonal or economic type.

13. Sometimes compensated for by an interest in the grandchildren, which permits them partially to recover the role of the vigorous parent.

14. The essential point is not that there are other authorities—in every society there are extrafamilial influences in socialization—but that, because of specialization and individualistic enterprise, they are *competing* authorities. Because they make a living by their work and are specalists in socializaton, some authorities have a competitive advantage over parents who are amateurs or at best merely general practitioners.

15. Margaret Mead, *Social Organization of Manua*, 84, Honolulu, Bernice P. Bishop Museum Bulletin 76, 1930. Large heterogeneous households early accustom the child to expect emotional rewards from many different persons. D. M. Spencer, "The Composition of the Family as a Factor in the Behavior of Children in Fijian Society," *Sociometry*, (1939) 2: 47–55.

16. The principle of substitution is widespread in familism, as shown by the wide distribution of adoption, levirate, sororate, and classificatory kinship nomenclature.

17. M. Mead, *Coming of Age in Samoa*, 200 ff.

18. Cf., e.g., L. K. Frank, "The Management of Tensions," *Amer. J. Sociol.*, March 1928, 33: 706–22; M. Mead, *op. cit.*, 216–217, 222–23.
19. "Even among the essentially 'unrepressed' Trobrianders the parent is never the confidant in matters of sex." Bronislaw Malinowski, *Sex and Reproduction in Savage Society*, 36 (note), London, 1927, p. 36n. Cf. the interesting article, "Intrusive Parents," *The Commentator*, September 1938, which opposes frank sex discussion between parents and children.
20. For further evidence of this incompatibility, see the writer's "Reproductive Institutions and the Pressure for Population," *(Brit.) Sociol. Rev.*; July 1937, 29: 289–306.

PART III. THE FAMILY AND SOCIAL CHANGE

# Synopsis and Evaluation of Theories Concerning Family Evolution

*Panos D. Bardis*

> *"A prima descendit origine mundi*
> *Causarum series."*
>
> LUCAN, *Pharsalia*, VI, 608

## Introduction

In his *Themistocles,* Plutarch asserts: "So very difficult a matter is it to trace and find out the truth of anything by history." And in his *Sertorius,* he adds: "It is no great wonder if in long process of time, while fortune takes her course hither and thither, numerous coincidences should spontaneously occur. If the number and variety of subjects to be wrought upon be infinite, it is all the more easy for fortune, with such an abundance of material, to effect this similarity of results." On the other hand, Thucydides, in his *Historia* (1, ii, 2), expresses an opinion which generated the well-known phrase, "History repeats itself," namely: "I shall be content if those shall pronounce my *History* useful who desire to give a view of events as they did really happen, and as they are very likely, in accordance with human nature, to repeat themselves at some future time—if not exactly the same, yet very similar."

These or other analogous controversial statements will undoubtedly come to mind whenever an effort is made to determine the origin of the family and reconstruct its more or less recondite evolutionary stages. Indeed, as the following discussion indicates, there is very little agreement among the scholars who, with impressive indefatigability, have explored this subject.

From *Social Science*, January, 1963. Reprinted by permission.

## Bachofen

Johann Jakob Bachofen (1815–1887), for example, the famous Swiss jurist, philologist, and classicist who in 1861 published *Das Mutterrecht*,[1] believed that human society began with hetaerism or promiscuity (sexual communism or extreme sexual permissiveness), which was succeeded by *Gynakokratie* (gynecocracy, or a society ruled by women), which was finally superseded by the patriarchate (a culture in which the male has higher social status, and in which descent, inheritance, and succession are usually reckoned through the father, while residence is patrilocal and women and children are subordinated to the ruling male).

That our earliest ancestors actually lived in a state of hetaerism is indicated, Bachofen contended, by the fact that fatherhood was originally unrecognized—all children belonged to the entire group —as well as by what he considered as survivals of a transition period from sexual communism to pair marriage. These survivals were temple prostitution and the *jus primae noctis*.

Of these, the first, which is also known as religious prostitution and sacred harlotry, refers to the practice of having women function as religious prostitutes in the temple. In this way, according to the author of *Das Mutterrecht*, the favor of the gods was believed to be won anew, since temporary prostitution expiated the breaking of natural law by entering marriage, which is characterized by sexual exclusiveness.

The *jus primae noctis* (law of the first night), on the other hand, which is sometimes referred to as *droit de seigneur* (right of the Lord), is a practice found in various primitive societies and probably in medieval Europe. This law gave the chief of the tribe, the priest, the lord, or some other leader the right to sleep with the bride on the first night after her marriage.

The theory concerning the second stage, that of *Mutterrecht* or mother right, was based on a reinterpretation necessitated by accumulating anthropological research which indicated that certain folkways and mores among primitives were incompatible with patriarchal theory. After asserting that mother right was typical of some societies, Bachofen theorized that matriarchy everywhere preceded patriarchy. His main arguments were as follows: First, there is no conclusive anthropological evidence that patriliny was succeeded by matriliny. Second, many patrilineal societies include features that seem to constitute vestiges of earlier matrilineal cultures. Third, analogous patrilineal vestiges are quite uncommon among matrilineal societies.

Fourth, patrilineal cultures in general appear more advanced than matrilineal cultures, thus indicating that the latter preceded the former. Fifth, primitives must have been unfamiliar with the nature of biological paternity. Sixth, the association of mother and child has always been physically obvious. And seventh, among early nomadic peoples, the father seems to have been excluded from the family group.

Believing that social evolution consists in transcending the material or animal-like aspects of the human race, or in increasingly dominating the laws of matter, and thus gradually spiritualizing and humanizing mankind, Bachofen concluded that the matriarchate was superseded by the patriarchate. According to him, the most genuinely spiritual power of the male family head was attained in ancient Rome. There, and only there, we find the ideal of *potestas* over wife and children, the highest type of human law, which facilitated the prevalence of the corresponding concept of a unified political *imperium* so relentlessly and unremittingly pursued in the Eternal City.

## Maine

In the same year that Bachofen's *Das Mutterrecht* appeared, Sir Henry J. Sumner Maine (1822–1888), an English lawyer and historian who contributed considerably to ethnological jurisprudence, who was the first scholar to employ the historical method in the study of legal phenomena, who was one of the founders of comparative law and the philosophical study of institutions, and whose definitions of territorial tie and blood bond influenced Lewis Henry Morgan's work, published his classic study, *Ancient Law*.

In this work Maine cautioned scientific researchers against attributing antiquity and universality to certain primitive customs and, unlike Bachofen, averred that a matriarchal stage in social evolution never existed; on the contrary, the patriarchate has always been prevalent. The establishment of private property, he added, and mother right are positively incompatible.

His description of the patriarchate was as follows:

"The eldest male parent—the eldest ascendant—is absolutely supreme in his household. His dominion extends to life and death, and is as unqualified over his children and their houses as over his slaves; indeed the relations of sonship and serfdom appear to differ in little beyond the higher capacity which the child in blood possesses of becoming one day the head of a family himself. The flocks and herds of the children are the flocks and herds of the father, and the possessions of the parent, which he holds in a representative rather than in a proprietary character, are equally divided at his death among his descendants in the first degree, the eldest son sometimes receiving a double share under the name of birthright, but more generally endowed with no hereditary advantage beyond an honorary precedence."[2]

With reference to the evidence concerning the patriarchal theory, he stated:

"The effect of the evidence derived from comparative jurisprudence is to establish that view of the primeval condition of the human race which is known as the Patriarchal Theory. . . . this theory was originally based on the Scriptural history of the Hebrew patriarchs . . . its connexion with Scripture rather militated than otherwise against its reception as a complete theory, since the majority of the inquirers who till recently addressed themselves with most earnestness to the colligation of social phenomena, were either influenced by the strongest prejudice against Hebrew antiquities or by the strongest desire to construct their system without the assistance of religious records. . . . indeed the difficulty, at the present stage of the inquiry, is to know where to stop, to say of what races of men it is *not* allowable to lay down that the society in which they are united was originally organized on the patriarchal model."[3]

In the same passage, Maine quotes and interprets a few lines from Homer's *Odyssey* in this manner:

"If I were attempting for the more special purposes of the jurist to express compendiously the characteristics of the situation in which mankind disclose themselves at the dawn of their history, I should be satisfied to quote a few verses from the *Odyssey* of Homer: . . . 'They have neither assemblies for consultation nor *themistes*, but every one exercises jurisdiction over his wives and his children, and they pay no regard to one another.' These lines are applied to the Cyclops, and it may not perhaps be an altogether fanciful idea when I suggest that the Cyclops is Homer's type of an alien and less advanced civilisation; for the almost physical loathing which a primitive community feels for men of widely different manners from its own usually expresses itself by describing them as monsters, such as giants, or even (which is almost always the case in Oriental mythology) as demons. However that may be, the verses condense in themselves the sum of the hints which are given us by legal antiquities."[4]

Maine's theory of family evolution is also presented in his tracing of the development of cultures from those with group relations and tradition determining rights and obligations to those where legal power and contract were the dominant forces. This is the classic "Mainean shift" epitomized in his own phrase "from status to contract." According to Maine, the shift is especially noticeable after the period of urbanization, when kinship bonds become less strong. In his own words: "The contrast may be most forcibly expressed by saying that the *unit* of an ancient society was the Family, of a modern society the Individual."[5] More specifically, when social evolution began, kinship and the family constituted the foundation of social organization. The most ancient legal systems, therefore, were concerned with the collectivity and not with the individual, whose life constituted a mere continuation of the existence of his ancestors. In this way, the ideal of liberty became reinforced as human society moved from status to contract, or as the individual gained power at the expense of the family group. When, for instance, the family was powerful in relation to the state, woman's social status was extremely low. But when familism declined and the state became stronger, her position was improved considerably. In other words, civil law now begins to take account of the individual, the family no longer being considered as the unit. Adding that marriage had its origin in the family and not vice versa, Maine also predicted further encroachments on the family by the state, as the latter grew in power, and as individualism became a more popular ideology.

## Morgan

Lewis Henry Morgan (1818–1881), a lawyer of Rochester, New York, became a prominent ethnographer and social evolutionist through his firsthand acquaintance with the Iroquois and other American Indians. His studies of their family customs enabled him to collect kinship data on more than two hundred different societies, which he discussed in *Systems of Consanguinity and Affinity of the Human Family*, a book published in 1870. Being the first work of its kind and one of the most brilliant and original anthropological achievements, this treatise established the study of kinship as a branch of comparative sociology. Here Morgan distinguished between two basic types of kinship nomenclature, namely, the classificatory and descriptive systems. The former represents a kinship system in which main emphasis is placed on kin solidarity rather than on exact genealogical relationships. The remoteness of a blood relationship, therefore, does not diminish its importance. The term *father*, for example, may refer not only to the male parent, but also to his brothers. On the other hand, the descriptive system, as is typical of Western cultures, includes specific kinship terms to designate specific individual relationships.

Another important treatise by Morgan is his *Ancient Society*, which was published six years later. This work constituted a synthesis of the social history of Oceania, the Indians of America, and classical Greece and Rome. Believing in uniform laws of social evolution, and beginning with the Australians and Polynesians, Morgan divided all human history into three great stages of "human progress," that is, savagery, barbarism, and civilization. As he wrote in his *Ancient Society*, "So essentially identical are the arts, institutions, and mode of life in the same status upon all continents, that the archaic form of the principal domestic institutions of the Greeks and Romans must even now be sought in the corresponding institutions of the American aborigines."[6]

Influenced by Charles Darwin, he developed his evolutionary scheme sufficiently to include various social institutions. The family, for instance, Morgan asserted, followed these stages: promiscuity, punalua, polygamy (commencing with matriliny and ending with patriliny), and monogamy. This is what Morgan himself called "Sequence of Institutions Connected with the Family," referring to the first stage as "Promiscuous Intercourse."

That promiscuity had actually existed, Morgan was never certain. He merely claimed that such an assumption was made quite logical by the stages that followed later, confessing that he deduced "Promiscuous Intercourse" at the theoretical level, since it lies concealed in mankind's misty antiquity beyond the reach of certain knowledge.

He did claim, however, to have found conclusive evidence of the punaluan family among the Indians of North America. This family system, which is also known as group marriage, involves a group of brothers sharing their wives in common or a group of sisters sharing their husbands in common. At this stage, the clan becomes the domestic institution and also the basic unit of social structure.

Matriliny, on the other hand, must have preceded patriliny, since paternity was at first uncertain. But later, as fatherhood became more certain, and as economic progress led to the accumulation of property, the male parent must have resented the exclusion of his offspring from inheriting his goods. The rules of descent and inheritance thus became patrilineal.

### Westermarck

Edward A. Westermarck (1862–1939), a Finnish sociologist and brilliant student of the types and history of human marriage, rejected primitive promiscuity and declared that, by nature, man has always been monogamous. His theories were presented in his classic work, *The History of Human Marriage,* which was published in 1891, and which, although rather outdated, still constitutes a valuable source of descriptive information regarding the family systems of innumerable cultures around the world.

In the first volume of this treatise, Westermarck writes:

"It is often said that the human race must have originally lived in a state of promiscuity, where individual marriage did not exist, where all the men in a horde or tribe had indiscriminately access to all the women, and where the children born of these unions belonged to the community at large. This opinion has been expressed by Bachofen, McLennan, Morgan, Lord Avebury, Giraud-Teulon, Lippert, Kohler, Post, Wilken, Kropotkin, Wilutzky, Bloch, and many others."[7]

Such an assumption, however, was completely unjustifiable, Westermarck asserted uncompromisingly. In his own words:

"I shall not merely endeavor to show that the supposed survivals of ancient promiscuity really are no such survivals at all, but also indicate how the customs in question may be explained.

"The evidence adduced in support of the hypothesis of promiscuity flows from two different sources. First, there are in books of ancient and modern writers notices of peoples who are said to live or to have lived promiscuously. Second, there are certain customs which are assumed to be relics from an earlier stage of civilisation when marriage did not exist."[8]

In one of his most interesting passages, he attacks the first source of evidence in this manner:

"Considering how uncertain the information is which people give about the sexual relations of their own neighbours, we must be careful not to accept as trustworthy evidence the statements made by classical writers with reference to more or less distant tribes of which they evidently possessed very little knowledge. In the very chapter where Pliny states that among the Garamantians men and women lived in promiscuous intercourse he tells us of another African tribe, the Blemmyans, that they were said to have no head and to have the mouth and eyes in the breast. I have never seen this statement quoted in any book on human anatomy, and can see no reason to assume that our author was so much better acquainted with the sexual habits of the Garamantians than he was with the personal appearance of the Blemmyans."[9]

Concerning the second source of evidence, Westermarck contended that the customs considered as survivals from an earlier state of sexual communism were actually due to other causes. The *jus primae noctis*, for example, was not really accorded to a king, chief, priest, or other leader because the sexual exclusiveness of marriage had put an end to promiscuity, but because, in certain cultures at least, the bridegroom wished to protect himself from pollution by hymenal blood to which the king, chief, or priest was believed to be not susceptible. In other cultures, where the priest functioned as a substitute, the common belief was that the marriage would thus be sanctified and fertility would be ensured. And, of course, it would be a great honor if the king himself performed the rite.

An additional argument, of a biological nature, had been inspired by Darwin, who had stated that the extreme jealousy of the male among the most highly developed apes made sexual communism quite unlikely.

Similarly, Westermarck cited numerous anthropological studies to disprove the theory of original promiscuity. For instance, he pointed out that "Giraud-Teulon refers to Dapper's description of the kingdom of Bornu, in which the people are said to have neither law, nor religion nor any proper names, and to possess their women and children in common, and the king is said to be so rich that all his utensils are made of gold. This does not sound very convincing. Dr. Post has found no people in Africa living in a state of promiscuity."[10] And he concluded: "Legends of this sort can no more be regarded as evidence of primitive promiscuity than the second chapter of Genesis can be quoted in proof of primitive monogamy. They may be simply due to the tendency of the popular mind to ascribe almost any great institution to a wise legislator or ruler, if not to direct divine intervention."[11]

Regarding Morgan's hypothesis of the punaluan stage, Westermarck objected that "so far as I can see, this hypothesis is not only unfounded but contrary to all reasonable assumptions. Among other things it presupposes unrestricted sexual intercourse between brothers and sisters, which is found nowhere among existing savages and is utterly inconsistent with the strict exogamy which prevails among most peoples who have a classificatory system of relationship terms."[12] His additional argument was that housemates feel a natural repugnance to coitus between each other. Incest tabu, of course, is not instinctive, he explained; the sexual appetite is merely diminished as a result of constant and prolonged association, especially when such association begins in childhood.

He was equally critical of the matrilineal interpretation of various family customs. "Nor must we take for granted," he maintained, "that a certain prominence given to the maternal uncle by a people with patrilineal descent is an indication of the former prevalence of maternal descent. The reckoning of descent either through the father or through the mother does not imply that the nearest blood-ties on the other side are ignored."[13]

Among his arguments for his own theory of natural monogamy were selected examples involving the anthropoids,[14] as well as his assertion that peoples at the stage of food gathering and hunting, who were considered economically most primitive by the social evolutionists, were predominantly monogamous. In the last volume of his *History*, he also concluded that if "the causes to which monogamy in the most progressive societies owes its origin will continue to operate with constantly growing force, if especially the regard for the feelings of women, and the women's influence on legislation, will increase, the laws of monogamy are not likely to be changed. It is certainly difficult to imagine a time when Western civilisation would legalise the marriage of one man with several women simultaneously."[15]

## Spencer

Herbert Spencer (1820–1903), an English liberal who dealt extensively with the concepts of evolution and the organic state, applied biological theories to social phenomena. Conceiving of evolution as a process by which a differentiated and complex whole results from an undifferentiated and simple one, he developed an optimistic theory of social progress, predicting peace and prosperity as a result of the industrial revolution. He also suggested that the state do not interfere in economic activities to any extent, thus becoming an uncompromising foe of socialism.

He was equally uncompromising concerning the theory of primitive promiscuity. In his great work, *The Principles of Sociology*, he declared: "I do not think the evidence shows that promiscuity ever existed in an unqualified form, and it appears to me that even had it so existed, the name 'communal marriage' would not convey a true conception of it."[16] On the contrary, influenced by Darwin's theory of the transmission of acquired traits, he asserted that monogamy, especially in the more advanced societies, was innate. This form of family organization, he explained, is appealingly definite and simple. Besides, it has been dictated by nature itself, which has created an approximately equal number of males and females. And he added: "The same marital relation occurs in the simplest groups and in the most compound groups. A strict monogamy is observed by the miserable Wood Veddahs, living so widely scattered that they can scarcely be said to have reached the social state; and the wandering Bushmen, similarly low, though not debarred from polygyny, are usually monogamic. Certain settled and more advanced peoples, too, are monogamic; as instance those of Port Dory."[17]

Spencer also maintained that the evolution of Homo sapiens has rendered propagation a less dominant task in the life of the individual. More specifically, the reasons are three: First, the number of offspring has declined. Second, the period of youth has become considerably longer. And third, the period between the cessation of propagation and death is also much longer now. Consequently, the development and advancement of the individual are more feasible at the present time.

However, although Spencer identified the ancient social unit with the family, which has recently been replaced by the individual, and although he accordingly predicted the gradual decline of the family institution, he rejected the political emancipation of woman, asserting that her activities should be confined to the home. Regarding the same subject, he theorized that woman's social status is inversely proportional to the degree of militarism in a given society.

## Briffault

Finally, Robert Briffault, in his famous three-volume treatise, *The Mothers*, which was published in 1927, attacked Westermarck's theory of primitive monogamy, maintaining that this form of marriage constitutes the fourth stage in the evolution of the family, the other three being original group marriage, matriarchy, and patriarchy. "It would be difficult," he wrote, "for any hypothesis to be so uniformly and directly in contradiction with the facts upon which it may be supposed to depend for evidence than the theological doctrine of primitive monogamy. Whatever the variability of the practice of polygyny among uncultured peoples, no monogamous primitive society is known."[18] Besides, he added, as far as nature is concerned, the function of the male in both the plant and animal kingdoms is to impregnate as many females as possible. And monogamy limits this function. He also asserted that, if, unlike Westermarck, we do not confine our research to a few cases, we will find that anthropoids are not actually monogamous. Then, he explained that primitive monogamy is not genuine monogamy, since it is determined by economic, not moral, factors. Finally, he pointed out that wife hospitality (the practice of a host's permitting a guest sexual access to his wife), the levirate (the practice of permitting or requiring a man to marry the widow of his brother, or of another close relative), and the sororate (a man's marrying his wife's sister, on either a mandatory or permissive basis, after the wife's death) are indicative of an early stage of group marriage.

Polyandry and polygyny, on the other hand, according to Briffault, are not distinct forms of family organization, but merely phases of group marriage. In other words, depending on the particular circumstances, group marriage may develop into polyandry or polygyny. Polyandry, for instance, usually evolves in matriarchal cultures, as in certain parts of Tibet, which were organized both matriarchally and gynecocratically. In brief, group marriage is the source, not the result, of polygamy.

Regarding matriarchy, Briffault stated that we should not conceive of this stage as the opposite of patriarchy, with the male having low social status—similar to that of the female in patriarchy. In the first volume of *The Mothers*, he wrote: "The characteristics of societies of a matriarchal type are by no means a simple inversion of the parts respectively played by the sexes in a patriarchal society. In the most primitive human societies there is nothing equivalent to the domination which, in advanced societies, is exercised by individuals, by classes, by one sex over the other. The notion of such domination is entirely foreign to primitive humanity; the conception of authority is not understood. . . . A social order involving such a domination, . . . can exist only in advanced economic conditions where private property has acquired a paramount importance; to impute that organisation to primitive society, where private property scarcely exists, is an anachronism. The development of durable private property, of wealth, the desire of the constitutionally predatory male to possess it and to transmit it to his descendants, are, in fact, the most common causes of the change from matriarchal to patriarchal institutions."[19]

Briffault also argued that, in the animal kingdom, patriarchy is completely nonexistent. Moreover, the maternal instinct typical of the more advanced mammals led to the development of maternal love among primitive women, which became a permanent force long before the periodic sex drive generated heterosexual love. The mother-child bond was further intensified by the long period of dependence on the part of the young, resulting from the prolonged immaturity of the human offspring. In this way, the mother and her children formed a relatively strong and permanent social unit, while a corresponding father group was nonexistent. The unity of the mother group was first threatened when the male child reached puberty and began to make sexual approaches to his sisters. Such behavior was strongly discouraged by the jealous mother, who forced her sons to seek mates outside their mother group, while the male outsiders that mated with her daughters were required to become loyal members of her cohesive social unit. According to Briffault, however, when the mother's authority expanded and finally included property rights, it became the Achilles' tendon of matriarchy, which was thus superseded by patriarchy and, ultimately by monogamy.

## Evaluation

In brief, the above theories of family evolution dealt with systems presented in primarily three ways. First, the various evolutionary stages were conceived of as actual deviations from the Christian ideal of monogamy. Second, on the basis of atypical existing primitive family systems, earlier stages were reconstructed of which present examples are not in existence. And third, beginning with the "family" life of the anthropoids, various Homo sapiens family stages were constructed.

These theories dominated anthropology, sociology, and other social sciences until Franz Boas, the father of American historical anthropology, and his students began to combat unilinear evolutionism by means of extensive ethnological research. Because of such investigation, these theories were soon rejected by virtually all serious social scientists.

In the present section, some of the limitations of unilinear evolutionism, which inevitably led to its downfall, will be selected at random and discussed briefly.

Bachofen, for instance, relied on mythology so extensively that, quite frequently, *Das Mutterrecht* sounds like a work of art rather than a scientific treatise. Moreover, he often attributed social consequences to biological phenomena in rather uncritical fashion, as in the case of ignorance of paternity among primitives. First of all, this argument, even if such ignorance ever prevailed, is not exactly relevant. Then, ethnological research has demonstrated that descent is associated primarily with group membership, not with recognition of kinship. Certain Australian primitives, who are completely unaware of biological fatherhood, still emphasize patrilineal descent. Additional field work in anthropology has also indicated that the father's membership in the human family is practically universal.

And many of the so-called survivals of matrilineal cultures have been rather satisfactorily explained by means of arguments different from those presented in *Das Mutterecht*. Bachofen's presentation, however, seemed so logical that his theory was accepted long after 1861, when his classic work was first published. This is indicated by numerous later publications, including A. Bastian's *Rechtsverhältnisse der verschiedenen Völker der Erde*, which appeared in 1872, Ludwig Gumplowicz' *Grundriss der Sociologie*, published in 1885, and *Étude sur la condition de la femme dans le droit ancien et moderne*, by Paul Gide, a French legal scholar, who spoke of *"une première période de désordre, et pour ainsi dire, de chaos moral, où les saintes lois de la famille étaient inconnues et où la femme, libre de tout lien, se trouvait livrée en même temps à la plus complète indépendence et à la plus honteuse abjection."*[20]

Like Bachofen, Maine often presented arguments from mythology, as if the ancient tragedies, epic poems, and other literary works were objective ethnological treatises. We have already mentioned that part of Maine's evidence concerning primitive patriarchy was based on a few Homeric verses dealing with the legend of the Cyclopes. For many reasons, however, the legend itself cannot be seriously cited as an adequate source of anthropological evidence, especially because, as a whole, in the body of classical literature, it presents innumerable inconsistencies and contradictions. For instance, according to some ancient authors, the gigantic Cyclopes, whom Vergil compared with tall trees in his *Aeneis* (III, 680), lived in Lycia, but according to others, in Sicily. Furthermore, certain poets spoke of large groups of Cyclopes, whereas Hesiod, in his *Theogonia* (139 ff.), stated that there were only three, namely, Arges, Brontes, and Steropes. In the same poem (144 ff.), Hesiod explained that the Cyclopes' name was due to the one and only *round eye* (*cyclos*, circle; *ops*, eye) which they had in the center of the forehead, while another etymological account gives the prehistoric colossal *circular* structures, such as the Treasury of Atreus at Mycenae, as the origin of the Cyclopes' name—incidentally, we cannot seriously assert that the Romans were *giants* or *devils*, simply because the Germans popularly call the ancient Roman walls *Riesenmauer* (Giants' Walls) and *Teufelsmauer* (Devil's Walls). Again, in his *Georgica* (IV, 173), Vergil refers to the Cyclopes as smiths and mere assistants of Hephaestus. Finally, most historians now attribute the ancient cyclopean structures to the Pelasgi, the prehistoric inhabitants of Greece, while classical authors habitually referred to all enormous architectural monuments as the work of the Cyclopes—for example, Euripides in his *Hercules Furens* (15), Pausanias in his *Periegesis* (II, 25), Seneca in his *Hercules Furens* (996), and P. Papinius Statius in his *Thebais* (IV, 151). Accordingly, Maine's argument is about as logical as a biologist's contention that, judging by the Cyclopes, only a few thousand years ago, Homo sapiens evolved from a race of one-eyed giants—in *Genesis* 6:4, we also read that "There were giants in the earth in those days."

Westmarck's assertion concerning incest is about equally unreasonable. First of all, ethnographic data demonstrate that marriage with a housemate is often favored, as among the Angmagsalik Eskimo, who permit marriage between children that have been reared together. This assertion is also contradicted by the fairly common preference for sororate and levirate unions, which may involve members of the same extended family. Then, the enduring attachment between spouses is not an unusual occurrence. Finally, innumerable clinical studies prove not only that incestuous inclinations are often present in the nuclear family, but also that such inclinations are constantly combated by both individual repression and social control.

Similarly, Briffault's arguments are not always logical. His contention, for instance, that the natural function of the male, in both the plant and animal kingdoms, is to impregnate the largest possible number of females, and that this function is limited by monogamy, is unreasonable; for in monogamy, as in polyandry, polygyny, hetaerism, and so forth, the period of gestation is always nine months and remains the same even when the female has coitus quite frequently. Briffault's other conclusion, namely, that polyandry is generated by group marriage, is not supported by anthropological research; for if group marriage were universal in the past, as Briffault asserted, why should the remnants of polyandry be so uncommon at the present time? Moreover, if it could prevail only in cultures in which matriarchy was dominant until recently, why is it nonexistent in most societies that seem to have been matriarchal in the past?

At any rate, we should conclude that "All of these attempts to reconstruct the earlier forms of organization of the family remain at best only elaborate hypotheses."[21] And, in brief, the reasons may be outlined as follows:

First, the postulation of the evolutionary stages is arbitrary.

Second, because of the bias of our own social norms, the evolutionists have often concluded that the earlier forms of family organization constituted the exact antithesis of modern family systems—for example, primitive promiscuity.

Third, conclusive evidence concerning such evolutionary stages is not available.

Fourth, the argument of survivals is unacceptable, since, according to recent ethnological research, these customs are functioning institutions.

Fifth, ethnological research has also demonstrated that matrilineal cultures are not always less advanced. Among primitive societies, we find the patrilineal Witoto of Amazonia, the matrilineal Kutchin of northern Canada, and the bilateral Andamanese pygmies. On the other hand, in the civilized areas of the world, we find the patrilineal Chinese, the matrilineal Brahman Navars of India, and the bilateral Syrian Christians. It is true, of course, that matrilineal cultures in general are more primitive than patrilineal ones. But it is also true that the difference is not considerable, that the similarities are very great, and that the difference may indicate nothing more than the fact that the patrilineal and bilateral Europeans and Asians have recently influenced the rest of the world extensively.

Sixth, combinations of family systems are anything but uncommon.

Seventh, not infrequently, the social status which accompanies polygamy is considered more important in various cultures than the relationship between the two spouses.

And eighth, not all inferences from the anthropoids can be accepted unquestioningly, since, if we define instinct as an "inherited invariable predisposition to perform certain *complex* acts," we must conclude that, unlike lower species, Homo sapiens has no instincts.

## Notes

1. Johann Jakob Bachofen, *Das Mutterrecht: eine Untersuchung über die Gynaikokratie der alten Welt nach iherer religiosen und rechtlichen Natur,* Stuttgart: Krais and Hoffmann, 1861.
2. Sir Henry J. Sumner Maine, *Ancient Law,* New York: E. P. Dutton and Company, no date, p. 102.
3. *Ibid.,* p. 101.
4. *Ibid.,* pp. 102–103.
5. *Ibid.,* p. 104.
6. Lewis Henry Morgan, *Ancient Society, or Researches in the Lines of Human Progress from Savagery, Through Barbarism to Cicivilation,* New York: Henry Holt Company, 1877, p. 18.
7. Edward A. Westermarck, *The History of Human Marriage,* fifth edition, New York: The Allerton Book Company, 1922, Volume I, p. 103.
8. *Ibid.,* pp. 104–105.
9. *Ibid.,* p. 110.
10. *Ibid.,* pp. 123–124.
11. *Ibid.,* p. 106.
12. *Ibid.,* p. 240.
13. *Ibid.,* p. 277.

14. *Idem*, "On Primitive Marriage, A Rejoinder to Mr. V. F. Calverton," *American Journal of Sociology*, 41 (March 1936), pp. 565–589.
15. *Idem, The History of Human Marriage, op. cit.*, Volume III, p. 106.
16. Herbert Spencer, *The Principles of Sociology*, New York: D. Appleton and Company, 1897, Volume I, p. 644.
17. *Ibid.*, p. 686.
18. Robert Briffault, *The Mothers: The Matriarchal Theory of Social Origins*, New York: Macmillan, 1927, Volume II, p. 303.
19. *Ibid.*, Volume I, pp. 433–434.
20. Paul Gide, *Étude sur la condition de la femme dans le droit ancien et moderne*, second edition, Paris: 1885, p. 20.
21. Margaret Mead, "Family: Primitive," in Edwin R. A. Seligman, editor, *Encyclopedia of the Social Sciences*, New York: Macmillan, 1931, Volume VI, p. 65.

# The Family in a Changing Society

*Ernest W. Burgess*

## ABSTRACT

The American family presents an external picture of diversity and instability. When viewed in the context of the social change from rural to urban conditions of life, a trend is revealed to the companionship type of family, adapted to urbanization and exemplifying the American ideals of democracy, freedom, and self-expression. The seeming instability of the family is largely a symptom of this transition which may be regarded as a vast social experiment in which adaptability becomes more significant for success in marriage and family living than a rigid stability. This experiment provides a favorable condition for studies on marriage and the family and for the utilization of their findings by their public.

The title of this symposium "The American Family" may seem a misnomer. In this country the patterns of family life are so numerous and varied that it appears more appropriate to speak of American families rather than of any homogeneous entity, as implied by the term *"the* American family."

Never before in human history has any society been composed of so many divergent types of families. Families differ by sections of the country, by communities within the city, by ethnic and religious groups, by economic and social classes, and by vocations. They are different according to the family life-cycle and by number and role of family members. They vary by the locus of authority within the family and by widely different styles of life. There are the families of the Hopi Indian (primitive maternal), of the old Amish of Pennsylvania (patriarchal), of the Ozark mountaineers (kinship control), of the Italian immigrant (semipatriarchal), the rooming-house (eman-

From *The American Journal of Sociology,* 1948, 53(6), pp. 417–422. Reprinted by permission of The University of Chicago Press. © 1948 by the University of Chicago Press.

cipated), the lower middle class (patricentric), the apartment house (equalitarian), and the suburban (matricentric).

## Unity in Diversity

With due recognition of all the diversity in American families, it is still possible and desirable to posit the concept of *the* American family. In a sense it is an ideal construction in that it attempts to concentrate attention upon what is distinctive of families in the United States in comparison with those of other countries. These differential characteristics are largely in terms of process rather than of structure and represent relative, rather than absolute, differences from families in other cultures. Chief among these distinctive trends are the following:

1. *Modifiability and adaptability* in response to conditions of rapid social change
2. *Urbanization*, not merely in the sense that the proportion of families living in cities is increasing but that rural, as well as urban, families are adopting the urban way of life
3. *Secularization*, with the declining control of religion and with the increasing role of material comforts, labor-saving devices, and other mechanical contrivances like the automobile, the radio, and television
4. *Instability*, as evidenced by the continuing increase in divorce, reaching in 1945 the proportion of one for every three marriages
5. *Specialization*, on the functions of the giving and receiving of affection, bearing and rearing of children, and personality development, which followed the loss of extrinsic functions, such as economic production, education, religious training, and protection
6. The *trend to companionship*, with emphasis upon consensus, common interests, democratic relations, and personal happiness of family members

These distinctive trends in the American family will not be elaborated. Certain of them, however, will receive additional comment at appropriate places in this paper.

## The Family and Society

With all the variations in American families, it is apparent that they are all in greater or less degree in a process of change toward an emerging type of family that is perhaps most aptly described as the "companionship" form. This term emphasizes the point that the essential bonds in the family are now found more and more in the interpersonal relationship of its members, as compared with those of law, custom, public opinion, and duty in the older institutional forms of the family.

The point is not that companionship, affection, and happiness are absent from the institutional family. They exist there in greater or less degree, but they are not its primary aims. The central objectives of the institutional family are children, status, and the fulfilment of its social and economic function in society.

The distinctive characteristics of the American family, as of the family in any society, are a resultant of (1) survivals from earlier forms of the family, developing under prior or different economic and social conditions; (2) the existing social and economic situation; and (3) the prevailing and evolving ideology of the society.

*1. Survivals.* The American family has had a rich and varied historical heritage, with strands going back to all European countries and to the religious ideologies of the Catholic, Jewish, and Protestant faiths. What is distinctive in the American family, however, has resulted from its role, first, in the early rural situation of the pioneer period, and, second, in the modern urban environment.

The growth of democracy in the family proceeded in interaction with the development of democracy in society. Pioneer conditions promoted the emancipation both of women and of youth from subordination to the family and to the community. Arrangements for marriage passed from the supervision of parents into the control of young people.

The rural family of the United States before World War I, however, had progressed toward, but had not achieved, democratic relations among its members. Control was centered in the father and husband as the head of the farm economy, with strict discipline and with familistic objectives still tending to be dominant over its members. Children were appraised in terms of their value for farm activities, and land tenure and farm operations were closely interrelated with family organization and objectives.

*2. The Evolving Urban Environment.* The modern city, growing up around the factory and serving as a trade center for a wide area, provided the necessary conditions for the development of the distinctive characteristics of the American family. It still further promoted the equality of family members and their democratic interrelationships, initiated and fostered to a certain degree by the rural pioneer environment. In the urban community the family lost the extrinsic functions which it had possessed from time immemorial and which continued, although in steadily diminishing degrees, in the rural family. The urban family ceased to be, to any appreciable extent, a unity of economic production. This change made possible a relaxation of authority and regimentation by the family head. Then, too, the actual or potential employment of wife and children outside the home signified their economic independence and created a new basis for family relations. In the city the members of the family tended to engage in recreational activities separately, in their appropriate sex and age groups. Each generation witnessed a decline of parental control over children.

This increased freedom and individualization of family members and their release from the strict supervision of the rural neighborhood was naturally reflected in the instability of the family. The divorce rate has averaged a 3 per cent increase each year since the Civil War.

Urbanization involves much more than the concentration and growth of population. It includes commercialization of activities, particularly recreational; specialization of vocations and interests; the development of new devices of communication: telephone, telegraph, motion picture, radio, the daily newspaper, and magazines of mass circulation. All these still further promote the urbanization and secularization of families residing not only in cities but even in remote rural settlements.

3. *The Ideology of American Society.* Democracy, freedom, and opportunity for self-expression are central concepts in the American ideology. The frontier situation favored their expression in the social, economic, and political life of the people. As they found articulation in the American creed, they reinforced existing tendencies toward democracy and companionship within the family.

Urban life in its economic aspects provided less opportunity than did the rural environment for the exemplification of the American ideology. For example, the development of big business and enormous industries decreased the opportunities for the husband and father to run his own business. But the city greatly increased the economic freedom and independence of the wife and children by providing employment outside the home. The social conditions of the modern city led to the emancipation of family members from the institutional controls of the rural family. The urban family tended to become an affectional and cultural group, united by the interpersonal relations of its members.

### The Family in Process

The paradox between the unity and the diversity of the American family can be understood in large part by the conception of the family in process. This means, first of all, that it is in transition from earlier and existing divergent forms to an emergent generic type and, second, that it is in experimentation and is developing a variety of patterns corresponding to the subcultures in American society.

*1. The Family in Transition.* Much of what is termed the "instability" of the American family arises from the shift to the democratic companionship type from the old-time rural family of this country and the transplanted old-world family forms of immigrant groups.

Many of the current problems within the family are to be explained by the resulting conflicting conceptions in expectations and roles of husbands and wives and of parents and children. The husband may expect his wife to be a devoted household slave like his mother, while she aspires to a career or to social or civic activities outside the home. Immigrant parents attempt to enforce old-world standards of behavior upon their children, who are determined to be American in appearance, behavior, and ideas.

*2. The Family in Experimentation.* The changes taking place in the family have constituted a vast experiment in democracy. Hundreds of thousands of husbands and wives, parents and children, have participated in it. Couples have refused to follow the pattern of the marriages of their parents and are engaged in working out new designs of family living more or less of their own devising. This behavior has been fully in accord with the ideals and practices of democracy and has exemplified the American ideology of individual initiative and opportunity for self-expression.

This experiment in family formation, while apparently proceeding by individual couples, has been essentially collectivistic rather than pluralistic behavior. Each couple has naturally cherished the illusion that it was acting on its own. To be sure, individual initiative and risk-taking were involved.[1] Many individual ventures have ended in disaster. But actually it has been a collective experiment in the sense that the couples were acting under the stimulus of current criticisms of family life and were attempting to realize in their marriage the new conceptions of family living disseminated by the current literature, presented by the marriages of friends, or developed in discussion by groups of young people.

### Adaptability Versus Stability

In the past, stability has been the great value exemplified by the family and expected of it by society. This was true because the family was the basic institution in a static society. American society, however, is not static but dynamic. The virtue of its institutions do not inhere in their rigid stability but in their adaptability to a rapid tempo of social change.

The findings of two recent studies underscore the significance of adaptability for the American family. Angell began his study of the family in the depression with the hypothesis that its degree of integration would determine its success or failure in adjustment to this crisis.[2] He found, however, that he needed to introduce the concept of adaptability to explain why certain families, highly integrated and stable before the depression, failed, and why some moderately integrated families succeeded, in adjusting to the crises. A restudy of these cases indicated that adaptability was more significant than integration in enabling families to adjust to the depression.

Another study[3] arrived at a similar conclusion. In predicting success and failure in marriage, data were secured from couples during the engagement period. Certain couples with low prediction scores were later found to be well adjusted in their marriage. The explanation seemed to lie in the adaptability of one or both members of the couple, which enabled them to meet and solve successfully difficult problems as they developed in the marriage.

Adaptability as a personal characteristic has three components. One is psychogenic and represents the degree of flexibility in the emotional reaction of a person to a shift from an accustomed to a different situation. The second component is the tendency of the person as culturally or educationally determined to act in an appropriate way when entering a new situation. The third component of adaptability is the possession of knowledge and skills which make for successful adjustments to a new condition.

Successful marriage in modern society with its divergent personalities, diversity of cultural backgrounds, and changing conditions depends more and more upon the adaptability of husbands and wives and parents and children. The crucial matter, then, becomes the question of the adaptability of the family as a group, which may be something different from the adaptability of its members.

The growing adaptability of the companionship family makes for its stability in the long run. But it is a stability of a different kind from that of family organization in the past, which was in large part due to the external social pressures of public opinion, the mores, and law. The stability of the companionship family arises from the strength of the interpersonal relations of its members, as manifested in affection, rapport, common interests and objectives.

Flexibility of personality is not sufficient to insure adaptability of the family to a changing society. Its members should also be culturally and educationally oriented to the necessity for making adjustments. For example, the prospects of successful marriage would be greatly improved if husbands on entering wedded life were as predisposed in attitudes as are wives to be adjustable in the marital relation. Finally, adaptability in marriage and family living demands knowledge and skills on the part of family members. These are no longer transmitted adequately by tradition in the family. They can be acquired, of course, the hard way by experience. They can best be obtained through education and counseling based upon the findings of social science research.

## The Family and Social Science Research

The instability of the American family as evidenced by its rising divorce rate is, in general, incidental to the trial-and-error method by which divorced persons ultimately find happiness in a successful remarriage.[4] But trial and error is a wasteful procedure. It involves tragic losses both to husbands and wives and to their children. So far as possible, it should be replaced by a more rational and less risk-taking planning.

The solution, however, does not lie fundamentally in legislation. Laws, within limits, may be helpful as in the insuring of economic and social security, the improvement of housing and nutrition, in the exemptions from income taxes for wives and children, and in family allowances for children.

The state and federal governments have taken steps to undergird the economic base of the family and are likely to be called upon for further aid. But assistance to young people entering marriage and to the family in attaining its cultural objectives is coming from other institutions and agencies.

The school and the church have for some time shown a growing interest in assuming responsibility for education for marriage and family life. This is most marked in colleges and universities, a large majority of which, upon demand of the student body, now offer one or more courses in the family, family relations, marriage and the family, and preparation for marriage. High schools are experimenting with different types of courses in human relations and in family relations or with the introduction of family-life education material in existing courses. Churches, through Sunday school classes, young peoples' societies, young married couples' clubs, and Sunday evening forums, have promoted programs in family-life education. Community programs have been organized under the auspices of the Y.M.C.A., the Y.W.C.A., settlements, social centers, associations for family living, parent-child study associations, and other agencies.

Marriage and family counseling are developing under both older and newer auspices. The public still turns to the minister, the physician, and the lawyer for assistance upon spiritual, physical, and legal aspects of marriage. Theological, medical, and law schools are beginning to realize their responsibilities for training their students for this activity. The family social case workers, particularly those with psychiatric training, are at present the persons best trained professionally for marriage and family counseling. The identification in the public mind of family-service societies with relief-giving has largely limited this service to dependent families, although in some cities special provision has been made to extend marriage and family counseling on a fee basis to middle-class clientele.

Beginning with the Institute of Family Relations in Los Angeles, established in 1930, and the Marriage Council of Philadelphia two years later, marriage-counseling centers under independent auspices are now functioning in an increasing number of our largest cities, in some smaller communities, and in a growing number of colleges and universities.

The growing disposition of young people is, as we have seen, to make their own plans for marriage and family living. They are, at the same time, interested in the resources available in education, in counseling, and in the findings of research in the psychological and social sciences. Leaders in the family-life educational and counseling movement are also looking to research to provide the knowledge which they may use in giving more efficient service.

Later in this symposium Dr. Nimkoff summarizes recent research trends in the study of the family and points the way to further studies. This paper attempts only to state the role of research in relation to the solution of the problems of the family in our modern society. Its role is to provide the knowledge which an increasing number of young people are desirous of using in planning marriage and parenthood.

The outstanding evidence of this attitude and expectation is the reliance upon science of upper- and middle-class parents in the rearing of children. Their diet is determined upon the advice of a pediatrician, and their rearing is guided by the latest book on child psychology. This is a wide and significant departure from the older policy of bringing up the child according to methods carried down by tradition in the family.

A second illustration is the growing interest of young people in the factors making for the wise selection of a mate and for success or failure in marriage as derived from psychological and sociological studies.

A third significant fact is the widespread public interest in A. C. Kinsey's book, *Sexual Behavior in the Human Male*, containing the first report of sex behavior of 5,300 male Americans, based upon a very complete schedule and a carefully organized interview.

These are but three of the indications of the receptivity of intelligent young people to the findings of the psychological and social sciences and of their willingness to utilize them in planning for marriage and parenthood. In short, these activities are being taken out of the realm of the mores and are being transferred to the domain of science.

The findings of research do not, in and of themselves, provide the data for a design for marriage and family life. It is, however, the function of social science research to collect and to analyze the fund of experience of young people in their various experiments in achieving happiness in marriage and family life. Therefore, these findings of research should be made available to them through books, magazines, and newspapers; through motion pictures and radio; and through marriage counseling and programs of family-life education.

In conclusion, the main points of this paper may be briefly summarized. The American family, both in its apparent variety and in its essential unity, needs to be viewed in the perspective of social change. It is in transition from older rural institutional forms to a democratic companionship type of family relations adapted to an urban environment. This great change in the mores is a vast social experiment, participated in by hundreds of thousands of families under the collective stimulation of the American ideology of democracy, freedom, and self-expression. This experimental situation places the emphasis upon the adaptability rather than upon the rigid stability of the family. This experiment provides an unusual opportunity for the study of the family in transition. Moreover, participants in the experiment are demonstrating an increasing interest in utilizing research findings in designing their own patterns for marriage and family life.

## Notes

1. See Floyd Dell, *Love in Greenwich Village* (New York: Doubleday, Doran & Co., 1926).
2. Robert C. Angell, *The Family Encounters the Depression* (New York: Charles Scribner's Sons, 1936).
3. See E. W. Burgess and Paul Wallin, "Engagement and Marriage," chapter on "Adaptability" (unpublished manuscript).
4. Harvey J. Locke, "Predicting Marital Adjustment by Comparing a Divorced and a Happily Married Group," *American Sociological Review*, XII (1947), 187–91.

# Recent Studies of Change in the Japanese Family

*Takashi Nakano*

To begin with we should note that any study of change in the Japanese family must go back over three periods—the pre-Meiji period, the Meiji and post-Meiji period and the post-second world war period. And, in fact, recent sociological studies in Japanese family cover not only the latter stage but the others as well. It would hardly be possible to attempt a complete survey of the trends of these studies[1] in this paper, since considerable background knowledge is needed of the peculiar characteristics of the Japanese family system and of the special concepts employed. Nevertheless, some of the more important aspects can be discussed here.

As is well known, the family and the village are the two fields of Japanese sociology in which sociological research had already made a great deal of progress, even before the war. These two fields overlap to a large extent. With the possible exception of the first family sociologist, T. Toda, the family sociologists who have made the most important contributions, such as K. Ariga and K. Kitano, are also the rural sociologists. Their studies of the Japanese family have been carried out in relation to the village, and particularly in relation to the *ie*, or traditional family system, and the *dozoku*, which is a sort of special institutional group composed of several *ie*.[2]

## The 'IE' As a Social System

With the revision of the Civil Law in 1947, the *ie* system disappeared from Japanese law. The press and educational circles preached democracy and the ideal of the modern family, and the

From *International Social Science Journal*, 1962, 14(3), pp. 527–538. Reproduced with the permission of UNESCO.

change from the *ie* to the modern family became the most popular theme of study. And, indeed, family life as controlled by the *ie* system in the past has undergone very conspicuous changes during the process of modernization that has been going on since the Meiji period and particularly since the last war. However, it can be questioned whether it is proper to regard the *ie* and the *dozoku* merely as feudalistic survivals or residues. Ariga, in *The Analysis of Feudal Survivals* (1949) and in other essays, has pointed out that we should pay more attention to the difference between the feudal system of Europe and that of Japan, and that the *ie* and the *dozoku* existed within the particular characteristics of the age; even the Meiji and the post-Meiji periods are no exception in this respect. Kitano stated that the *ie* and the *dozoku* were not peculiar to the feudal system.[3] Although they existed within the feudal system, they themselves were not feudalism, but rather resembled the patrimonialism developed from patriarchalism (in the sense of Max Weber's use of the term).

T. Kawashima, law sociologist, pointed out that the 'familistic principle of life' is the basic rule of Japanese society and a traditional characteristic of the structure of Japanese society.[4] Here let us examine this point, limiting the scope of discussion to the inner aspects of the *ie*. Though Kawashima regards the *ie* itself as a family system, he makes a distinction between the 'family system of the feudal warriors (= of Confucianism, which was particularly influential to their norm)' and the 'family system of common people.' And he points out that the Family Law (1898), a part of the Meiji Civil Law, referred only to the former. Thus, the family system of the feudal warrior was legally enforced as the family system of the nation. However, since the system was somewhat modified by elements of the modern law, the *ie* system of the Meiji Civil Lar is said to be 'semi-feudalistic' though it may not be proper to call it 'feudalistic.'[5] To differentiate, Kawashima gives the following information: that the family property belonged to the *ie* head (*kachyo*) himself; and that the children of a certain age (male, 30 years; female, 25 years) could marry legitimately without the consent of their parents.

Kawashima, in making the distinction between the *ie* system of the feudal warrior and that of the common people, rightly rejects the view that the *ie* system of the Meiji Civil Law was the only national tradition.

Since the pre-war years, sociologists have been studying the *ie* in the actual life of the common people, not the legal *ie*. And K. Ariga, since the publication of his essay, *The Labour Service of the Nago* (1933), has paid special attention to one feature of *ie*, that is, that it can include a special resident servant as a member besides the family of the *ie* head. Originally, relationships in each *ie,* or between several *ie,* were not limited to parent-child relations as they are today, but included a special master-servant relationship: a would-be servant leaves his *ie* of birth when very young and becomes a member of his master's *ie,* thus making himself a *ko* of the master whose social role is termed *oya.* The term *oya-ko* meant originally the personal relationship between the head and the follower in the labour system. However, since this also included children of the head and of others in the family, the concept of employment relationship alone is not enough to explain it. The grown-up resident servant forms a *bunke* or *bekke* (branch family) separated from the *ie* of the head as in the case of the *umi-no-ko* (*ko* by birth), except for the heir, who is one of the children of the *ie* head. An *umi-no-ko* becomes the head of a *bunke* of kin relations, and a foster *ko* (i.e., a resident servant) becomes the first head of the servant-*bunke.* The original *ie* is called *honke* (main family). Each *ie* is maintained supergenerationally, both in the main family and in the branch family. And the relationships between these *honke,* kin-*bunke,* and servant-*bunke* are also maintained supergenerationally. A group which is called the *dozoku* is made up of these *ie.* The *dozoku* is analogous to the patri-clan, but we cannot call it a patrilineal kin group just as we cannot say that the *ie* is always identical with family. It is, we might say, a patri-clan that is internally stratified by occupation or social class, and which recruits members to subordinate strata through a process akin to fosterage in Western societies.

Before the Tokugawa period, the *ie* of the feudal warriors, like that of the farmers and merchants, could include the resident servants who had a *ko*-role, and a *bunke* could be established for them, forming a unit of the *dozoku.* With the bureaucratization of the governing organs during the Tokugawa period, the *ie* of the feudal warriors was no longer able to divide off from itself a *bunke* for the resident servants. Similarly, in the *ie* of the merchants in large-scale business the tendency to exclude non-relative elements from the owner's *ie* and its *dozoku* followed from the rationalization of the enterprise[6]

However, the *ie* as well as the *dozoku* is a group which can essentially contain non-kinship elements, as can be seen in the farming or the merchant community. Sometimes the *ie* is composed of its head and his family, and sometimes it contains resident servants and their families. The *ie* as an institutionalized group, originally was perhaps only for the head and his family. However, once a *ie* is formed, whether it be a *honke* or *bunke*, it becomes a special group which tries to maintain and develop permanently the political, economic, religious and other functions of the *ie*. All the members of the *ie*, from the head to the resident servants, have to contribute to the realization of the aims of the *ie* in their given role. Even the head does not have power as an individual (which is why we do not use the term 'patriarch' in this paper). He is only the representative of the will of the *ie*, and he himself is a servant to the ancestor who is the symbol of that will. The role and status of each member is determined by the type of responsibility incumbent upon him with respect to the realization of the aims of the *ie*. Those who carry the responsibility of maintaining the *ie* throughout their lives are called the *chokkei* (or *chakkei*) members of the *ie*, and the rest are called the *bokei* members. Customarily, *bokei* means only the relatives of the head, i.e., the head's family. It should be noted here that, although the concepts are frequently confused, *chokkei* or *bokei* membership of the *ie* is to be distinguished from the concept of *chokkei-shin* (lineal ascendent and descendant) or *bokei-shin* (collateral relative) of the Law on Relations. The third kind of *ie* member is the foster resident servant. The *bokei* members and the resident servants either separated from the original *ie* to form a branch group away from a main family, or left the *ie* at such occasions as marriage accompanied by change of *ie* or as a result of exclusion by sanctions, etc. Among the foster resident servants of a merchant, only certain selected ones can join the *dozoku* of the head as the head of servant-*bunke*.

### The 'IE' and the 'Dozoku'

Ariga, Kitano and many other sociologists have done a great deal of research on the *ie* and *dozoku* among farmers, and Ariga and the present author have worked on the same subjects in merchant communities. Since space does not allow of discussion of all these studies, we must confine ourselves to one particular book on the problem.[7] This book is the collective work of fourteen authors—ten sociologists and four socio-economic historians. Most of them dealt with the *ie* and *dozoku* of the farmers, the merchants and the Buddhist priests in the Tokugawa period (1603–1868). In order to elucidate the essential character of the *ie* system which still controls family life in Japan, it was necessary to make sociological studies of the *ie* period which had not been influenced either by the European idea of family or by

the Meiji Civil Law. The sociologists obtained good results by applying the theory and the method of analysis used in research dealing
with contemporary *ie* and *dozoku*. The present writer's essay, *The
Study of Ie in Sociology*, in this book summarizes the work done
between 1933 and 1958.

In the same book, Ariga analyses *The Idea of the Ancestor in
Japan* making use of his famous pre-war intensive case study of Ishigami Village, and the post-war study of the Tokugawa-period data of
a Osaka merchant *dozoku*, the 'konoike.' He showed that the genealogy of the *ie* itself (which means the supergenerational continuance
of each *ie*) and its relation to the *honke*, were symbolized by two
types of ancestor. They are the ancestor of the *ie* itself and the
ancestor that antedates the establishment of the *ie*, in other words
the ancestor of the *honke*. Although we may use the word genealogy,
it does not mean in this context the descent of individuals in the
kinship system. When we speak of the 'descent of the *ie*' we refer to
the relationship from which the *ie* was originally derived and on
which it still depends.

Kitano, in the same volume, re-examined his well-known pre-war
study of the mountain village, Yuzurihara, and analysed the structure
of the farming *ie* of the early eighteenth century. There it was found
that the *chokkei* members constituted 80 per cent of each *ie*, the
*bokei* members 14 per cent and the resident servants 6 per cent.
However, few *ie* included all three: many *ie* were made up of only
*chokkei* members. If they contained *bokei*, they seldom contained
the resident servants, and vice versa. Only in very rare cases did
members other than *chokkei* have a spouse. These phenomena are
due to the fact the *ie* had no necessity for a large labour force since
the cultivated acreage was small. According to Kitano's theory as set
out in the essay (1956) mentioned above, the *ie* can exist only as a
constituent unit of the *dozoku*. He holds that only this could ensure
the continuity of the *ie*. Ariga, on the other hand, in later writings
stated that the need to perpetuate the Japanese family as an institutional nucleus, *ie*, originated from the fact that ultimately the family
had to assume the responsibility of ensuring the livelihood of its
members because of the absence of a system of social security in the
political structure of past Japanese society.[8] Thus the *dozoku* came
into existence in order to strengthen the continuance of each *ie*. He
also pointed out that especially since the beginning of modern times
there has been a strong influence exerted in favour of the perpetua-
tion of the *ie*, even when it was separated from the *dozoku*.

## The Life Cycle of the 'IE'

T. Koyanna's essay,[9] threw light on the 'family life cycle' found in the *ie* system by using the records of certain villages over a period of 60 years during the nineteenth century. He classifies the family, according to its structure, in seven categories, and tries to show the process of shift among the seven types statistically. These seven types of family are: (a) only one member; (b) household couple only; (c) household couple and children; (d) household couple and young couple; (e) (d) plus the lineal ascendants; (f) (e) plus the lineal descendants; (g) (f) plus the collateral relatives. And the change of the family structure pattern usually followed the circuit:

(c) 26 per cent → (d) 50 per cent → (g) 45 per cent → (f) 61 per cent → (c)

In other words 26 per cent of type (c) moved on to type (d), 50 per cent of type (d) moved on to type (g), and so on.

This preliminary theory of the Japanese life cycle shows the several waves of family continuation within the *ie* system. This was referred to by E. Suzuki (1942) and K. Morioka (1953), and was corroborated with considerable positive evidence by Koyama. The *ie* keeps its members longer, or sends them away earlier, or recruits a member from other *ie*, depending upon its management, or its external conditions. These phenomena complicated the changing process of the *ie* member structure. They are the important factors. We should not overlook the fact that the number of *ie* members is recruited and adjusted by adding not only the *bokei* members but also the resident servants.

Now, we must consider the fact that Kawashima's essay to which we referred earlier makes no mention of one of the important points concerning the modification in the Meiji Civil Law of the *ie* system according to the principles of modern law. Sociological studies have proved that it was essential to the *ie* and *dozoku* to be able to include non-kinship elements, not only during the Tokugawa and pre-Tokugawa periods but even in the modern period as well. Nevertheless, the Meiji Civil Law legally excluded and refused recognition to the non-kinship elements, that is, the resident servant in the *ie*, and the servant's *bunke* in the *dozoku*. This change of the *ie* system marks its modernization, and corresponds to the popularization of the modern contract of employment. With the wider acceptation of the Meiji Civil Law, the *ie* system came to mean simply the family system of the *ie head*.

Such phenomena in owner-employee and manager-employee relationships as have been described as 'familism in human management' or the 'fictitious family relation' in fact appear to be related to this change in the *ie* system. However, even after the feudal period in Japan, the *ie* system which could include servants continued to exist. After the enforcement of the Meiji Civil Law, the two types of the *ie* system existed together in law and custom, in formal organization and informal organization, in the large enterprises of modern capitalism and in small affairs managed by the *ie*, and they influenced and supplemented each other. This tendency favoured the rapid development of capitalism in Japan even under conditions of poverty. The democratization of the family system by the revision of the civil law after the second world war brought a marked change to the family in the cities, and saw the development from the *ie* characterized in the Meiji Civil Law to the modern family, backed still more by industrial modernization and the improvement of the national standard of living. In the villages the change has not been so conspicuous because there has been no basic change in small management by the *ie*, though the bonds of the *dozoku* are weakening. As T. Takeuchi reported in 1954[10] two types of *bunke* are to be seen in modern times when the *honke* separates from its *bunke* in the same village. One type is the *bunke* which depends on the *honke* to a great extent, as in the past, and the other is that established by the sons other than the heir almost without financial help from the parents. Especially when these sons abandon farming and leave the village, the *dozoku* relationship loses its importance. This new tendency has become more and more conspicuous since the war.

The modern Japanese family, which can be regarded as a kind of extended family, began to take on the characteristics of the nuclear family. In such circumstances G. P. Murdock's theory of the family[11] came to be widely accepted by Japanese sociologists. But Ariga held on the contrary that the theory of the nuclear family was an attempt to explain the family in other cultures by using the modern European family as a standard. Referring to the nuclear family as a basic unit of the extended family, Kitano rephrased it as the 'small family as a nucleus.' I think it is necessary to rephrase it as 'familial nucleus' and distinguish it as a unit of structure from the nuclear family as an ideal type of family of a particular period and area or of a particular culture. In research we may discover a sectional structure of the family at a given point in time, but this is really a kind of extended family controlled by the *ie*, a part of which externally looks as if it is a nuclear family. In fact, we may simply be observing a stage of the family life cycle, as in the case of a newly established *bunke,* or when the heir of the house happens to remain unmarried after the former householders' deaths. Thus, it is necessary to distinguish the structural types which may occur at certain points in time from the qualitative ideal type of family within the culture. K. Morioka[12] and the present author[13] have both discussed the question, and Koyama's essay (1959) previously mentioned also gave some attention to it, though in the work edited by Koyama[14] in 1960 there seems to be some confusion about this point.

The first half of *The Study of Modern Family* reports the results of the family survey done by the Society for the Study of Family Problems from 1956 to 1957. Three sections of the Tokyo metropolitan area—one mountain village, one suburban village and one apartment house district in the former Tokyo City—were chosen as the sample area. Koyama classifies the family structure according to the seven types given earlier in this paper and regards types (a) to (c) as the nuclear family and types (a) to (g) as the extended family. Of the mountain village families, 58 per cent can be classified as belonging to types (a) to (c), and of the apartment families 79 per cent.

Koyama also carried out a survey using a questionnaire asking whether, and if so to what extent, the traditional family consciousness was maintained. The persons questioned in each case were the householder and his wife. Some of the results were as follows: Those who approve of sharing the same house with their married child and his or her spouse: mountain village 72 per cent, apartment district 19 per cent; those who think that the eldest son is responsible for supporting the parents: mountain village 82 per cent, apartment district 20 per cent.

Answers to other questions show the same contrast. The suburban village represented an intermediate attitude. The answers to these questions were quantified and the individual's total points calculated. Family consciousness was classified as follows: the modern type $(+5 +3)$, the intermediate type $(+2 -2)$, and the traditional type $(-3 -5)$. The correlations between these three types and the 'family type' were examined in each case.

The correlations turned out to be very low. Both in the mountain village and the suburban village the traditional type of consciousness was strong regardless of the 'family type.' In the mountain village, the nuclear family showed the traditional type more than the rest. The extended family of the non-farmer of the suburban village showed both the modern and traditional types more than the nuclear family. Most of the nuclear family showed the intermediate type.

| | Mountain village | | Apartment district | |
|---|---|---|---|---|
| | Extended family | Nuclear family | Extended family | Nuclear family |
| Traditional | 68.1 | 75.5 | 12.7 | 6.9 |
| Intermediate | 31.9 | 23.6 | 55.6 | 60.6 |
| Modern | – | 0.9 | 31.7 | 32.5 |
| TOTAL | 100.0 | 100.0 | 100.0 | 100.0 |

The following two reasons are given by Koyama to explain these results. First, a change in family consciousness does not accompany change of 'family type' because the conditions of life implied by such a change are not fully accepted. Secondly, differences of 'family type' mentioned here are mostly those which occur in the family life cycle. Moreover, the attitudes and conduct of family life are determined not only by the family structure at one time but also by the conditions of life of the family as seen in the perspective of past, present and future.

T. Fuse in 1956–57 conducted a survey on the extended family and nuclear family. He suggests that there are three kinds of nuclear family. They are: (1) the nuclear family formed by a son, other than the heir, leaving his parents' family—which corresponds to the *ie* immediately after the formation of a *bunke*; (b) the nuclear family composed of the household couple and the unmarried children after the death of the householder's parents who lived together; and (c) the nuclear family consisting of the couple only, their children having grown up and left the house. He regards (a) and (b) as two stages in the life cycle of the extended family and sees only (c) as the modern nuclear family. However, I think it is possible that (a) and (b) could include some modern nuclear families and that (c) could be a part of an extended family forming a separate household for convenience sake; although Fuse was right in pointing out that the typical *ie* (a kind of extended family) often has the outward appearance of a nuclear family at one point of its life cycle.

Nevertheless, Fuse goes on to say that we can regard the urban family as a modern family in so far as it has the construction of a nuclear family. The following facts noted in this study do not necessarily accord with his argument, but they are of interest. In 22 per cent of the nuclear family cases, and 38 per cent of the extended family, the couple have one bedroom for themselves alone. Twenty-nine per cent of the couples who had an opportunity to go out by themselves for recreation are found in the nuclear family, and 37

per cent in the extended family. It is noteworthy that the family of
the extended family type has favourable conditions for the couple's
privacy and partnership.

The results of a study conducted by K. Tominaga is a ward of
Tokyo (82 per cent of the families in this ward had moved into it
since 1945) were as follows:

Extended family: parents or a parent of husband living with the
    couple, 11 per cent; parents or a parent of wife living with the
    couple, 9 per cent; eldest son and his wife living with the couple,
    5 per cent.
Nuclear family: 76 per cent (including 14 per cent who remit some
    money to husband's parents living separately).

Of course, this is an heuristic classification of the family at the time
of the research. Therefore we may think that the nuclear family as
the ideal type is less widespread than the nuclear family of this list,
and that the family controlled by the *ie* as the ideal type could be
less than the extended family here.

Tominaga also carried out an attitude survey among housewives
of the various social strata of urban families, contrasting their evaluation of the traditional *ie* family system with the 'value of modern
family.' The results indicated that the traditional system generally
lost ground in the big cities; that the 'feudalistic and familistic'
ideology is kept more in the upper stratum than the middle; and
that more members of the lower stratum than of the middle wanted
to stay in the same house with the young couple, or to receive economic support in their old age from their children. We can confirm
from the data in this essay of Tominaga that the *ie* system is not
merely a question of ideology but also a matter of daily life.

## Family Change in Modern Japan

The change of the family in modern Japan is, of course, greatly
accelerated by change in the conditions of life. Even the white-collar
workers of Tokyo would continue to expect benefits from the *ie*
system if such problems as security, especially in old age, and housing, especially for younger couples, were not settled otherwise. And
this is much more so with people engaged in farming or small home
industries. What they really need is not enlightenment with regard
to the ideals of the democratic family but the betterment of actual
living conditions.

Ariga's essay 'Since the BreakDown of the Large Family'[15] is a report of supplementary research to his famous monograph, *The Large Family System and the Nago System in Ishigami, Ninohe Country, Nanbu District,* published in 1939. (The term 'large family system' here corresponds to the concept of 'a compound type of *ie* and its *dozoku*' which Ariga has employed since 1943.) This mountain village, Ishigami, consisted of one *dozoku*. How did the *dozoku*, whose *honke* was the compound type of *ie* (that is, containing *bokei* members and resident servants with their wives), come to break down? The earlier research had been conducted in 1935, but by the time of its publication (1939) the management of the *honke*, which had the *oya*-role as the big landlord, became difficult because of war-time controls. Whereas in the past the *honke* had apportioned the land (fields, mountains and residential land) to the tenant's *ie* which had the *ko*-role, or *nago*, in return for their labour without payment, during the war the *honke* began to sell the fields to the *nago* at half price. Thus, the 42 acres of fields owned by the *honke* in 1935 had decreased to 25 acres at the end of the war (1945). The *nago* had not sufficient money to buy residential land other than cultivated land, and this kept them traditionally and customarily in the role and status of *nago*. Therefore, they were under an obligation to provide the *honke* with labour, although they could not fulfil this obligation because of the general lack of labour during the war. During the land reform after the war, the *nago* generally defied the *honke* and refused to provide the labour that was due for the residential land and mountain forests apportioned to them. The land reform in this village was conducted under the leadership of the Farmers' Association. The *honke* readily fell in with the decision of the Land Reform Committee, and the area of the fields owned by the *honke* decreased to 7 acres or so after the reform. The committee concentrated on purchasing the exploitable forest of the landlord, and did not feel keenly the necessity of releasing the residential land. At that time the *honke* owned 220 acres of forests of which 17 acres were released by the order of the committee and the rest released voluntarily. Only th residential land of the *nago* was left in the hands of the *honke*. It was decided that the rent should be paid in cash. But the *honke* according to his traditional *oya* role did not demand even the rent. However, as time passed the *nago* began voluntarily to offer their labour again to the *honke*. For this service the *honke*, contrary to the custom of the past, paid the nago. The *heir* of the *honke* died at the end of the war. After the war his younger brother, repatriated from Saghalien, succeeded him. The new leader of the *honke* endeavoured

to rebuild his *ie* with the aid of his two younger brothers. He purchased a power-driven plough, the first to be seen in this village,
a power-driven threshing machine, and then a rice-hulling and
selecting machine. The *nago* allowed to use these machines owned
by the *honke* if they paid the fuel costs, and those who were unable
to pay the fee offered their labour instead. Thus, the people of this
mountain village came to recognize the efficiency of mechanized
farming. Mechanization of farming started in 1955 even among the
*nago*. Thus the 'large family' broke down, and the so-called 'feudalistic' *honke* took the lead in introducing mechanization.

Nii-ike, a small community in Okayama Prefecture, is an ordinary
Japanese village.[16] After the investigation conducted (1950–54) by the
University of Michigan group, this village once again became the
subject of a study, carried out this time by a group of sociologists and
rural economists headed by Y. Okada.[17] The report of the investigation (1956–59) shows how aid for farm mechanization provided by
the Asia Foundation brought changes into this village as a result of
the use of a small motor plough. Chapter 6 of the report deals with
the changes which took place in the family life of this village made
up of small-scale farmers' *ie*.

The most conspicuous change in the allotment of labour was
brought about through the use of the motor plough by each *ie*. The
threshing machine, the rice-selecting machine, and the spraying and
spreading machines used to prevent damage by blight and pests were
owned and used by a co-operative system made up of several *ie*. With
the introduction of the motor plough the women were no longer
needed for the work of cultivation. Dissatisfaction spread among the
old men who had hitherto been in charge of the oxen used for cultivation, since the work had to be taken over by the young people.
Small-scale poultry breeding was formerly the job of the old or
married women but it became a job for men—and particularly for
young men—as artificial methods of rearing chickens, and large-scale
egg production and marketing were introduced. Thus, the older
women lost a source of additional income. In housekeeping, the
change from the well to piped water decreased the women's hours
of work by as much as 15 or 20 per cent, particularly in regard to
cooking and cleaning. Though extra laundry was required, the work
involved was made considerably easier.

Thus, the amount of spare time for women, and particularly the
housewives, increased by about 30 per cent, and the older men
enjoyed about 20 per cent more free time. The spare time of the
householder, however, increased by no more than 8 per cent, and in

some cases decreased by 6 per cent. The aged men used their extra leisure for recreation or for pilgrimages to Shinto shrines. The husbands began to take agricultural courses, and the wives cooking courses. The women particularly began to read more newspapers and books than before and to attend meetings of an educational nature. Thus, they acquired greater opportunities of contacts outside the home. This opened the way, though only little by little, to improvements in the status of women. The new social tension between the old, who had lost their role in farm management, and the younger generation took the place of the older tension between the controlling elders and the dissatisfied young. However, succession to the divided farm land as the property of *ie* is still the foundation of the *ie* system. Which means that it is difficult to further farm mechanization without promoting greater co-operation in farm management.

The success of the role structure analysis by K. Morioka and K. Kakizaki in this study of farm families was largely due to the fact that two researchers (Kakizaki and A. Kawamoto) lived in the village for three years.

Other interesting investigations of interfamily relationships have been reported by K. and M. Tamura, Division of Sociology, National Institute of Mental Health.

We may conclude with the remark that the extremely delicate and complex structure of the Japanese family and the changes to which it is subject can only be investigated by long and intensive study carried out by students who win the confidence of the people sufficiently to be able to report fully on their actual living conditions.

# Notes

1. For an inclusive list of recent studies on the Japanese family see: K. Morioka, '*A Bibliography on the Sociology of Family, 1945–59*,' *The Journal of Social Science*, Tokyo, 1960 (International Christian University Publications II, B. 1).
2. Although I shall explain both *ie* and *dozoku* in this paper, more detailed information may be gained from: Ariga *et al.*, *The Japanese Family, Transactions of the Second World Congress of Sociology*, 1958; and Ariga, *Family in Japan, Marriage and Family Living*, edited by Nimkoff.
3. 'The *Dozoku* System and Feudalistic Survivals', in: Society of Humanities (ed.), *Feudalistic Survivals*, 1951.
4. *The Familistic Structure of Japanese Society*, 1948.
5. T. Kawashima, *The Family System as Ideology*, 1957.
6. T. Nakano, 'The Change in the *Dozoku* in the Merchant Community,' *Japanese Sociological Review*, Vol. 12, No. 2, 1961.
7. *The Ie: Its Structural Analysis*, edited by Kitano and Y. Okada in 1959.

8. 'The *Ie* System and the Social Welfare,' *The Social Work*, Vol. 38, No. 9, 1955; 'Family and *Ie*,' *Philosophy*, Vol. 38, 1960 (Keio University Publications).
9. *The Ie: Its Structural Analysis.*
10. *Dynamics of Rural Family.*
11. *Social Structure*, 1949.
12. 'Structure and Function of the Family,' 1957, in *Koza Shyakaigaku*, Vol. 4.
13. *Family and Kinship.*
14. *The Study of Modern Family*, 1960.
15. In *Shinano* (1958), a local magazine for historians and folklorists, Nagano Prefecture.
16. Nii-ike was introduced widely by R. Beardsley *et al., Village Japan*, University of Chicago Press, 1959.
17. *The Analysis of Japanese Farm Mechanization—An Experiment at Nii-ike*, 1960.

# Changes in the Colonial and Modern American Family Systems

*Panos D. Bardis*

> *Felix qui potuit rerum cognoscere causas,*
> *Atque metus omnes et inexorabile fatum.*
> Vergil

## Introduction

In his *Marriage Analysis*, Harold T. Christensen states that the American family has been undergoing these main changes: more and earlier marriages, greater family disorganization, acceptance of re-marriage, declining birth rates, partial loss of family functions, changing sex roles, and increasing individualism.[1] Burgess and Locke add that "the family is changing from the institutional to the companionship form."[2]

In the present discussion, emphasis is placed on certain of the changes in the American family, from the colonial times to the present day.

## The Early American Family

In colonial times, in view of the pioneer conditions that prevailed in the typical community, young men and women were permitted to associate with one another rather freely. Parents, however, expected their children's courtship to be fairly short. In addition, romantic love was usually discouraged. At least three forces led to the disapproval of romantic love affairs: the strict Puritan morality, the fierce struggle for existence, and the realistic stress on the economic aspects of marriage contracts.

An unusual form of courtship was *bundling*, which was introduced from Europe by the Dutch and the English, and was practiced

---

From *Social Science*, April, 1963. Reprinted by permission.

mainly by the lower social classes in new England. This custom, which became dominant chiefly in the second half of the eighteenth century, consisted in permitting lovers to court in bed, at least partly dressed and often in the presence of other family members.

The acceptance of this type of courtship was due to the following reasons: first, the prevailing hospitality in pioneer times; second, the predominance of one-room cabins, which resulted in the relative absence of privacy; and third, the fact that sitting up at night was inadvisable, in view of the very limited supply of candles and fuel. Indeed, according to a poem dealing with bundling:

> "Since in a bed a man and maid
>     May bundle and be chaste,
> It does no good to burn out wood,
>     It is a needless waste."

But, obviously, not every couple could both "bundle and be chaste." Washington Irving has observed: "wherever the practice of bundling prevailed, there was an amazing number of sturdy brats annually born . . . without the license of the law, or the benefit of clergy." Undoubtedly, numberless couples must have lost their self-control in such situations. And few must have been as wise as the British lieutenant who, when he stopped at a cabin and was asked to bundle with young Jemima, refused most emphatically, preferring to sit up all night long.

Later, bundling began to decline, and this "is to be attributed largely to the increase of wealth which made possible larger houses and less rigorous conditions of life."[3] Its decline was further accelerated by the intemperance and excesses that accompanied this practice, as well as by the protests of numerous respected leaders.

Concerning his own courtship adventures, David Crockett (1786–1836), the celebrated American politician and frontiersman, confessed that, when he attempted to speak of his love to the first woman that ever attracted him, his heart "would get right smack up in my throat and choak me like a cold potato." And then, when he managed to express his feelings and the maid told him that she was engaged to another man, he was completely stunned, overwhelmed, and stupefied. "This news," he said, "was worse to me than war, pestilence, or famine; but still I knowed I could not help myself. I saw quick enough my cake was dough, and I tried to cool off as fast as possible."

The same pioneer conditions were partly responsible for the relative freedom that characterized mate choice. Indeed, despite "the seeming parental tyranny that prevailed in colonial days young women seem to have exercised considerable independence in love affairs."[4]

Still, parents and masters, who usually placed main emphasis on the economic aspects of marriage, often influenced mate selection extensively.

Then, miscegenation, in spite of the absence of restrictions with reference to interclass unions, was definitely forbidden. In 1698, for instance, Pennsylvania's Chester County Court prohibited marriage between Negroes and whites. Similarly, a Massachusetts law of 1705 imposed a fine of fifty pounds on those officiating at white-Negro or white-mulatto unions. In general, white-Indian marriages were also tabu. Needless to add, all this does not mean that persons of racially mixed ancestry, because of illicit unions, were nonexistent.

An additional restriction dealt with incest. The law specified certain degrees of affinity and consanguinity within which marriage was prohibited. Offenders were commonly punished most severely, one of the penalties consisting in wearing a capital *I*, which represented incest.

Colonial laws further required the publication of matrimonial intention. This was usually done by reading an announcement at a public meeting or by posting a written notice in a public place.

Another feature of the early American family was the colonial village's emphasis on marriage. Bachelors and maids were often rejected and penalized in various ways. Plymouth and Hartford, for example, taxed single men much more heavily than married ones. To render bachelorhood ludicrous, the government of Eastham, Massachusetts, also ordered the following in 1695: "Every unmarried man in the township shall kill six blackbirds or three crows while he remains single; as a penalty for not doing it, shall not be married until he obey this order." It is no wonder, therefore, that such attitudes, combined with the many needs generated by the prevailing conditions, often led to hasty marriages. Not infrequently, a lonely man merely proposed to a woman whom he had just met for the first time, thus securing a desperately needed mate and housekeeper on the very same day!

Such attitudes further made early marriage desirable. Thus, one "finds unmarried women of twenty-five referred to in the literature as 'ancient maids.'"[5] Even at twenty a woman was regarded as a "stale maid." Both sexes, therefore, usually married when quite young—girls very often at the age of thirteen—as a result of which, in places such as North Carolina, one could find many grandmothers of twenty-seven! Of course, in view of the scarcity of women and the abundance of free land, this practice was not unwise.

The predominant form of marriage in colonial days was not the sacramental, but the civil type. "This was owing partly to the fact that certain colonists had resided in Holland, where civil marriage existed, and others had come at the time of the Cromwell Civil Marriage Act. Hostility to papism was keen in the English colonies."[6] Accordingly, it was the magistrate, not the clergyman, that officiated at marriages. In fact, a Boston clergyman who dared perform a wedding ceremony was taken to court and tried for his offense.

Countless marriages involved widows and widowers, since the death rate was exceedingly high in those days. Besides, because of their property and experience, widows were among the most desirable potential spouses. In Plymouth, the widow Susanna White married Edward Winslow only seven weeks after his wife's death. And Isaac Winslow, needing a spouse most urgently, proposed to a certain woman a few hours after burying his wife.

Not many years after the wedding, households, which started with small groups of parents and children, "often grew by the addition of indentured or wage-earning servants, unattached female relatives, and sometimes married sons with their wives and children."[7] But these were not households of the patriarchal type found in Europe. Since, in numerous cases, "young people never returned to the paternal home or even saw their families again, after they had set out toward the frontier on horseback or by wagon,"[8] the father's authority was undermined considerably. In other words, social and geographical mobility, resulting from the Protestant ethic, individualism, political democracy, and the frontier environment, led to the gradual decline of patriarchy. The individual thus replaced the family as the basic unit of society in the New World.

Unlike the father's status, woman's position tended to improve as a result of the spirit generated by such forces. According to Groves and Groves, the "new conditions on this side of the ocean made it difficult from the first to maintain the patriarchal control of daughters."[9] Besides, her companionship, hard work, and creation of additional workers through reproduction rendered a wife most useful. Then, women's high death rate—usually caused by childbirth and backbreaking labor—made them scarcer, thus raising their status further. Such scarcity was especially prevalent in the western regions of the country. That is why, occasionally, heroic efforts were made to supply men in this area with unattached women from the eastern sections of the New World. At any rate, these conditions led to many freedoms on the part of women. The economic rights of daughters, for instance, were virtually identical to those of their brothers. Moreover, not only husbands, but also wives were in general permitted by the law to divorce their spouses. A few women, like Salem's Mrs. Goose, even worked outside the home, operating shops or stores of various types.

Still, women's emancipation was not complete. In the sphere of religious matters, men continued to be dominant. Fornication and adultery led to the imposition of more severe penalties on females than on their male partners. The practice of witchcraft among women was punished inhumanly. And in 1699, Virginia formally forbade its female population to vote.

In general, both in the South and in the North, women functioned primarily as diligent and industrious housekeepers. The making of clothes, the preparation of food, the rearing of children, and the like constituted their chief activities. Not infrequently, they also worked in the fields, helping their men and servants.

It was only in the South, however, that chivalry became dominant. And even there romance, courtesy, and respect for women were typical of the upper classes, not of Negroes and poor whites, also. The reasons for the rise of this unusual phenomenon were at least three: first, the shortage of women, which made them more valuable; second, the presence of slavery, which freed women of manual labor; and third, the plantation system, which created wealth and leisure for the South's aristocracy.

Infinitely less fortunate were those women in New England who were accused of witchcraft—unlike the superstitious Puritans of the North, the Episcopalians of the South were so liberal that witch trials in Dixie Land were virtually nonexistent. Such persecutions were also less common in New York, due to the influence of the Dutch and their intellectuals, Bekker, Grevius, Weyer, and others—in Holland witch trials ended in 1610.

The usual penalties for witchcraft in the North were whipping, banishment, and execution. One of the most celebrated trials in this area involved Alse Young, the first American witch to be hung—in Connecticut, on May 26, 1647. Other famous trials were those of Margaret Jones in Boston and of Governor Richard Bellingham's sister at Salem, both of whom were executed.

Salem's trials were among the most notorious and infamous in all witchcraft history. It was there that one of Nathaniel Hawthorne's ancestors, Judge Hawthorne, who was an uncompromising believer in sorcery and demonology, tormented Sarah Good with a most satanical cross-examination—Sarah was hung on July 19, 1692. Concerning another innocent victim, Rebecca Nurse, who was executed on the same day, Whittier wrote:

> "O Christian martyr, who for Truth could die
> When all about thee owned the hideous lie,
> The world redeemed from Superstition's sway
> Is breathing freer for thy sake today."

"Witch-prickers," often male ones, stripped accused women before or during each such trial and examined their bodies most minutely. The purpose of this scrutiny was to ascertain the possible existence of *stigmata diaboli* or witch's marks. Polymastia (having extra breasts) and polythelia (having extra nipples) were accepted as definite signs of witchcraft. An examination of this type is described in Cotton Mather's *Wonders of the Invisible World* (1693), where he states that the "witch-prickers" of Salem, who searched Bridget Bishop in 1692, "found a preternatural teat upon her body." Needless to add, Bridget was executed on June 10, 1692.

Cotton Mather (1662–1728) himself, the son of Harvard's President Increase Mather, was the successful minister of Boston's North Church who encouraged the persecution of witches and Salem's witchcraft trials. In his *Memorable Providences Relating to Witchcrafts and Possessions* (1689), he averred that "there is both a God and a Devil and witchcraft." He further denounced witchcraft as "the most nefarious high treason against the Majesty on high," and suggested that a "witch is not to be endured in heaven or on earth." His definition of witchcraft was: "the doing of strange, and for the most part ill, things by the help of evil spirits, covenanting with . . . the woeful children of men." With fanaticism, he added: "So horrid and hellish is the crime of witchcraft, that were God's thoughts as our thoughts, or God's way as our ways, it could be no other but unpardonable." In 1692, in "The Return of Several Ministers" (VIII), he encouraged the Salem trials as follows: "we cannot but humbly recommend unto the Government, the speedy and vigorous prosecution of such as have rendered themselves obnoxious, according to the directions given in the laws of God and the wholesome statutes of the English nation for the detection of witchcrafts." And in his famous *Diary*, he referred to the same subject in this way: "The Devils, after a most preternatural manner, by the dreadful judgment of heaven, took a bodily possession of many people in

Salem, and the adjacent places; and the houses of the poor people began to be filled with the horrid cries of persons tormented by evil spirits." It is no wonder, therefore, that, when New England had gradually become less superstitious, Harvard refused to appoint the incorrigible Mather as its new President. It was then that the frustrated and humiliated archenemy of witchcraft persuaded Elihu Yale to found a new school at New Haven, Connecticut.

Regarding family size in early America, James H. S. Bossard has stated the following: "Families of ten or twelve were quite common; twenty or twenty-five children in one family were not rare enough to occasion comment."[10] Benjamin Franklin, for instance, came from a family of seventeen, and Boston's Green, a printer, produced thirty children. Also prolific was Sara Thayer, who died in 1751, and who was eulogized as follows:

"Also she was a fruitful vine,
The truth I may relate—
Fourteen was of her body born
And lived to man's estate.

"From these did spring a numerous race,
One hundred thirty-two;
Sixty and six each sex alike,
So I declare to you."

This characteristic, resulting from limited knowledge of birth control and the importance of children as potential workers, tended to reinforce the family members' security. In other words, ordinarily, no individual dependend exclusively on one or very few relatives. Thus, the death of a person seldom constituted a major psychological or economic catastrophe for the rest of the family. Nevertheless, in view of the rather primitive medical conditions that prevailed at that time, we should not conclude that the early American family was much larger than the one which is typical of the United States today.

Indeed, child mortality was quite high. The specific reasons for this were as follows: first, rigorous geographical conditions; second, inadequate housing; third, the rule of baptizing children on the first Sunday after birth, even if the water and the church were exceedingly cold; fourth, the small number of available physicians; fifth, the often charlatanic methods of treating children's diseases; sixth, poor sanitation; seventh, certain curious practices, such as the effort to toughen children's feet by keeping them wet as long as possible—

for instance, by wearing shoes with thin soles; and eighth, widespread child labor.

This last began at a very early age, since there was a great deal of hard work to be done in the rather forbidding and inhospitable new environment, and since the Puritans conceived of work as a virtue. Two other reasons were the influence of the Hebrews and the tendency among the aristocrats to utilize child labor. Especially unfortunate were children coming from very poor families, who were often sold as apprentices. In the South, one of the organizations making extensive use of child labor was Virginia's London Company, some of whose workers were children that had been kidnaped in Europe.

The home, like the school and the law, also placed extreme emphasis on discipline. Corporal punishment was usually administered most generously. This, of course, is not surprising, since most early Americans agreed with preacher John Robinson, who asserted: "there is in all children . . . a stubberness and stoutness of minde arising from naturall pride which must in the first place be broken and beaten down." Respect for one's parents and grandparents was further stressed in every possible way. Accordingly, a Long Island lass of eleven considered it necessary to open one of her letters in this way: "Ever Honored Grandfather: Sir." And she closed thus: "Your most obedient and Duty full Granddaughter Pegga Treadwell." Moreover, a New York law stated: "If any Child or Children, above sixteen years of age . . . shall smite their Natural Father or Mother, unless provoked . . . that Child, or those Children so offending shall be put to Death." In Boston, another law, passed as early as 1657, read as follows: "complaints are made that several persons have received hurt by boys . . . playing at football in the streets, these therefore are to enjoin that none be found at that game in any of the streets . . . under the penalty of 20s."

The religious training of children was equally strict. According to the diary of Boston's Judge Sewall, one day his little daughter began to cry, as "she was afraid she should goe to Hell, her Sins were not pardon'd. . . . Her Mother asked her whether she pray'd. She answered yes but fear'd her prayers were not heard because her Sins were not pardon'd." Sam, however, the judge's ten-year-old son, was less receptive at first, when his father began to give him a rather morbid and macabre lecture on religion and death. The little boy, complained Sewall in frustration, "seemed not much to mind, eating an Aple." Cotton Mather's daughter had a similar experience when she was only four! In her father's words: "I took my little daughter

Katy into my study and there told my child that I am to dy shortly and she must, when I am dead, remember everything I now said to her. I sett before her the sinfull condition of her nature, and charged her to pray in secret places every day."

At least two factors explain the emphasis placed on this sort of religious training. To begin with, the prevalent belief was that children were wicked by nature—Jonathan Edwards called them vipers, and Whitfield described them as rattlesnakes. The other belief was that children were miniature adults.

The educational training of children was more advanced in the North, since in this area there were many more public and private schools than in the South. Besides, by 1649, with the exception of Rhode Island, all New England colonies had made a certain amount of education compulsory. It was in the South, then, that the educational role of the home was more extensive. Still, among the upper classes, it was not the parents themselves, but nurses, governesses, and tutors that were responsible for the child's training. In general, boys in early America were taught the three R's, Euclid, and Latin, while girls were usually given much less training, most of which consisted of sewing, dancing, and the like. After all, as the voters of Northampton decided in 1788, it was a waste of money to attempt to educate girls! Consequently, Mrs. Adams complained: "I regret the trifling, narrow, contracted education of the females of my own country." It is revealing to add that, when the rather erudite wife of Connecticut's Governor Hopkins lost her mind, Governor Winthrop asserted that, if she had devoted herself to her domestic responsibilities, instead of participating "in such things as are proper for men, whose minds are stronger, etc., she had kept her wits." It was only in the nineteenth century that such convictions became sufficiently weak to permit additional training for girls.

In the area of manners, innumerable manuals supplied children with detailed instructions such as the following: "Sing not, hum not, wiggle not. Spit nowhere in the room but in the corner, and wipe it with thy foot." Boys and girls were also advised: "When any speak to thee, stand up. Say not I have heard it before. . . . Snigger not; never question the Truth of it." And a didactic poem suggested:

> "Defile, not thy lips with eating much,
> As a Pigge eating draffe;
> Eate softly and drinke mannerlye,
> Take heed you do not quaffe.
> Scratche not thy head with thy fyngers."

During this period, divorce was much less common than at the present time. In Connecticut the grounds for dissolving marriage were desertion, adultery, and fraudulent contract. The grounds in Massachusetts were similar, namely, cruel treatment of the wife, desertion, and adultery committed by the female spouse, but not by the male.

Another difference was the emphasis which early Americans placed on the family as an economic unit. According to Hart and Hart, "The home was the factory during the first two centuries after our ancestors began to settle America."[11] And it was the household rather than the family which, particularly in the South, functioned as an economic unit. Furthermore, in the plantation system of Dixie Land, the size, isolation, and self-sufficiency of the household were greater than in New England. Southern male heirs also enjoyed more inheritance privileges than their Northern counterparts, since primogeniture and other male-centered property rights in New England were soon abandoned almost completely. Concerning a typical Southern estate of the self-sufficing type, Calhoun informs us that George Washington "had a smithy, charcoal-burners, brickmakers, carpenters, masons, a flour-mill, coopers, and a vessel to carry produce to market. He also employed shoemakers and operated a weaving establishment."[12] Needless to add that kinsmen often cooperated extensively, not only in economic matters, but in others as well, in view of the relative absence of agencies that might deprive the family of its functions.

In another passage, dealing with morality in early America, Calhoun states that, according to Groton church records, "until 1803 whenever a child was born less than seven months after marriage a public confession had to be made before the whole congregation."[13] Obviously, the faithful found such confessions most interesting and fascinating, since church attendance increased considerably whenever sinners confessed their offenses. One may further conclude that sex immorality was perhaps promoted rather than diminished by this sort of sensationalism. Other penalties consisted in fines, imprisonment, whipping, branding, the wearing of the scarlet letter, and the use of pillories and stocks. One of those punished by confinement to the stocks was a captain who, in public and on Sunday, dared kiss his wife upon his return from a three years' voyage! Women, of course, were ordinarily punished more severely. And adultery, especially when it was committed for the second time, was considered a most serious crime—much more serious than fornication. In fact, in very early times, it was often punished by death in virtually all

New England colonies. Such was the Puritan moral code. Increase Mather protested most vociferously even against what he called "Gynecandrical Dancing," while in 1642 Governor Bradford declared that too many single and married people in Plymouth were hopelessly and incorrigibly wicked.

In the South, however, the laws dealing with immorality were much more liberal. One of the reasons for such liberalism was the presence of Negro women, whom white men were usually tempted to exploit. In this part of the country, writes Mowrer, before the Civil War, concubinage involving colored women "was a common, if not a sanctioned, practice."[14] White mistresses were also common. In fact, several governors kept paramours quite openly, while it was not unusual among upper class men to recognize their illegitimate offspring.

## The Modern American Family

Marriage in the United States at the present time is ordinarily based on romantic love and individual choice of mate through dating. Moreover, the average age at first marriage is lower for both sexes than it was a few decades ago. And interethnic, interclass, and interreligious unions are much more numerous now than in the past.

Parents, too, have become more democratic. Their authority, even that of the father, has declined extensively. Thus, decisions are commonly made, not by the father alone, but through discussions involving the husband, his wife, and, not infrequently, their more mature offspring.

As a result of the feminist movement and other forces, one of the most spectacular changes may be seen in the social status of the fair sex. Although Thomas Jefferson, despite his liberal convictions, believed that women should not participate in the world of politics, men such as Thomas Paine, Ralph Waldo Emerson, John Greenleaf Whittier, and others supported feminism with enthusiasm. So in 1848 the first American women's rights convention took place at Seneca Falls, New York, where it was called by Elizabeth Cady Stanton and Lucretia Mott. Through the "Declaration of Sentiments," drawn up by this convention, women complained: man has made woman, "if married, in the eye of the law civilly dead;" "He has taken from her all right in property"; "He has so framed the law of divorce . . . as to be wholly regardless of the happiness of women"; "He has monopolized nearly all profitable employments"; and "He has denied her the facilities for obtaining a thorough education."

Such protests led to the gradual emancipation of women. For instance, "The first woman in government service was Clara Barton, who became a clerk in the Pension Office in 1854."[15] Previously—in 1833—the first institutions of higher education had opened their doors to female students. Then, in 1837, the first measures were taken to remove women's property disabilities. Another economic freedom consisted in their gainful employment outside the home, which, even for married women, was accelerated dramatically by both World Wars. Moreover, as early as 1868, the territory of Wyoming permitted its women to vote. But it was President Wilson who, in spite of his rather antifeminist attitudes, in September 1918 recommended a constitutional amendment that would give the female population the right to vote. The amendment, which, the President believed, would help win the war, was adopted in 1920.

All this, of course, does not mean that complete equality between the sexes has now been attained. On the contrary, this is still a man-centered world, and, strangely enough, even at the present time there are many women who seem to approve of a certain degree of discrimination against their own sex.

Women's emancipation constitutes one of the main reasons why family size has declined. As the birth rate decreases and childlessness increases, although infant mortality has diminished appreciably, the small nuclear family becomes more dominant. Needless to add that the extended type cannot be maintained in our society, in view of the prevailing geographical mobility and the higher educational and occupational achievements of the younger generation.

The freedom gained by the female population is only one of the factors explaining the modern birth control movement and the resulting limited family size. More specifically, the reasons for birth control may be outlined as follows:

1. The aforementioned emancipation of women, which has rendered them much less reproduction minded.

2. The economic insecurity generated by industrialization.

3. The often exorbitant expenses involved in child rearing. The passing of the frontier and the adoption of laws against child labor have changed the preadolescent and, to some extent, the adolescent into liabilities. Even childbirth itself has become more expensive, since it now usually takes place in a hospital.

4. The prevailing budgeting complex, because of which even children must be budgeted through planned parenthood.

5. The educational and other advantages enjoyed by children coming from small families.

6. The vertical social mobility which parents ordinarily empha-size at the expense of having children.

7. The decline of religiosity and the corresponding prevalence of secularism, due to which a child's birth is no longer regarded as an act of God. In 1931 even the Federal Council of Churches expressed its approval of birth control.

8. Recognition of birth control by the medical profession—the American Medical Association recognized this practice officially in 1937.

9. The increase in the number of birth control clinics.

10. The legal approval in all states, except for Connecticut and Massachusetts, of medical advice concerning contraception for reasons of health.

11. More extensive education, which tends to liberalize the population in many respects, including acceptance of birth control.

12. The philosophy of individualism.

Regarding the history of modern birth control, one may assert that, as a social movement, it began in England in 1823. It was Francis Place, a worker, who in that year distributed for the first time his so-called "diabolical handbills." These were leaflets advocating the reduction of family size as a panacea for the problem of poverty.

Five years later, under Francis Place's influence, the United States adopted the birth control movement. Then, in 1832, appeared the first American work on the subject, authored by a physician, namely, Charles Knowlton's *Fruits of Philosophy*. In 1914, another controversial work on contraception was published. Mrs. Margaret Sanger's *Family Limitation*. This brave public health nurse also established the American Birth Control League and, in 1916, the first birth control clinic. Moreover, Sanger was one of the leaders who organized the Geneva World Population Conference of 1927. Part of the history of the movement she presented in her famous autobiography, *My Fight for Birth Control*, which appeared in 1931. Two other developments were the founding of a monthly journal, the *Birth Control Review*, in 1917, and the organization of the Voluntary Parenthood League, in 1919.

Not all groups have been enthusiastic about the birth control movement. On December 31, 1930, *Casti Connubii*, the encyclical of Pope Pius XI, declared: "since the conjugal act is destined primarily for the begetting of children, those who in exercising it deliberately frustrate its natural power and purpose sin against nature and commit a deed which is shameful and intrinsically vicious. . . . Onan . . . did this, and the Lord killed him for it."

As far as children are concerned, one of the most important developments has been the child welfare movement. In 1899, for example, the National Conference of Charities and Corrections suggested numerous ways of promoting the welfare of children. Ten years later, Theodore Roosevelt called the first White House Conference, which emphasized the principles of prevention, foster homes, adequate record keeping, and so forth. It also recommended the following: "A bill is pending in Congress for the establishment of a Federal Children's Bureau to collect and disseminate information affecting the welfare of children. In our judgment the establishment of such a Bureau is desirable." This measure was adopted in 1912. The Children's Code Movement, aimed at the unification, coordination, and improvement of laws dealing with child welfare, was first organized in Ohio, in 1911.

Regarding the functions of the family, it may be asserted that its economic, educational, religious, recreational, and protective tasks have been reduced considerably.

For instance, while the early American household functioned as a unit of production and consumption, today virtually all economic goods are manufactured outside of the home. The making of clothes, baking, canning, preserving, and the like are no longer prevalent domestic activities. Even consumption—as in the case of meals—often takes place outside. Then, the typical housewife's work has been rendered much easier, due to the use of innumerable modern household appliances.

Next, the educational function has been taken over by the school, since social complexity necessitates highly specialized training. The time element alone reveals the immensity of this change: in colonial days, children ordinarily attended school for about three months, not nine or ten, as they do at the present time; now education typically begins at an earlier age and ends at a later one; and children nowadays spend a greater part of the day in school. Furthermore, a larger proportion of young people are now enrolled in high schools and institutions of higher education.

Similarly, religious activities have become much less common, especially among the urban and Protestant segments of the population. For example, saying grace at meals, reading the Holy Scriptures, attending church, and the like are emphasized less today, in view of the influence of war, modern economic conditions, and the spirit of secularism and hedonism. Then, religious training usually takes place, not at home, but in churches and Sunday schools.

World War II, by partially dissolving the family, also led to the development of new recreational habits among lonely soldiers, working wives, and neglected children. Extended leisure time has further contributed to this change. And recreational pursuits, even among members of one and the same family, are becoming more and more heterogeneous. Therefore, the government and private business have responded to the trend by organizing facilities and activities such as the following: city parks, picnic areas, baseball diamonds, tennis courts, swimming pools, skating rinks, bowling alleys, drama, music, dancing, crafts, and so forth. Even schools and churches have, to a certain extent, become recreational centers.

In addition, the protective functions of the family have been transferred, at least partially, to the government, as well as to various private social agencies and insurance companies. To illustrate, it is the police and fire departments that now protect the family. The sick are treated in hospitals. And the juvenile court system, introduced in 1899, assumes responsibility for child discipline.

Finally, immorality, divorce, and other forms of individual and social disorganization have become more extensive. The anonymity of the urban community now "is an invitation to prostitution and illicit unions that offer temporary, and sometimes permanent, substitutes for marriage and family life."[16] War, economic crises, crowding in the city, the emancipation of women and young people, commercialized recreation, the automobile, modern methods of contraception, Freud's theories, certain types of literature, and countless other forces have also reinforced the prevailing disorganization.

### Summary

In brief, some of the main changes in the American family are as follows: first, individual choice of mate based on romantic love; second, decline in parental authority; third, emancipation of women; fourth, reduced family size; fifth, emphasis on child welfare; sixth, decline in the economic, educational, religious, recreational, and protective functions of the family; and seventh, prevalence of various forms of disorganization.

### Conclusion

When dealing with changes in the family, it seems necessary to add a few words regarding the past, present, and future of this institution, as follows:

1. It appears that, at the present time, we lack sufficient data

whose synthesis would facilitate the construction of satisfactory supersystems concerning family evolution. This, however, does not mean that regularity, which renders scientific research meaningful, is not present in this area. On the contrary, as in other social spheres, a certain degree of regularity or recurrence is typical of family phenomena.

2. It seems that, in view of man's nature, as well as of the conditions prevailing on our planet, the family is a virtually indestructible institution, which, throughout history, has been capable of surviving formidable crises, seemingly insoluble problems, and cataclysmic catastrophes. In addition, even during periods of decadence, it remains exceedingly influential in numerous respects.

3. The concept of *social telesis,* as Lester F. Ward, America's pioneer sociologist, would suggest, constitutes an indispensable tool, if the world of the family is to be transformed consciously, intelligently, creatively.

4. Needless to add, such telesis would be incomplete and ineffectual, if not based on the cooperation of all social institutions.

5. Undoubtedly, family life education is a most valuable instrument, and it will be rendered more valuable and efficacious, if we place greater emphasis on its more serious, objective, scientific aspects.

6. Stressing some knowledge of the history of the family would diminish parochialism and provincialism in this area, while at the same time it would supply invaluable insights into familial phenomena.

7. The often meaningless debate between "old-fashioned sentimentalists" and "Plutarchian types,"[7] rather fashionable among family experts at the present time, should be discouraged, since it is primarily based on *a priori* arguments. Instead, main emphasis should be placed upon an objective evaluation of each family characteristic, which should then, and only then, be reinforced or combated, depending on its unemotionally and empirically ascertained merits. After all, change is inevitable—"*panta rei,*" asserted Heraclitus, the "Obscure and Weeping Philosopher" of Ephesus. And "no man can enter into the same river twice." In an industrial society, for instance, it is futile and unavailing to attempt the resurrection of familism, with all of its ramifications. But its complete rejection, without scientific justification, seems also unwise. Why should the "new" and "present" be accepted unquestioningly? Are "novelty" and "presence" the sole criteria of worth, value, and excellence? All situations were "new" and "present" once. But have all situations

or constellations of social forces been *equally* desirable, beneficial, salutary, and creative? Think of Egypt and the Fourth Dynasty with the three pyramids and *The Book of the Dead,* the Twelfth Dynasty which introduced a Golden Age, and Cleopatra and her defeat in Actium. Think of United Israel and Abraham's entrance via Haran to Canaan, the settlement in the Promised Land, and the rise of the Hebrew Monarchy. Think of Greece and the Homeric times, the Golden Age of Pericles, and the Peloponnesian War. And think of Rome and the period of the *Casa Romuli,* the Carthaginian Wars, and Gaius Julius Caesar crossing the Rubicon after exclaiming: *"Jacta est alea."*

8. Objective, extensive, and sufficiently coordinated family research may easily lead to the construction, at least for each social system, of an ideal-typical *Homo domesticus* characterized by attitudes and behavior regarded as highly desirable by scientific investigators. This construct or abstraction may then be presented to the members of the respective social system as a goal to be pursued and approximated.

9. Finally, the present author is convinced that research and teaching emphasizing the discovery and internalization of fundamental principles of the "A causes B" type would achieve much more than any other approach. After all, it is not only true that, as Francis Bacon asserted, *"scientia potestas est,"* but also that *"scientia est per causas scire."*

## Notes

1. Harold T. Christensen, *Marriage Analysis,* second edition, New York: The Ronald Press, 1958, pp. 48–65.
2. Ernest W. Burgess and Harvey J. Locke, *The Family,* second edition, New York: American Book Company, 1960, p. 450.
3. Arthur W. Calhoun, *A Social History of the American Family,* New York: Barnes and Noble, Inc., 1945, Volume I, p. 132.
4. *Ibid.,* p. 55.
5. Meyer F. Nimkoff, *Marriage and the Family,* New York: Houghton Mifflin Company, 1947, p. 77.
6. Clifford Kirkpatrick, *The Family,* New York: The Ronald Press, 1955, p. 114.
7. Stuart A. Queen, Robert W. Habenstein, and John B. Adams, *The Family in Various Cultures,* second edition, New York: J. B. Lippincott Company, 1961, p. 272.
8. Andrew G. Truxal and Francis E. Merrill, *The Family in American Culture,* New York: Prentice-Hall, Inc., 1947, p. 99.
9. Ernest R. Groves and Gladys Hoagland Groves, *The Contemporary American Family,* New York: J. B. Lippincott Company, 1947, p. 144.

10. James H. S. Bossard, *The Sociology of Child Development*, revised edition, New York: Harper and Brothers, 1954, p. 623.
11. Hornell Hart and Ella B. Hart, *Personality and the Family*, revised edition, New York: D. C. Heath and Company, 1941, p. 244.
12. Calhoun, *op. cit.*, p. 229.
13. *Ibid.*, p. 132.
14. Ernest R. Mowrer, *The Family*, Chicago: The University of Chicago Press, 1932, p. 259.
15. Una Bernard Sait, *New Horizons for the Family*, New York: Macmillan, 1938, pp. 421–422.
16. Ray F. Baber, *Marriage and the Family*, first edition, New York: McGraw-Hill Book Company, 1939, p. 11.
17. Carle C. Zimmerman, *Family and Civilization*, New York: Harper and Brothers, 1947, pp. 786 *et passim*.

# PART IV. CROSS–CULTURAL FAMILY SYSTEMS

# The Family System of Rajputs in Pakistan

*Mahfooz A. Kanwar*

The degree of illiteracy among Rajputs prevented us from using a written questionnaire. Instead we conducted an interviewing procedure and the information was randomly verified by the author. The author was greatly helped by the knowledge of his interviewee's language. Through some choudhries (head men or influential men) we got together in Bathaks (places for men to gossip, smoke and relax) mostly in the evenings. We asked them questions on 'what,' 'why,' and 'how' do they do their things. We were helped by some friends to record the conversation. We were able to talk to some women and we questioned men about females and their roles in Rajput families. The Rajput family in general seems to be very stable. The present generation has seen a greater trend toward education; education among rural Rajputs is still meant for boys more than for girls. The extended family is maintained. The father is given the highest authority in family affairs; oldest brother is respected by younger brothers; and man is dominant over woman. [The author conducted this study in four Rajput villages in Multan in December–January, 1968, 1969.]

The Rajputs[1] in Pakistan are Muslims; most of them in India are Hindus. Both Hindu and Muslim Rajputs have the same ancestry. Some of them were converted from Hinduism to Islam by the Moghal Emperors. Although this process of conversion began with the marriage of Akber, a Muslim King, to Man Singh's Sister, a Hindu Rajput girl, it did not materialize greatly until Aurangzeb became the Emperor. Akber was the third (or fourth if we count his father Himanyoun twice as he was overthrown by Sher Shah Suri) Moghal Emperor in India and was considered to be the greatest and most liberal in the Moghal Empire. Aurangzeb was the sixth king and was considered to be one of the most conservative Moghal Emperors. It does not seem to be appropriate for us here to go into the full history of Rajputs and their ancestry, their great contribution to India's cultural, military and political history, their relationship to India's caste system and societal heirarchy, and their conversion to Islam and the history after that. Therefore, from here on we shall concentrate on the family system of Muslim Rajputs in West Pakistan. Most of them are populated in the districts of Multan, Montgomery, Muzaffar Garh, Dera Ghazi Khan and Mian Wali. A large number of them is still uneducated and their main professions or occupations are farming and military service.

The Rajput family in general is patriarchal, patrilineal and patrilocal. Although Islam gives a privilege to a Muslim man to become polygamous, a Muslim Rajput in Pakistan, like his counterpart in India, is generally monogamous. Moreover, after the 1958 revolution in Pakistan everyone had to be monogamous. The husband and/or father is the head of the family and there is no threat in sight to his position in the home. The Rajputs have been able to maintain kinship families. The parents, children and grandchildren live under one roof, eat in the same kitchen and seek their guidance from the grandfather or father. The sons are expected to, and most of them do, give their earnings to their fathers. The sons and their individual families are expected to perpetuate the large family with their parents and unmarried sisters. The emphasis on the kinship family is mainly because of the traditional practice of holding family property in common. However, the division of property does not occur if the brothers, after their father has died, are unable to live together either because of some kind of tensions or sheer jealousy between them or their wives or because of the different occupations of brothers.

When a division of property occurs, the situation among the Rajputs is unlike that of the Chinese before the Communist takeover
In case of property division among Chinese, "each brother separated his straight line descendents from the larger group and established a new branch of the family with himself as patriarch. Such a move permitted younger brothers to attain the status of family head which otherwise would be denied to them. . . ."[2] Some Rajput younger brothers do seem to become the heads of their individual families, none of them want to separate his straight line descendents from their original group. Although they separate from each other, for the most practical purposes, they live together. When it happens, the property is equally divided among brothers with a token share for their sisters. Islam provides that

> Men shall have a share in what their parents and kinsmen leave; and women shall have a share in what their parents and kinsmen leave; whether it be little or much, they are legally entitled to their share.[3]

The Quran further says that:

> A male shall inherit twice as much as a female. If there be more
> than two girls, they shall have two-thirds of the inheritance; but
> if there be only one, she shall inherit the half. Parents shall
> inherit a sixth each, if the deceased have a child; but if he leave
> no children and his parents be his heirs, his mother shall have
> a third. If he have two brothers, his mother shall have a sixth
> after payment of his debts and any legacies he may have be-
> queathed.[4]

Similar was the provision in Pakistan's last constitution and we do not
expect a great change in the new constitution expected to be ready
sometime this year. Theoretically, the sisters are entitled to get their
share and they can claim it by a court action if the brothers refuse
to recognize it. However, the Rajput sisters generally do not take
this share. They voluntarily "donate" their shares to their brothers.
This happens because of the general belief and as we heard some
sisters say that two acres together are more useful and productive
than if they are divided. Moreover, in case of their father's death,
the brothers are expected to arrange dowry for unmarried sisters
and if the sisters demand their share in their father's property, which
is in most cases a piece of land, they risk their brother's resentment
and thus the dowry. At the time of marriage, as we were told by
some sisters and daughters, the presence of guardians—parents, and/
or brothers, uncles and others—and the dowry seem to be more important than the share in the father's property and absence of these
people and dowry. Furthermore, this is a general custom among
Rajputs that after the marriage the girl would accept the patrilocal
system but within a matter of weeks, she will visit her parents and/or
brothers and other relatives. When she leaves again for her inlaws'
place, she expects to receive more dowry. Although the amount of
this "giving" becomes smaller and smaller, as the time goes by, it
never ends completely. On the other hand if she had taken her share
in her father's property, she may not, as we mentioned earlier, get
all this and she may lose her brothers and other relatives, as there are
still many more ties between them all than in any western society
and thus may become cheap in her inlaws' eyes. Although she had
brought some amount of property into her husband's home, if she
loses her brothers and other relatives, she risks her position in her
new home, because this and all other property belongs to her husband. If some parents, however, leave their daughters with no
brother, then it is altogether a different matter. She takes her share

and it does not really matter a great deal whether or not she will risk the resentments from uncles or others.

## Mate Selection and Marriage

Generally there are two systems of mate selection: arranged marriages and love marriages. There are some other ways in between these two. In case of arranged marriages, the spouses are selected by parents or others other than the spouses themselves. Both of them see each other in the first night, i.e., after they are married to each other. In the love marriage both spouses select each other with little or no consultation with parents or others. The first system is more common in Pakistan and other eastern societies and the second in Canada and other western societies. In between these two extreme systems, there are other modified ways of mate selection. Parents make the mate selection with the consent of the parties concerned and the spouses concerned select each other with the permission or consent of their respective parents. Sometimes an agent does the mate matching consulting with the parents and/or the persons concerned.

The Rajput family generally falls in the first category. The parents are the main discussants in mate selection and the girls and boys generally accept their parents' decision. However, there is some indication and even some examples for mate selection made by the parents with the consent of their sons and daughters. This is done mostly among the educated or comparatively well off Rajputs. Custom of purely arranged marriages still continues to remain well established and maintained in rural areas where most of the Rajputs still live. There the arranged marriage is a well established fact of life. A Westerner may wonder about this custom. This practice has some well accepted reasons behind it: for example, it is believed that if you love someone before marriage, you are not objective in making decisions about marriage and other things. On the other hand, your parents are not in love with the other party and therefore can avoid becoming subjective in the decision making process. Secondly, as they believe, your parents know you probably more than you know yourself especially in cases of early marriages which were again very common among Rajputs until recently. As they do know you more, they will do a better job in mate selection for you. Thirdly, they love you and the family ties are still very strong; they would not do anything bad for you. Fourthly, the marriage is considered as a gift from the parents or from the family and you do not reject a gift from anybody, especially your parents. Fifthly, they believe that love begins after marriage and therefore premarital love is not required. Sixthly, Rajputs are still endogamous. They make their mate selection from within Rajputs to keep their blood "pure" or to keep the coming generation "pure" Rajputs. Therefore, they usually make the mate selection for their sons and daughters from close relatives or other known Rajputs. This mere fact of pure Rajput, more than education, beauty, etc., will satisfy the parties concerned. However, there is some evidence, especially among educated Rajputs, that the young folks are looking for something more than pure Rajput blood. This has not yet become a popular custom. Finally, Muslim Rajputs, like any other Muslim, believe that mate selection is done by God. It is written in your fate who you will marry and you cannot challenge God's decision. He knows better than anybody else who is best for you.

Marriage among Rajputs is not only a union of two persons but also an alliance of two families. A Rajput family, as we mentioned earlier, is a patrilocal; it is not a neolocal. Family tradition counts more than their individual considerations and they have been socialized to accept this. A Muslim lady from India explains the importance of family for young people who are ready to marry. She notes that

> [Marriage] is considered a family project where the older and wiser members of the family are given the privilege of finding a healthy, industrious, intelligent and efficient girl who can be regarded as lovable by all members of the family and not just her husband. Likewise, a boy who cannot get along with his own family is looked upon with a little trepidation. Hence a marriage is not a selfish personal relationship that excludes consideration of generations to come.[5]

This fits quite well the situation among Rajputs in Pakistan. Consideration of dowry, mutual aid, and pure Rajput blood give all the importance to the families involved. Parents of course do their best in making sure that the union is the best anyone can make regarding the character of the girl and boy, equal or near equal social and economic status of the two families, ability of the boy and girl to be efficient husband and wife and so on. Ownership of land, or Zamindari, is also one of the considerations by both families, especially by the family of the girl. In cases of first and/or second cousin (mother's side) marriages, not only the families know each other well but also the spouses know each other well. A great many Rajputs marry the

daughters of their maternal uncles but very few marry the daughters
of their paternal uncles. In these situations the processes of decision
making and adjustment are much easier than the marriage taking
place among strangers.

## Marriage Ceremony and Dowry

Dowry among Rajputs in Pakistan is paid by the girl's parents.
Dowry payments have their significance. As was mentioned earlier,
the Rajput daughters and sisters generally do not demand their share
in their father's property; dowry is given partly in lieu of that, partly
to enhance the girl's prestige in her inlaw's eyes and partly to maintain the prestige of her father's family. It has been established and
maintained as a popular custom for a long time and therefore anyone
who would try to ignore it, would risk putting his honor and prestige
on the line. It of course differs in amount, quantity and quality from
family to family according to their economic and social status. Being
a popular tradition, it forces especially the people who are among the
lower ladders of economic status to take a loan, sell some property
and do almost anything to arrange dowry for their daughters and
sisters. We have known some cases where the parents have been
financially ruined by dowry and cases where the parents have taken
loan which they have not been able to pay off for quite some time.
On the other hand, as we pointed out earlier, it has some positive
effects on both families. It helps the girl to have prestige in her new
family. It becomes a great help for her new family to start a better
life. It gives her some portion of her share in her father's property,
and so on. Among Rajputs the dowry is in cash, utensils, clothing,
jewelry, furniture and animals like a cow or buffalo. Although there
is a law in West Pakistan which restricts the exhibition of dowry,
this custom is still as popular as ever. We are told by a few educated
Rajputs that this custom should be abolished. On the other hand, a
great many of them indicated clearly that this custom is very good
and must stay. This is probably not limited to Rajputs only, this
seems to be a popular custom in the whole Indian sub-continent.
Similar seems to be the case in relation to the share of the daughters
in their father's property and the arranged marriages. Dr. Swarn
Hooja recently conducted a study in Delhi, India and got similar
reactions from Indian people.

It is found that ninety-two per cent of the people in the group
are against abolition of the dowry system; six per cent favor

partial abolition and two per cent complete abolition. As regards a share in property, 100 per cent are against any share of
property to the daughter. On their opinion as to the nature of
marriage, here again 100 per cent favour arranged marriages.[6]

Insofar as marriage ceremony, it is considered to be one of the
greatest and most important moments of their lives. In some cases
the engagement takes place while the spouses are still children; in
others when the boys and girls are in their mid teens. We did not
find any definite age of boys and girls getting engaged, i.e. engagement arranged by their parents. However, we did observe a common
trend that engagement should take place at least one or two years
before marriage so that the families can get prepared or complete
the incomplete dowry which in some cases begins to be prepared at
an early age of the girl. This period also gives enough time to both
of the families to know each other and to find out not only about the
boy and girl but also about the history of both families especially
if they are strangers to each other. Once everything is in order, the
date for marriage is set. Usually the representatives of the boy's
family go to the girl's family to set the date and to ask them how
many people they can bring in the wedding party. The day comes
and the wedding party goes to the girl's family. If the girl's family
is an urban one usually a hotel is booked for a day according to the
status of the family. All the expenses are paid by the host family.
The boy and the girl accept each other separately at two different
places—the boy generally in a mosque and the girl at home. One
meal and two teas are served and the boy with his wedding party
take the girl to his home. If the girl's family is a rural one the wedding party stays for two to three days, usually three. Almost every
Rajput village and small town has a large place which in some
villages belongs to the whole village and in others belongs to a richer
Rajput. In any case, this is a place for men to sit together, gossip,
play and smoke water pipes. At times of someone's wedding it is used
for the wedding party to stay. There is a great amount of mutual aid
and cooperation among most Rajputs in someone's marriage, as there
is in times of birth, death and other occasions. The cots, sheets and
blankets are gathered from each other and so are the plates and other
things for kitchen and dining. People volunteer for service in and
outside the house. Usually the wedding parties are big in number;
there are some with few people depending on the family's economic
as well as social standing. Generally there is some kind of day and
night entertainment, for women inside the home and for men out-

side. The people give some amount of money to the boy and girl—not as a loan but in the hope that when their sons and daughters get married, they would receive this mutual aid as well. For these and other reasons the marriage becomes a community affair as it is a family function among Rajputs.[7]

## Divorce and Remarriage

Divorce procedures among Rajputs are pretty well in line with those of the rest of Pakistani Muslims. As a result of social, political and legal changes in Pakistan,[8] three pronouncements of talaq (divorce) are not the rule of the game any more. Therefore, the Rajputs, like anyone else in Pakistan, would have to go through the courts. Among all four villages where we conducted our study, we found only one divorce case. In this case, the divorce was initiated by the parents of the girl rather than the girl herself on the basis of cruelty of her husband. The divorce was given by the court and thus enmity between two families was created. The divorce is regarded as not only tragic for the couple but also for both families. The woman, especially an uneducated villager, does not have any place to go except her parents. Although both families hurt their prestige and the man is frowned upon, it is the divorced woman who suffers most. Lack of divorce among Rajputs seems to be because of arranged marriages, marriage being a family (both families and even the whole clan) affair and the fear of having no chance for remarriage. The couples in their differences, are generally approached by both families, other relatives and friends and in some cases by the clan (Brotheri) leaders and the problem is resolved. Moreover, male dominance or husband dominance is still the accepted rule in the family and this almost rules out the initiation by women for divorce. The case of adultery by husband is regarded less harmful to family prestige than the wife's. We can safely say that there are found more murders than divorces in case of adultery committed by the wife. The author in another study[9] observed that Rajputs are the fourth highest committing murders in West Pakistan and there was a high ratio of Rajputs committing murder because of women.[10]

Although Muslim Rajputs still carry some Hindu customs, they stick mostly to Islamic norms in relation to remarriage. Among Hindus, for instance, "A man can marry a younger sister of his wife, but not her elder sister. Where widow remarriage is allowed, a man may marry the widow of his deceased elder brother, but not that of a younger brother."[11] A Muslim Rajput can marry a younger or elder sister of his deceased wife. Similarly he can and does marry the widow of his deceased elder as well as younger brother. A brother is positively encouraged to marry his deceased brother's widow to keep the property within the family, to keep their person (as she belongs to the family) and also because in many cases the family finds it difficult to arrange another girl for the living brother.

## Notes

1. The word Rajput consists of two sub words—"Raj" meaning king or kingdom and "Put" (poot) meaning son. Hence Rajput means a son of a king. This refers to the history of India when there were many Rajput states owned and governed by the Rajputs. There is no independent Rajput state at the present time; however, there are still some Rajput Princes like Maharaja Jaipur. The Rajputs are also referred to as warriors.
2. Gerald R. Leslie, *The Family in Social Context*, New York (Oxford University Press, 1967) p. 90.
3. *The Koran*, Translated by N. J. Dawood, Harmondsworth, Middlesex, Penguin Books, 1966, p. 357.
4. *Ibid.*, p. 358.
5. George Kurian, *The Family—A Cross-Cultural View*, New York, Selected Academic Readings, 1969, p. KUG–5A.
6. George Kurian, *Ibid.*, p. KUG–17A.
7. The author attended twenty-six Rajput weddings; twenty-one in villages and five in cities. Most of them were attended before the period in which the research was done for this article.
8. M. A. Kanwar, *Changing Conceptions of the State in Islamic Nations*, an unpublished Masters Thesis, Department of Sociology, University of Waterloo, 1968.
9. M. A. Kanwar, *A Comparative Study of Rural and Urban Murders*, an unpublished Masters Thesis, Department of Sociology, University of the Prujab, Lahore, West Pakistan, 1964, p. 25.
10. We conducted this study dealing with seventeen districts including the ones where Rajputs are heavily populated. M. A. Kanwar, *Ibid.*, p. 1.
11. George Kurian, "Mate Selection and Marriage: Some Changing Trends With Special Reference to India," an unpublished article quoting S. C. Dube, "Men's and Women's Role in India, A Sociological View," *Women of Asia*, (U.N.E.S.C.O. 1960), p. 181.

# The Family in the Philippine Islands

*Panos D. Bardis*

The population of the ancient Philippine Islands consisted of three racial groups, namely, the Negritos (Itas, Inagta), the Malays, and the Indonesians. After centuries of intermarriage, the inhabitants of these islands were transformed into a fairly homogeneous group and, consequently, the Philippines were no longer disturbed by serious racial conflicts.[1] Linguistic heterogeneity, however, is still typical of the Filipinos, who are speaking eight languages and eighty-seven different dialects.[2]

In 1521, when Magellan arrived in the Philippine Islands, the natives had an idolatrous religion, which placed main emphasis on ancestor worship, and a monogamous family system.[3] The social position of their women was unique in the entire Orient. Despite her geographical proximity to the kimono maiden of Japan, the "lily-footed" dame of China, and the veiled lady of India, the Filipino woman experienced neither seclusion, nor oppression, nor servitude.[4] On the contrary, her socio-economic status was very high.[5] She enjoyed approximately the same privileges and rights as her husband and, when the latter died, she inherited half of their joined gains. Furthermore, in several communities, the wife of a chief was permitted to succeed her husband in his important position, as soon as his death occurred.[6]

In the mountainous areas of the Philippine Islands, the women spent most of their time working hard in the rice fields. Housekeeping was not their main task. Agriculture was their primary occupation and, without the women's hard labor, it would be impossible

From *Alpha Kappa Deltan*, Spring 1956, Vol. 26, No. 3, pp. 20–24. Reprinted by permission of Professor Bardis.

for this productive activity to go on. As a result of such hard work, birth rates were very low and the women aged very early.[7]

In this region, young boys and girls enjoyed considerable sexual freedom. The latter formed groups and occupied huts which constituted places of courtship and experimental mating. The girls' huts were visited by boys who usually had intimate physical contacts with the girls in order to facilitate mate selection. Here the final choice of one's mate was based on compatibility, which was determined primarily by the pregnancy of the girl. In this way, mate selection took place without parental influence. This custom, which was common among aristocratic families, also dominated the mountain communities, even during the beginning of the twentieth century.[8]

In the majority of the Philippine communities, the courtship custom known as *binalata* was of the following nature:

After the young couple had selected each other, the boy informed the girl's parents or guardians about his decision to marry her. Then the parents of both parties met to make arrangements concerning the marriage of their children. Before the wedding day, the boy sent a daily gift to his girl and, on the eve of their wedding, the final gift, which consisted of the price for the wedding dress. The bridegroom also gave his bride a dowry in the form of a house, land, money, or other articles of value.[9]

On the wedding day, the couple attended a banquet during which they partook of food from the same plate and drank from the same glass. After the banquet, they were blessed by a priestess, who then threw the javelin to kill the animal for the sacrifice. When the dancing and praying that followed the banquet were completed, the ceremony ended with the undressing of the newly weds.[10]

In her new home, the wife was respected and usually enjoyed many privileges. In case of discord, for instance, the husband assumed the role of a priest and repeated the wedding ceremony, praying to the Almighty for peace and harmony. But if conciliation were still impossible, then the case was brought before a jury composed of the community's older men. After considering the case carefully, these men decided who was the culprit. If it were the woman, the dowry was returned to her husband; but if she were innocent, she was allowed to keep it.[11]

In 1565, when the Philippines were conquered by the Spaniards, the faith, customs, and laws of Spain were introduced into many islands. Accordingly, the culture of the natives began to change tremendously, especially in the area of religion. By 1924, for instance, ninety-two per cent of the Filipinos were Christians, the remainder being primarily Mohammedans, Buddhists, and pagans.[12] Education was also influenced considerably, since the Catholic priests were eager to teach the natives reading in order that they might be able to read religious books. Writing, however, was discouraged by both priests and parents. The former did so merely because they wished to prevent intercommunication among the natives, whereas the latter disapproved of writing in order to keep their daughters from communicating with boys.[13]

During the Spanish occupation, the Philippines entered a period of rapid population growth. This growth was due to the following factors:

1. The Catholic Church was opposed to birth control.[14]
2. The high death rates spurred the natives toward large families in order to overcome the losses.[15] It was only recently that successful scientific measures were taken against the high mortality rates.[16]
3. The islands have been mainly agrarian. By 1919, of the 120,000 square miles of rich tropical land, 14,000 had been touched by a plow—the Philippines can hold 70 million people.[17]
4. Children were desired since they could help in the fields.[18]

As a result of these influences, the population of the Philippines grew rapidly, reading 10,314,310 in 1918. Six years later, it was 11,-541,841.[19] By 1939, the population of the Philippines had grown to 16,000,303.[20]

The influence of the Catholic Church manifested itself in the area of courtship also. During this period, chastity was highly prized and praised. Young girls were trained to be obedient, submissive, and quiet, and they were given daily lectures on how to save their souls from the eternal fire. Consequently, they gradually began to conceive of the members of the opposite sex as dangerous devils. Furthermore, the young woman scarcely ever left her home. In her presence, adults carefully avoided conversations dealing with love. Dancing was forbidden. Her dress should not be ostentatious. Chaperonage was very common and, in general, the young woman led a strictly moral and conservative life.[21]

Under such circumstances, a young man was forced to employ glances, sighs, handkerchiefs, parading in front of a girl's home, night serenades below her window, letters, and flowers in order to convince her of the fact that he was not a dangerous devil and that his love was sincere. If he were more courageous, he visited the girl's parents and, after greeting them reverently, he spoke to them about their daughter. If the young man were a *persona grata*, the young

THE FAMILY IN THE PHILIPPINE ISLANDS

lady would soon appear in the hall. If, however, he were not agreeable to the family, the girl pretended to be sick and stayed in her room. In the former case, the young woman usually sat in the opposite corner of the hall, thus enabling her parents to hear the entire conversation. Such Draconian measures were dictated by the fact that mate selection had to be conducted very carefully, since the Catholic Church did not permit divorce. Furthermore, because the jilted girl was usually discredited very much, parents considered it their duty to protect their daughters as much as possible.[22]

In case the parents disapproved of a young man, whereas their daughter persisted in displaying interest in him, the girl was usually beaten and whipped, or else she was sent to a convent or dormitory for girls, where no visitors were allowed to see her. If, however, marriage seemed to be desirable, the suitor's parents or guardians, sometimes accompanied by the influential elders of the town, came to the girl's house to ask for her hand. When, after mutual consultations, the two families agreed to the marriage of their children, preparations were made and the affair ended with a spectacular wedding ceremony.[23]

In her new home, the status of the wife was raised considerably. Here she was not only the queen of her family, but also her husband's adviser or co-worker in the business in which he was engaged. Of course, her work was usually light, but her reward was very generous, consisting of the greater part, and sometimes all, of the husband's earnings, which were turned over to her. Furthermore, the married woman was allowed by the law to retain the ownership of her inherited property, the husband acting merely as her administrator. Daughters also shared equally with their brothers the wealth which was left by their parents.[24]

If the Catholic faith in the Philippine Islands constitutes a symbol of four centuries of Spanish sovereignty, the English language is a symbol of a half century of American influence.[25] As a result of American sovereignty, by 1905, there were 3,000 Filipino and 1,000 American teachers in the Philippines where 500,000 pupils were attending public primary schools.[26] In 1917, the number of girls enrolled in the primary and intermediary grades of public schools was 234,905.[27] Accordingly, the literacy rate was 60 per cent of the entire population in 1924,[28] while in 1939, 48 per cent of the population over 10 years of age could read and write.[29] Moreover, women were soon admitted to the State University, and in 1912 the first Filipino woman doctor graduated from this school. In 1927, the State University awarded degrees to 231 women, among whom there

however, was adopted as late as April 30, 1937.[31]
were 12 physicians, 7 dentists, and 22 pharmacists.[30] Woman suffrage,

Despite America's influence, both in the educational and the economic spheres—before World War II, the Philippines had the second highest standard of living in the Orient, Japan having the highest[32] —the family system in this area remained rather conservative. During the first decades of the twentieth century, the women disapproved of Occidental ultra-modernism, preferring to be good mothers and loyal wives rather.[33] Children were expected to display extreme respect for their elders and especially for their parents whose hands they were required to kiss after saying their evening prayers.[34] Family ties were very strong and even distant relatives were permitted to visit one's home frequently and to stay there for a fairly long time.[35] This custom is typical of the professional classes also, even at present. That is why there are few poorhouses in the Philippines. People there say: "every poor person is a relative to someone."[36] Economically, however, the family was more modern, since the wife remained almost as influential as her husband in the area of business activities.[37]

Filipino women have also organized several clubs of their own. In 1919, there were 50 women's clubs engaged in social settlement work, the improvement of health conditions, the prevention of infant mortality, and the like. By 1924, the membership of these clubs was 12,000.[38]

At present, marriage is less frequently arranged, and even young ladies are enjoying more freedom. "The old devices of courtship have been thrown into the discard, for the young woman nowadays meets her men friends . . . at social clubs, . . . school rooms, . . . and the cinematographs."[39] Dating of the American type, however, is not very common in the Philippines, due to the influence of the Malay-Latin-Chinese forces, which still dominate certain aspects of social life in these islands.

## Notes

1. Francis Burton Harrison, *The Corner-Stone of Philippine Independence* (New York: The Century Company, 1922), p. 13; David Bernstein, *The Philippine Story* (New York: Farrar, Straus and Company, 1947), pp. 12–13; Maria Paz Mendoza-Guazon. *The Development and Progress of the Filipino Women* (Manila: Bureau of Printing, 1928), p. 8; and Oliver C. Miller, "The Semi-civilized Tribes of the Philippine Islands," *Annals of the American Academy of Political and Social Science*, 18:41–63, July, 1901.
2. Bernstein, *op. cit.*, p. 3.

3. Mendoza-Guazon, *op. cit.*, pp. 9, 11.
4. Maximo M. Kalaw, *Self-Government in the Philippines* (New York: The Century Company, 1919), p. 173.
5. Charles Edward Russell, *The Outlook for the Philippines* (New York: The Century Company, 1922), p. 37.
6. Kalaw, *loc. cit.*
7. Felix M. Keesing and Marie Keesing, *Taming Philippine Headhunters* (Stanford University Press, 1934), pp. 191–92.
8. *Ibid.*, pp. 50–51.
9. Russell, *op. cit.*, pp. 37–40; and Mendoza-Guazon, *op. cit.*, pp. 11–12.
10. *Ibid.*, pp. 12–13.
11. *Ibid.*, pp. 13–15.
12. *Ibid.*, pp. 15–16: Frank Wilkes Pyle, *An Ancient People and Their Problems* (Washington, D.C.: Philippine Press Bureau, 1920), p. 3; Kalaw, *loc. cit.*: Frederic S. Marquardt, *Before Bataan and After* (New York: Bobbs-Merrill Company, 1943), pp. 28–29; Jose P. Melencio, *Arguments Against Philippine Independence and Their Answers* (Washington, D.C.: Philippine Press Bureau, 1919), p. 10; Vincente G. Bunuan, *Arguments for Immediate Philippine Independence* (Washington, D.C.: Philippine Press Bureau, 1924), p. 29; Bernstein, *op. cit.*, p. 20; and Charles C. Pierce, "The Races of the Philippines—The Tagals," *Annals of the American Academy of Political and Social Science*, 18:25, July, 1901.
13. Mendoza-Guazon, *op. cit.*, pp. 16–17.
14. Bernstein, *op. cit.*, p. 13.
15. *Ibid.*
16. Elpidio Quirino, *The New Philippine Ideology* (Manila: Bureau of Printing, 1949), pp. 95–96.
17. Kalaw, *op. cit.*, p. 175; and Prescott F. Jernegan, *A Short History of the Philippines* (New York: D. Appleton and Company, 1917), pp. 279–80.
18. Willystine Goodsell, *Problems of the Family* (New York: The Century Company, 1930), p. 19.
19. Bunuan, *op. cit.*, p. 32.
20. Bernstein, *op cit.*, p. 3.
21. Mendoza-Guazon, *op. cit.*, pp. 19–20.
22. *Ibid.*, pp. 20–21.
23. *Ibid.*, pp. 21–25.
24. *Ibid.*, pp. 26–29.
25. Bernstein, *op. cit.*, p. 20; and Marquardt, *op. cit.*, pp. 36–38.
26. Jernegan, *op. cit.*, pp. 277–79.
27. Kalaw, *op. cit.*, p. 175.
28. Bunuan, *op. cit.*, pp. 26–27.
29. Joseph Ralston Hayden, *The Philippines: A Study in National Development* (New York: Macmillan Company, 1942), p. 204.
30. Mendoza-Guazon, *op. cit.*, p. 37.
31. Hayden, *op. cit.*, p. 203.
32. Bernstein, *op. cit.*, p. 15.
33. Bunuan, *op. cit.*, p. 32.
34. Russell, *op. cit.*, pp. 63–64.
35. Charles Burke Elliott, *The Philippines* (Indianapolis: Bobbs-Merrill Company, 1917), p. 110.
36. Bernstein, *op. cit.*, p. 24.
37. Elliott, *loc. cit.*: Mendoza-Guazon, *op. cit.*, pp. 41–42; and Kalaw, *op. cit.*, pp. 173–74.
38. *Ibid.*, p. 174; Hayden, *op. cit.*, pp. 651–52; and Bunuan, *op. cit.*, p. 31.
39. Mendoza-Guazon, *op. cit.*, p. 44.

# Marriage and Family Life among Negroes

*G. Franklin Edwards*

## Introduction

This article analyzes from available demographic data, chiefly those of the 1960 Census of Population, the marital status and family characteristics of the nonwhite population.[1] Its major concern is with changes in these characteristics occurring during the 1950–1960 decade. In this respect, it extends a previously reported study of comparable characteristics for the nonwhite population during the 1940–1950 decade.[2]

On the assumption that marital status and family characteristics are related to the organization of community life and have an important influence on the personality and life chances of members of the family, comparable data to those reported for nonwhites are furnished also for whites. This is followed to establish the extent to which the characteristics observed for nonwhites are similar to or diverge from the same characteristics of the majority group.[3]

The article begins with a discussion of marital status and considers in turn: types of families and household relationships, reproductive behavior and children in families, and other characteristics.

## Marital Status

*General.* The marriage rate during the 1950's was high, though not so high as during the preceding decade. The approximately 42 million married couples in 1960 were 5.6 million more than existed in 1950, an increase of 15 per cent for the period.[4] The percentage

From *The Journal of Negro Education*, 1963, 32 (4), pp. 451–465. Reprinted by permission of the editor and author.

increase in number of persons married over the decade was 15.7 and 13.5 for white males and females, respectively, and 12.4 and 15.7 for nonwhite males and females, respectively.[5]

It can be observed from Table I that between 1950 and 1960 the percentage of the male population 14 years of age and over married increased by two percentage points and, conversely, the percentage of single persons dropped by 1.5 percentage points. For females, the percentage married remained constant, but there was a reduction of a percentage point for single persons.

TABLE I

Marital Status, by Sex and Color, Total Population 14 Years of Age and Over, 1960 and 1950, by Per Cent

| Color | 1960 | | | | | | | | | |
|---|---|---|---|---|---|---|---|---|---|---|
| | | Male | | | | | Female | | | |
| | Total | S | M | W | D | Total | S | M | W | D |
| Total | 100.0 | 24.9 | 69.6 | 3.4 | 2.1 | 100.1 | 19.0 | 66.0 | 12.2 | 2.9 |
| White | 100.0 | 24.3 | 70.3 | 3.3 | 2.1 | 100.0 | 18.6 | 66.7 | 11.9 | 2.8 |
| Nonwhite | 100.0 | 30.2 | 62.8 | 4.6 | 2.4 | 99.7 | 21.9 | 60.5 | 13.7 | 3.6 |
| | | | 1950 | | | | | | | |
| Total | 100.0 | 26.4 | 67.5 | 4.1 | 2.0 | 100.0 | 20.0 | 65.8 | 11.8 | 2.4 |
| White | 100.0 | 26.1 | 67.9 | 4.0 | 2.0 | 100.0 | 19.9 | 66.2 | 11.5 | 2.4 |
| Nonwhite | 100.0 | 28.5 | 64.4 | 5.2 | 1.9 | 100.0 | 20.7 | 62.0 | 14.6 | 2.7 |
| | | | Difference 1960–1950 | | | | | | | |
| Total | | —1.5 | 2.1 | —0.7 | 0.1 | | —1.0 | 0.2 | 0.4 | 0.5 |
| White | | —1.8 | 2.4 | —0.7 | 0.1 | | —1.3 | 0.5 | 0.4 | 0.4 |
| Nonwhite | | 1.7 | —1.6 | —0.6 | 0.5 | | 1.2 | —1.5 | —0.9 | —0.1 |

Source: U.S. Census of Population, 1960, U.S. Summary (Detailed Characteristics), PC(1)–1D, Table 177, pp. 436–437.

Virtually all of the percentage increase in married persons and decrease in the percentage single over the decade resulted from the marital behavior of whites, especially white males among whom the percentages married and single showed most change. Among both nonwhite males and females a reverse pattern to the general trend was observed, with an increase in the percentage single and decrease in the percentage married for the decade.

The figures given in Table I include among the percentage married many persons who were not living with a spouse either because of marital discord or for "other" reasons.[6] As shown by Table II, this percentage was sizeable, being especially marked for nonwhites. Whereas in 1960 only 4.0 and 4.5 per cent of white males and females, respectively, enumerated as married lived apart from their spouses, the comparable percentage for nonwhite males was 15.4 and for nonwhite females 20.1. Thus, proportionately, nearly four times as many nonwhite males as white males and 4.5 times as many non-white as white females, though enumerated as married, were living apart from their mates.

TABLE II

Married Persons and Presence of Spouse, Total Population 14 years of Age and Over, According to Color, 1960 and 1950, by Per Cent

| | | Males Married | | | | Females Married | | |
| | | | Spouse Absent | | | | Spouse Absent | |
| | Total | Spouse Present | Sep-arated | Other | Total | Spouse Present | Sep-arated | Other |
|---|---|---|---|---|---|---|---|---|
| | | | | 1960 | | | | |
| White | 100.0 | 96.0 | 1.4 | 2.6 | 100.0 | 95.5 | 2.0 | 2.5 |
| Nonwhite | 100.0 | 84.5 | 8.7 | 6.7 | 100.0 | 79.9 | 14.1 | 6.0 |
| | | | | 1950 | | | | |
| White | 100.0 | 94.9 | 2.3 | 2.8 | 100.0 | 96.0 | 1.9 | 2.1 |
| Nonwhite | 100.0 | 85.2 | 9.3 | 5.5 | 100.0 | 82.0 | 13.9 | 4.1 |

Source: Computed from U.S. Census of Population, 1960, U.S. Summary (Detailed Characteristics), op. cit., Table 178, pp. 439–440.

There was little change between 1950 and 1960 in the overall percentage of white males and females separated from their spouses. Similarly, there was no significant increase during the decade in over-all percentage of nonwhite males apart from their spouses; but nonwhite females showed a 2.1 percentage point increase for the period, contributed mainly by the larger percentage living apart for "other reasons." One interesting fact to be observed in Table II is that whereas among whites of each sex separation for "other" reasons is the larger component in the total percentage of married persons apart from their spouses, among nonwhites the reverse is true. For each of the sexes among nonwhites and for each of the census periods reported, separation resulting from marital discord was the larger component. The tendency to be separated because of domestic in-felicity is especially marked among nonwhite females, the percentage separated for this reason in 1960 being twice as large as the percentage separated for "other" reasons and in 1950 three times as large.

These statistics indicate that nonwhite families are more likely to be broken than are white families. The difference in the percentage of white and nonwhite marriages terminated by divorce is small, but this is not the case as regards separations resulting from marital conflict. Nor do separations and divorce give a complete picture of the greater propensity of nonwhite marriages to become broken. Death contributes a considerable measure to the observed white-nonwhite differential in broken family units. In 1930, 3.3 and 4.6 per cent of white and nonwhite males, respectively, were widowers; and 11.9 and 13.7 per cent of white and nonwhite females, respectively, were widows. This larger percentage of widows, as compared with widowers, results from the lower death rate of women and their longer life span and has an important bearing on family economics, as many widows, particularly nonwhite, are left with children to support.

The significance of widowhood for nonwhite females goes beyond their larger percentage as compared with whites. Nonwhite females become widows at an earlier age than white females. In 1960, one-fifth of all nonwhite females (19.5%) between 14 and 35 years of age as compared with 6.9 per cent of white females of the same age group were widows.

By summing the percentages of persons not living with a spouse because of separation, divorce or death, one notes that the total percentage is more than twice as high for nonwhite males as for white males (15.7 as compared with 6.8 per cent), and almost twice as large for nonwhite females as for white females (31.2 as compared with 16.7 per cent).

The greater instability of nonwhite marriages may be documented further from statistics on remarriages. Among "persons ever married," 21 percent of nonwhite females and 22 per cent of nonwhite males have been married more than once. The comparable percentages are 13.2 and 13.4 for the white males and females, respectively.[7] A larger percentage of persons married more than once is found among those now living with a spouse as compared with those who, though married more than once, are now divorced, widowed, separated or living apart for "other" reasons. This pattern in remarriage holds for both whites and nonwhites. But the percentage of persons married more than once not now living with a spouse is significantly higher for nonwhites than for whites.

*Type of Area.* Marital status varies by area, with different patterns existing for males and females in the proportions married according to farm or nonfarm residence. Generally, the highest proportion of males married is found in urban areas and the highest proportion of females married is found in rural areas. These patterns result mainly from differences in sex ratios which are high in rural areas and low in urban areas.

It will be observed from Table III that this generally expected marital pattern held for whites, among whom the percentage of males married in urban areas was three percentage points higher than the comparable percentage for rural farm males. The percentage of rural white females married was 7.6 percentage points higher than the comparable percentage for urban females. The white rural nonfarm population, among both males and females, occupied an intermediate position in the proportion married.

TABLE III

Marital Status of the White and Nonwhite Population 14 Years of Age and Over, Type of Area, by Per Cent, 1960

| Area and Color | Population 14 Years of Age and Over | | | | | | | | | |
|---|---|---|---|---|---|---|---|---|---|---|
| | | Male | | | | | Female | | | |
| | Total | S | M | W | D | Total | S | M | W | D |
| *Urban* | 100.0 | 24.1 | 70.2 | 3.4 | 2.3 | 100.0 | 19.4 | 64.5 | 12.8 | 3.4 |
| White | 100.0 | 23.6 | 70.8 | 3.3 | 2.3 | 100.0 | 19.2 | 64.9 | 12.6 | 3.3 |
| Nonwhite | 100.0 | 28.0 | 64.7 | 4.5 | 2.8 | 100.0 | 20.6 | 61.1 | 13.9 | 4.3 |
| Diff. W.-Nw. | | —4.4 | 6.1 | —1.2 | —0.5 | | —1.4 | 3.8 | —1.3 | —1.0 |
| *Rural Nonfarm* | 100.0 | 26.0 | 68.7 | 3.4 | 1.9 | 100.0 | 17.2 | 69.7 | 11.2 | 1.8 |
| White | 100.0 | 25.0 | 69.9 | 3.2 | 1.9 | 100.0 | 16.5 | 70.8 | 10.9 | 1.8 |
| Nonwhite | 100.0 | 36.2 | 57.2 | 4.8 | 1.7 | 100.0 | 24.7 | 58.7 | 14.9 | 1.7 |
| Diff. W.-Nw. | | —12.2 | 12.7 | —1.6 | 0.2 | | —8.2 | 12.1 | —4.0 | 0.1 |
| *Rural Farm* | 100.0 | 29.5 | 66.2 | 3.2 | 1.1 | 100.0 | 20.0 | 71.1 | 8.1 | 0.8 |
| White | 100.0 | 28.6 | 67.1 | 3.1 | 1.2 | 100.0 | 18.9 | 72.5 | 7.9 | 0.8 |
| Nonwhite | 100.0 | 38.0 | 57.2 | 4.0 | 0.8 | 100.0 | 29.9 | 59.5 | 9.9 | 0.7 |
| Diff. W.-Nw. | | —9.4 | 9.9 | —0.9 | 0.4 | | —11.0 | 13.0 | —2.0 | 0.1 |

Source: *U.S. Census of Population, 1960, U.S. Summary* (Detailed Characteristics), *op. cit.,* Table 176, pp. 424–435.

The observed pattern of having a larger proportion of males married in urban areas held for the nonwhite population, among which this proportion was 7.5 percentage points higher than the comparable percentage in rural nonfarm and rural farm areas. The expected relationship did not hold for nonwhite females, however, as the proportion of females married was slightly higher in urban than in rural farm and rural nonfarm areas. That this is so bears a relationship to the heavy migration of nonwhites from rural areas during the 1950s. Doubtless many young nonwhite married couples left the open country for cities during the period and, equally important, a large number of nonwhite males of marriageable age migrated to urban centers.

There is one further fact which doubtlessly operated to influence the relatively small percentage of nonwhite females married in rural areas. A substantial proportion of this population (24%) is between the ages of 14 and 20, an age group in which marriage rates are not high for the lower end of the age distribution even in rural areas. (The comparable proportion of white rural females in this age group is 14.0 per cent.)

Marital status patterns of whites and nonwhites in each type of area show that proportionately more white males and females are married and larger percentages of nonwhite males and females are single. The two color groups show least differences, among both males and females, in urban areas. The white-nonwhite difference is greatest between males in rural nonfarm areas and between females in rural farm areas.

*Regions.* The marital patterns observed for regions in Table IV are similar to those reported for the country as a whole and for farm and nonfarm areas. In each of the regions there is a larger proportion of the total population, as compared with nonwhites, married and a smaller proportion single. This relationship holds for both sexes. The difference between the percentages of the total and nonwhite population widowed and divorced in each region is negligible when compared with differentials in the proportions single and married.

Nonwhite males vary least from the total population in the proportions single and married in the Northeast and North Central regions.[8] These are highly urbanized regions, and, as previously observed, the marital status of nonwhites shows greatest similarity to that of the total population in urban areas. The differentials are much greater between total and nonwhite males in the South and West. As previously observed, migration of nonwhites out of the South played an important part in this result.

The percentage point difference between the total population and nonwhite population in the proportion married in the South more than doubled between 1950 and 1960 (3.6 as compared with 7.6), owing mainly to a reduction of 2.8 percentage points in the proportion of nonwhites married. A similar magnitude was observed

TABLE IV

Marital Status of the Total and Nonwhite Population 14 years of Age and Over
According to Region, by Per Cent, 1960

| Region and Color | Population 14 Years of Age and Over | | | | | | | | | |
| | Male | | | | | Female | | | | |
| | Total | S | M | W | D | Total | S | M | W | D |
| --- | --- | --- | --- | --- | --- | --- | --- | --- | --- | --- |
| *Northeast* | | | | | | | | | | |
| Total | 100.0 | 25.7 | 69.1 | 3.9 | 1.4 | 100.0 | 21.4 | 63.8 | 12.7 | 2.0 |
| Nonwhite | 100.0 | 29.6 | 64.5 | 4.2 | 1.8 | 100.0 | 23.1 | 61.5 | 12.5 | 2.9 |
| Diff. T-Nw. | | —3.9 | 4.6 | —0.3 | —0.4 | | —1.7 | 2.3 | 0.2 | —0.9 |
| *North Central* | | | | | | | | | | |
| Total | 100.0 | 24.0 | 70.3 | 3.5 | 2.2 | 100.0 | 18.6 | 66.8 | 11.8 | 2.9 |
| Nonwhite | 100.0 | 27.0 | 64.6 | 4.5 | 3.9 | 100.0 | 18.9 | 62.8 | 12.6 | 5.7 |
| Diff. T-Nw. | | —3.0 | 5.7 | —1.0 | —1.7 | | —0.3 | 4.0 | —0.8 | —2.8 |
| *South* | | | | | | | | | | |
| Total | 100.0 | 25.4 | 69.5 | 3.1 | 2.0 | 100.0 | 18.3 | 66.4 | 12.5 | 2.8 |
| Nonwhite | 100.0 | 31.3 | 61.9 | 4.9 | 1.8 | 100.0 | 23.0 | 58.8 | 15.4 | 2.8 |
| Diff. T-Nw. | | —5.9 | 7.6 | —1.8 | 0.2 | | —4.7 | 7.6 | —2.9 | |
| *West* | | | | | | | | | | |
| Total | 100.0 | 24.9 | 68.9 | 2.8 | 3.5 | 100.0 | 16.7 | 67.9 | 11.0 | 4.4 |
| Nonwhite | 100.0 | 32.4 | 60.4 | 3.5 | 3.7 | 100.0 | 20.2 | 65.1 | 9.4 | 5.3 |
| Diff. T-Nw. | | —7.5 | 8.5 | —0.7 | —0.2 | | —3.5 | 2.8 | 1.6 | —0.9 |

*Source: U.S. Census of Population, 1960, U.S. Summary* (Detailed Characteristics), *op. cit.*, Table 242, pp. 651–657.

in the proportions single, for which the percentage point difference
increased from 2.3 in 1950 to 5.9 in 1960.

The greatest variation between the total population and the nonwhite in marital status of males existed in the West, a result chiefly
of the relatively small proportion of nonwhite males married. The
same condition was true in 1950. The West is the only region in
which the number of nonwhite males exceeds the number of nonwhite females.[9] Much of this excess of nonwhite male population
is owing to the migration of single males to the region.

Among females, the nonwhite marital pattern most closely resembled that of the total population in the Northeast. The greatest
variation between the two by region was in the South.

## Types of Families and Household Relationships

The approximately 45 million families in the United States in
1960 were 6.6 million more such units than existed in 1950, an in-

crease of 19 per cent. The number of white units increased by 5.8 million units or 16.4 per cent. The 4.1 million nonwhite family units in 1960 represented an increase of 732,000 since 1950, an increase of 21 per cent.[10]

White and nonwhite families differed in composition, especially as regards the family head and presence of children. For both color groups husband-wife families dominated, as shown in Table V. Approximately 9 of 10 white families were headed by a male whose spouse is present in the home; but only three of four nonwhite families are of this type. Only one in eleven white families is headed by a female, but one in five among nonwhites has a female head.

TABLE V

White and Nonwhite Families in the United States According to Type, by Per Cent, 1960 and 1950

| Type of Family | White | 1960 Non-white | Diff. W-Nw. | White | 1950 Non-white | Diff. W-Nw. |
|---|---|---|---|---|---|---|
| Husband-wife | 88 | 74 | 14 | 87 | 78 | 9 |
| Other Male Head | 3 | 5 | — 2 | 4 | 4 | — |
| Female Head | 9 | 21 | —12 | 9 | 18 | —9 |
| All Families | 100 | 100 | | 100 | 100 | |

Source: U.S. Census of Population, 1960, U.S. Summary (Detailed Characteristics), op. cit., Table 186, p. 464.

The percentage with "Other Male Head" did not vary much for the two groups.

It may be observed from Table V that the type of family remained remarkably constant among whites during the 1950–1960 decade, a condition which did not hold for nonwhites. Husband-wife families among nonwhites declined four percentage points during the period, while the families with a female head increased by three percentage points.

The average size of white family units, as observed from Table VI, was smaller than the average for nonwhite units in both 1960 and 1950. The difference between the two groups in average size increased during the decade. For both census periods reported the average size of the nonwhite family was larger for each type of family, with the greatest difference occurring for families with "Female Head," in which category nonwhite families in 1960 averaged one more member than white units (4.04 as compared with 2.93). A part

of the difference in average family size for families of all types resulted from the presence of "own children under 18" in the home.
Whites averaged 1.3 such children and nonwhites 1.7 children.

*Household Relationships.* There were more than 52.8 households
in the United States in 1960, an increase of one-quarter in the number of such since 1950. White households accounted for 47 million
of the total and increased by 24 per cent during the decade, while
nonwhite households numbered five million, an increase of 30 per
cent for the same period.[11]

TABLE VI

Average Number of Family Members by Type of Family and Color,
Conterminous United States, 1960 and 1950

| Type of Family | Average Number of Family Members | | | |
| | 1960 | | 1950 | |
| | White | Nonwhite | White | Nonwhite |
| --- | --- | --- | --- | --- |
| Husband-wife | 3.66 | 4.41 | 3.61 | 4.16 |
| Other Male Head | 2.82 | 3.56 | 3.05 | 3.63 |
| Female Head | 2.93 | 4.04 | 3.06 | 3.82 |
| All Families | 3.58 | 4.30 | 3.54 | 4.07 |

*Source: U.S. Census of Population, 1960, U.S. Summary* (Detailed Characteristics), *op. cit.*, Table 187, p. 469.

TABLE VII

Percentage Distribution of Persons in White and Nonwhite Households
by Relationship to Head, United States, 1960 and 1950

| Relationship to Head | 1960 | | | | 1950 | | | |
| | White | | Nonwhite | | White | | Nonwhite | |
| | M | F | M | F | M | F | M | F |
| --- | --- | --- | --- | --- | --- | --- | --- | --- |
| Head | 51.2 | 9.7 | 37.9 | 13.3 | 51.9 | 8.3 | 40.8 | 11.6 |
| Wife | — | 45.1 | — | 30.1 | — | 46.5 | — | 32.3 |
| Child | 40.2 | 36.5 | 42.3 | 39.4 | 39.1 | 34.9 | 38.9 | 35.6 |
| Grandchild | 1.0 | 0.9 | 5.2 | 4.7 | 1.7 | 1.5 | 5.8 | 5.2 |
| Parent of Head | 0.7 | 2.2 | 0.5 | 1.9 | 1.1 | 2.8 | 0.7 | 2.5 |
| Other Relatives | 2.1 | 2.5 | 5.8 | 6.0 | 3.7 | 3.7 | 7.1 | 7.2 |
| Lodger | 1.3 | 1.0 | 3.6 | 2.3 | 2.4 | 1.8 | 6.5 | 4.8 |
| Res. Employee | 0.1 | 0.2 | 0.1 | 0.5 | 0.2 | 0.4 | 0.3 | 0.7 |

*Source: U.S. Census of Population, 1960, U.S. Summary* (Detailed Characteristics), *op. cit.* Table 183, pp. 457–458.

Table VII shows the percentage distribution of persons in white and nonwhite households for 1960 and 1950. Some rather significant changes, particularly in the composition of nonwhite households, occurred over the decade.

*Head.* There was a significantly larger percentage of white male heads of households than nonwhite heads in both 1960 and 1950. But the difference between the percentages for the two groups was larger in 1960 than ten years earlier, owing mainly to a reduction in the percentage of nonwhite male heads. Conversely, though there was an increase in the percentage of women serving as heads for both groups, nonwhites had a higher proportion of female heads in both periods. One nonwhite household in seven in 1960 was headed by a female as compared with one in ten white households having such a head.

*Wife.* White women were present in the home more often as wives for both census periods.

*Children and Grandchildren.* Nonwhite households contained a larger proportion of children than did white households in 1960. This held for households headed by a male as well as those with a female head. Ten years earlier there was little difference in the proportion of children in white and nonwhite households. The larger proportion of nonwhite children in 1960 doubtless results from the continued higher birth rate of nonwhites during the 1950s.

In 1950, nonwhite households, proportionately, had three and one-half times as many grandchildren as white households. The proportion became five times as large by 1960. The difference in proportions for the two periods resulted mainly from a reduction in the proportion of grandchildren in white households.

*Other Relatives.* The proportion of "Parents of Head" in the household of both color groups was reduced over the decade. Whites had a slightly larger proportion for each of the census years reported.

There was a sharp reduction in the presence of "other relatives" (cousins, aunts, etc.) in both white and nonwhite households. Nonwhite households, however, had proportionately two and one-half times as many "other relatives" in 1960 as did white households, which was an increase over the relative proportion of twice as many in 1950.

The presence of a large number of grandchildren and "other relatives" suggests that the nonwhite family retains much of the primary group characteristics of rural families. It suggests also that with the movement to cities nonwhites have provided housing for relatives who either could not find adequate shelter or were unable to pay for separate accommodations. The reduction in the proportion of "other relatives" in nonwhite households in the 1960s as compared with the 1940s doubtless indicates that the acute housing shortage which faced nonwhites was abated.

*Lodgers.* A sharp reduction in the percentage of lodgers in white and nonwhite households occurred during the 1950s. The proportion of lodgers in nonwhite households in 1960, however, was twice as large as the proportion in white households. As lodgers often are taken in for economic reasons—to help with rental payments, for example—the reduction in the percentage of this group in nonwhite households suggests that their contribution to the economic welfare of the family was not so necessary as formerly.

TABLE VIII

Own Children Under 5 Per 1,000 Women 15 to 49 Years Old,
According to Marital Status and Color
Conterminous United States,
1960 and 1950

| | Children Under 5 Years | | | |
|---|---|---|---|---|
| | 1960 | | 1950 | |
| Color | Per 1,000 Women | Per 1,000 ever Married | Per 1,000 Women | Per 1,000 ever Married |
| White | 464 | 592 | 404 | 525 |
| Nonwhite | 520 | 698 | 396 | 516 |

*Source: U.S. Census of Population, 1960, U.S. Summary* (Detailed Characteristics), *op. cit.*, Table 193, p. 486.

## Reproduction and Children in Families

Crude birth rates in the 1950s were below those of the war and immediate post-war years. Already by the late 1940s the birth rate of whites had begun to decline from its wartime peak. The decline continued in general during the 1950s and by 1961 was 22.2 per 1,000 population, well below the 1947 rate of 26 per thousand. Nonwhite rates, in contrast, continued high during the fifties and reached a peak of 35.4 per thousand in 1956. Since that date there has been a drop in the nonwhite rate, which was 31.6 in 1961—still well above the comparable rate for whites.[12]

The fertility ratios of both whites and nonwhites for the Conterminous United States were higher in 1960 than in 1950. Whereas the ratio of children under 5 to women of reproductive age was slightly higher for whites than nonwhites in 1950, it was much higher for nonwhites in 1960, reflecting the divergent tendency of white and nonwhite birth rates during the 1950s. These fertility ratios are shown in Table VIII.

Despite the fact that nonwhite women ever married averaged more children per woman than white women of the same status, the difference was affected by the large number of children borne by some nonwhite women. A larger percentage of nonwhite than white women (21.3 as compared with 16.0) had not given birth to a child. Larger percentages of white women had had one, two, three and four children. But the proportions of nonwhite women with five and six children were much larger than the comparable percentages of white women with these order parities, and the percentage of nonwhite women with seven or more children was more than three times as large as the comparable percentage for white women.[13]

Much the same pattern is observed for the number of own children under 18 present in the homes of married couples. Approximately two-fifths each of all white and nonwhite married couples had no child under 18 present in the home. The percentage of white couples having one, two and three such children, respectively, exceeded the comparable percentage for nonwhites. But the nonwhite percentage having four or more children was twice as large as the comparable percentage for whites.[14]

Earlier it was observed that a larger percentage of nonwhite, as compared with white, families are broken by separation, divorce and death. One consequence of this is that many children in nonwhite families live with one parent only, usually the mother. Table IX shows that only approximately two of three nonwhite children under 18 as compared with nine of ten white children of the same age are living with both parents.

In each type of area the percentage of white children living with both parents is consistently higher than the comparable percentage of nonwhite children. The least variation between the two color groups occurs in rural areas where the percentage for whites is one-fifth larger than that for nonwhites.

## Other Characteristics

*Education of Head.* The educational attainment of heads of nonwhite families is greatly inferior to the level reached by heads of

TABLE IX

Percentage of White and Nonwhite Children Under 18 Living with Both
Parents, United States, Urban and Rural, 1960

| | Children Under 18 with Both Parents | | |
| Area | White | Nonwhite | Difference White-Nonwhite |
| --- | --- | --- | --- |
| United States | 90.0 | 66.3 | 23.7 |
| Urban | 89.7 | 64.9 | 24.8 |
| Rural Nonfarm | 89.9 | 67.3 | 22.6 |
| Rural Farm | 93.4 | 73.5 | 19.9 |

Source: U.S. Census of Population, 1960, Social and Economic Characteristics (PC(1)–1(C), Table 79, p. 210.

white families. Almost one-half (48.5%) of all nonwhite heads had
not finished elementary school. Only 19.2 per cent of white heads
failed to reach the eighth grade. Even in urban areas two out of five
nonwhite family heads failed to reach the last year of elementary
school, while 70 per cent and 80 per cent of the nonwhite heads in
rural nonfarm and rural farm areas, respectively, had their schooling
terminated before they reached that level. (The comparable percentages of whites were: urban, 16.4; rural nonfarm, 24.7; and rural
farm, 28.6) At the other extreme, only 4.1 per cent of nonwhite heads
had some college education (1 to 3 years) and 3.2 per cent had four
years or more. The percentages of whites reaching these levels were:
one to three years of college (10.0 per cent) and four years or more
(10.5 per cent).[15]

The low level of educational achievement by nonwhite heads has
obvious implications for the cultural life to which the child is
exposed in the home and doubtless for motivating the child in his
school work. It also is related to the labor force participation and
income of nonwhites.

Labor Force. The economic fluctuations of the 1950s resulted in
a divergence of white and nonwhite male labor force rates. The
percentages of both white and nonwhite males in the labor force
in 1960 showed a decline from the comparable percentages for 1950,
but the nonwhite decline was greater than the white. In 1960, 72
per cent of nonwhite males 14 years of age and over were in the
labor force as compared with 78.0 per cent of whites of the same
age group. The comparable percentages for 1950 were nonwhite
76.5 and white 79.2.[16]

These gross statistics do not reveal the full extent of the degree of participation of the two groups. Nonwhites experience heavier unemployment and underemployment. The percentage of nonwhite males unemployed (8.8%) was nearly twice as high as the comparable percentage of 4.6 for white males. It should be observed, further, that 16 per cent of nonwhite males in the civilian labor force, but only 11 per cent of the white males, were part-time workers. Approximately one-third of white male part-time workers and 18 per cent of nonwhite workers in this category were under twenty years of age. This suggests that a large proportion of older males among non-whites were without full-time employment.

A sharp contrast existed in the occupations followed by the heads of white and nonwhite families. Forty per cent of all white heads, as contrasted with 13 per cent of nonwhite heads, were white collar workers. Another fifth of white male heads, but only a tenth of nonwhite heads, were skilled craftsmen. Thus, three of five heads of white families were professional, managerial, clerical or skilled workers, while only one in four nonwhite heads was in one of these occupational categories.

Among female workers the trend toward the convergence of white and nonwhite labor force participation rates, observed for the 1940s, continued during the 1950s. The percentage of white and nonwhite women in the labor force increased during the 1950s in contrast to the decline observed for males of both color groups. The forty-two per cent of nonwhite females in the labor force in 1960 represents a five percentage point increase over 1950, while the 34 per cent of white females in the labor force in 1960 represents a six percentage point increase for white women during the decade.

A larger percentage of nonwhite females in the labor force, as compared with white females, were unemployed (8.5 as compared with 4.9), and one-third of all nonwhite females, as compared with one-quarter of white females, were part-time workers.

In connection with labor force participation, it should be pointed out that nonwhite families had a larger percentage of units in which two members of the family were in the labor force (nonwhite, 33.2%; white, 29.8%). The same relationship held for family units with three or more workers in the labor force (nonwhite, 10.2%; white, 6.8%).

*Family Income.* In view of the relative labor force participation rates and the occupations followed by the heads of white and non-white families, it is not surprising that the median income of non-white families is far less than the median for white families. In

1959, the median income of $3,161 for nonwhite families was only approximately 54 per cent of the median of $5,893 for whites. The percentage of the white median represented by the median for non-whites in 1959 was about the same as the relationship between the respective medians ten years earlier.

There was a considerable variation in the relationship between white and nonwhite income by type of area. In urban areas, non-white income was 58 per cent of white income; in rural nonfarm areas, 40 per cent; and in rural farm areas, 36 per cent.

There also was a marked variation among nonwhite families in income by type of family. Husband-wife families had the highest median, $3,633 and families with a "Female Head" the lowest, $1,734. Those families with "Other Male Head" had a median income of $3,168.

The relatively small money income of nonwhite families is indi-cated by the fact that nearly one-half of them (47.9%) earned less than $3,000 in 1959. The comparable percentage for whites was 18.6. At the other extreme, one white family in six earned $10,000 or more annually, as compared with one in twenty-five nonwhite families.[17]

### Summary and Conclusions

This analysis reveals that during the 1950s the nonwhite family, considered in relation to white families, did not make any substan-tial gains toward closing the gaps which were noted between the two in 1950. In many respects the nonwhite family lost ground, but the dominant picture is that the relative status of the nonwhite family was unchanged during the decade.

The single most important fact observed is that nonwhites became more highly urban during the decade, thus continuing a trend set in motion on a large scale a half century ago. Seventy-five per cent of all nonwhite families are found in urban places as compared with 70 per cent of white families. Only 6.5 per cent of all nonwhite families remain in rural areas (comparable percentage of white fam-ilies, 7.4). Migration out of the South continued for nonwhite units.

For many of the characteristics observed, white-nonwhite family differences were least in urban areas or in highly urbanized regions. This held for the proportion of the population married (both males and females), income, and the fertility ratio. The larger percentage of nonwhite families living in their own household and the smaller proportion of subfamilies in 1960 as compared with 1950 indicate that the tight housing situation which resulted in considerable "doubling" during the 1950s was relieved. This point is supported by the smaller proportion of "other relatives" and lodgers in nonwhite households.

While nonwhite families were 9.4 per cent of all families, they were only 7.9 per cent of families with both husband and wife present in the home. On the other hand, they represented 21.0 per cent of all families with a female head. The large number of family units headed by a female indicates the persistence of many of the characteristics observed for nonwhite units during earlier periods.

The proportion of nonwhite units broken by separation, divorce, and death remained high in 1960, and the difference between white and nonwhite "broken" units was larger in 1960 than in 1950. The birth rate of nonwhites remained high in the 1950s and the difference in white and nonwhite fertility ratios was broadened during the period. The average family size of nonwhites remained considerably larger than that of whites in each type of area.

Though the income of nonwhite families relative to white families was about the same in 1959 as in 1949, nonwhite males and females experienced greater unemployment and underemployment than whites in the 1950s. Nonwhites continue to have a larger percentage of units with two or more persons in the labor force. A larger proportion of nonwhite females, as compared with white females, was in the labor force. The gains made by nonwhite male workers during the 1950s were not maintained during the 1960s.

The present status of nonwhite family life has an important bearing on the prospects and life chances of the nonwhite child. In general, there is a greater probability that he will enjoy less economic and emotional support than the white child as he attempts to reach the objectives set for members of the society. In many cases, owing to the negating influences of family life, the objectives to which nonwhite children aspire will not be very high.

There is a further lesson to be learned from the experiences of nonwhite families during the 1940s and 1950s. Improvement of nonwhite family life in terms of those values posited by the society as desirable is tied to the larger economic and social forces which operate. Full employment of the war and immediate post-war years provided opportunities for the improvement of nonwhite family life which were not present in the 1950s. The deeply embedded patterns of disorganization in nonwhite family life which have existed for a full century cannot be eliminated by specialized efforts aimed at family education, nor under any circumstance can they be corrected in a short period. Equal access to employment opportunities, education, housing and the other values of the society for nonwhites provides the only sound basis for convergence of white and nonwhite family patterns.

## Notes

1. Virtually all data on the characteristics discussed in the 1960 *Census of Population* are reported for nonwhite rather than for Negroes. Negro families, however, comprise an overwhelming majority (93%) of all nonwhite families. The Negro percentage of the nonwhite may vary by region and for some of the characteristics discussed.
2. See, G. Franklin Edwards, "Marital Status and General Family Characteristics of the Nonwhite Population," *Journal of Negro Education*, 22:280–296, Summer 1953.
3. A definitive analysis of the similarities and divergent patterns of white and nonwhite marital status, family and household characteristics from 1950 census data is found in Paul G. Glick, *American Families*, New York: John Wiley and Sons, Inc., 1957.
4. These figures are for the "Conterminous United States," which is defined as the territory included in the 1950 and earlier censuses.
5. U.S. Bureau of the Census, *U.S. Census of Population: 1960, U.S. Summary* (Detailed Characteristics). Final Report PC (1)–1D. U.S. Government Printing Office, Washington, D.C., 1963, Table 177, p. 436–437.
6. This category includes married persons employed and living away from home, those with spouses absent in the armed forces, immigrants whose spouses remained in other areas, husbands or wives of inmates in institutions, married persons (other than separated) who were living in group quarters, and all other persons whose place of residence was not the same as that of their spouse. *U. S. Census of Population: 1960 U.S. Summary* (Detailed Characteristics) *op. cit.*, p. XX.
7. *Ibid.*, Table 176, pp. 424–428.
8. Eighty per cent of the population of the Northeast and 69 per cent of the population of the North Central Region are urban. The East North Central portion of the North Central Region, however, is 73 per cent urban. This contains the largest proportion of nonwhites in the region. The nonwhite population is 96 per cent urban in the Northeast and 95 per cent urban in the East North Central states.
9. Among Negroes, the number of males exceeded the number of females in the ages between 15 and 30. *U.S. Census of Population: 1960, U.S. Summary* (Detailed Characteristics), *op. cit.*, Table 233, p. 618.
10. All figures are for the Conterminous United States. Computed from *U.S. Census of Population: 1960, U.S. Summary* (Detailed Characteristics), *op. cit.*, Table 186, p. 464.
11. Computed from Table 183, *U.S. Census of Population, 1960, U.S. Summary* (Detailed Characteristics), *op. cit.*, pp. 457–458.
12. "Birth Rate, Down; Baby Count, Up," *Population Profile*, Population Reference Bureau, Washington, D.C., December 26, 1962, p. 4.
13. *U.S. Census of Population, 1960, U.S. Summary* (Detailed Characteristics), *op. cit.*, Table 191, p. 483.
14. Bureau of the Census, *Current Population Reports*, Series P-20, No. 106, "Household and Family Characteristics: March, 1960," Table 18, p. 9.
15. *U.S. Census of Population, 1960 ,U.S. Summary* (Detailed Characteristics), Table 188, p. 470.
16. The data of this section are taken from: *U.S. Census of Population, 1960, U.S. Summary* (Detailed Characteristics), *op. cit.*, Tables 194 and 195, pp. 487–500.
17. Based upon data furnished in *Ibid.*, Tables 224 and 225, pp. 594–603.

# The Hawaiian Family

*Panos D. Bardis*

The Hawaiians constitute a branch of the Polynesian family, which includes the Maori of New Zealand, the Samoans, the Tongans, the Tahitians, the Cook islanders, and the Marquesans. These people originally emigrated from India and other Asiatic areas and inhabited the island groups between Sumatra and Luzon. By the first centuries of the Christian era, when they began to organize expeditions into the Pacific, they were already a mixed race. During the sixth century A.D., many of them reached the Hawaiian Islands and for about half a thousand years remained there in complete isolation. Then began a period of great voyages which lasted between the eleventh and fifteenth centuries. These voyages were followed by a new period of isolation which was interrupted in 1778, when Cook visited the Hawaiian Islands. At that time the population of these islands was about 300,000, but the coming of the haole (whites, i.e., foreigners) disrupted adjustment between the natives and their resources, and the population soon began to decline rapidly. The number 300,000 was reached again in 1925, when the economy of the islands was already capitalistic.

Before Cook's visit, Hawaii had a feudal system characterized by a precise hierarchy, the chieftain (alii) and priest (kahuna) class controlling the commoners (makaainna) almost completely. The language of these natives, a variant of that spoken by the Polynesians and one of the most musical in the world—because it had only seven consonants and every syllable ended in a vowel—had never assumed a practical written form.

According to L. H. Morgan, in ancient times the Hawaiians were

From *Archive of Economic and Social Sciences*, July–September, 1958, Vol. 38, No. 3, pp. 381–385. Reprinted by permission of Professor Bardis.

promiscuous. When the evils of promiscuity were perceived, however, a new family type, the Punaluan (Hawaiian word for "dear friend"), was invented. Under this system, "the brothers are the common husbands of several sisters, but not of their own."[1] Nevertheless, it is doubtful whether promiscuity was ever in existence in these islands. Morgan's assumption was merely based on the Hawaiian practice according to which children called every man "father." He believed, therefore, that each generation married promiscuously within itself and that all young men and women were mates, while the members of the older generation were their fathers. This interpretation, however, seems incorrect, in view of the fact that the word "father," to the Hawaiians, meant merely a member of the older generation, not a biological father. In other words, this term was employed for the purpose of distinguishing between generations, not between family members.

In old Hawaii, as in ancient Egypt and Peru, dynastic incest, in the form of brother-sister marriages, was prevalent. The purpose of this practice, which was dominant even during the last decades of the nineteenth century, was to preserve the purity of the royal line.

Among the lower classes the family was not strictly organized. Both spouses were free to terminate their partnership at will, since divorce was not forbidden and the form which it usually assumed was mere quitting. Female infanticide and abortion were also very common—cases of infanticide were reported even as recently as 1860.

The women of Hawaii did not enjoy a high socio-economic status. Their usual activities consisted in the care and early training of children, the plaiting of mats, and the preparation of clothing from bark cloth. Sex hospitality was very prevalent and women were frequently lent to sailors and other visitors. Visitors could also buy young girls at a very low price. Such purchases occurred not only in 1792, during Vancouver's visit, but also as late as 1820.

In 1820, when the first New England missionaries arrived in Hawaii, the Christian faith began to spread among the natives quite rapidly. The acceptance of the new religion, however, was superficial. The missionaries, although they had been successful in inducing the natives to cover a greater area of their skin with conservative clothing, were unable to control immorality. Indeed, the Christian standards of chastity were rejected almost completely The Hawaiians, for instance, continued to participate in mourning ceremonies which, especially after a chief's death, were accompanied by an orgy of sexual license. Moreover, they still played u m e and k i l u, two native games which involved sexual relations, and they still danced the h u l a, which the missionaries considered highly erotic, but were unable to suppress. In fact, such attitudes toward sex were not only maintained, but also reinforced, due to the frequent visits of lascivious sailors, who were attracted to the islands by the practice of sex hospitality. Consequently, the missionaries' work became more difficult and more dangerous. In 1825, for example, when Reverend William Richards and Reverend Hiram Bingham protested against sex hospitality, a group of frustrated American sailors did not hesitate to employ physical violence against both of them. It is little wonder, therefore, that during the second half of the nineteenth century Iwilei, near Honolulu Harbor, became one of the most notorious brothel districts in the entire Pacific.

As a result of such international and interracial contacts, mixed marriages soon became very common in Hawaii.[2] This may be indicated by the fact that, although there were only 2,119 foreign residents in the islands in 1853, the number of those who were part-Hawaiians was 983—the total population in the same year was 73,134. Later the number of foreigners began to increase rapidly and by 1941, those of Japanese descent constituted the largest racial group in Hawaii. By 1948, however, the number of the Japanese was 176,280, whereas that of Caucasians was 180,480, and that of the Hawaiians only 10,650. In the same year there were 30,530 Chinese in the islands. The entire population of Hawaii—which was 300,000 in 1778, and 82,035 in 1850—had risen to 423,330 in 1940. In the same year the 179,000 residents of Honolulu—15,000 in 1875—represented 40 per cent of the entire population. Only 8 years later this number rose to 277,129—51.3 per cent of all inhabitants. It is no wonder, therefore, that at present this fairly Americanized city is in transition, with 20,000 of its residents—mostly Orientals—living in slums.

The Americanization of Hawaii has been promoted not only by the presence of Americans in the islands, but also by its modernized education. In 1853, for instance, the legislature began to encourage the study of the English language, and by the next year, there were already 10 English schools in the islands. Interest in the education of Hawaiian girls was also increased during this period. Consequently, in 1859 the first school for girls was founded in the city of Honolulu by Catholic Sisters of the Sacred Heart. In the same year Miss Maria Ogden founded the Makiki Family School for women, also in Honolulu. One year later the legislative assembly authorized the board of education to establish girls' "family schools" for domestic training in the English language. As a result of this policy, by 1868 there were 9 such schools in Hawaii, with 300 pupils.

These educational developments soon helped Hawaii's women to gain freedom and independence. Their status was especially raised when they became economically emancipated. Due to this emancipation, notwithstanding the conservative ideologies of the thousands of Oriental immigrants, the family of Hawaii became more liberal. At the same time the percentage of interracial marriages began to increase very rapidly and by 1934 it was as high as 30.1 per cent. The divorce rate also increased considerably. Furthermore, the Hawaiian-born boys and girls began to rebel against the custom of arranged marriage, which their parents had transplanted to Hawaii from China and Japan, most of them now preferring individual choice of mate and American courtship patterns.

In general, due to modernized education, urbanization, the introduction of Western athletics and other types of recreation, and the tremendous influence exercised by thousands of American servicemen stationed in this area during World War II, the Hawaiians soon became the most Westernized Oceanic group. As a result of this rapid and radical transformation, even the various churches were forced to adopt less conservative measures. At present, for example, most of the denominations no longer disapprove of native music and dancing.

Nevertheless, it would be incorrect to conclude that the Hawaiian family has become as liberal as the American. It is true, of course, that around 1930, when the Hawaiian-born began to rebel against their Chinese and Japanese parents and the Oriental practice of arranged marriage, this and other conservative family customs entered a period of rapid decline. Arranged marriage, however, has not disappeared completely. Some Hawaiian-born males have even practiced Japanese yoshi, a custom according to which the oldest daughter of a family that has only female children marries matrilocally and her husband takes her name.[3] Between 1931 and 1936, for instance, the Governor of Hawaii issued 96 decrees of change of name to Hawaiian-born Japanese, 35 of whom mentioned yoshi as the reason. Furthermore, Hawaii has also had a few cases of Japanese shinju, i.e., double suicide for love. In 1938, for example, a Hawaiian-born Japanese couple committed shinju when their immigrant parents disapproved of their relationship. It is interesting to note that the letters left behind by these two young people indicated considerable influence by American courtship patterns and romantic ideals.

In brief, the Hawaiian family is in transition.[4] The conflict between the conservative ideals of Oriental immigrants and the American ways of the Hawaiian-born is still going on. The latter, however, are already more dominant and it is almost certain that the Hawaiian family will soon be as liberal as the American.


## Notes

1. C. N. Starcke. *The Primitive Family in Its Origin and Development*, New York: D. Appleton and Company, 1889, p. 176.
2. Concerning the attitudes of Hawaiians toward various races and nationalities, see Panos D. Bardis, "Social Distance Among Foreign Students," *Sociology and Social Research*, 41 (November–December, 1956), p. 113.
3. "The practice of naming a man after his wife" is known as gyneconymy. See Panos D. Bardis, "Four New Concepts in Family Sociology," *Alpha Kappa Deltan*, 27 (Winter, 1957), p. 16.
4. Panos D. Bardis, "Attitudes Toward Dating Among Foreign Students in America," *Marriage and Family Living*, 18 (November, 1956), pp. 342–343.

# On Portuguese Family Structure

*Emilio Willems*

This paper[1] is an attempt to examine certain relationships between family structure and social class in contemporary Portuguese
society. We are promarily concerned with two structural variables,
namely the locus of authority in the family and its structural range
beyond the limits of the nuclear or conjugal core unit. In other
words, the questions we propose to raise are these: who is subordinate to whom, and what consanguine, affinal and ceremonial
relatives of a given individual are actually tied to him by reciprocal
obligations and privileges.

Our basic hypothesis that these two structural variables are functions of social class, is predicated upon the Brazilian model of the
historical, patripotestal, extended family which is regarded as integral part of the Portuguese heritage. Here authority is concentrated
and vested in the oldest male who exercises considerable control
over his unmarried and married children, their wives and children.
An elaborate set of rules places very definite restrictions on female
behavior outside the narrow circle of family and kin group, and
limits contact between persons of different sex not closely related
to one another, to carefully defined and rigidly controlled situations.
Thus the sexes are segregated early, the women secluded and female
behavior restricted by rather complex canons of chaperonage. The
rules of kinship solidarity extend to a variable number of collateral
relatives of any particular family head, especially to the families of
his siblings and their linear descendents' families. These groups
include baptismal godparents, and if such ritual relationships happen to coincide with consanguine or affinal ones they tend to reinforce these beyond the ordinary degree of kinship solidarity.

From *International Journal of Comparative Sociology*, September, 1962, 3(2),
pp. 65–79. Reprinted by permission of the Editor, I.J.C.S.

The closest approximation to this model is found only in the traditional family structure of the landed upper class of Brazilian society. Gilberto Freyre has shown that Brazilian "rural patriarchalism" already changed under the impact of nineteenth century urbanization. (Freyre, 1936). It has since undergone further changes of the kind that may be expected in a society which is rapidly becoming industrialized. The family of the working class, both rural and urban, is not, and probably never was, either patripostal or extended. It lacks the centripetal power of the latifundium with its associate political incentives for concerted action on the part of the kinship group. In contrast with the upper and middle class family, the lower class family is loosely integrated and relatively unstable. Norms concerning sex, courtship, marriage, child rearing, economic obligations and care for the old and invalid are rather vaguely defined and subject to local and individual variations. (Willems, 1952:65–78; 1953)

## The Family of the Portuguese Bourgeoisie

The descriptive model of the traditional Brazilian family applies, *mutatis mutandis,* to the Portuguese upper class family. Like its Brazilian counterpart it is patripotestal, even in contemporary urban society which is still predominantly preindustrial. What Moigénie had to say about the "women of Lisbon" did no justice at all to the lower classes, or to the peasantry, as we shall see, but it was certainly meant to include all strata of Portuguese bourgeoisie.

> Formerly—half a century ago—the women of Lisbon exhibited some characteristics of Circassian harem inmates. They never descended from their carriages, not even to buy a scarf or a soft drink. They concealed and veiled themselves.
> It was prohibited to look around and smile. Social disgrace hung over a lady who caught a cold during a drive. She had to refrain from sneezing in order not to be regarded as uncouth. Dancing parties were parades of statues and conversations parades of monosyllables.
> Whenever they knew how to read, they were unable to go beyond the prayer book. When they could cook, they were only permitted to make sweets. A lady who sang either fell into complete disrepute, or was at least regarded as *comical,* which was a grave insult at that time. It was morally bad for a woman to attend a theatrical performance outside her private box, where she was expected to sit haughtily and silent in Olympian stiffness. (Moigénie, 1924:246)

Nowadays, the great granddaughters of Moigénie's grand ladies go to high school and college as a matter of course. There are women lawyers and women doctors, saleswomen and female clerks, and grade school is predominantly taught by women. Yet in the early thirties, provincial capitals like Beja, still exhibited some of the Moorish traits depicted by Moigénie. Upper class women were almost never seen in the streets and stores. Strangely enough, they appeared not even in church. Purchases were mediated by servants who carried samples of merchandise home, where the lady of the house did her picking. Courtship was restricted to few occasions, such as public feasts, trade fairs, hunting parties and family picnics. Had the lovers reached an understanding their contacts were not allowed to go beyond the verbal stage wherein the lover talked from the sidewalk to the girl who stood at a window of the first floor. Only engaged couples were allowed in the fiancee's home, naturally always in the presence of elder relatives. Furthermore, mating was highly assortative or homogamous: the local "elites" were not only class-conscious, but also likely to repudiate strangers from other provinces or regions as potential family members.

Doubtlessly, both married and unmarried women are now seen in the streets, and the relations between the sexes are less restricted but otherwise Beja of 1954 is still very much like Beja of 1930. Women never appear in cafés where men spend most of their leisure time. Even in downtown Lisbon, the patrons of the numerous cafés are almost all men. The changes which have taken place in the middle and upper class family, appear to be, as in Brazil, rather peripheral. The patripotestal traditions are still intact; hymenolatry and the "virginity complex," associated with well defined double standards of sex morals and family honor, are virtually indistinguishable from analogous phenomena in Brazil.

Although the neolocal, conjugal family undoubtedly prevails over any form of joint household, Ego is usually part of an extensive and closely knit group of kinsfolk. Two examples taken from the upper class of Porto, a city of 258,000 inhabitants (in 1940) may illustrate the structural intricacies of such kin groups.

## Case 1

Ego, his wife and children, as well as his married sister, her husband and children joined their parental household thus conforming to the wishes of the father.

As in some other cases, Ego's family feels more closely attached to the maternal than to the paternal line. There are a number of ritual celebrations such as birthdays, Christmas, Epiphany, New Year, which bring Ego's family together with his maternal grandmother, her siblings and their spouses and offspring. The *ceia de Natal* (Christmas supper), the most elaborate and solidarity-reinforcing event of the annual cycle, assembles the living and deceased members of the group. After the living have retired to bed, the table is rearranged, food and wine are served and the lights left burning for the dead who are thus invited to have their share.

Each summer the whole kin group meets on the beach or in some resort town for a period of vacation. Economic assistance and promotion of business interests are of course major objectives of the group. In-group marriages are common, and sometimes they are arranged to assuage the financial worries of a hard-pressed branch of the group. As a matter of fact, the numerous gatherings and celebrations are looked upon as suitable opportunities for courtship under the subtle and astute influence of older relatives. Five in-group marriages occurred, and all participants were still alive in 1954. (1) Ego himself married a daughter of his maternal grandmother's brother. (2) Ego's sister married a brother of his maternal grandmother's brother's wife. The three other marriages took place between (3) a son of Ego's maternal grandmother's brother, and a daughter of Ego's maternal grandmother's brother's wife's sister; (4) another son of Ego's maternal grandmother's brother's one of the two daughters, of Ego's maternal grandmother's brother; (5) another daughter of Ego's maternal grandmother's (second) brother, and a son of Ego's maternal grandmother's first brother's wife's sister.

In addition to being in-group or even consanguine marriages, three of these unions reveal a tendency toward what might be called *cumulative connubial association* of otherwise unrelated families. Marriages 2, 3, and 5 took place between one of Ego's maternal relatives and persons whose families had already been attached to Ego's family by a previous marriage. The principle inherent in these marriages may tentatively be formulated as *particularized homogamous mating.* Case 2 illustrates this aspect even more pointedly.

## Case 2

In contrast with the first case its consanguine marriages are bilaterally oriented. Three such marriages took place:
1. Ego (female) married one of her father's half-brothers.

2. Ego's brother married a daughter of one of his mother's three sisters.
3. The daughter of one of Ego's father's half-brothers married a son born to the previous couple.

For many years Ego's family of orientation shared the residence of a family of the same (upper middle-class) level. In the course of time relationships between the two families became intimate enough to constitute a mutually desirable mating circle for their younger members. As a matter of fact, four members of Ego's family married into family B.

1. Ego's sister married a son of Armando's (head of B) brother.
2. A daughter of one of Ego's father's five brothers married one of Armando's sons.
3. A daughter of another of Ego's father's brothers married Armando's second son.
4. One of Ego's mother's sister's sons married the daughter of Armando's wife's sister.

Furthermore, a son born to family number 4 married a daughter of Armando's wife's sister's son.

Particularized homogamous mating, of which some other instances could be observed, rests upon the tendency toward selective restriction of a given mating circle, not merely to the same social class but to a limited number of families or kinship groups which, on the basis of reciprocal *confiança* (trust), have engaged in social intercourse. It seems noteworthy that, at least in the upper strata of Porto, such mating circles counteract, to a certain extent, the secludedness of their female members who are allowed considerable leeway in their domestic contacts with both related and unrelated male members of the circle. The effectiveness of these mating circles is guaranteed as long as the "social life" of their members is centered around the interrelated kinship aggregates.

There is little doubt that Portuguese society, except in the lower classes, is still family ridden, and nowhere is familism more conspicuous than among the upper urban strata of the provinces. Two main factors seem to act as integrative forces in the Portuguese family structure:

1. Economic pursuits and prospects tend to develop within kinship aggregates.
2. Secludedness of the women limits mating to the confines of domestic meeting grounds.

There is evidence that in the past family and kinship heavily encroached on political institutions. Until far into the nineteenth century the local political power structure frequently gravitated around rival kinship groups. (Descamp, 1935: 39–43) To the extent that the national government was able to tighten political controls, the power of these kinship aggregates tended to fade away. Eventually the establishment of a totalitarian regime eliminated parties and political feuds on the local level. At the present time scarcely any vestige of political familism can be discovered.

## The Peasant and the Proletarian Family

The structural differences between the family of the bourgeoisie and the working class are reflected by a complete absence of seclusion of the lower class women. Heavy male emigration, a relatively high natural increase rate (about 1.p.c. between 1940 and 1950), combined with an extremely low income per capita, have forced the women, both married and unmarried, to become breadwinners to an extent which is hardly paralleled by any other European country except perhaps Spain. In the Portuguese working class there is hardly any menial job which is not habitually performed by women. In and around the central market of Lisbon women dominate the streets and stalls as carriers, sellers and buyers of produce. All imaginable kinds of wares are peddled by women in the streets of Lisbon and Porto. Even female stevedores may be seen unloading fishing vessels in the port of Lisbon. Writing in 1935, Descamps noted that "it is the woman who administers, pays taxes, discharges her obligations to the civil registrar, and solves litigations with neighbors." (Descamps, 1935:273)

A similar situation prevails in Portuguese rural society. Below the level of the upper class of absentee owners whose way of life is hardly different from that of the urban bourgeoisie, two strata may be distinguished, a middle class of small landowners and a landless proletariat, but the shrinking size of many holdings makes it virtually impossible to draw a sharp line of demarcation between these two classes.

The small landowner participates in the traditional subsistence economy and to a varying degree in a market economy. He belongs to a local political structure, the village community, and he lives in what some anthropologists have called a "semi-autonomous folk culture." (Fallers, 1961: 108 ff) In other words, he is a peasant and his family is the Portuguese peasant family.

As among the urban workers, sexual division of labor as an institutional arrangement appears to be limited to the household. Outside the household there are few menial occupations or tasks which are not habitually performed by men *and* women, both married and unmarried. Not only do the women participate in practically all kinds of work related to agriculture, they also cut wood, take care of the cattle and build houses. In Beira Baixa, for example, engaged girls are expected to help their fiancés building the traditional stone house which is going to be their home.

Under such conditions the life of the peasant woman can hardly be more secluded than that of the male members of the household. Chaperonage can only be provided to the extent that women move and work in teams. Yet frequently the work groups include men, a fact which facilitates contact and intimacy to an extent which would constitute a grave violation of the sex mores of the bourgeoisie. Indeed, in rural areas courtship is traditionally tied in with certain phases and varieties of work. In most rural areas of Portugal, courtship usually begins with the *derriço*, a phase of secret rendezvous during which the lovers become acquainted with each other. Should they decide on marriage, the swain appears henceforward at the door of the girl's home. In the eyes of the families and the village ( the lovers, who are now *conversados*, have indicated the seriousness of their intentions. To complete the courtship cycle, the young man secures the unpaid services of a go-between who negotiates an agreement with the girl's family. Once a final understanding has been achieved, the lovers are *prometidos* (engaged) and the fiancé is admitted to the girl's home. Economic conditions are such that two, three or more years may elapse between *derriço* and marriage.

Premarital sexual intercourse seems to be a rather common occurrence in rural Portugal. Although frowned upon by the church and public opinion, its practice is probably rooted in ancient folk customs.[2] If the girl becomes pregnant, marriage is apt to ensue very soon, certainly before the birth of the child. It is generally felt, however, that the presence of an illegitimate child does not preclude marriage with somebody else, especially if a substantial dowry is to be expected. Likewise, a dowry or even personal qualities are held to be acceptable compensations for the loss of virginity. In fact, it has been flatly denied that at least in the Alentejo province peasants attribute any value at all to virginity. (Gonçalves, 1922:57) Whatever regional variations there may be regarding the valuation of virginity, they certainly do not suggest any attempt to emulate the sex mores of the upper classes.

Further support for our hypothesis concerning class-conditioned

variants in the family structure was found in the very definite matripotestal slant of the Portuguese peasant family. In the ethnographic
literature there are references to the "matriarchate of the Minho,"
(Descamps, 1935: 84; 191–92; 273; 459–60) but little about other
provinces. The assumption is that a continuous emigration of lower
class males over a period of at least a hundred years has had marked
effects upon the status of the female members of the family. In fact,
some supporting evidence is to be found in descriptive studies of
the nineteenth century. (Macedo, 1974:261) Yet even in provinces
which played a minor role in the history of emigration, matripotestal
tendencies have been recorded. In the Alentejo, for example, one of
the southernmost provinces housewives are clearly in charge of budg-
etary planning and financial expenditures. (Picão, 1947:135) In
some regions such as Trás-os-Montes, which Poinsard considered as
the bulwark of Portuguese patriarchalism (Poinsard, 1910), the situation is somewhat different, although the patriarchal idyl is marred
by certain matrilineal and matriolocal tendencies. The matripotestal
slant of the Alentejo peasant family is further emphasized by matrilineal accretions to the nuclear family unit. It is almost invariably
the wife who determines which invalid, old or poor relatives are to
be accepted as permanent members of the household. And she refuses to put up with anybody except members of her own family of
orientation. The husband has no choice in the matter, mainly because he, as well as his relatives, realize that dependence on charity
would be preferable to their joining his household. (Picáo, 1947:
136–37) Likewise, a childless couple will adopt a youngster from the
wife's family of orientation, preferably one of her sister's children.

Many of our interviewees felt that the matripotestal trend in the
contemporary peasant family is to be regarded as a comparatively
recent development. One author attributes the "decay of paternal
authority" to seasonal migrations in which numerous family heads
have been forced to take part for economic reasons. (Craveiro, 1949:
142) The assertion that the matripotestal trend is recent, at least in
southern Portugal, is also supported by the fact that it has not yet
affected the status of widows who, by communal consent, are not
allowed to remarry. The idea that a widow should spend the rest of
her life in perpetual mourning, as well as the underlying emotions
expressed by ribald folk stanzas[3] strongly suggest patriarchal origin.
It would seem that, if more time had elapsed, matripotestal influences would have modified the status of widows as they actually did
in northern Portugal. The custom of insulting a remarrying widow
with a cacophonous mock serenade during nine consecutive nights

following the marriage ceremony, certainly indicates communal disapproval, yet in the north widows do remarry in spite of such inconveniences. Of course, this aspect calls for further inquiry.

Matripotestal tendencies have also encroached upon the family of Trás-os-Montes, the most isolated and conservative of all Portuguese provinces. Among the lower strata of the Mofreira region married couples are sometimes unable to establish a neolocal household, nor is a joint household with either family of orientation deemed economically feasible. Each spouse instead remains in the parental household which continues to receive the benefits of his or her economic cooperation. The husband spends the nights with his wife in her parental home, and the days with his own family of orientation. If children are born, it is the mother's family that assumes responsibility for their upbringing. Aside from occasional visits to the father's home, the children are under the authority of their mother and her family. However, as soon as death vacates one of the parental homes, husband, wife and children establish a common household. I suggest that this structural arrangement be designated *bipartite* or *ambilocal* family.

Portuguese villages are traditionally endogamous, and the fine which in some regions the young villagers jokingly collect from outmarrying individuals, may be interpreted as a survival of stricter sanctions. Indeed there are recorded cases of mutually hostile villages whose inhabitants forcefully prevent people from inter-marrying (Descamps, 1935:17). In the relatively rare instances of exogamous marriages the rule of residence is strictly matrilocal (Dias, 1953:137).

In the Minho province, inheritance of names and property frequently follows matrilineal rules. Descamps found that "the women constitute the most stable part of the population. There are also numerous cases where the female line prevails so far as names and inheritance are concerned. Nowadays, official records require family names, yet in the current language of the people only first names are known. One does not say "José, filho de Pedro," but, "José, filho de Maria," or "simply "o José de Maria." If he marries Luisa, he becomes "o José de Luisa." And the latter becomes a "Luisa do José de Maria." (Descamps, 1935:70).

In northern Portugal, a son sometimes inherits his father's name, while a daughter is named after her mother. As a rule, the name of the *casa* (house) including all movable and immovable property, prevails over individual names. Thus, when the *casa* is inherited by a daughter, her husband not only moves into the casa but takes her name as well. (Dias, 1953:134)

A further matripotestal element may be seen in the status of the widow in communal structures of the Minho. She inherits the position which the husband held as a full-fledged member of the local *junta* or assembly of voters. (Dias, 1948:56) Such rights, however, are denied to widows in communities with similar structures in Trás-os-Montes. (Dias, 1953:145)

Another aspect of the Portuguese peasant family concerns the structural arrangements which are related to population pressure and the relative scarcity of land. How does the peasant family react to this problem?

It ought to be borne in mind that in the culture under scrutiny, as probably in most peasant cultures, landownership represents a focal value. Not only is it economically relevant, it is, to put it plainly, the thing that makes life worth living, above and beyond the economic security it may provide. Even emigration to foreign countries has been conceived of as a device to retain or to recuperate, under increasingly difficult economic conditions, the status attached to landownership in the native community. This is illustrated by the number of returning migrants, usually called "Brazilians" who invest their savings in a prestige-carrying *quinta*, a kind of farm owned by the rural gentry.

It is not surprising at all, therefore, that most aspects of the family structure are subordinate to the question of how to keep or expand the family property. As the land is divided upon the death of its owner, many of the inheriting children receive less than necessary to make a living. At any rate, whether the inherited property is too small or barely large enough to raise a family, the owner will make every conceivable effort to buy additional land. If this can be accomplished by keeping unmarried sons and daughters on the farm, the expansion of the family land, with its inherent rewards in terms of prestige and status improvement, is then recognized as the supreme goal which is to be pursued to the detriment of individual goals. As this can be achieved only by keeping consumption at the level of the barest minimum, extreme frugality must be accepted as a way of life. As soon as a small fund has been accumulated, it is immediately invested in the purchase of additional land.[4] Ultimately, the concerted effort of the family will of course revert into the benefit of the inheriting children. Their contributions in terms of labor are thus not one-sided obligations, but based upon expectations of delayed reciprocity.

Frequently the parental holdings or their rate of increase are too small to anticipate a distribution commensurable with the initial minimal needs of a neolocal household. In such cases, a young man is allowed to accept wage earning part-time jobs. He may obtain some additional cash by raising sheep on the family pastures. If he is a hard worker he may be able to accumulate a few thousand *escudos* which will help him establish a household of his own. In most cases, this turns out to be a time-consuming process, and late marriage is the rule rather than the exception among peasants. (Teixeira, 1940:3–7)

Marriage usually involves some distribution of parental property. Daughters receive a dowry whose value is measured in *lençoes* (bed sheets), although the dowry is by no means to be considered as a *conditio sine qua non*. If no surplus land is available for a marrying son, he may be given some animals or agricultural machinery. Many newly established households receive weekly contributions in flour, vegetables and meat from either spouse's family or orientation.

Whenever the number of unmarried children exceeds the labor demand of a household, some of them are allowed to accept jobs in distant places. They are expected to save money and to return to the village sooner or later. The numerous servantry which is found in middle and upper class urban homes is largely recruited from peasant families. These girls regularly contribute a considerable part of their wages to the parental household. Their loyalty to family and village is reflected by the observance of homogamous rules of courtship which limit suitable choices to spatially circumscribed mating circles. Most of these girls, as well as the majority of the men, are unable to conceive of marriage as divorced from family and community.

In some parts of the North, especially in the Minho, the eldest son is expected to take over the economic responsibilities of the deceased father.

Sometimes, local customs prevent the division of family holdings, as in certain parts of the Minho and Trás-os-Montes. Only one son, usually the eldest, is allowed to marry. To keep the family small, the father tends to postpone such a decision as long as possible. The marying son inherits the parental property undivided, yet he is expected to assume responsibility for his unmarried siblings who come to share the privileges and duties of his household. There is no evidence that such a household ever becomes a *de facto* fraternal polyandry. As the unmarried male members of the family may obtain sexual gratification within the village celibacy is not felt to be an intolerable burden.[5]

It is expected that all valid members of such a joint family work for the common household, but usually the unmarried males are allowed to fatten a few sheep on the family pastures and to keep the profit obtained from the sale of these animals.

While the occurrence of this kind of joint family is restricted to a few regions, the *famille-souche*, as described by Le Play, is found all over Portugal. Both types are sanctioned by special provisions of the Civil Code which explicitly recognizes the *Sociedade Familiar*.[6] According to its stipulations, the *Sociedade* comprehends the

> "use of and the income from the property of its members, and the products of their labor and industry, and the possessions which the members own individually." (Article 1284)

Furthermore, the code defines the economic responsibilities which the *Sociedade* assumes toward its individual members. (Article 1285) The fact that the law recognizes a *tacit* constitution of the *Sociedade Familiar* after a year of spontaneous sharing of residence and food, income and expenditure, gains and losses, indicates that its legal structure was merely superposed upon an already existing social institution.[7]

In many villages of the Minho and Trás-os-Montes the fraternal joint household was formerly the only existing family type. Since World War I there has been an increasing number of men who prefer marriage and economic insecurity to celibacy and the security of a joint household. Although they would legally be entitled to a share of the parental estate, *if* they requested dissolution of the *Sociedade Familiar*, no such case could be discovered. In one community of Trás-os-Montes, Dias found fourteen neolocal families living precariously on inferior tracts of land which hitherto had not been cultivated at all. Economic insecurity as well as the fact that the heads of these families are not entitled to membership in the communal council indicate that the breach of the traditional family structure has had stratifying effects on a formerly non-stratified community. (Dias, 1953:136–37)

Increasing population pressure and scarcity of arable land make it impossible for a large proportion of peasants to earn a living merely by cultivating their own holdings or to keep their unmarried children on the farm. As indicated already many are forced to seek, at least temporarily, employment in nearby cities or towns. Since industry offers few opportunities, domestic services, agricultural wage earning and emigration appear to be the most frequently chosen solution of a problem of mounting gravity. Many small landowners leave their farms for several months every year to work for large landholders, mainly in the southern part of Portugal. In the meanwhile their own farms are worked by their wives and younger children. As they grow up, they may take the place of their father. Among the seasonal migrants there are numerous groups of unmarried women who, under the leadership of a *manageira,* hire themselves out to harvest the wheat and rice crops of the southern latifundia. The *manageira* is a middle-aged woman, often a widow, who is expected to maintain at least a semblance of respectability. Needless to say the conditions under which seasonal migrants work and live are miserable even by local standards. Seasonal migration has probably contributed to a gradual weakening of the patripotestal traditions of the peasant family in Portugal.

Finally a very large proportion of people of peasant stock are landless rural laborers. According to the national census of 1953, 388,633 or 49.1 per cent of all heads of agricultural families of Portugal were found to be in that category. Most of these rural laborers live in villages associated with or located on latifundia. Upon studying such a village in the Alentejo province, Descamps wrote that "people seldom marry. Two young people may establish a household; sometimes they separate and sometimes they live together all their life. When there are two or three children, the parents may decide on a civil marriage." (Descamps, 1935:213) Our own survey of Canhestros, another Alentejo village, confirmed Descamps' observations. The range of permissible alternatives concerning courtship and marriage is wide and loosely defined. Church control is almost non-existent. Canhestros with its 700 inhabitants, has neither church nor priest, and most marriages are of the common-law type. Frequently, a young couple does not even bother about securing parental assent to establishing a household, an attitude that would scarcely be conceivable among landowning peasants. The extended family is conspicuously absent, and complaints about insufficient care for the old and invalid members of the family are common. All inhabitants of Canhestros are rural laborers who earn cash wages on the surrounding latifundia. They are not given any land to cultivate, as they would in Latin America under similar conditions.

The question as to whether or not the family of the lower rural classes of Portugal is to be classified as peasant family, is not easy to answer. The people are certainly of peasant stock, their way of life is very similar to that of peasants, but they are neither landowners nor engaged in subsistence farming, although their occupation is exclusively concerned with agriculture. Politically and economically, they are completely dependent upon the latifundia owners of the region. A considerable degree of anomic relationships found within the family seems to be incompatible with the structure of the genuine peasant family. Future attempts towards classification should probably be preceded by more intensive research. This suggestion applies to the migratory as well as to the sedentary portion of the rural laborers of Portugal.

## Ceremonial Kinship

The institution of the *compadrio* (co-parenthood) constitutes a triangular relationship between the baptismal godparents and godchild on the one hand, and between the biological parents and the co-parents on the other. *Compadre* and *comadre* are, according to Catholic church norms, "spiritual parents" of the godchild.[8] Theirs is the responsibility to see that the godchild is brought up as a good Catholic, but the mores go beyond such spiritual relationship and impose economic responsibilities in the case of a premature death of either or both biological parents. Marriages between baptismal godparents and godchild are prohibited by church law and custom. In some parts of Portugal (in Trás-os-Montes for example) people believe that a child born out of an incestuous relationship between godparent and godchild becomes a werewolf. (Vasconcellos, 1882: 264) Marriages or sexual intercourse between godparents and biological parents are likewise regarded as incestuous, and any offspring of such a union will be a werewolf unless this fate is prevented by the ritual burning of the first shirt worn by such a child. (Vasconcellos, 1882:264)

The prohibition of carnal relationships between co-parents and biological parents does not imply avoidance. Much on the contrary, friendship, mutual trust and cooperation are regarded as desirable traits of ceremonial kinship ties. Within such a group the male members are addressed as *compadres*, the female members as *comadres*. Co-parents may belong to the same social class or to a superordinate class. In the former case either previously existing friendship or blood relationships determine the choice of the godparents. However, if these belong to a superordinate class, the biological father is apt to be an actual or potential employee of the godfather, and the relationship tends to be of the patronal kind.

Whether relatives or not, godparents are supposed to be at least one generation removed from the godchild. The choice of an older brother or somebody else belonging to the generation of the godchild is frowned upon as "lack of respect." In fact, the parish priests refuse to accept godparents whose age precludes effective fulfillment of responsibilities toward the godchild.

A further prerequisite for the choice of suitable godparents is the absence of love relationships between them, for this would mean a violation of incest rules. Nor should the choice of the godmother fall upon a pregnant woman because this would spell "bad luck" for the unborn child, while the fate of the godchild would not be affected by the state of pregnancy. (Braga, 1924:38)

The sacredness of ceremonial kinship ties has been pointed out many times. It would seem that, particularly in the more isolated provinces, the *compadrio* almost supersedes consanguine relationship. Descamps noted that "the ties between two compadres are more sacred than those relating two brothers to each other. In fact, it happens that two brothers quarrel and go on quarreling all their life, but the friendship between two compadres is indissoluble. The only way to reconcile two quarreling brothers is to make them compadres. It is a true *artificial kinship* superseding blood relationships." (Descamps, 1935:192–193) The *campadrio* may thus perform the additional function of straightening out brittle family relationships. With the exception of the grandparents, relatives who become godparents are addressed as *padrinhos e madrinhas* by their godchildren.

The relationship between godparents and godchildren are ritualized by the *pedido de bencao* (literally: request for blessing) and the *folar*. Among the peasantry at least, whenever a godchild meets a godparent he greets him with a ceremonial *"bencao, padrinho,"* and the godparent answers: *"Deus te abençoe."* (God bless you). Formerly, the *folar* was a kind of bread, which the afilhado offered to his padrinho on Easter Sunday, but nowadays it may be any gift, which is promptly repaid by a return gift. This ceremonial exchange of gifts apparently serves the function of reconfirming mutual responsibilities. In northern Portugal the day following the marriage ceremony, bridegroom and bride take the *fatia* (usually a *pão-de-ló* or sponge cake) to their padrinhos' houses. This act marks the formal termination of the responsibilities which baptismal padrinhos assume towards their godchildren. However, a "good" padrinho never ceases to aid his afilhados in difficult situations.

In return for any past or future benefit which an afilhado receives from his padrinho, he is expected to recognize and respect his authority as a potential father, but he has no responsibilities towards his godparents if these become old, sick or invalid. When a padrinho dies, his afilhados carry the coffin to the grave. There is an official mourning period which may extend up to six months during which the women wear black dresses and the men a black ribbon on their lapels.

Godparents are expected to be generous. A generous padrinho offers clothes, money and sometimes jewelry to his godchildren. It is not unusual for a good padrinho to contribute towards the education and marriage of his afilhado. And he may help him to find a job if he is in a position to do so. The emoluments connected with the baptism of a child are the responsibility of his padrinho, but among the peasants of the Minho the father of the child repays the generosity of his compadre with a gift whose value is equal to such ceremonial expenditures.

In emergency situations, especially when an unbaptized child is dying, a saint may be chosen as padrinho, if nobody else is available. One cannot let a child die without supernatural protection, for *quem não tem padrinho morre mouro* (The one who has no godfather dies as a Moor).

The obligations imposed by the compadrio are not always taken as seriously as the foregoing description seems to imply. Above all, there are regional differences affecting the expectations which people attach to the choice of a godparent. Alentejo province seems to be the *terra de compadres* par excellence where obligations are apt to be discharged in conformity with traditional norms. This probably applies to the more isolated regions in general, but among the owners of minifundia, as well as the migrant and the landless rural proletarians little, if anything, may be expected from a compadrio relationship, unless it cuts across class lines. Even so, a big landowner is likely to have scores of godchildren among his laborers, and the example of Canhestros seems to indicate that the institution is hardly more than a gesture of condescendence on the part of the *latifundiários*. Many of our peasant interviewees stressed the importance of the compadrio, but at the same time they complained about an increasing tendency to ignore the responsibilities inherent in the compadrio relationship. In the cities, the compadre de *ocasião* seems to prevail, i.e. one chooses baptismal godparents merely to fulfill a church requirement, but a *padrinho* is no longer expected to fulfill the obligations of a substitute father.

## Conclusions

The Portuguese upper class has retained, in spite of peripheral changes, its patripotestal and extended character. Sometimes it is a joint family in the residential sense of the term, for a married son with his wife and children may continue to live in his parents' household. However, most households are neolocal, but related families tend to form a closely knit unit which appears functionally adapted to urban life, mainly by promoting the business interests of its members and by providing financial aid to younger or unsuccessful members of the group. The attractiveness of these services is enhanced by the limited opportunities of an essentially pre-industrial setting. Consanguine marriages are common, and connubial associations between unrelated kingroups are reinforced by repeated intermarriages of their members. Within rigidly drawn class lines mating circles are established which offer opportunities for social intercourse, and thus counteract the traditional secludedness of the women.

The sex mores of the peasantry and the proletariat are different, and in some respects diametrically opposed to those of the urban middle and upper classes. Full participation of the women in breadwinning activities preclude the sort of male dominance which is still the prevailing pattern in Portuguese bourgeoisie. The matripotestal slant of the peasant family in some regions seems to be due to seasonal migrations or emigration to foreign lands of numerous family heads and unmarried sons. The value attributed to land ownership above and beyond its economic significance tends to delay marriage of adult children who prefer to work for the parental household in order to increase their share of inherited land. Whenever the family holding is too small to absorb domestic labor, unmarried sons and daughters are allowed, at least temporarily, to hire themselves out on wage-earning jobs. However, they are expected to remain loyal to family and village, and to aid the parental household by turning over part of their wages.

Two types of the joint family were observed in Portugal. One is the *famille-souche*, or stem family, and the other may be called fraternal family in which unmarried sons live together with the nuclear family of the brother who inherits the family holding undivided. While the former type prevails in all parts of rural Portugal, the latter is restricted to certain regions of the north. Both types are recognized by the legal institution of the *Sociedade Familiar*. In contrast to the tightly integrated peasant family, the family of the rural and urban proletariat is loosely structured and relatively unstable, with a strong tendency towards anomie.

While ceremonial kinship ties are weak or non-existent in other classes they have retained considerable vitality among the peasantry.

Surrounded by prohibitions and magical beliefs, they still perform the functions of expanding the family circle and of reinforcing existing kinship ties whenever ceremonial kinship coincides with biological or affinal kin relationships.

# References

BRAGA, ALBERTO V., 1924, *Dos Guimaraes: Tradiçoes e usanças populares*. Espozende.

CRAVEIRO, MARIA ANGELA ALVES DE SOUZA, 1949, *Monografia de S. Vincente da Bairo*. Lisboa: Instituto de Serviço Social. MS.

DESCAMPS, PAUL, 1935, *Le Portugal: La vie sociale actuelle*. Paris: Firmin-Didot.

DIAS, JORGE, 1948, *Vilarinho da Furna. Uma aldeia comunitária*. Pôrto: Instituto para a Alta Cultura. Centro de Estudos de Etnologia Peninsular.

——— 1953, *Rio de Onor. Comunitarismo agro-pastoril*. Pôrto: Instituto para a Alta Cultura. Centro de Estudos de Etnologia Peninsular.

FALLERS, L. A., 1961, "Are African Cultivators to be Called Peasants"? *Current Anthropology*, Volume 2, No. 2.

FREYRE, GILBERTO, 1936, *Sobrados e mucambos: decadência do patriarchado rural no Brasil*. S. Paulo: Companhia Editora Nacional.

GONCALVES, LUIS DA CUNHA, 1922, *A vida rural do Alentejo*. Coimbra.

LEZON, D. MANUAL, 1903, *El derecho consuetudinario de Galicia*. Madrid: Imprenta del Asilo de Huerfanos.

MACEDO, ANTONIO DA COSTA DE SOUZA DE, 1874, *No Minho*. Lisbôa: Imprensa Nacional.

MOIGENIE, VICTOR DE, 1924, *A mulher em Portugal*. Pôrto: A. Figueirinhas.

PICAO, JOSE DA SILVA, 1947, *Através dos campos: usos e costumes agricoloalenteianos*. Lisbôa: Neogravura.

POINSARD, LEON, 1910, Le Portugal inconnu. *La Science Sociale*, 25:

TEIXEIRA, CARLOS, 1940, *A mulher portuguesa e o seu papel bio-sociológico*. Porto: Congresso Nacional de Ciências da Populaçao.

VASCONCELLOS, J. LEITE DE, 1882, *Tradiçoes populares de Portugal*. Porto:

WILLEMS, EMILIO, 1952, *Buzios Island. A Caiçara Community in Southern Brazil*, Monographs of the American Ethnological Society XX. Locust Valley, New York: J. J. Augustin.

——— 1953, "The structure of the Brazilian Family." *Social Forces*, 31:339–345.

# Notes

1. The field work upon which the present paper is based was carried out during the months of June, July and August, 1954. It was made possible by grants from the Social Science Research Council and the Institute of Research and Training in the Social Sciences of Vanderbilt University. The field trip was preceded by a careful survey of Portuguese ethnographic literature.

2. Since the early sixteenth century the *Constituiçoes Episcopais* of the Roman Catholic Church insisted on prohibiting sexual intercourse among engaged persons. Apparently the church has never been able to eradicate this practice. At the present time, premarital intercourse seems to be most common where church control has been traditionally weak.

3. The emotions are sexual jealousy and contempt for whom has been "used" by a predecessor.

4. This tendency counteracts, to a limited extent, the excessive fragmentation of rural holdings which are customarily distributed among outmarrying children. Even so, a law was inacted to prevent the division of holdings inferior to one hectare. (Affonso, 1944:165–66)

5. In most villages some sort of prostitution is accepted as an "inevitable evil." The village whore may be a young girl who has been deserted by her seducer, or a widowed or deserted woman without a family to lean upon. In sharp contrast with Brazil, a girl who engages in a number of informal affairs for the sake of material gain may eventually find a husband if she is discreet enough not to incur the ostracism of her family. At any rate, "women who do a favor," as people call notorious village whores, resort to prostitution to supplement their meager income which is derived from some respectable occupation.

6. Article 1281 of the Civil Code stipulates that "a family association is one which may be organized among siblings, or among parents and major children."

7. Similar recognition was given to the Compania Familiar Galega, the extended rural family of the Spanish province of Galicia whose culture closely resembles that of Portugal. (Lezón, 1903:29–30)

8. Only the institution of the *baptismal* compadrio has been considered in the present paper.

# Home and Family [of Mennonites in Paraguay]

*J. Winfield Fretz*

Among Mennonite social institutions in South America the family occupies by far the most important place. It is the chief source of population increase and the main agency for training children and transmitting traditions and culture from generation to generation. In the geographically and culturally isolated areas where the Mennonite communities are located, the family takes on a doubly important role which may be characterized by its sanctity, unity, and permanence. It stands in sharp contrast to the atomized family of more highly urbanized and secularized societies. While the Mennonite family possesses stability, it must not be concluded that stability is necessarily synonymous with happiness.

The average size of a Mennonite family in Paraguay in 1967 was 5.3. In Menno the families were largest, with an average of 6.0 per

Vital Family Statistics
Five Mennonite Colonies in Paraguay

| Colony | Inhabitants | Families | 1967 Marriages | Births | Deaths | Average Family Size |
|--------|------------|----------|----------------|--------|--------|---------------------|
| Menno | 5179 | 863 | 45 | 224 | 22 | 6.0 |
| Fernheim | 2631 | 535 | 21 | 77 | 12 | 4.9 |
| Neuland | 1370 | 306 | 7 | 41 | 7 | 4.5 |
| Friesland | 921 | 187 | 9 | 23 | 2 | 4.9 |
| Volendam | 638 | 148 | 3 | 22 | 5 | 4.3 |
| Total | 10739 | 2039 | 85 | 387 | 48 | 5.3 |

From *Pilgrims in Paraguay* by J. Winfield Fretz. Copyright 1953 by Mennonite Publishing House, Scottdale, Pa. Used by permission.

family, whereas in Volendam families were smallest. Here the average was 4.3.

## Family Organization

When speaking of South American Mennonites, it must be borne in mind that they do not all fit into the same mold. There is variation from colony to colony. The Mennonites who came from Canada in 1926 and again in 1948 show much less change in family ideals and structure than those who came from Russia and encountered all of the fragmenting effects of being violently uprooted. More than three fourths of the 2,600 Mennonite families in Paraguay have experienced the tensions and terrors resulting from war, famine, and revolution. Most of them have had to undergo years of wandering, followed by the strain of colonizing in a new geographical and cultural environment as penniless refugees. The experiences encountered in these disrupted years have required tremendous adjustments, and naturally introduced some unconventional ideas and practices. In spite of these required accommodations, the large majority of Mennonites still hold to the traditional and conventional Christian views of the family.

The father is the unquestioned head of the family, and in case of death is normally succeeded by the oldest son. The family can be said to be patriarchal, but it is not a tyrannical nor absolute patriarchy. The father, while the highest authority in the family, never-the-less has limits to his power. The extent and use of his authority is defined in the Scriptures in such passages as: "Husbands, love your wives, and be not bitter against them,"[1] and "Likewise, ye husbands, dwell with them according to knowledge, giving honour unto the wife, as unto the weaker vessel, and as being heirs together of the grace of life; that your prayers be not hindered."[2] This means that family administration is to be seasoned and governed by Christian love. Religious mottoes such as: "Christ is the head of this house," found on the walls of Mennonite homes, serve as constant reminders to parents and children alike that all are under the care and direction of a higher authority.

Marriage is sacred and the rules of courtship and marriage are rather well defined. The conventional dating pattern common in North America is neither practiced nor tolerated in the South American colonies. Young people may fraternize informally at times of church gatherings, such as weddings, funerals, and religious holidays, but the idea of a young man or woman dating many different individuals is as unfamiliar to the young people in the colonies as it was to our grandparents.

## Home and Family

Long engagements are discouraged, and in the more conservative groups, not permitted. It is customary for the minister to announce engagements at the close of a Sunday morning worship service. The normal period of engagement is from two to six months. All weddings must be announced at least two weeks before the wedding, and engagements are to be announced as soon as they are made. The typical couple, after it announces its engagement, visits around in the homes of the community during the weeks preceding the wedding. On the evening before the wedding, the young people gather for what is called Polterabend. In North America, the closest comparison is a shower for the bride. At this social occasion those who come bring wedding gifts, and remain for an evening of fun. The program usually includes recitations consisting of original humorous verses written by one of the local wits about the wedding couple, group singing of folk songs, and playing of folk games. Several guitars and violins are usually brought together to provide instrumental music and add to the singing and general merriment.

The wedding day, which is usually set for a Thursday or a Saturday, is an important occasion for a whole village, in fact, often for a large share of an entire colony. It is customary to invite all families in the village of the bride, and if the groom is from a neighboring village, the people from that village are invited also. In one of the older colonies, the writer was told by a recent bride's father that his family had invited seventy-four families and over 400 guests attended. At this particular wedding the guests consumed an entire beef, forty large cakes, and two giant kettles of *Borscht*.[3] Not all wedding meals are this elaborate. Sometimes only coffee, *Zwieback*, and cookies are served.

The wedding ceremony is a simple yet impressive service. It is customary to have at least two ministers at the wedding. The service is very much like a normal service. It is begun with the singing of one or two hymns. This is followed by two sermons, a short and a long one. Next the vows are exchanged. Choir music is interspersed throughout the service. The marriage party does not exchange rings. The writer was told that among the Mennonites from Russia this custom had been dropped as a result of the difficult experiences encountered during the years of famine and civil war. The Canadian

Mennonites never adopted the custom because of opposition to the wearing of jewelry as contrary to Christian simplicity.

While all marriages are sacred and it is impossible to be married without a minister, not all of the colony people are church members. There is some variation among the colonies on the matter of eligibility for marriage. Where Mennonites came from Russia, it is the practice of ministers to marry couples who are not necessarily baptized church members, although naturally an effort is made to have all candidates for marriage accept the Christian vows and join the church. In Menno, Bergthal, and Sommerfeld church membership is a prerequisite both to marriage and the right to hold colony property.

Family devotions seem to be rather widely practiced, although one gathers the impression that in many cases it is routinely formal. Grace is always said before meals—sometimes silently, sometimes audibly spoken or sung: sometimes it is a memorized prayer, and sometimes a spontaneous one. The practice of using a daily devotional calendar is widespread.[4] In visiting Mennonite homes, the writer seldom discovered the direct use of the Bible in family devotions.

## Women and Children

While the father is the head of the house, the mother is generally highly revered by the children, who seem to be easily and strictly disciplined by either parent. The mother appears to defer to the father in the matter of discipline, as in most other things. A North American visitor is likely to be impressed with the way the woman of the house plays the role of servant. In the writer's many home calls, the woman was seldom present during the visit, and in most instances, where the visit took place over mealtime, only the husband and the guest were seated at the table. The wife generally served the food but only in a few instances did she take part in the conversation. If the visit occurred during midmorning or afternoon, she would generally serve coffee and freshly baked bread or rolls.

All women in Mennonite villages do a great deal of work. They commonly cook for large families, do the family sewing and mending, care for the garden, and do the family laundry by hand or with a crudely built homemade washer. Women commonly look after the poultry and do the milking twice a day. During harvest they also help in the fields, especially in the Chaco during cottonpicking time. There are practically no labor saving devices and no household conveniences. In all Paraguay, there are in the colonies only a few private Mennonite homes that have inside bathrooms with modern plumbing fixtures.

Statistics on Appliances and Motor Vehicles in
Five Mennonite Colonies in 1967

| Colony | Refrigerators | Radios | Trucks | Autos & Jeeps |
|--------|--------------|--------|--------|---------------|
| Menno | 195 | 265 | 18 | 32 |
| Fernheim | 192 | 229 | 52 | 16 |
| Neuland | 57 | 149 | 4 | 20 |
| Friesland | 59 | 68 | 5 | 9 |
| Volendam | 28 | 78 | 1 | 3 |
| Total | 531 | 789 | 80 | 80 |

A person from the highly mechanized and comfortably furnished homes of North America who visits Paraguayan Mennonite homes, feels as if he were suddenly projected into eighteenth-century colonial homes. Few Paraguayan colony housewives enjoy such laborsaving devices as a vacuum cleaner, power washing machine, electric iron, pressure cooker, central heating system, deep freezer, or family automobile. (Mechanization in a modest way began in the late 1950's and as the accompanying table indicates, grew steadily in the 1960's.) The Mennonite home in Paraguay is simple, although generally attractively furnished. It is a relatively self-sufficient producing and consuming unit. There are comparatively few things bought. By far the largest number of items used, such as food, clothing, and furniture, are still produced in the home. This naturally restricts the variety of foods and the number of family conveniences.

In this setting it is obvious that large families are welcomed because children are an asset to both husband and wife. Sons and daughters begin assuming work assignments at a very early age. By the time children are thirteen or fourteen years old, they generally do the job of a grown person. Boys in early adolescence consider it a privilege to be put in charge of a team of horses or in some other way given the responsibility of an adult.

Girls from an early age are required to share in the daily family chores. Water must be drawn from the village or family well for man and beast. Mandioca, the Paraguayan staple vegetable, a substitute for potatoes, must almost daily be dug from the ground, washed, and peeled. The universal task of preparing meals, doing dishes, and cleaning house must, of course, be done daily in Paraguay as everywhere else, except that in Paraguay these chores are more burdensome. Children are given many of these routine duties. The Mennonite families are definitely not child-centered, nor can they be said to be equalitarian in the sense that all members share in the decision-making of the family. Children are definitely pushed in the background when visitors come. They do not customarily eat with adult guests. When children are small, adults generally do not take them to church services.

In the homes of those who came more recently from Russia, one notices a greater degree of equality between children and parents than among the Old Colony Mennonite families. One may suppose that this is due to the different philosophies of education as well as to the liberalizing influences experienced in Russia, and the years of interrupted family life and social upheaval. The shyness and suppression of the children is due in part to isolation and limited social contacts, and in part to the widely held idea among Mennonites that children should be seen but not heard.

## Housing

Mennonite houses in Paraguay are of two distinct architectural types, and are made of two distinct building materials. The first Mennonites in Paraguay were those in the Chaco. All of the Chaco Mennonites built their houses of adobe bricks made out of native clay. The Menno colonists, however, erected many two-story houses as they had been accustomed to doing in Canada. Their sister colonies, Sommerfeld and Bergthal in eastern Paraguay, also erected some two-story houses in 1948, but used wood instead of mud brick as building material. They also commonly excavated basements which is something not done in the Chaco or in Friesland and in Volendam. This may be due in part to the extremely porous soil and to the scarcity of cement. The Friesland and Volendam Mennonites also in eastern Paraguay, where wood is plentiful, have not constructed their houses of wood, but of adobe brick. Neither have they made basements under their homes, although this would have been possible because of the loamy soil. In Fernheim and in Neuland practically all houses are single story adobe brick dwellings.

The interior arrangement of the houses seems to be modeled in part after the pattern previously used, and partly as an accommodation to the environmental conditions. Those coming from Canada modeled after the typical Canadian Mennonite farm home: the kitchen, pantry, livingroom, and perhaps one bedroom downstairs and the rest of the bedrooms upstairs. The Mennonites from Russia, almost without exception, built simple, single-story, three or four-room dwellings. They adopted the native Paraguayan patterns to a greater extent than have the Mennonites from Canada.

There are a variety of interior arrangements and sizes, and yet there is a remarkable uniformity to the houses. They are, with a few exceptions, generally made by the people themselves or possibly with the help of Indian or Paraguayan labor. After the bricks are molded and dried for a few days, they are laid up on walls and plastered with mud. Many of the families whitewash the walls in order to make them more attractive. It is common for houses to have small porches to provide shade in summer and protection from dust storms in winter.

While made of the same substance as that used by Paraguayans, the houses are different in style. The Mennonite homes are much larger and provide more room and greater privacy to family members. The kitchen is generally a small building at a little distance from the main house, or at best it is at one end of the house, often separated by a breezeway. Sometimes it is not much more than an outside oven with a roof overhead as shelter from sun and rain. The interior of the homes seems to have few closets or cupboards. Beds, tables, chests of drawers, benches, chairs, and many other household articles are made by hand in the homes. No furniture was brought along from either Canada or Europe. Most of it was made either by the occupants of the house or by a local carpenter in one of the villages. Such comforts as innerspring mattresses are not to be found in colony homes. Mattresses are generally filled with various types of dried local straws, hulls, or other materials suitable for stuffing.

People who have not experienced the life of the Mennonite house-wife in Paraguay have little idea of the burdens under which she has lived and labored. (In 1967 earthern floors were the rare thing rather than common.) In these early days earthern floors constantly developed holes and rough places on the surface. In dry weather they became dusty and naturally caused children playing on the floor to become quickly soiled. It will seem strange to North Americans, especially the younger generation, when told that the best preserva-tive of these earthen floors was a mixture of fresh cow manure and earth in a one to three ratio. This mixture was periodically smeared over the earthen floors. It laid the dust, smoothed the surface, and gave it a freshly enameled appearance. This same mixture was also used for outside walls of the house. Naturally the task of applying this mud-manure mixture was not a pleasant one, yet it needed to be done every few weeks by the women who wanted to keep their houses neat and in order. Fortunately, there was no offensive odor from this inexpensive floor finish. In a few of the wealthier homes, floors were painted with regular oil paint. The earthern floors were disease bearers. Many of the small children contracted hookworm as early as two years of age, partially, it was believed, because of much direct contact with the earth. The cure, although not a pleasant one for little children, was a day's fasting, plus medicine, and a restricted diet. Today earthen floors in Mennonite houses are the exception rather than the rule.

The colony women naturally desire improvements and relief from the burdensome strains and limitations that come with pioneering. One of the luxuries that women cherish is that of a smooth wooden floor in the house. Running water, of course, is still not found in the homes. Washing is done over the tub and the scrubbing board. In this dry, dusty climate, children naturally get dirty easily, and clothing requires frequent washing. Dry-cleaning services are of course not available in the colonies.

Self-sufficiency is thus reflected by the fact that the building material for the entire house is found directly on the premises or near to it. This includes the mud for the bricks, window frames made out of wood that has been cleared from the land, and roofs out of native thatch found in open grasslands. Joints are made without nails; doors, latches, and knobs are made out of various types of native woods. Ovens are constructed either indoors, or outdoors with burnt brick from ground that was taken from the farmer's land.

The Mennonite homes stand in contrast to the Paraguayan homes because of their larger size, their better-kept condition, and their generally neat appearance. Substantial sheds and stables for implements, wagons, and animals are found on every Mennonite farm, reflecting pride in ownership and responsible stewardship for property. The typical rural Paraguayan house is made of adobe brick walls and split palm posts or thatch for roofs. The house generally consists of two small rooms, separated by an open space of six or eight feet and sheltered by a kind of porch under which a hammock is frequently slung. The walls are smeared inside and outside with mud, and sometimes whitewashed. The typical rural Paraguayan house is seldom fenced in—it seems to rise naturally out of the surrounding landscape. The native trees, shrubs, and bushes give it a kind of rustic "Old Kentucky Home" appearance. The dogs, goats, pigs, chickens, and family pets share the dwellings with about as much freedom as do the children.

In contrast to this, Mennonite women take pride in having artistically arranged and enclosed flower gardens and borders along walks, houses, and fences. This distinction between Mennonite and Paraguayan homes is obvious to any visitor who travels through Paraguay. The house reflects pride of ownership and suggests also its importance as the family center and the little kingdom of each kinship group.

Every visitor to the South American Mennonites is deeply impressed with how much progress has been made in the few years that Mennonites have lived there. It is amazing how much has been done with so little. Equally impressive is the good spirit that prevails in the lives of so many individuals. In spite of all the difficulties, the handicaps, and the poverty, one does not hear a great deal of complaining. Naturally all long, work, and pray for a better and brighter day. The great majority of Mennonites in Paraguay are grateful for the priceless possessions of freedom, peace, and bread. New families are again being started without the terror and fear of being ruthlessly torn apart. Children are again being raised without the agonizing thought of having them indoctrinated with atheism or taught to be spies for the state against their parents. Economic conditions, although exceedingly severe, are accepted because of the hope of a better day. The struggles and hardships of life tend to bind families together into solid social units. The religious faith of the parents and the awareness of heroic achievements of pioneering forefathers in other days all help to encourage the younger generation to persevere and move ahead.

## Family Disorganization

There are two general reasons for family disorganization. One cause is voluntary, the other involuntary. Families that have been broken as a result of the misfortunes of revolution, war, and forced migration are involuntarily broken. Those cases of family disorganization that come about as a result of free choice by one or both parents may be called voluntarily broken homes. The term suggests families that have been broken as a result of desertion, divorce, or full separation.

Of the latter type, there is comparatively little among Mennonites in Paraguay, in spite of the strenuous experiences that approximately 75 per cent of the families in Paraguay have encountered. There are only a few cases of separation on record. Divorce is almost unheard of and is generally unthinkable in the older colonies, although among the recent refugees there are several families where parental relationships are broken or loosely defined. There are a number of unhappily married families, but this is by no means unique among the families in Paraguay. Marriage is accepted as a life contract without any thought of severing the marriage bonds. Men and women who are unhappily married tend to endure each other and work out adjustments, by which means they get along even if not exactly on a romantic basis.

A very genuine moral problem is caused by the large number of families that have come to Paraguay without fathers since 1947. In Russia, from 1933 to 1938, a large number of men were snatched out of homes and sent to prisons and concentration camps. This happened again during the war years of 1941 and 1945.

There are a large percentage of widows, many of them with children, in the new colonies of Volendam and Neuland. For instance at one period in the early history of Neuland, out of 641 families 253, or 40 per cent, were without fathers. In 1951 there were still 177 women who were in some way separated from their husbands and not remarried. In this same colony there were thirty-two men separated from their wives and children. These conditions have given rise to many acute family problems. Among them is the practice of common law marriages; namely, the practice of men and women living together without benefit of legal or religious sanction. The practice cannot be approved, but when one sees the plight of broken families it is not easy to condemn some of these who so choose to alleviate their problems. In Neuland alone there were thirty-five men and 37 women illegally living together as common law husbands and wives. In Volendam, the second new, although smaller colony, the number is proportionately as great. These people are forbidden to remarry by Paraguayan law, unless there is evidence of death on the part of one party. Evidence of death is, of course, difficult to obtain in the case of those whose partners are still un-accounted for in Russia.

The Mennonite churches in Paraguay have attempted to work out a compromise arrangement whereby remarriage is permitted after a waiting period of seven years. If, during this time, neither husband nor wife hears anything from his or her legal partner, either party may then remarry. This practice is not encouraged, but rather tolerated. There are many brave souls among the bereft who still blindly hope for the return of their loved one. In Paraguay one is often reminded of Longfellow's legendary poem, "Evangeline." In Russia and in South America there still are many Mennonite Evangelines searching for their Gabriels.

## Intermarriages

The abnormal situation in the imbalance of the sexes has given rise to a greater than usual tendency toward marriage between Mennonite women and non-Mennonite men. This is especially the case in the cities. This is true not only in Paraguay, but also in the cities of Curitiba and Sao Paulo in Brazil, in Montevideo, Uruguay, and in Buenos Aires, Argentina. Such marriages do not occur so frequently with native Paraguayans or Brazilians, but more frequently with those of German stock who happen to be living in the cities where Mennonite girls work. This situation may correct itself as the ratio of men to women tends to equalize within the next generation.

An interesting aspect of Mennonite family life in South America is the practice of intermarriage within Mennonite groups. Such marriages may take place between individuals from different colonies belonging to the same group, or between individuals of the same colony belonging to different church groups, such as the General Conference, Evangelical Mennonite Brethren, or Mennonite Brethren. In South America the Mennonites show the same behavior pattern as those in North America. Most marriages occur within a church group of a single colony. There is the tendency and the tradition of frowning upon marriage outside the immediate church and colony group. It has been both the tradition and a rigidly enforced church rule that marriage outside the Mennonite Church, and sometimes even outside the specific church group, automatically results in church discipline. Usually it has meant a temporary loss of church membership for the offending party.

The General Conference has permitted intermarriage of its members without penalty, but the Mennonite Brethren and Menno churches have opposed exogamous marriage.[5] In South America, this strict practice of marriage within the group is undergoing changes. Prior to the coming of the 1947–48 groups, there was practically no intermarriage between Fernheim and Menno people. Since the coming of the recent immigrants, intermarriage on a colony basis has increased considerably. During the first four years in Neuland, there are five marriages between individuals from Neuland and Menno. Of these five, three men are from Menno and two girls are from Neuland. In two cases, the wife joined the Menno church, and in one case, the couple belongs to no church. In another case, the wife belongs to the Mennonite Brethren and the husband to the Menno church, but the wife plans to join the General Conference Church. In the fifth case, the wife from Menno is joining the General Conference Church.

During the first four years of Neuland's history there have been over forty marriages between individuals in Neuland and Fernheim. Thus there is growing evidence that intermarriage, both colony-wise and church conference-wise, is taking place in Paraguay. The number of marriages between Mennonites and non-Mennonites in the Paraguayan colonies is practically nil. Family life is thus stabilized even where there is intermarriage on a colony and a denominational basis. Where individuals from different church groups marry, they tend to affiliate with one or the other, although some in the General Conference and Mennonite Brethren have heretofore retained membership in their respective groups. This practice is discouraged in both churches.

## Notes

1. Colossians 3:19.
2. I Peter 3:7.
3. *Borscht* is a specially prepared meat and vegetable soup. It is a universally favorite dish among all Mennonites with a Russian background.
4. This German devotional calendar is somewhat similar to the popular devotional booklet *The Upper Room*, so widely used in North America. It contains Scripture references and homilies for daily use.
5. In South America one is reminded of Kansas in the early part of the twentieth century when marriage was severely frowned upon and practically forbidden between Mennonites of Swiss, Dutch, and Prussian background, even though all were members of the same church conference. Only in recent decades has this situation changed. Even now marriage between Mennonite conference groups is still the exception in North America.

# Trial Marriage in the Andes

*Richard Price*

In this paper[1] I shall first offer a sketch of pre-Columbian marriage in highland Peru, indicating that our sources permit a more comprehensive description than has generally been accepted (Rowe 1946: 285). Then, with the aid of field data from a modern Quechua community, I shall review contemporary Andean marriage patterns, stressing continuity through time. Finally, I will suggest some reasons why so-called "trial marriage," despite more than four centuries of active opposition by the Church and ridicule by the non-Indian highland population, has continued to flourish since before the Inca empire.

Using available ethnohistorical sources, we can discern a "basic pattern" for Quechua marriage which applies equally well to pre-Columbian and contemporary Andean Indians. This pattern includes relatively free adolescent sex relations, a yearlong premarital trial period marked by patrilocal residence and cohabitation of the couple and permitting socially sanctioned separation at any time, and subsequently a marriage ceremony which is binding for life. I hope to demonstrate that neither the Inca nor Roman Catholic marriage ceremonies differed in sociological function from their indigenous precursors and that the "basic pattern" has persisted, relatively unchanged but for this substitution of ceremonies, since before the coming of the Inca.

## Inca Marriage

Among the commoners of the Inca empire, premarital sex relations were common and socially sanctioned. Pedro Pizarro and Cieza

From *Ethnology*, 1965, 4(3), pp. 310–322. Reprinted by permission of the editor, Ethnology.

de Leon, eyewitnesses writing in 1570 and 1550 respectively, both contrast conjugal faithfulness with widespread premarital promiscuity (Pizzaro 1917: 170; Cieza de Leon 1864: 363). Arriaga (1920: 50) noted that Indians readily admitted adultery in confession, "pero la simple fornicación de ninguna manera la tienan por pecado." Father Cobo, perhaps the most reliable chronicler, goes into more detail. Parents allowed complete liberty to their teenage daughters, and no amount of sexual excess was considered offensive or reprehensible. Virginity was considered a definite stagma since "las que estaban doncellas no habian sido de nadie queridas" (Cobo 1893: iii, 37–38). Further evidence that love and marriage were not simply controlled by the state comes from reports of the widespread use of love magic, including potions, charms, and foods, and from a description of two forms of divination practiced by young men in search of a partner (Arriaga 1920: 62–63). Father Murua provides the major conflicting testimony when, in his chapter on crime and punishment, he lists tortures—frequently resulting in death—for both adulterers an done who "tenia exceso con su mujer antes que el Inga se la diese, y al que la tomaba de su motivo" (Murua 1946: 220). It is difficult, however, to reconcile this information with Murua's own reports (cited below), in a chapter on marriage, of publicly sanctioned premarital relations throughout the Inca realm. Perhaps these laws applied only to the nobility; perhaps they were simply never applied. In any case, the great weight of positive testimony leaves little doubt that the commoners of the Inca empire enjoyed and took advantage of considerable premarital sexual liberty.

The earliest reference to "trial marriage," as the Spaniards called a widespread "diabolical" custom of the Indians, dates from 1539, less than a decade after Pizarro's landing (Valcárcel 1945: 146–147). A Church document of the early 1550s described *pantanacuy*, a period of premarital cohabitation during which the prospective bride is tested for responsibility and household skills, and which is followed—if she proves satisfactory—by a definitive indigenous wedding including ritual exchanges of gifts, etc. To the discouragement of the Augustinian missionaries, newly converted Indians refused to submit to the Catholic marriage rite until they had enjoyed this "trial" period (Romero 1923: 86). In 1575 a civil decree, promulgated by the Viceroy Toledo, ordered exemplary punishment for all Indians who persisted in this "custumbre tan nociva y perniciosa a su converción, policía, y cristianidad." And as if it were not enough that the Indians lived for a time premaritally "just as if they were married in fact," Toledo adds with annoyance that they actually

held this custom necessary to their permanent conjugal "paz, con-
tento, y amistad" (Romero 1923: 88–89). The Church again condemned this practice in 1585, and more strongly in 1613, recom-
mending punishment of malingerers (Romero 1923: 86–87). Finally,
in 1649, the Archbishop of Lima, surveying the Indian scene, sol-
emnly noted that marriage not preceded by *tincunakuspa*, i.e., by
"trial marriage," is "very rare today" (Romero 1923: 88).

Several chroniclers offer additional evidence of this practice.
Murua, writing in 1590, reported that single men and women before
deciding to marry, lived together "mucho tiempo por via de prueba,"
and that this seemed in no way a sin to them (Murua 1946: 290).
Arriaga, writing several years later, briefly discussed *tincunakuspa*,
without which, he laments, marriage is "very rare." On one occasion,
while passing through a town, he saw an Indian violently oppose the
mariage of his sister on the sole grounds that the couple had not had
previous sexual relations, and he reports another Indian, in quarreling with his wife, as taunting her for having married without ever
having had other lovers (Arriaga 1920: 59). Finally, according to
Cobo (1893: iii, 38), an Indian, in order to find out whether a woman
can "bien servir y regalar," generally lived with her for several
months, or even years, and married only if content, otherwise choos-
ing another.

In summary, after a period of considerable adolescent sexual liberty, the commoners of the empire entered into a "trial" relationship
which tested the girl's work abilities and the couple's general compatibility. Residence, though never specified, was probably patrilocal
because of the emphasis on testing the girl. The duration of the trial
period apparently varied regionally from a few months to several
years. The custom is spoken of as generalized over the whole Inca
realm, and specific references attest to its vigor in places as scattered
as Huamachuco in the northern Peruvian Andes and among the
Collas on the shores of Lake Titicaca (Romero 1923: 85; Murua
1946: 290).

The marriage ceremony which the Inca imposed on his subjects
took place once a year in the plaza of every village in the empire
(for the best descriptions see Cobo 1893: iv, 182; Murua 1946: 244;
Santillan 1927: 22; Bandera 1557: 100; Peñalosa 1885: 60). Here
the men and women of marriageable age stood facing each other in
two rows in front of a visiting government official. Each man, beginning with local dignitaries, selected a girl and placed her behind
him with her hands on his shoulders. The couples then received
together the official blessing of the Inca's representative. Thus con-

cluded, marriages were completely indissoluble, with the imposition
of the death penalty even for adultery. The state provided a house,
tools, and fields for the newlyweds, and the man immediately entered
the ranks of taxpaying adults.

There was more to this apparently arbitrary pairing of partners
than meets the eye. Murua (1946: 244) relates how, prior to this
ceremony, a groom, or sometimes his parents unbeknownst to him,
solicited his prospective parents-in-law, bearing coca, alcohol, and
other gifts, and states that their acceptance was always respected at
the subsequent official ceremony. In most cases, therefore, the Inca
ceremony merely legalized unions which had already been arraaged
between families according to traditional local customs. Of course, it
also insured that every subject marry, and it perhaps also provided
for interlocality marriages in the case of surplus males or females
(Puga 1955: 147–148). Murua's affirmation that prior contracted
arrangements were respected and his description of the just settlement by the Inca's representative of disputes between rival pre-
tenders at this ceremony are neither fully supported nor completely
contradicted by the other chroniclers, none of whom, unfortunately,
enters into comparable detail about choice and prearrangement.
Cobo (1893: iv, 181) implies corroboration. Peñalosa and Bandera
remain silent. Santillan (1927: 22) and Molina (1873: 177) seem to
miss the point, affirming that the women given at the ceremony are
accepted without resistance. Poma de Ayala (1936: 300) summarily
denies choice. Most modern commentators, including Means (1931:
361) and Baudin (1955: 230), accept both prearrangement and
choice.

Cobo (1893: iv, 182) and Murua (1946: 240–241) describe additional ceremonies which followed the official pairing and involved
the families of both partners. Murua (1946: 244) explicitly states
that after the official lineup the Indians "do their own wedding and
celebration among themselves." At the home of the girl, in the presence of relatives of both partners, there were ritual exchanges of
food, drink, clothing, and other gifts accompanied by speeches and
ceremonials. Thereafter the whole party drank and danced their way
to the home of the groom's parents for a continued celebration.
Variations are reported for different provinces, but it seems clear
that the official lineup was followed by some local marriage ceremony throughout the empire (cf. Rowe 1946: 285).

The foregoing facts suggest the widespread occurrence in the
Andes, probably antedating the Inca conquests, of a "basic pattern"
of sex and marriage practices characterized by considerable adoles-

cent sexual liberty, by a trial period of premarital cohabitation with the possibility of separation, and by a folk ceremony, varying by region, which confirmed the prearrangements of the parties concerned. In this context the Incas merely interposed a supplementary ceremony—a public and secular one—which neither eliminated nor disturbed the traditional usages. In the post-Conquest period, as we shall see, the public ceremony of the Incas was replaced by the wedding rites of the Church without significantly altering either the form or the function of the pre-Columbian marriage pattern.

## Modern Andean Marriage

Trial marriage, usually followed today by a Catholic wedding, is still almost universal among the Quechua. It is described in practically identical terms for sites as scattered as Hualcan (Stein 1961: 141–144) and Puno (Baurricaud 1962: 169–174). In surveying the ethnographic literature I encountered only one Indian community in which it appears to be completely absent. The people of Q'ero, a community not far from the ancient Inca capital which has minimal contact with the Catholic Church and is isolated from *mestizo* interference, condone premarital freedom, have a definitive marriage ceremony, and forbid divorce (Nuñez del Prado 1958: 21–27), but they do not practice premarital patrilocal residence. They thus appear to preserve all the elements of the ancient basic pattern except trial mariage. The wedding ceremony, moreover, is not a Catholic rite but a functionally equivalent local version consisting of an exchange of formal phrases and a ritual sharing of coca. I am tempted to suggest that Q'ero has somehow managed to preserve not only a pre-Columbian but a pre-Inca ceremony—of the kind described by Fathers Murua and Cobo as following the public pairing-off.

A second contemporary case which likewise fits the basic pattern is reported by Solano (1944: 69–70). Here trial marriage is terminated by two distinct ceremonies: an indigenous one marked by a highly formalized dancing ritual and the display of gifts on a special table, to which the Indians are reported to attach the greatest importance, and a Catholic rite performed once a year during Lent, when itinerant missionaries perform a mass marriage. The parallel to the dual ceremonies of the Inca is immediately apparent, and it seems possible that a pre-Inca local rite has survived here as in Q'ero.

The coexistence of these wedding ceremonies here and the ready substitution of Catholic for Inca or indigenous ceremonies in most

other areas point to the same conclusion. The functional inter-
changeability of the rites has permitted both their unobtrusive
coexistence wherever the traditional practices did not contradict
current values or laws, as under the Incas, and their easy serial substitution whenever pressures, such as those from the Church, have
been brought to bear against the earlier forms.

Two geographically marginal cases also deserve mention. The
neighboring Aymara to the south enjoy great adolescent sexual liberty and apparently practice some form of trial marriage. Their
marriage ceremony is not definitive, however, for Tschopik (1946:
545–546) speaks of easy and fairly frequent divorce. The lack of substantial data on Aymara marriage and divorce limits speculation, but
it seems at least possible that the modern Aymara pattern is a fairly
recent corruption of that formerly shared with the Quechua (Bandelier 1910: 147) and that trial marriage is merely being increasingly
abused, as Rouma (1913: 58–59) reports for areas of the Bolivian
highlands. Farther north in the Andes, the Moguex and Paez, before
their Catholic wedding, practice a form of trial marriage, called
*amaño*, which sounds remarkably like the Quechua institution (Hernandez de Alba 1946: 948; Pittier de Fabrega 1907). Unfortunately,
the data are again very limited, and it is unclear whether there is
postmarital separation or divorce.

The extreme poverty of published ethnographic data bearing on
Andean trial marriage should by now be obvious. Although Peruvian
folklorists rarely tire of this quaint subject, we have yet to read an
adequate description or analysis.[2] While the following sketch cannot
fill this ethnographic gap, it will  attempt to present a balanced
summary of the "basic pattern" in a modern highland community
where I did field research for three months in 1961.[3]

## Marriage in Vicos

The community of Vicos rests in an intermontane valley, two
miles high, in the north central Andes of Peru. The numerous publications of the Cornell-Peru Project at Vicos render an introduction
to the community unnecessary. Suffice it to say that the 2,000 or
more Vicosinos, in spite of the changes of the past decade, remain
well ensconced in the culture shared by their several million contemporary Quechua brothers.

Vicos courtship features considerable sexual freedom, often violent
horseplay, and quiet exchanges of presents. Courting most often
occurs during fiestas, visits to the market, certain agricultural activi-

ties, or while herding sheep on the mountain slopes. Significantly, these situations all permit maximum freedom from parental or family observation. Serious courtship begins late. The onset of puberty is delayed until seventeen or eighteen years of age for males and only about six months earlier for females, perhaps because of the stresses of high altitude and inadequate nutrition (Newman 1961). Moreover, physiological puberty is not a ritual occasion and signals no change in social status. In brief, this marked retardation of puberty allows for the antecedent near-completion of the socialization process, leaving the courting Vicosino free from other new obligations. The extensive teasing, horseplay, and mock battles between the sexes which mark this period of the life cycle, furthermore, are more than a passing phase, for throughout their active life husband and wife continue playfully to pummel, pinch, and wrestle with each other in much the same rough way they did as late adolescents.[4] Courtship is thus doubly important in Vicos. Marked by unusual intensity before marriage, its attitudes and behavior later become part of the permanent conjugal relationship.

Adolescents freely choose their own marriage partners in modern Vicos. Men seek responsible, hardworking girls who have mastered the household skills, can help them in the fields, and possess a sunny disposition. Romantic love plays an important role, and beauty is appreciated; men prefer rosy-cheeked, full-bodied women who take care of their appearance, especially their hair. Virginity is of little consequence, although unusually loose premarital relations are considered a reliable prediction of marital infidelity. Women look for physical strength, responsibility, and general potential as a provider for their family. Men having some acquaintance with spoken Spanish are especially sought after today. The relative wealth of the families seems more important to parents than to children, who tend to think more in terms of economic potential. Most Vicosinos marry women about two years their junior, and those rare unions with age differences of more than a decade cause considerable unfavorable comment.

Despite improved roads and increasing contact with the outside world, Vicos remains about 75 per cent endogamous, and this figure surpasses 95 per cent if the area within ten miles of the community is considered. Marriage prohibitions extend to members of the father's and mother's *castas* (named patrilineages or more often sibs), to certain ritual kin (particularly *compadres* of baptism or marriage), and to various other consanguineal and affinal relatives as dictated by the canon law. While there is some marriage, despite

Church disapproval, between second cousins who are not of the prohibited *castas*, unions between *compadres*, whether formalized or not, are clearly a crime against the community. *Ashmanaki*, the cohabitation of *compadres*, is believed to cause severe agricultural blight or crop-damaging torrential rains, and it was formerly punished by public whippings, for which payment of a fine and public disgrace are substituted today. Furthermore, numerous folktales relate the exploits of the *qeqe* (literally "sickness"), a frightening nocturnal figure into which women living in *ashmanaki* are transformed. While the offender's decapitated body snores loudly through a corn cob stuck in its gaping esophagus, the head of the *qeqe* flies through the night air making spine-tingling supernatural noises.

For the great majority of Vicosinos, Roman Catholic marriage is preceded by a period of patrilocal cohabitation known locally as *watanaki*, literally "having a year together." During the period 1951–1960, out of some 100 church weddings 93 per cent were preceded by *watanaki*. Among the several ways of entering *watanaki* which Vicosinos distinguish, formal *ashipa* ("to look for") and informal *topakipa* ("to meet") represent two extremes.

*Ashipa* has several variations. In the past, a young man's parents often suggested a partner or even secretly arranged the union with her family, and the couple's first sexual relations with each other occurred only after final approval of the match by both families. The couple was shut in a room for the night, while their families drank and celebrated outside; in the morning the children had the option of terminating the union then and there. In contemporary Vicos, the young man generally informs his parents that he wishes to enter *watanaki* with a particular girl, with whom he has almost certainly been carrying on clandestine sexual relations for some time. The parents usually simply give their consent, but there may first be a family conference, as more often occurred in the past. Such a meeting includes the young man's *parientes*, who have already participated in his earlier life-crisis rites of baptism and first haircutting. (This kin-group, although bilateral, reflects the strength of the patrilineal principles in Vicos by emphasizing the paternal and maternal *castas*.)

Once family approval is won, the young man's mother and father (or in his absence some other male relative) visit the parents of the girl. This first solicitation is carried out after dark and is accompanied by gifts of cooked guinea pig and potatoes, coca, chicha, and alcohol, varying with the wealth of the family and the formality of the visit. The girl's family rarely accepts on this first visit, even if the match pleases them. Normally they feign complete surprise and indignation, followed by considerable good-humored defamation of the proposed suitor, who is staunchly defended by his own parents. In the past, a conference of the girl's *parientes* often followed this first solicitation, but today the girl's family is usually prepared for the visit and has already resolved their differences of opinion regarding the suitor. The second or third visit, often accompanied only by gifts of alcohol, usually brings success, although there have been several cases of yearlong unsuccessful solicitations. The only practical means of marrying in spite of parents' refusals—running away to the coast—occurs only about 2 per cent of the time. Upon acceptance by her parents, the girl accompanies her prospective inlaws to their home and begins *watanaki* with their son.

The most informal entrance into *watanaki—topakipa—*is also the most popular in modern Vicos, where it appears to have considerable antiquity. Both sets of parents are simply presented with a *fait accompli*, and there is little that they or their relatives can do about it. *Topakipa* most frequently begins after a major fiesta, when a man finds his son passed out on the floor with a girl. The father, accompanied by his son, conducts an immediate solicitation of the girl's parents, bearing hastily assembled gifts of coca and alcohol. Although both fathers may be outraged, they generally give their belated consent and content themselves with angry invectives about each other's children or about the disrespect for parents nowadays. In a more extreme form of *topakipa*, the youth's parents are completely excluded from the solicitation, and the suitor demands the girl's hand directly from her father. Occasionally there is no solicitation whatsoever. Whatever the details, however, *topakipa* is always distinguished by the exclusive initiative of the couple involved.

Only about 7 per cent of contemporary marriages are not preceded by *watanaki*, and these arise from unusual circumstances. Highly desirable men, usually Spanish-speaking army veterans, have occasionally been inveigled into quick marriages by girls' families who are afraid lest they lose their prize catch to another woman. Several particularly desirable women have likewise been convinced to marry quickly. Very recently a lonely Vicosino serving in the army wrote home asking his family to have a wife waiting for him upon his return. In short, marriage without *watanaki* seems of only peripheral importance.[5]

Regardless of the mode of initiation, a couple once in *watanaki* has a good chance of remaining together for life. During the 1951–60 period, 83 per cent of the couples living in *watanaki* for the first time confirmed their unions with church ceremonies, and, with the exception of one woman who needed three tries, the remainder all married after a second *watanaki*. The average duration of *watanaki* during this same ten-year period was just under fifteen months. The age at entrance averaged 23 years for men and 22 for women.

Residence in *watanaki* is usually patrilocal, but if the girl's family lacks an active male the couple may move in with them. The young man continues to work the family fields by his father's side, and he remains economically, as well as in matters of authority, under the full protection of his parents. In more formal cases of *watanaki*, particularly in the past, the boy made periodic visits to his future parents-in-law, hauling wood, helping in their fields, and sometimes substituting for the girl's father as a hacienda peon. The boy's mother and her potential daughter-in-law maintain constant contact and co-operate in cooking, washing, spinning, and other household chores. The newcomer undergoes continual surveillance and a rigorous testing of the household skills she acquired during her long apprenticeship at her mother's side. Her behavior toward her future mother-in-law is generally marked by reserve and respect.

Throughout *watanaki* the relatives of both partners make an effort to interact socially, utilizing such occasions as baptisms, funerals, and other family ceremonies. For the immediate families of the couple, practical arrangements for the future wedding provide many opportunities for mutual visiting, which is often accompanied by exchanges of small gifts. In the past, marriage *padrinos* were usually chosen at a formal ceremony involving the *parientes* of both partners, but today the mother of the girl usually indicates her preference at a meeting of the parents early in *watanaki*. The majority of marriage *padrinos* are related Vicosinos, although about a third are *mestizos* from the nearest town. The latter convey prestige, may make possible a more impressive ceremony complete with brass band, and can often help the couple in their later relations with the Spanish-speaking outside world. With the naming of the *padrinos*, the girl's family fades into the background until the wedding. The formal solicitation of the proposed *padrinos*, which includes gifts of ceremonial foods and alcohol, is a prerogative of the parents of the prospective groom, and it is they who conduct all subsequent business transactions.

Ties of marriage *compadrazgo* are strong in Vicos. Years after the ceremony the godchild may still haul wood or perform other services for his aging *padrinos*, and it is they more often than the parents who intercede if the couple has conjugal difficulties. A generation ago *padrinos* still publicly whipped their adulterous godchildren, tied naked to a rock in the central plaza. A marriage *padrino* not only gains prestige and a certain kind of old-age insurance from his position; his new *compadres* must fete him with gifts of sheep, chickens, food, and alcohol, all in considerable quantities. In return, he must share, about equally with the groom's father, the total cost of the wedding, which today invariably exceeds the cash value of the gifts he receives.

Late in *watanaki*, the boy's father sets the date of the wedding in consultation with the *padrino*. Economic problems, however, often delay the ceremony indefinitely. The saving of cash, which is necessary for new clothing, special food and drink, church fees, etc., is never easy for Vicosinos. Furthermore, relatives must have time to prepare the traditional gifts of household equipment, and the immediate families must reconcile themselves to parting with the fields and animals which will be given to the newly married couple. Finally, time is needed for the young man, aided by his paternal kin, to construct a new house near that of his family, with which it often shares a common patio. This is commonly done during *watanaki*, although it is sometimes deferred until after the church ceremony.

Separation is socially sanctioned at any time during *watanaki*, although the girl's family often applies increasing pressure for marriage once children have been born. Children born during a broken *watanaki* carry no social stigma in the eyes of the community. They merely accompany their mother when she returns to her parents, and upon her eventual marriage become assimilated, with full inheritance rights, into her new household. A definitive separation, especially if it occurs on an unpleasant note, results in extreme avoidance behavior between the members of the two families, who may not resume normal social intercourse until several years after the girl's remarriage to another man.

A variety of circumstances can lead to separation, which terminates about one *watanaki* in six. Infidelity on the part of the girl, often while the man is in the army, dissatisfaction of the boy's parents, particularly his mother, with the girl's work habits, and incompatibility between the two families are common reasons for sending the girl away. Less frequently the girl's family shows its dissatisfaction with the suitor or his parents by taking their daughter home. Once in *watanaki*, a couple wishing to marry can usually prevail over hesitant parents. Most separations today are initiated by the couple themselves, even in the face of strong parental influence.

When no separation occurs, *watanaki* culminates in either a private church ceremony or in a mass marriage following the yearly *ronda*—a series of unannounced "roundups," of couples who, by the Church's definition, are living in sin. The choice is influenced by both social and economic considerations. A large private wedding wins prestige but involves great expense for its extensive and colorful fiesta. The *ronda* ceremony costs only 10 per cent as much but involves only minimal celebrations; no dancing, for example, is allowed, since mass weddings always occur during Lent.

The mechanics of the *ronda* are dramatic. During January and February the fifteen members of the *varayoq*, the local civil-religious hierarchy, keep their eyes and ears open for all scandalous information and amorous gossip. They put this reconnaissance to the test during the final weeks of Lent, when they make unannounced midnight descents on the homes, portable brush herding huts, and open fields of Vicos. Their objective is to capture all unmarried couples found sleeping together, whether they are well advanced in a publicly acknowledged *watanaki* or are merely having their first fling together in a corn field. These raids net about ten couples a year on the average, but not always without difficulty. Physical force combined with well planned strategy may be necessary to capture a recalcitrant youth surprised in a pre-*watanaki* affair, and stories of particularly clever or fantastic *ronda* evasions circulate widely. Once caught, the couple waits in a temporary prison until their *padrino*, sometimes hastily chosen and solicited by the boy's parents, arrives to vouch for them. In front of their captors, they must promise to marry each other, either in a reasonably immediate private ceremony or in the mass wedding which follows several days later.

The *varayoq*, encouraged by the local priest and the *mestizo* authorities, take great pride in the effectiveness of their raids. Nevertheless, couples living in *watanaki* for less than a year at the time of the *ronda* can usually arrange with the authorities in advance to be left untouched. Thus a certain balance is achieved; the Church grudgingly tolerates *watanaki* if it ends in a Catholic marriage, and the community wholeheartedly participates in the Catholic sacrament provided it is preceded by a *watanaki* of appropriate duration. Community opinion does not, however, sanction a second *ronda* evasion, and very few couples remain in *watanaki* for more than two years. The mechanics of the *ronda* help explain two facts: the fifteen-month average duration of *watanaki* and the striking concentration of both private and mass weddings in the period immediately following the raids. Only 15 per cent of Vicos marriages over the past decade have occurred in months other than March and April. These *rondas*, which occur widely throughout the Andes, recall strikingly the annual forced marriages of the Inca.

The Church ceremony marks the entrance of a Vicosino couple into the adult world. Various kinds of property—land, tools, animals, clothing—which have been earmarked for the children from time to time ever since their first haircutting ceremony now become theirs in fact. The establishment of an independent household, which usually follows quickly upon marriage, marks relative liberation from the authority of the parents. Significantly, a man can enter the ranks of the *varayoq* only after he has been married in a church ceremony. And only then can a male, heretofore referred to as a "boy," be called *nuna*, "man"[6] Permanent separations after marriage are rare, with an incidence in Vicos of perhaps 2 or 3 per cent, but adultery, despite severe punishments, seems fairly frequent.

Within the cultural context of Vicos, I think we can distinguish at least five major functions of *watanaki*:

(1) *Watanaki* permits the carefully supervised introduction of the girl into the unfamiliar *casta* with which she will pass much of her life and which will give a patronym to her children. The 50 or more *castas* of Vicos, in addition to their strict rule of exogamy, show considerable economic solidarity, tend to form residential clusters within which much work and social intercourse occurs, and demonstrate their unity in fights, humiliations, and fiestas. *Watanaki* allows the newcomer, under the tutelage of her future mother-in-law, to be gradually inducted into an important, and often initially hostile, kin group.

(2) *Watanaki* witnesses the gradual but methodical creation of a whole network of new kinship relationships of permanent importance to both families. From the first meeting of both *parientes* (kindreds) at the traditional *padrino*-naming ceremony through the subsequent visits and formalized exchanges of gifts the future affinal relatives make every effort to relate socially and to observe suitable amenities. On the night preceding the wedding the couple and their *padrino* traditionally visited all the homes of both *parientes* for brief hand-kissing ceremonies called *bendición*. After the wedding, the ties between the families continue to grow, and affinal kin call freely upon each other for both work and ceremonial support. Affinal ties are further reinforced after the birth of children through the network of *compadrazgo* relationships. In fact, the standard term of address between co-parents-in-law is *cumpadri* or *cumadri*. *Watanaki* thus initiates the transformation of two potentially hostile

families into a unified kin group of major importance. By the time of the church ceremony, the creation of the *parientes* of the couple's unborn children already rests on a strong foundation.

(3) *Watanaki* also provides an opportunity for major economic adjustments. Both families are given time to prepare gifts of land, animals, and tools, to accumulate the considerable sum of money often needed for the wedding ceremony, and in the case of the groom to construct a house. Moreover, the frequent procrastination and repeated postponements of the wedding date, for want of ready cash, are rendered more readily acceptable by the fact of *watanaki*, in which the couple already live essentially as man and wife.

(4) *Watanaki* is also important as a trial marriage. The possibility of separation, despite its actual infrequency, lends the institution the flavor of a trial period which many commentators have mistaken for its sole function. The work ability, responsibility, and faithfulness of the girl, and to a lesser extent the qualities of the young man, are put to the test, as is the compatibility of the two families. In short, this living together for a period of many months, in close simulation of real marriage, offers the couple an excellent opportunity to assess their mutual feelings before taking the irreversible step of church marriage.

(5) *Watanaki* likewise mediates the transition from adolescence to adulthood. The young couple acquire certain of the social and sexual advantages of adult status without as yet assuming its full responsibilities. Economic independence and release from parental authority come only with marriage. It is not surprising that many Vicosinos consider *watanaki* the happiest period of their lives. As an introduction to the assumption of full adult responsibilities, *watanaki* represents the final step in the socialization process.

## Bibliography

ARRIAGA, PABLO JOSEPH DE. 1920. La extripación de la idolatria en el Perú. Lima.

BANDELIER, A. F. 1910. The Islands of Titicaca and Kosti. New York.

BANDERA, DAMIAN DE LA. 1557. Relacion general de la disposicion y calidad de la provincia de Guamanga, llamada San Joan de la Frontera, y de la vivienda y costumbres de los naturales della. Relaciones Geographicas de Indias (Madrid, 1885) 1: 96–103.

BAUDIN, L. 1955. La vie quotidienne au temps des derniers Incas. Paris.

BAURRICAUD, F. 1962. Changements à Puno. Paris.

CIEZA DE LEON, P. DE. 1864. The Travels of Pedro de Leon, A.D. 1532–52, ed.

C. R. Markham. Hakluyt Soc., ser. 2, No. 33. London.

COBO, BARNABE. 1893. Historia del Nuevo Mundo. Sevilla.

HERNANDEZ DE ALBA, G. 1946. The Highland Tribes of Southern Colombia. Bulletins of the Bureau of American Ethnology 143: ii, 915–960.

LABARRE, W. 1948. The Aymara Indians of the Lake Titicaca Plateau. Memoirs of the American Anthropological Association 68: 1–250.

MACLEAN Y ESTENOS, R. 1952. Sirvinacuy o Tincunacuspa. Perú Indígena 2: iv, 4–12.

MEANS, P. A. 1931. Ancient Civilizations of the Andes. New York.

MOLINA, CRISTOBAL DE. 1873. The Fables and Rites of the Yncas, ed. C. R. Markham, London.

MURUA, MARTIN DE. 1946. Historia del origen y genealogía real de los Reyes Incas del Perú. Madrid.

NEWMAN, MARSHALL. 1961. Personal Communication.

NUNEZ DEL PRADO, O. 1958. El hombre y la familia: su matrimonia y organizacion politica en Q'ero. Cuzco.

OSBORNE, H. 1952. Indians of the Andes. London.

PENALOSA, MERCADO DE. 1885. Relacion de la provincia de los Pacajes. Relaciones Geográficas de Indias 2: 51–63. Madrid.

PITTIER DE FABREGA, H. 1907. Ethnographic and Linguistic Notes on the Paez Indians. Memoirs of the American Anthropological Society 1: 301–356.

PIZARRO, PEDRO. 1917. Descubrimiento y conquista del Perú. Lima.

POMA DE AYALA, F. H. 1936. Nueva corónica y buen gobierno. Paris.

PUGA, M. 1955. Los Incas. Mexico.

ROMERO, C. A. 1923. Tincunakuspa. Inca: Revista Trimestral de Estudios Antropologicos 1: 83–91.

ROUMA, G. 1913. Les Indiens Quitchouas et Aymaras des hauts plateaux de la Bolivie. Bruxelles.

ROWE, J. H. 1946. Inca Culture at the Time of the Spanish Conquest. Bulletins of the Bureau of American Ethnology 143: ii, 183–330.

SANTILLAN, FERNANDO DE. 1927. Historia de los Incas y relacion de su gobierno. Lima.

SOLANO, S. 1944. Sobre el matrimonio indígena. Boletín Indigenista 4: 68–73.

STEIN, W. 1961. Hualcan: Life in the Highlands of Peru. Ithaca.

TSCHOPIK, H. 1946. The Aymara. Bulletins of the Bureau of American Ethnology 143: ii, 501–574.

VALCARCEL, L. 1945. Ruta cultural del Perú. México.

# Notes

1. This paper was written with the support of United States Public Health Service fellowship 1–F1–MH–22,007,01. I am indebted to Evon Z. Vogt for advice on an earlier, extended version. George Collier, George L. Price, Sally Price, and John M. Whiting also made helpful suggestions.
2. The article by MacLean y Estenós (1952), the most important recent commentator, is typical. It includes: (a) a discussion of Indian "psychology," drawing on such data as the dancing, drinking, and laughter following the death of a child and its contrast with the melancholy and crying at a cow's

death, (b) an historical review of the institution drawn almost exclusively
from Romero (1923), and (c) a cursory comparison of supposedly similar practices in the Ukraine, Ceylon, and Iceland. For additional references see Bibli-
ografia del Folklore Peruano, Lima, 1960.
3. This field research was supported by the Columbia-Cornell-Harvard Summer
Field Studies Program, sponsored by the Carnegie Corporation. I am grateful
to field leaders Paul and Polly Doughty, to director Allan Holmberg, and to
the staff of the Cornell-Peru Project for aid throughout the summer.
4. For similar patterns, compare the discussion of Aymara courtship by LaBarre
(1948: 129).
5. There is some evidence that marriage not preceded by *watanaki* was considerably more frequent in Vicos two generations ago, but further field work is
needed before this interesting possibility can be assessed.
6. Among the neighboring Aymara the verb "to marry" means literally "to become a person" (Tschopik 1946: 550).

# Mate Selection in Collective Settlements

*Yonina Talmon*

*This paper presents an analysis of second generation "exogamy" in the Kibbutzim in Israel. It combines and coordinates an elucidation of social system functions with a developmental-motivational interpretation. Examination of this case study provides a crucial test of theories of mate selection. In addition it enables us to go beyond the specific problem of mate selection and deal with the more general theoretical problem of the relations between functional and causal analysis.*

Sociologists and psychologists who studied the second generation in the Kibbutzim in Israel have all noted that children born and bred in the same Kibbutz, do not marry one another as adults. Attempts to account for this phenomenon are usually based on the assumption that it is an exogamous extension of a self-imposed incest taboo generated by the collective system of education. In the Kibbutz, children are brought up together in peer groups which substitute, to a large extent, for their families.[1] Children in the same peer group live in close proximity, interact constantly and share most of their daily experiences from birth to maturity. It is assumed that much like biological siblings, members of the peer group develop an incest taboo that neutralizes their sexual interest in each other, and that this prohibition of sexual relations and marriage within the peer group is somehow extended to all children born and reared in the same Kibbutz.[2] This explanation, which is based on an analogy to the genesis and extension of the incest taboo in the elementary family, is plausible but tells us very little about the origin of the exogamous tendency or about the mechanisms that maintain and

From *American Sociological Review*, August, 1964, Vol. 29, No. 4, pp. 491–508. Reprinted by permission of the American Sociological Association.

stabilize it. It ignores altogether the structural implications of exogamy and does not deal with its effects on the social system.

Theories of incest and exogamy fall into two major categories:
first, those that deal with these mate selection patterns in terms of
social system functions and emphasize their effect on intra-group or
inter-group solidarity, and second, those of the psychological-genetic
variety that deal with this problem primarily on the motivational
level. Very few explanations of incest and exogamy attempt to combine the two approaches in a systematic way. The Kibbutz presents
us with the rare opportunity to observe exogamy in *statu nascendi*
and follow the dynamic process of its initial development and crys-
tallization. Since exogamy in the Kibbutz is not an established and
taken-for-granted injunction but an emergent pattern, it enables us
to examine closely the intricate interplay between social structure
and individual volition. The main purpose of this paper is to relate,
coordinate and integrate the two basic perspectives and deal with
the problem on both levels of analysis.

## Second Generation "Exogamy"

My analysis of second-generation exogamy is based on the sociological study of mate selection and marriage patterns of the second
generation in three long established Kibbutzim. This study is part
of a larger research project carried out in a representative sample of
12 of the Kibbutzim affiliated with one of the four Federations of
Kibbutzim.[3] The project combined sociological and anthropological
field methods. The data obtained from questionnaires, from various
types of interviews and from analysis of written material were examined and carefully interpreted by direct observation. The present
analysis is based primarily on the special inquiry focused on marriage patterns of the second generation, but the more comprehensive
investigation supplied many insights and provided a considerable
amount of corroborative evidence.

I shall first sum up the facts revealed by our inquiry:

1. Among the *125 couples* we examined, there was not one instance in which both mates were reared from birth in the same peer
group. In four cases husband and wife were born in the same Kibbutz but reared in different peer groups. In addition we found eight
couples in which one mate was born and raised in the Kibbutz while
the other entered the educational institutions of the Kibbutz at
diverse ages, ranging from three to fifteen. In six of these cases the
"outsider" came to the Kibbutz and was subjected to collective edu-

cation just before or after puberty. Only three of these "outsiders" joined the Kibbutz together with their parents; the others came as "external pupils" while their families continued to reside in town. In seven out of the eight couples the respective mates were reared in different peer groups. The single case of intra-peer group marriage occurred between a native and an "outsider" who was sent to the Kibbutz as an "external pupil" at the age of 15. The love affair between these two started after they left school and after an additional period of separation brought about by service in the army and study in town. In addition, 12 cases of intermarriage occurred between second generation members born and reared in different Kibbutzim.

Thus, in-migrants who undergo only part of their socialization in the Kibbutz and remain semi-outsiders in it and members of the second generation of other Kibbutzim seem to be more acceptable mates than full insiders.

2. Our data on *erotic attachments and sexual relations* are scantier and less reliable than our data on marriage. The pattern of distribution of love affairs, however, seems to parallel closely the pattern of distribution of marriages. We have not come across even one love affair or one instance of publicly known sexual relations between members of the same peer group who were co-socialized from birth or through most of their childhood. A small number of love affairs occurred between members of different peer groups, and a somewhat larger number between a native and an outsider who entered collective institutions at a later age and between second generation members of different Kibbutzim. The very rare cases of intra-group affairs involve an "outsider" who came to the Kibbutz as an "external pupil" long after puberty. These affairs did not occur during the period of study and started only after completion of secondary school.

The tendency to avoid in-group sexual relations and marriage is, then, strongest between members of the same age group. It is somewhat weaker between members of different age groups and between second generation members of different Kibbutzim. Age of entry into the Kibbutz educational system is yet another factor: the tendency toward out-group erotic relationships is strongest among those socialized in the Kibbutz since earliest infancy. In-migrants who undergo only part of their socialization in the Kibbutz are partly outsiders and as such are more desirable than insiders. Our data underline the importance of relations within the peer group, which appear to be at the core of the matter. It should be emphasized, however, that the tendency to avoid intra-second generation erotic relationships is almost as strong as the tendency to avoid intra-peer group erotic relationships. With few exceptions, love affairs and marital unions are extra-second generation.

3. We did not make a full study of the *demographic aspects* of our problem, but we did examine the possibility that the exogamous tendency may be a function of such demographic factors as age, sex and number of available prospective mates in the second generation.[4] Our data indicate that while the limited number of suitable second-generation candidates is an important factor, it is certainly not the only or even the major factor operative here. The exogamous tendency appears in all Kibbutzim irrespective of the number of available second-generation members of a marriageable age. The unmarried members of the second generation in our sample could have chosen from about 20 to 60 second generation members who were within the acceptable age range, yet almost invariably they by-passed this pool of prospective mates and sought erotic gratification and marriage outside it.

4. A careful analysis of our data led to the conclusion that the tendency to out-group mate selection in the Kibbutz *is an attitudinal and behavioral trend and not an institutionalized normative pattern.* This tendency differs radically from full-fledged incest taboos and exogamic injunctions, which regulate mate selection by means of explicit norms and negative sanctions.

Scrutiny of the literature on incest and exogamy in different societies[5] reveals a great deal of variation as to explicitness of norms, stringency of prohibitions and severity of sanctions. The breach may be defined as sinful and punishment relegated to automatic mystical retribution.[6] It may be defined as criminal and subject to penal sanctions. It is viewed in some cases as merely scandalous and disreputable and subject to diffuse public disapproval and derision.[7] It may invoke extreme rage, horror and revulsion, or merely embarrassment and scorn. This variation should not obscure the fact that infractions of the core taboos and injunctions are hardly ever condoned and almost invariably incur more or less severe negative sanctions.[8]

The second-generation tendency toward out-group mate selection in the Kibbutz is not backed by any formal or informal prescriptions or proscriptions, and it is not buttressed by any institutionalized sanctions or inducements. The rare cases of intra-second generation affairs and marriages attract attention and comment but are not considered in any sense illegitimate or irregular. These unions are fully accepted by parents, friends and public opinion, without even a shade of censure or unease. Not only is proscription or negative evaluation of intra-second generation marriage completely absent, but as I shall show later, many of the parents prefer intra-second generation marriage above any other pattern. This difference between a non-normative trend and a fully institutionalized normative pattern is so fundamental that the two phenomena should not be designated by the same term without due reservations. To underline this basic distinction. I have consistently put such terms as "incest," "endogamy" and "exogamy" in quotes when I apply them to mate selection trends in the Kibbutz.

These findings concerning the prevalence, range and significance of the "exogamous" tendency among members of the second generation in the Kibbutz indicate that this is a self-imposed limitation which cannot be accounted for by either demographic or normative pressures. This brings into even sharper relief the twin questions originally posed: What are the social functions of this "exogamous" tendency? What are its sources and its functions at the level of individual personality?

## Patterns of Marriage

The tendency of the second generation toward out-group marriage cannot be studied in isolation. Avoidances should be examined in conjunction with preferences and related to the overall distribution of marital choice categories. The first step toward such an analysis is a detailed examination of the group membership of all the spouses in our sample. Classification of these couples in this respect yields an "endogamy"-"exogamy" continuum, a graded series between two polar extremes.

1. *Intra-second generation marriage:* (a) Intra-peer group marriage—marriage between members of the second generation who were brought up in the same peer group. (b) Inter-peer group marriage—intermarriage between members of the second generation who were brought up in different peer groups. Such unions are "exogamous" with respect to the peer group but "endogamous" with respect to the second generation.

2. *Intra-Kibbutz marriage*—Intermarriage between members of the second generation of a given Kibbutz and candidates for membership or members who have joined their Kibbutz at later stages of its development. Such unions are "exogamous" from the point of view of the second generation but "endogamous" from the point of view of membership in the Kibbutz.

3. *Inter-Kibbutz marriage*—Intermarriage between members of the second generation of a given Kibbutz and members of other Kibbutzim. Contacts between the Kibbutzim occur either within the framework of the Federation[9] to which they are affiliated or within the framework of the regional organization that unites all the Kibbutzim in the region.

4. *Intra-Movement marriage*—Intermarriage between members of the second generation of a given Kibbutz and members of the youth movements that share the ideology of the Kibbutzim and channel their members to settlement in them. There are many institutionalized contacts between the Kibbutzim and the youth movements from which they recruit most of their new members. The youth movements send groups of prospective settlers to establish Kibbutzim for preparatory training; such groups may reside and work in the Kibbutz for periods ranging from a few months to two years. Second-generation members often serve as instructors and organizers in youth groups and nuclei of prospective settlers in town. Such unions are "exogamous" with respect to the Kibbutzim concerned but "endogamous" with respect to the collective movement as a whole.

5. *Extra-Movement marriage*—Intermarriage between members of the second generation and outsiders who are not members of the collective movement and do not share its ideology. Such outsiders are either hired professional workers—mostly teachers, but occasionally a resident doctor or an engineer—who reside in the Kibbutz temporarily but are not members and are not committed to its ideology, or outsiders who have no direct contact and no affinity with the Kibbutz ideology and way of life. Members of the second generation meet the latter type of outsiders primarily during the period of compulsory service in the Israeli army.

In our sample of 125 couples the distribution of marriage patterns is as follows:

|  | Per cent |
|---|---|
| 1. *Intra-second generation:* | |
| (a) Intra-peer group | 0 |
| (b) Inter-peer group | 3 |
| 2. *Intra-Kibbutz* | 31 |
| 3. *Inter-Kibbutz* | 23 |
| 4. *Intra-Movement* | 27 |
| 5. *Extra-Movement* | 16 |
|  | 100 |
|  | (125) |

These results are tentative and should be viewed with great caution. In Many cases, it was not easy to determine the group membership of the spouse at the time of marriage, especially among couples who left the Kibbutz to join another Kibbutz or left the collective movement altogether. There is, in addition, considerable variation among the Kibbutzim in our sample, and we are by no means certain that our results are representative of other Kibbutzim. Yet, the pattern we found does not seem atypical and may well give a good indication of the major trends.

Most marriages are concentrated in the intermediate range of the typology; 81 per cent are of the intra-Kibbutz, inter-Kibbutz or intra-movement types. Both intra-second generation marriage and extra-movement marriage, the polar extremes, are less prevalent than the intermediate types. Examination of the distribution of the marriage patterns in terms of this typology locates the specific problem in a wider context. Instead of focusing exclusively on the near-absence of type 1 we can examine it as part of the total constellation of marital choice categories.

## The Social Functions of Marriage Patterns

The voluminous literature on the functions of marriage patterns in different societies clearly indicates that these patterns have a crucial effect on the social system.[10] Marriage brings about a re-arrangement of the social structure by segregating and interlinking sub-groups within it. It bears directly on the cohesion and continuity of the social system. What, then, are the functions of the extra-second generation marriage patterns from the point of view of any single Kibbutz and from the point of view of the movement as a whole?

Close scrutiny of our data reveals that the extra-second generation marriage patterns have a number of important functions on the *local level*. The intra-Kibbutz pattern is an important mechanism for *reinforcing membership ties by kinship ties*. The nuclei of settlers and the candidates for membership who join the Kibbutz during later stages of its development remain marginal for a long time. Direct confrontation with the realities of life in the Kibbutz has a corrosive effect on their commitment to stay in it. Their absorption is a prolonged and difficult process, and many drop out at first. Marriage to a son or a daughter of an old-timer consolidates the new member's ties to the established Kibbutz and reinforces his identification with it. The marital bond and the newly acquired kinship affiliations turn the newcomer, still a semi-outsider, into an insider and facilitate his adjustment.

Closely related to the function of reinforcing membership ties is the function of *recruiting new members*. The extra-Kibbutz patterns are an important external source of additional members. Both sons and daughters are expected to stay on in their Kibbutz after their marriage and to prevail on their spouses to join them there. The Kibbutzim in our sample have gained a considerable number of additional members through marriage—the ratio of gain to loss is about three to one. Established Kibbutzim suffer from a shortage of manpower, and the flow of new members drawn into it by extra-Kibbutz marriage is very welcome.

Thus, membership and kinship are, in a very important sense, complementary. The Kibbutz, however, is based on the primacy of membership ties over kinship affiliations and it cannot afford to let kinship gain an upper hand.[11] All established Kibbutzim face the problem of the gradual re-emergence of wider kinship ties within them. Relatives often form united blocks and conduct a covert struggle for particularistic interests.[12] Occasionally such blocks become quite powerful and exert a considerable influence on communal affairs. Predominance of kinship ties over ties of membership undermines the primacy of collective considerations and engenders internecine strife. The established Kibbutzim have devised many mechanisms to limit the enfluence of kinship groups. One function of the extra-second generation marriage patterns is *to check the emergence and consolidation of large and powerful kinship groupings within the Kibbutz*. When intermarriage occurs between a member of the second generation and a newcomer or an outsider, only one spouse has his family of orientation and his siblings' families living with him in the same community, while marriage between members of the second generation would proliferate kinship ties within the Kibbutz.

The extra-second generation patterns also *link different subgroups in the Kibbutz*; marrying out *bridges the intergeneration cleavage*. The educational system partly segregates the second generation from the rest of the Kibbutz. The children's society has its autonomous arrangements and children live within this semi-separate framework uninterruptedly throughout the long process of socialization. They share with their age mates most of the formative experiences of infancy, childhood and adolescence; internal relations within the peer group are more frequent and more continuous than relations with outsiders. Members of the second generation are highly conscious of their special position in their Kibbutz and often tend to keep to themselves. Extra-second generation marriage mitigates this intense in-group solidarity after maturity. Marrying out propels members of the second generation outside their group and bolsters their external ties.

Extra-second generation marriage bridges the gap between sub-groups within the Kibbutz in yet another way. *Marrying out checks the consolidation of the emergent stratification system.* The founders of the Kibbutz usually enjoy a privileged position in terms of pres-tige and power. The kinship ties produced by any considerable number of "endogamous" marriages between their children would reinforce in-group solidarity among them and enhance the consoli-dation of the old-timers into a separate and dominant group. The extra-second generation patterns counteract this tendency to closure and exclusion. Through their children, the established old-timers are linked to less established and more marginal members. Extra-second generation marriage is thus *an equalizing mechanism* of major importance.

The functions of the prevalent mate selection patterns for the *movement as a whole* are even more evident. The inter-Kibbutz and intra-movement patterns counteract the strong separatist tendencies of the local communities by cutting across the boundaries between them and by strengthening their ties to the youth movements. The function of inter-Kibbutzim unions as *living links between distinct communities* is particularly noticeable in the cases of inter-collective "adoption." The Federations have recently developed a system whereby each established Kibbutz "adopts" a newly founded Kib-butz and pledges itself to assist it until it is able to manage on its own. Intermarriage links the long-established and newly founded Kibbutzim together and gradually reinforces the pseudo-kinship ties entailed in "adoption." Parents and relatives of members of the sec-ond generation who have gone over to new Kibbutzim maintain frequent and close ties with them and eventually come into contact with other members as well. Since the assistance scheme affects the well-being of their close kin, members of the established Kibbutz become personally committed to it and press for a strong alliance between the two communities. Cross-cutting kinship affiliations transform "adoption" into a comprehensive and lasting partnership.[13]

Of similar importance is the *revitalization and renewal of relations with the youth movements.* Established Kibbutzim tend to settle down and lose much of their revolutionary zeal. The sense of be-longing to a revolutionary movement becomes less pervasive and less urgent; growing involvement in local affairs brings about a concomitant limitation of the horizons of identification and partici- pation. There is an increasing tendency toward contraction of com- mitment and withdrawal from the movement. Estrangement occurs also because of the gradual shift in relations between the estab- lished Kibbutz and the youth movements. The dependence of the established Kibbutz on the youth movements for new members diminishes and at the same time the movement's claims on it grow manifoldly. The established Kibbutzim realize the importance of supporting the youth movements, yet they cannot help feeling hard- pressed and overburdened when confronted with demands to send more youth leaders to the cities and to participate more actively in the training programs. Intra-movement marriage links the youth movements with the Kibbutzim and emphasizes the unity of the collective movement that encompasses them all.

Finally, intra-movement and extra-movement marriages *bridge the gap between Kibbutzim and other sectors of the society.* In many notable cases, they provide very valuable personal links with other elite groups. Unions contracted between members of the second generation and military, political and intellectual leaders or their close kin cement the manifold ties between the Kibbutzim and both the pivotal and secondary elites of Israeli society. Extra-movement unions curb separatist tendencies and create solidarities that tran- scend the local units and reinforce wider ranging unities.

So far, I have analyzed only the *positive* functions of the extra- second generation marriage patterns, disregarding the fact that to a lesser or greater degree they all constitute a *threat to local continuity.* Intra-second generation marriage is the pattern most conducive to local continuity. Both spouses are natives of the Kibbutz and share a common commitment and attachment to it. Their staying on in the Kibbutz after marriage is safeguarded also by the fact that all their close relatives and friends reside there. A new member's ties to the Kibbutz are weaker and more vulnerable—he is much more prone to leave and to draw his spouse out of the Kibbutz.

The threat to local continuity is even more noticeable in the inter- Kibbutz and intra-movement patterns. A union between a member of the second generation and a member of another Kibbutz or a member of a nucleus of prospective settlers engenders a conflict of loyalties. When members of two established Kibbutzim intermarry, they tend to spend a trial period in each community and settle in the one that is more congenial to both spouses. But intermarriage with a member of a new Kibbutz, or with a member of a nucleus of settlers that is about to found its own Kibbutz, creates cross pressures and counter-claims with no institutionalized solution. Members of the second generation are often attracted by the numerous openings offered to them in the new Kibbutz. They also feel that it is their duty to help the newly founded Kibbutz rather than return to the fairly prosperous community established by their parents. In spite of their commitment to their native village and in spite of the pressure put on them by their parents, the conflict is often resolved in favor of the new Kibbutz.

Extra-movement marriages are the greatest hazard from the point of view of continuity. Some of the hired professional workers who marry into the Kibbutz become attached to it and wish to join as members in their own right. This also happens occasionally with outsiders who have had no affinity and no direct contact with the collective movement prior to marriage. Yet more often than not, extra-movement marriages lead to desertion of the Kibbutz and dissociation from the movement. This happens more often when the second-generation member is a woman; in spite of the fact that both sons and daughters are expected to stay in their native Kibbutz, wives follow their husbands more than husbands follow their wives. Linkage of a couple to the Kibbutz through a son is therefore less vulnerable than linkage through a daughter.[14]

The foregoing analysis of *functions and dysfunctions* enables us to weigh the effects of the marriage patterns on the social system. Intra-second generation marriage ensures local continuity, yet if it were prevalent, it would deprive the Kibbutz of important internal and external integrating mechanisms. It would lead to the consolidation of kinship blocks and to the hardening of the line dividing the old-timers from the newcomers and outsiders. It would separate the Kibbutz from the movement and from the society at large. At the other extreme, extra-movement marriage links the Kibbutz to the society at large, but this advantage is counterbalanced by heavy losses in terms of cohesion and continuity. *The intermediate marriage patterns combine in-group closure with intergroup linkage, and in this respect are more functional than the two polar types.* The most prevalent marriage patterns are those that safeguard the cohesion and continuity of the local community, yet at the same time promote the unity and growth of the movement as a whole.

The intermediate patterns provide a functional solution from the point of view of the elementary family as well. Extreme homogamy limits the possibilities of interchanges and complementariness; extreme heterogamy is inherently unstable, since it joins together spouses with conflicting loyalties and incompatible norms and aspirations. The intermediate patterns combine basic homogeneity with manageable differentiation: they enable members of the second generation to marry newcomers and outsiders without disrupting their matrix of interpersonal relations. It seems, then, that the intermediate patterns perform important functions for the social system on all levels.

## Institutional Mechanisms

The preceding analysis indicates that the net effect of the present distribution of marital choices is by and large favorable. This elucidation of functions supplies an indispensable starting point for a causal analysis, yet in and by itself it does not explain differential incidence. To account for the adoption of a certain institution it is not sufficient to show that it is in some sense "good" for society and serves its long-range interests.[15] Listing the beneficial or dire consequences of an institutional pattern from the observer's point of view does not in itself account for the actors' attitudes and behavior. Second-generation members are only partly aware of the considerations outlined above, and even if they do recognize them, that does not mean that they actually choose their mates to suit the best interests of their society. Mate selection is considered a purely personal and private matter and there is a strict ban against meddling in the process of choice. How, then, do the functional considerations impinge on the individuals directly concerned? How does the structure, or the "sake" of the Kibbutz interact, as it were, with individual volition? What are the efficient causes and the immediate determinants of action?

An examination of the social system from the point of view of *differential availability* of categories of prospective mates provides an important connecting link between the functional and causal analyses of marriage patterns. The fact that the Kibbutzim are not closed, self-sufficient communities but interconnected and interdependent units, operating within an active and proselytizing movement, is of utmost importance in this context. The strong separatist tendencies of the local communities are counterbalanced by external ties. There are first of all the federative affiliations based on an ideological-political affinity. Secondly there are the regional schemes that further cooperation between settlements situated in he same district and encompass Kibbutzim affiliated with different federations. Last but not least, we should take into consideration the manifold ties that connect the Kibbutzim with the overall structure of Israeli society.[16]

The exernal relations of the Kibbutz impinge directly on its internal organization. The youth movements supply the Kibbutz with reinforcements. The Kibbutz accommodates, in addition, transient members of the youth movements, who stay for varying periods to get their basic training or to lend a hand during the busy season. Many Kibbutzim have developed special institutions for immigrant youth who stay in the Kibbutz for a number of years, combining study and part-time work. In border settlements, units of a special formation of the army combine military duties and work. Even while staying in their native Kibbutz, members of the second generation are brought into institutionalized and more or less prolonged contact with groups of new members, candidates for membership and various kinds of transients, and these out-groups provide a pool of prospective mates. Activity on the regional, federative and national level further extends the range of participation and provides opportunities to develop durable and meaningful ties outside the confines of the local community[17]

Members of Kibbutzim and especially leaders of the movement are aware of the dangers of closure and separatism, and have devised ingenious mechanisms to link the different groups and different communities affiliated with the movement in common endeavors. Situational exigencies and ideological considerations have led to the expansion of the regional schemes beyond their original, rather limited scope. These schemes curtail local autonomy and have a considerable impact on the economic, social and cultural life of the participating communities. Large scale regional enterprises and institutions create a common meeting ground and bring the members of different Kibbutzim together. Most important, from the point of view of our special problem, are the regional secondary and vocational schools that draw out and bring together the adolescent youth growing up in these Kibbutzim. Several of the inter-Kibbutz marriages in our sample originated in friendships formed during study in such an inter-collective secondary school.

Many of the inter-Kibbutz and intra-movement unions are by-products of the newly developed scheme of federative assistance. A series of serious setbacks in the new settlements and a crisis of recruitment in the youth movements have led the Federations to intensify and widen the scope of federative cooperation. After completing their army service, members of the second generation are drafted for an additional year of service in a newly established

Kibbutz or in a youth movement training group. Recruitment is channeled primarily through "adoption," and most recruits serve in the new settlement adopted by their native Kibbutz. In addition, members of the second generation of a number of established Kibbutzim serve in new settlements that require considerable reinforcement to keep them going and consequently find adoption by only one established Kibbutz inadequate. Inter-Kibbutz second-generation teams participate also in maintaining their Federation's outposts in outlying, uninhabited and arid areas. They are engaged there in experimental cultivation and in preparation of the land for permanent settlement. A certain percentage of the annual quota of recruits serve as instructors and organizers of training groups in the youth movements.

Since service to a common cause and prolonged and close contacts breed affairs and lasting attachments, these schemes create ready opportunities for inter-group unions. The widening of the frameworks of cooperation results in a concomitant widening of the range of available mates. The three to three and one-half years of service in the army and in new settlements are concentrated in the beginning of adulthood, so that young people are taken out of the narrow confines of their Kibbutz at the time they begin to contemplate marriage. Maximal external contacts occur at the most marriageable age.

Influencing mate-choice is not an intended aim of the supplementary institutional mechanisms analyzed above. The established Kibbutzim view the intermarriages brought about by the regional and federative schemes with ambivalence and anxiety. Assistance schemes resulting in permanent settlement of a considerable number of second generation members in the new Kibbutzim evoke covert competition and acute tension. To avoid open conflict, some of the established Kibbutzim have reached an agreement with their adopted settlements that as long as the official ties of adoption last, second generation members will not be allowed to settle in the new Kibbutz or even volunteer for a second term of service in it. The established Kibbutzim press for deferment of the year of service in new Kibbutzim until members of the second generation reach a more mature age and are already married and settled down in their native villages. Most inter-Kibbutz and intra-movement marriages occur as *unintended, unanticipated and even undesired* consequences of organizational arrangements made for other purposes.

At times availability is an outcome of a *more conscious and purposeful design* to channel mate choice. The demographic policy of the Kibbutz is not uninfluenced by considerations of mate selection. Members of the Kibbutz are aware of the intra-second generation avoidance. They realized that intra-Kibbutz marriage is a safeguard against the desertion of the second generation to other communities and that the best way to ensure local continuity is to provide for their adult children a pool of suitable mates within their native village. They are partly aware also of the stabilizing effect that such marriages have on their new members. The timing of stages of demographic expansion by means of absorbing groups of new members, and the selection of such groups, are not unaffected by these considerations.

The Kibbutzim have lately become very concerned about the "undesirable" associations developed by members of the second generation during their army service. Service in the army throws the young recruits into direct and intense contact with all segments of Israeli society and provides them with an opportunity to develop attachments outside the aegis of the Kibbutz and the collective movement. The Kibbutzim try to limit the disruptive effects of these external contacts by channeling a certain quota of their recruits to the agricultural-military formation of the army, which maintains their contacts with the movement throughout the period of service. They make special efforts to keep in touch with members of the second generation who serve in other units and to maintain and strengthen their intra-movement ties.

The need to counteract extra-movement associations has led the Federations to design new inter-Kibbutz and intra-movement frameworks of encounter and interaction. An important instance of such indirect yet intentional channeling of mate choice is the ideological seminars and refresher courses, which are planned with matchmaking as one of their unofficial, yet tacitly recognized, aims. This gives rise to much bantering during the seminars and figures as a major theme in the humorous skits and songs presented at parties. At times the program of instruction and the lectures serve mainly as a convenient cover while the main purpose of the seminar is to provide a congenial atmosphere and ready opportunities for forming attachments. The channeling of mate choice is achieved by means of control over the frameworks of formal and informal interaction. *The prevalence of the intermediate patterns stems, at least in part, from institutional arrangements that make certain categories of mates more readily accessible.*

Analysis in terms of differential accessibility supplies an important clue, but not the full answer. Second generation members are more

available than any other categories of prospective mates. They interact closely and are within easy reach of each other, yet they do not
regard each other as erotically desirable. Our initial question is
still unanswered. How can we account for this sexual neutralization
on the motivational level?? What makes newcomers, outsiders and
strangers more desirable? How do these deep-lying tendencies develop during the process of maturation?

## Mate Selection and the Process of Maturation

The life of children in the Kibbutz is dominated from the outset
by *a division between the communal sphere represented by the peer
group and the private sphere represented by the family*. This division
determines the ecological patterning and the time rhythm of the
child's schedule and is maintained by the daily shifting from the
children's house to the parents' home. The family and the peer
group are dominated by different yet complementary principles.[18]
Relations between parents and small children are very intimate,
intense and highly eroticized. Expressions of love become more
restrained and less overt as the children grow up, but the relationship remains warm and affectionate. Throughout the process of
socialization the family supplies the child with uncontested love
and exclusive personal attention.

The atmosphere in the peer group is more neutral, less affectively
toned. A certain routine, diffuse general friendliness and overall
solidarity is emphasized, rather than love or intimacy. Everything
is shared and each child is entitled to the same amount of attention.
Relations in the peer group are based on a diffuse and all-embracing
internal solidarity that discourages exclusive friendships or love
affairs with it.[19] Love is anchored in the specifically personal and
private sphere; since it leads to preoccupation with inner emotional
states, it competes with involvement with the group and detracts
from dedicated commitment to collective goals. Romantic love is in
its very nature exclusive; it sets the lovers apart and separates them
from the rest of their comrades. The emphasis on commitment to
the group discourages dyadic withdrawal; members look askance at
intense friendships of any kind, and they occur infrequently.[20] Since
the child's personal need for exclusive intimate relations is from the
outset provided for outside the peer group rather than within it,
the formation of erotic attachments in adolescence and adulthood is
inhibited. The "exogamous" tendency should be viewed as one
manifestation of the *basic distinction between peers who are comrades and intimates who are "outsiders."*

Data on educational institutions in the Kibbutz enable us to probe
a little further *into the ways in which the peer groups neutralize
and inhibit sexual attraction between their members.* Relations between the sexes are de-eroticized not by means of strict restrictive
norms or enforced segregation, but by dealing with sexual problems
in a straightforward, objective and "rational" way and by minimizing the differentiation and distance between the sexes. Children of
different sexes share the same living quarters[21] and physical shame
is de-emphasized. There is very little differentiation between the
sexes in style of dress and demeanor and hardly any sex-differenti-
ated social activities. Interaction between age mates in the peer
group is much tighter and all-pervasive than interaction between
siblings. Siblings share only activities and experiences in the family,
and their participation is age and sex differentiated, but members
of the peer groups eat, study, work and play together as a group
most hours of the day and sleep together in the same room or in
adjoining rooms at night. We encounter here, then, very close propinquity and very intensive interaction between peers of different
sexes.

The de-eroticizing mechanisms described above operate throughout the process of socialization, but the norms regulating relations
between the sexes, as well as actual behavior, change during *different phases of maturation.*[22] Attitudes to childhood sexuality are permissive and sexual manifestations in young children are viewed as
normal. Living and sleeping quarters are bisexual during this stage.
Children of different sexes sleep in the same room, shower together,
play and run around in the nude and there is a considerable amount
of wrestling, tickling, exploring, soothing and caressing between
them. This close contact between the sexes continues until the second or third grade, and then decreases with age. Gradually, a sense
of sexual shame emerges, and a growing distance between the sexes.
Showers are taken separately. Sleeping arrangements are reshuffled;
from the fourth grade on room occupancy is unisexual. All group
activities remain bisexual but friendship becomes unisexual.

The onset of puberty brings about a conspicuous increase in
sexual shame and the development of considerable hostility between
the sexes. Girls take great pains to hide their nudity when undressing
and keep to themselves as much as possible. Members of both sexes
insist on sitting separately in the classroom and at all assemblies and
parties. They declare that they detest each other and are constantly
involved in petty quarrels. The girls regard the boys as immature
and uncouth and treat them with disdain, and the boys retaliate by
annoying the girls and poking fun at them. Much of this tension

stems from the differential rate of sexual maturation—girls reach puberty and manifest a renewed interest in sex a few years earlier than boys. This interest is directed to older students and to other young unmarried males in their Kibbutz and not to their peers. The boys react to this development with resentment and aggression. This hostility continues until the age of 14 or 15 and then recedes, as the boys catch up with the girls and the relations between them cease to be highly charged with tension. The intensity of physical shame decreases. Girls and boys conceal their nudity from each other but this is now done without much ado in a calm and mater-of-fact manner. The unity of the peer group is restored and relations between the sexes becomes easy, unconstrained and friendly. During most of their adolescence age mates interact with each other as asexual peers rather than as potential sex objects.

Attitudes toward adolescent sexuality are more restrictive than attitudes toward childhood sexuality. The educational ideology upheld by both teachers and parents maintains that adolescents should refrain from sexual relations until they finish secondary school. It is felt that preoccupation with sexual matters prevents full concentration on school activities and has a disruptive effect on the peer group and on the student society. The energies of the adolescents are channeled to work, to study and to hectic participation in extra-curricular group and inter-group activities. All social participation is group rather than couple centered.[23] Seductiveness, coquetry and flirtatiousness are strongly discouraged. Sex does not loom very large in the lives of these adolescents. Shifting relations and indiscriminate experimentation are not common, nor do many couples go steady.[24] There are only few infractions of the injunction against sexual intercourse. Couples who become engrossed in each other and neglect their duties are admonished by their educators and peers to restrain themselves and to "return to the fold."

During this stage interaction cutting across divisions between peer groups increases considerably. Inter-group cooperation is highly organized and much more intensive than in the primary school. The committees elected by the students have jurisdiction over all matters other than the purely academic ones. Interaction between members of different peer groups occurs also in youth movement activities and in the numerous cultural interest and discussion groups. In most established and well-to-do Kibbutzim there are, in addition, a students' choir, a students' orchestra and a students' paper, which require close cooperation among many students. Activity in age-heterogeneous groups leads to a student-society solidarity that complements and reinforces peer group solidarity. Students of the senior classes have a strong "generational" consciousness and view themselves as the representatives of the second generation in their Kibbutz.[25]

Another relevant feature of adolescent life is a change in the balance between the communal and family spheres. Young children are deeply dependent on their parents. They gradually outgrow this intense involvement and become attached to their age mates. Adolescents become firmly embedded in their peer group and in the students' society and drift away from their families. Their relations with their parents remain friendly and affectionate but no longer very intense or intimate. The oslidarities cultivated by communal education gain an upper hand and partly supersede family solidarity.

After graduation from secondary school, members of the second generation may engage in sexual relations with impunity and are given a free hand with respect to choice of mate. There is no objection to pre-marital sexual relations as long as they are not treated in a frivolous and off-hand way. The prevalent view of sexuality and marriage stresses personal autonomy and genuine intimacy, and it is felt that both sexual relations and marriage should be anchored in spontaneous love. The search for a mate draws members of the second generation away from their peers and away from all other members of the second generation. As noted before, the overwhelming majority of love affairs and marital unions are extra-second generation, and as far as we can judge, relations between adult members of the second generation are friendly and familiar but devoid of any signs of erotic tension. Members of the second generation view their relations with each other as "sexless" and erotically indifferent.[26]

How do members of the second generation account for their tendency to out-marriage? How does the transition from adolescence to adulthood lead to the emergence of "exogamy?" One of the most frequent reasons given by second generation members for their lack of sexual interest in each other is *overfamiliarity*. They firmly believe that overfamiliarity breeds sexual disinterest and that it is one of the main sources of "exogamy." Our second-generation respondents stressed that they knew each other "inside-out," or more figuratively, "We are like an open book to each other. We have read the story in the book over and over again and know all about it." That this is an important issue with them we learn also from the reasons they give for their interest in newcomers, outsiders and strangers.

They refer to the curiosity, excitement and anticipation that unfamiliar people evoke in them and to the exhilarating sense of
discovery and triumph they get when they establish a relationship
with one of them. They describe the unfolding of an affair as an
exchange of confidences and emphasize the importance of relating
and comparing different life histories. The affair with the outsider
is experienced as an *overcoming of distance between persons* and as
a growth of a newly won and unfamiliar sense of intimacy. The most
perceptive and introspective among our respondents regard their
affairs with unfamiliar persons also as a means of *self-discovery.* The
effort to bridge the gap and reach mutual understanding requires
self-scrutiny and brings about a heightened sense of self-awareness.
To quote one of them "We are all cut from the same mold. We
take each other and ourselves for granted. Reaching-out to an outsider has made me conscious of myself. I know now more clearly
what I am and what I stand for." The search for self-awareness and
genuine intimacy as distinct from mere familiarity is an insistent
and recurrent theme in many interviews.

Closely related to the issue of overfamiliarity is *the issue of privacy.*
The concern with privacy is very intense.[27] Adolescent couples are
very secretive about their relationships. The typical partners give
few overt indications of their relationship. They do not appear
together in public as a couple nor do they seek each other out
informally between classes or at work. All meetings are clandestine.
It would be unthinkable to show any physical sign of affection in the
presence of other people. This exaggerated secrecy disappears after
adolescence, but the concern with privacy remains very strong. As
one of our respondents put it "In the children's society everything
is 'ours.' This affair is mine. It is something of my own that I do
not want to share with others. I try to keep it to myself as much
as I can." Communal living and constant sharing of daily experiences with peers seems to breed a strong urge to seclude one's personal life and protect it from external intrusion. Maintenance of
secrecy is also a mechanism for dealing with stringent group control
against dyadic withdrawal.[28] The threat to group cohesion is less
evident if the relationship remains subdued and covert.

One of the major advantages of the extra-second generation over
the intra-second generation union is that it is *more amenable to
segregation and seclusion.* Members of the second generation are
part of a highly interconnected network of interpersonal relations.
Being the first-born of their Kibbutz they are at the center of public
attention. An amorous attachment between members of the second

generation attracts immediate notice and incessant comment. The courtship will be conducted with the whole community looking on. It is much easier to keep secrecy or at least to maintain a semblance of privacy when the partner is a newcomer or an outsider who has few or no contacts with the Kibbutz. Members of the second generation take great pains to guard knowledge of their extra-second generation affairs from public notice.

The aspirations and expectations of second-generation members concerning their mates often reflect the external influence of the ideals of romantic love derived from novels, poems, plays and films.[29] The quest for individuation and genuine intimacy, however, should not be attributed to illicit external influences. These concerns are anchored in the image of love and family life upheld by the Kibbutz and are therefore legitimate. Preoccupation with overfamiliarity and lack of privacy stems from the internal dynamics of the system and reflects the dilemma engendered by the interplay between the communal and private spheres of the Kibbutz.

The social and psychological dynamics engendering this quest for individuation are further clarified by considering the *relation between "exogamy" and the demand for local continuity.* Loyalty to the Kibbutz is defined in localized terms, and members of the second generation are pledged to stay in their native Kibbutz for the rest of their lives. This duty gives rise to serious problems that become particularly acute during the transition from adolescence to adulthood. The Kibbutz is part of a revolutionary movement that puts a premium on discontinuity and creative innovation. Since it still depends on reinforcements from the youth movements, it encourages young people to dissociate themselves from their parents and continues to glorify rebelion. At the same time, it expects its own second generation to stay on in their native villages and continue their parents' lifework there. Inheriting a revolution engenders an inevitable dilemma. The second generation is called upon *to continue and conserve in a movement committed to discontinuity.*[30] Most members of the second generation accept responsibility to their heritage and stay on in the Kibbutz, but their attitude toward continuity is very ambivalent.

The duty to stay on in the native village engenders a deep *fear of closure* because it implies blocked mobility and a curtailment of life chances. It imposes a drastic limitation on free choice of domicile, of career, of associates and of friends. The cultivation of external contacts and the period of service outside the Kibbutz mitigate local closure but at the same time accentuate the problems involved in local continuity. Resettlement in the Kibbutz after prolonged service outside it entails a difficult reorientation and readjustment. Many second generation members are loath to sever their external ties and to forego the more variegated opportunities offered by life outside their Kibbutz. Most of them feel cut off and hemmed in. They realize that the course of their lives is set from the outset and that their future is predetermined by membership in their home Kibbutz. The tendency to marry out is an attempt to counteract this limitation. The large majority of extra-second generation mates have been brought up outside the Kibbutz; they come from a different milieu and represent the outside world. "Exogamy" enables second generation members to extend their contacts beyond the narrow confines of the circle of people with whom they have been associated since they were born. It expresses their craving for new experiences and their groping for new contacts. Most important, perhaps, it affords them opportunities to explore on their own, to initiate and experiment. In short, out-group marriage enables the second generation to escape the in-group closure imposed on them by their education and by their commitment to continuity.

The relation between "exogamy" and the commitment to continuity is especially significant in the context of relations between the first and second generations. Parents and children are at cross purposes on this issue. Parents have a strong vested interest in "endogamy." Their major concern is to ensure that the new family will stay on in the Kibbutz. From the point of view of familial and local continuity, intra-second generation marriage is the safest solution, and it is in fact a first preference with many parents. They view with enthusiasm and anticipation any sign of attachment between their children and give them their full blessing. The tendency of their children to marry out is a source of constant anxiety to them, and they watch them with unease until they settle down. Parents are not supposed to have any say whatsoever in the matter, yet they cannot refrain from comments and covert pressure. They openly oppose the decision of their children to move to another Kibbutz and do their utmost to win them back. Their opposition to out-movement "exogamy" is particularly strong and stubborn in cases of extra-movement unions leading to desertion of the Kibbutz and estrangement from the movement.

The "exogamous" tendencies of the children should be examined in conjunction with the "endogamous" preferences of their parents. *In the confrontation between the generations the parents represent the tendency toward in-marriage, while the children represent the tendency toward out-marriage.* Viewed in this context, "exogamy" is, among other things, an attempt to cut loose from the parents and redefine relations with the first generation. Our material reveals many undertones of resentment and opposition to the parents' generation. Exogamy is often defended in terms of the right of the second generation to self-determination and free choice, irrespective of the wishes of the parents and the Kibbutz. The parents want to hold their children back and to tie them as securely as possible to their Kibbutz. The second generation has a strong urge to break out and explore the more variegated possibilities of the surrounding world. Exogamy is an attempt to dissociate from the first generation as a whole and from the parents. It expresses a quest for a separate and partly independent identity.[31]

This interpretation of "exogamy" throws additional light on the functions of the intermediate marriage patterns. These patterns are compromise solutions that enable members of the second generation to meet the pressures impinging on them half way and to work out the dilemma of continuity versus discontinuity.[32] Our study indicates that in the majority of cases the conflict is resolved in favor of continuity. Most members of the second generation either stay in their native Kibbutz or join another one. Joining a young frontier Kibbutz and starting anew there is essentially a re-enactment of the revolutionary deed of the parent generation. Although it breaks local continuity, it affirms the revolutionary tradition. The individual quest for a separate identity is an aspect of the revolutionary ideology and as such is not without normative support. Only a minority of the second generation marry outside the movement and dissociate themselves from it. Total estrangement is uncommon.

Our material did not allow full examination of the relation between choice of marital partner and degree of identification with the Kibbutz and the movement. Extra-movement unions, however, are more prevalent in less integrated Kibbutzim, in which a rebellious second generation rejects many of the tenets of the collectivist ideology, than in Kibbutzim in which the second generation is more loyal to the Kibbutz and its values. Only 6 per cent of marriages in the most integrated Kibbutz are extra-movement marriages, compared with 27 per cent in the least integrated one. In many cases a decision to marry outside the movement is not an accidental outcome of circumstances, but a culminating step in a long developmental process of dissociation; it reinforces a pre-existing estrangement.[33]

*By combining "exogamy" and "endogamy," the second generation reconciles dissociation with identification and maintains a flexible balance between rebellion and loyalty.*

Mate selection is thus a solution to the basic dilemma of individuation. The intermediate patterns make it possible for members of the second generation to maintain continuity without being totally hemmed in and encapsulated. The compromise between in- and out-marriage enables them to cut loose without losing their roots, to remain within the fold yet achieve distinctiveness.

## Conclusion

This case study highlights the importance of mate selection patterns as major integrating mechanisms. The thesis that marriage brings about a realignment of the social structure, and that it has a direct bearing on the cohesion and continuity of the social system, has been fully demonstrated with respect to kinship-dominated primitive and traditional societies. The social functions of mate selection are less evident when we turn to non-familistic societies. The decline in the strategic importance of kin lines, which reduces the impact of mate selection on the overall institutional structure, reduces also the need for stringent regulation of mate choice. Young people are given more leeway in their choice of marital partners and the channeling of selection becomes more indirect and covert. Spontaneous love is regarded as the most important basis of marriage, and mate selection is defined as a purely personal matter. Relegation of mate selection to the private sphere obscures its social functions. Small wonder that most theories of mate selection in modern societies deal with it as a process of interpersonal negotiation and minimize its repercussions on the social structure. Great emphasis is put on the "fit" and compatibility between personalities in terms of either complementary or similar character traits.[34]

The present study demonstrates the inadequacy of a purely interpersonal approach to the analysis of mate selection. The Kibbutz is a non-familistic revolutionary society. Kinship affiliations are irrelevant in most institutional spheres and there is no institutionalized normative regulation of mate choice. Yet marriage patterns have a direct impact on the cohesion and continuity of the social system; *they mesh closely with the overall institutional structure and serve as crucial integrating mechanisms even in non-familistic societies.*[35]

Analysis of the intermediate marriage patterns revealed that their main function is to maintain a delicate and flexible balance between in-group closure and intergroup connectedness. *Endogamy is essentially a segregating boundary maintaining mechanism,* safeguarding the internal uniformity and cohesion of the group and ensuring its continuity as a distinctive unit. *Exogamy is an interlinking associative mechanism,* connecting groups and cementing them together as segmental units within wider ranging unities. Ascendancy of endogamy leads to withdrawal from out-group commitments and to separatism. Ascendancy of exogamy leads to over-diffusion of attachments and to attenuation and withering of narrower loyalties. It engenders discord and conflicting commitments and threatens continuity. The intermediate patterns reconcile the drawing inward with the thrust outward. The centrifugal tendencies in exogamy are held in check by the centripetal drag of endogamy. *A combination of exogamy and endogamy militates against insulation yet safeguards distinctiveness.*

While I have emphasized the social functions of the patterns of mate selection, I have also examined the ways in which the marriage patterns meet the needs and interests of the individuals directly concerned. Developmental analysis has revealed that the interpersonal "fit" approach is inadequate even with respect to individual motivation. One of the most important conclusions of this study is that mate selection is a way of resolving the conflict between rebellion and loyalty. *The quest for the most intimate role partner is influenced by the way in which collective identification is counterpointed by individual identity.* The development of a lasting commitment to a spouse is intertwined with the process of defining and delimiting one's commitments to the collective.[36] Marriage involves an interplay between the life-stage transition of the individual and social processes. Individual choice has far-reaching repercussions on the social system and conversely, social system determinants channel and direct individual choice.[37]

And last, but perhaps most important, this study has dealt with the more general theoretical problem of *the relation between functional and causal analyses.* Starting from the assumption that elucidation of functions cannot in and by itself account for the distribution of the marriage patterns, I have sought the efficient, operative causes and direct determinants of action and spelled out the institutional mechanisms and devices that channel and influence mate choice. An important connecting link between the two modes of analysis is *purposeful action based on awareness of function.* The anticipation of future outcome contributes to the movement toward a goal so that this goal is, to some extent at least, a cause of its causes.[38] The Kibbutz is a planned society. So far as some of the institutional patterns affecting mate selection directly or indirectly are introduced with reference to their intended consequences, analysis of function leads to analysis of cause.

Another important connecting link between functional and causal analyses is *the degree of individual identification with society and its values*. Recognition that an institutional pattern serves the best interests of society would not, in itself, guarantee that it would be adopted and adhered to. Identification with the Kibbutz partially merges personal and collective goals. Hence the considerable congruence between individual needs and aspirations and long range societal interests, which leads to the development of a personal commitment to continuity.

But this is only part of the explanation. Marriage is not regulated by consciously held norms. Moreover, most functions of the marriage patterns are latent. Recognition of the issues involved is partial, vague and unequally distributed within the system. Even leaders and educators, who are more clearly conscious of the effects of mate selection on the social system than those directly concerned, recognize only some of the implications of the problem. Purposeful and conscious indirect control of mate selection is of only secondary importance. Channeling of mate choice occurs primarily as an unintended, unanticipated or even undesired consequence of *institutional arrangements made for other purposes*. The incidence of the marriage patterns is determined mainly by the framework and setting of interaction and by the interpersonal relations engendered by the social structure and by the system of socialization. The processes that influence mate choice stem from the internal dynamics of the system and reflect the *tensions and conflicting interests, the pressures and counter-pressures inherent in it*. Thus, elucidation of functions and examination of causes are partly overlapping yet partly independent modes of analysis.

## Notes

1. The main features of the collective settlements (Kvutzot or Kibbutzim) are common ownership of property except for a few personal belongings and communal organization of production and consumption. Members' needs are provided for by communal institutions on an equalitarian basis. All income goes into the common treasury; each member gets only a very small annual allowance for personal expenses. The community is run as a single economic unit and as a single household. Husband and wife have independent jobs.

Main meals are taken in the communal dining hall. In most Kibbutzim children live apart from their parents and are looked after by members assigned to this task. They spend a few hours every day with their parents and siblings, but from their birth on they sleep, eat and study in special children's houses. Each age group leads its own life and has its autonomous arrangements. The Kibbutz is governed by a general assembly, which convenes as a rule once a week, by a secretariat and by various committees. Each Kibbutz is affiliated to one of the Federations of Collectives. The Federations recruit most of their new members from youth movements that channel their members to settlement Kibbutzim.

2. See for instance Gerald Caplan, *Social Observation on the Emotional Life of Children in the Communal Settlements in Israel*, New York: Josiah Macy, Jr. Foundation, 1954; Melford Spiro, *Children of the Kibbutz*, Cambridge: Harvard University Press, 1958, pp. 326–336 and 347–350; see also his "Is the Family Universal?—The Israeli Case" in Norman W. Bell and Ezra F. Vogel (eds.), *A Modern Introduction to the Family*, Glencoe, Ill.: The Free Press, 1960, pp. 59–69; J. R. Fox, "Sibling Incest," *British Journal of Sociology*, 13 (June, 1962), pp. 128–150.

3. The project was conducted by the Research Seminar of the Sociology Department of the Hebrew University. Rivka Bar-Yoseph took an active part in the initial planning. Amitai Etzioni assisted me in directing the project in its first stage. The other main research assistants were Eli Ron, Moshe Sarell and Joseph Sheffer. Moshe Sarell and Erik Cohen took over from Amitai Etzioni in the second stage. The main research assistants were Uri Avner, Batsheva Bonné, Uri Hurwitz, Ziporah Stup and Rachel Shaco.

4. For an attempt to explain incest and exogamy in demographic-ecological terms, see Mariam Kreiselman Slater, "Ecological Factors in the Origin of Incest," *American Anthropologist*, 61 (December, 1959), pp. 1042–1058.

5. See George P. Murdock, *Social Structure*, New York: Macmillan, 1949, ch. 10; see also A. R. Radcliffe-Brown, "Introduction," in A. R. Radcliffe-Brown and W. C. Daryll Ford (eds.), *African Systems of Kinship and Marriage*, London: Oxford University Press, 1950, pp. 60–72; Kathleen E. Gough, "Incest Prohibitions and Rules of Exogamy," *International Archives of Ethnography*, 46 (1952), pp. 81–105; Brenda Seligman, "Incest and Exogamy—A Reconsideration." *American Anthropologist*, 52 (July, 1950), pp. 305–326; Talcott Parsons, "The Incest Taboo," *British Journal of Sociology*, 5 (June, 1954), pp. 101–117; Jack Goody, "A Comparative Approach to Incest and Adultery," *British Journal of Sociology*, 7 (December, 1956), pp. 286–305.

6. See David M. Schneider, "Political Organization, Supernatural Sanctions and Punishment for Incest on Yap," *American Anthropologist*, 59 (October, 1957), pp. 791–800 and Robert A. Levine, "Gusii Sex Offences—A Study of Social Control," *American Anthropologist*, 61 (December, 1959), pp. 965–990.

7. See Meyer Fortes, *The Web of Kinship Among the Tallensi*, London: Oxford University Press, 1949, p. 250.

8. See J. R. Fox, *op cit.* Fox tends to ignore the universality of negative sanctioning of the core taboos and injunctions and to overstress the extent of variation.

9. To simplify this typology, I have disregarded organizational and ideological divisions within the collective movement, so that intra-Federation and inter-Federation marriage patterns are not distinguished.

10. For analysis of the functions of intermarriage see Robert K. Merton, "Intermarriage and the Social Structure," *Psychiatry*, 4 (August, 1941), pp. 361–374; Kingsley Davis, "Intermarriage in Caste Societies," *American Anthropologist*, 43 (July, 1941), pp. 376–395; Meyer Fortes, *op cit.*; I. Schapera, "The Tsawana Conception of Incest" and E. E. Evans Prichard, "Nuer Rules of Exogamy and Incest," both in Meyer Fortes (ed.), *Social Structure*, Oxford: Clarendon Press, 1949, pp. 85–121; E. E. Evans-Pritchard, *Kinship and Mar-*

*riage among the Nuer*, Oxford: Clarendon Press, 1951; Claude Lévi-Strauss, *Les Structures Elémentaires de la Parenté*, Paris: Presses Universitaires de France, 1949; Talcott Parsons, *op. cit.*, pp. 101–117; and Jack Goody, *op. cit.*, See also William J. Goode, "The Theoretical Importance of Love," *American Sociological Review*, 24 (February, 1959), pp. 38–47.

11. For a fuller analysis of this problem see Yonina Talmon, "The Family in a Revolutionary Movement" in Meyer Nimkoff (ed.), *Comparative Family Systems*, Boston: Houghton-Mifflin, 1964 (forthcoming).

12. See Yonina Talmon-Garber, "The Family and the Social Placement of the Second Generation in Collective Settlements," *Megamoth*, 8 (1958), pp. 369–392 (in Hebrew).

13. For a recent restatement and development of the view that the incest taboo and exogamy diffuse attachment and harness it to larger coordinated aggregates, see Philip E. Slater, "On Social Regression," *American Sociological Review*, 28 June, 1963), pp. 339–364. For an analysis of the way in which estrangement within the group strengthens loyalties to wider ranging unities, see Max Gluckman, *Custom and Conflict in Africa*, Oxford: Basil Blackwell, 1955, ch. 3.

14. John A. Barnes, "Marriage and Residential Continuity," *American Anthropologist*, 62 (October, 1960), pp. 850–866; see also his "Land Rights and Kinship in Two Bremnes Hamlets," *Journal of the Royal Anthropological Institute*, 87 (1957), pp. 31–56.

15. See George C. Homans and David M. Schneider, *Marriage, Authority and Final Causes*, Glencoe, Ill.: The Free Press, 1955, pp. 3–20; see also Harry C. Bredemeier, "The Methodology of Functionalis," *American Sociological Review*, 20 (April, 1955), pp. 172–180, and Ronald P. Dore, "Function and Cause," *American Sociological Review*, 26 (December, 1961), pp. 843–853.

16. See Yonina Talmon and Erik Cohen, "Collective Settlements in the Negev," in Joseph Ben-David (ed.), *Agricultural Planning and the Village Community in Israel*, Paris: Unesco, 1964, pp. 58–95.

17. For comparative data on the influence of propinquity on mate selection see A. M. Katz and Reuben Hill, "Residential Propinquity and Marital Selection," *Marriage and Family Living*, 20 (February, 1958), pp. 27–35.

18. For an analysis of the division of functions between the family and the peer groups see Yonina Talmon, "The Family in a Revolutionary Movement," *op. cit.* and "Family and Collective Socialization in the Kibbutz," *Niv-Hakvutsah*, 8 (1959), pp. 2–52 (in Hebrew). See also Rivka Bar-Yoseph, "The Pattern of Early Socialization in the Collective Settlements in Israel," *Human Relations*, 12 (1959), pp. 345–360; Elizabeth Irvine, "Observations on the Aims and Methods of Child-Rearing in Communal Settlements in Israel," *Human Relations*, 5 (1952), pp. 247–275; Helen Faigin, "Social Behaviour of Young Children in the Kibbutz," *Journal of Abnormal Social Psychology*, 61 (1958), pp. 117–129; A. I. Rabin, "Infants and Children under Conditions of Intermittent Mothering," *American Journal of Orthopsychiatry*, 28 (July, 1958), pp. 577–586, and his "Attitudes of Kibbutz Children to Parents and Family," *American Journal of Orthopsychiatry*, 29 (January, 1959), pp. 172–179.

19. For analysis of the opposition between dyadic attachment and group solidarity see W. R. Bion, "Experiences in Groups," III, *Human Relations*, 2 (1949), pp. 13–22; see also Slater, *op. cit.*, pp. 348–361.

20. Shmuel Golan, *Collective Education*, Merchavia: Sifriat Poalim, 1961, pp. 204–214 (in Hebrew).

21. See Melford Spiro, *Children of the Kibbutz, op. cit.* It should be noted that the Kibbutz described by Spiro is affiliated with a Federation that pursues a much more extreme and more rigorous policy of sexual desegregation than the Federation in which we conducted our research. Kibbutzim affiliated to the orthodox religious Federation practice considerable segregation between

sexes. We are engaged now in a cross-Federation comparative study of mate selection which will enable us to examine the relation between intensity of heterosexual contact during the process of socialization and the development of "exogamy."

22. *Ibid.*, pp. 219–228, 275–283, 326–336.

23. For comparative data on heterosexual interaction during adolescence see Willard Waller, "The Rating and Dating Complex," *American Sociological Review*, 2 (October, 1937), pp. 727–734; Robert O. Blood, "A Retest of Waller's Rating Complex," *Marriage and Family Living*, 17 (1955), pp. 41–47.

24. See Robert D. Herman, "The Going Steady Complex," *Marriage and Family Living*, 17 (1955), pp. 36–40.

25. On the problem of generations see Karl Manheim's *Essays on the Sociology of Knowledge*, New York: Oxford University Press, 1959, pp. 276–321; see also Shmuel N. Eisenstadt, *From Generation to Generation*, Glencoe, Ill.: The Free Press, 1956, and Bruno Bettleheim, "The Problem of Generations" in Erik H. Erikson (ed.), *Youth: Change and Challenge*, New York: Basic Books, 1963, pp. 64–93.

26. Two different psychological hypotheses have been proposed concerning this neutralization of sexual attraction. Spiro bases his analysis on Freudian premises and assumes that sexual attraction between co-socialized children of opposite sex is inhibited and suppressed but persists subconsciously. Fox constructs a neo-Westermarckian model and assumes that intense heterosexual bodily contact before puberty extinguishes desire. Since our research does not supply data on subconscious motivation, I cannot resolve the problem of suppressed versus extinguished sexual attraction. Both hypotheses have only limited explanatory value: as they stand, neither can fully account for the genesis of second generation "exogamy." They explain the neutralization of sexual desire between members of the same peer group but not the generalization of attitudes engendered within the peer group to the second generation as a whole. See Spiro, *op. cit.*, pp. 347–350 and Fox, *op. cit.*, pp. 128–150.

27. See Spiro, *op. cit.*, pp. 334.

28. See Slater, *op. cit.*, pp. 348–353.

29. See Hugo G. Beigel, "Romantic Love," *American Sociological Review*, 16 (June, 1951), pp. 326–334, and Jackson Toby, "Romantic Love" in Harry C. Bredemeier and Jackson Toby (eds.), *Social Problems in America*, New York: John Wiley, 1960, pp. 461–467.

30. For a fuller analysis see Yonina Talmon-Garber, "Social Structure and Family Size," *op. cit.*, pp. 121–146; and Moshe Sarell, "The Second Generation in Collective Settlements," *Megamoth*, 11 (1961), pp. 123–132 (in Hebrew).

31. Mate selection is viewed as a resolution of conflicts in the process of identity formation in Maria H. Levinson and Daniel J. Levinson, "Jews Who Intermarry," *Yivo Annual*, 12 (1958/59), pp. 103–129; see also John E. Mayer, *Jewish-Gentile Courtships*, Glencoe, Ill.: The Free Press, 1961.

32. For a general discussion of the problem of identity and loyalty to a historical heritage, see Erik H. Erikson, "Youth, Fidelity and Diversity," in Erikson (ed.), *Youth: Change and Challenge, op. cit.*, pp. 1–23.

33. For a close analogy see the analysis of the "emancipated" type in Levinson and Levinson, *op. cit.*

34. See, for instance, Robert F. Winch, *Mate Selection*, New York: Harper, 1953; Irving Rosow, "Issues in the Concept of Need Complementarity," *Sociometry*, 20 (September, 954), pp. 216–223; Reuben Hill and Evelyne M. Duvall, *Family Development*, Chicago: J. B. Lippincott, 1957.

35. For an analysis of the social functions of love and marriage in modern societies see Goode, *op. cit.* and Slater, *op. cit.*

36. See Erikson, *op. cit.*, p. 20; see also his "The Problem of Ego Identity," in *Identity and the Life Cycle, Psychological Issues*, New York: International Universities Press, 1959, Vol. I, No. 1. In terms of Erikson's analysis of critical

life stage tasks, our case study indicates that the process of establishing intimacy is closely intertwined with the process of identity formation.

37. For an attempt to relate social, ideological and personal factors in the process
of choice see Alan Kerchoff and Keith E. Davies, "Value Consensus and Need
Complementarity in Mate Selection," *American Sociological Review*, 27
(June, 1962), pp. 295–304.

38. Cf. Dorothy Emmet, *Function, Purpose and Powers*, London: Macmillan,
1958; Carl G. Hempel, "The Logic of Functional Analysis," in Llewellyn
Gross (ed.), *Symposium on Sociological Theory*, Evanston, Ill.: Row Peterson,
1959, pp. 271–307; and Harold Fallding, "Functional Analysis in Sociology,"
*American Sociological Review*, 28 (February, 1963), pp. 5–13.

# Marriage and Adjustment in a Traditional Society: A Case Study of India

*George Kurian*

Patterns of mate selection vary from culture to culture. There are two extreme positions in mate selection; the first is the traditional arranged marriage where the prospective spouses are chosen by the respective families with very little opportunity for the young man and woman to take active part in the decision making. The other extreme is the self-choice marriage where the youngsters have ample opportunity to meet each other and find a suitable life partner with very little influence of the parents. The self-choice marriages based on the decisions taken by the young people are not always stable if only one cares to look at the increasing number of separations and divorces in modern urban families. Therefore, it is interesting to make some observations about arranged marriages with regard to their contribution to the stability in marriage. This paper is an attempt to discuss the changing patterns of arranged marriage. Here an attempt will also be made to compare arranged marriage with self-choice marriage to emphasize the advantages of a modified form of arranged marriage.

Among most people in India, irrespective of religious and regional differences, marriages are arranged by parents and close relatives. The custom continues to be well established in rural areas. In urban areas modification in mate selection is increasingly in evidence. The following statement by Taya Zinkin made in 1958, "India is a country of arranged marriages. Only aboriginals and modern elite marry for love,"[1] holds true for the whole of India today. It is also correct to say that arranged marriages are a way of life. In Europe, North America, and those areas in the world in which European settlers have established themselves, at present, a young man and woman are expected to have fallen in love and then married. In India probably the reverse is true: namely, one marries by arrangement and then falls in love.

An arranged marriage in India emphasizes the alliance between two families. On the other hand in Western society, the young man and woman make a decision on their own with or without the consent of the parents, depending on their ages and the closeness of their ties with the parents.

## Important Prerequisites

*Importance of Family Alliance.* Arranged marriage in its most traditional style allows almost no opportunity for the young man and his prospective bride to take an active part in the final decision about marriage. The decision is made by the parents and close relatives, giving primary consideration to the benefit of alliance of the two families. Until recently, a significant number of marriages in rural areas were arranged before the girls reached the age of puberty. Traditionally, if a marriage was delayed beyond puberty, it was a blemish for the family's reputation.

*Age.* In a recent study made in Dharwar area in Mysore State by Dr. D. A. Chekki, it was found that the majority of the women were married before the age of thirteen. He studied 257 females of all age groups. Of them 140 had married below the age of thirteen. However, it was significant to note that when the study was made, these women were over thirty-five years of age.[2] This means that prepuberty marriages are slowly disappearing even in areas where the custom was fairly well established.

The Child Marriage Restraint Act of 1929 prohibited the marriage of a male under eighteen years and a girl under fourteen years. The Hindu Marriage Act of 1955 accepts fifteen as the minimum age at marriage for a girl and eighteen for that of a boy.

*Endogamy.* Endogamy in India applies at different levels. First of all, most marriages take place only between families speaking the same language. This consideration is most important due to the linguistic-cultural features of each region. Therefore to marry someone who speaks a different language is even now very rare.

*Propinquity.* The fact that marriages take place in the same linguistic-cultural region makes propinquity in mate selection most important. Marriages are arranged only between families which are known to each other. Therefore, the affinal links extend to no more than about twenty-five miles in densely populated states, though in less dense areas the distance may be even more. In Dr. Chekki's study in Dharwar, he has taken special notice of this feature.

The average distance from which girls come as wives to Kalyan is 28.9 miles. . . . The affinal links stretch out in most cases from fifteen miles to a maximum of sixty miles. This indicates to a certain extent the geographical distribution of subcaste membership within the region.[3]

*Religious Endogamy.* As a rule, most people marry only within the same religion. Though the predominant majority of the people are Hindus, there are millions of Moslems, Christians, Sikhs, Jains, Buddhists and Zoroastrians, and others who form smaller groups. Marriage outside one's religion is still rare even in urban areas.

*Caste Endogamy.* As a rule, marriage takes place within the Jati or subcaste which are the actual social units. Occasionally one can find intercaste marriages. There are other variations which are of significance. One is preferential marriage which is in the form of cross-cousin marriage. The following statement of Professor Dube explains some of the important considerations in Hindu marriage:

Marriage must be within the caste, unions with certain speci- fied categories of kin should be avoided, and no marital ties should be established within the same *gotra* or clan. As a gen- eral rule caste endogamy has been respected, although certain hypergamous unions across caste lines have been permitted and eventually recognized. There is considerable variation in regard to the rules permitting marriage between specified categories of kin. Among the Hindus of North India cross-cousin marriages as well as uncle-niece marriages (those between a woman and her mother's brother only) are not permitted. Cross-cousin marriages are the general rule in the tribal communities and are allowed among both upper and lower castes in Western and Southern India. Moslems permit parallel-cousin marriages also. Among certain groups of the Hindus and Ardhra Pradesh and Karnatak in South India, maternal uncle and niece mar- riages are preferred, as they involve a cyclic change of hands in regard to substantial property. A man can marry a younger sister of his wife, but not her older sister. Where widow re- marriage is allowed, a man may marry the widow of his deceased elder brother, but not that of a younger brother. As a general rule, marriages between *sapirdas* (near kin who make ritual offering of balls made with flour to common ancestors) and between two persons of the same *gotra* (clan) are prohibited. Recent legislation has permitted marriage between certain

categories of relations in these two groups, having the pre-
scribed genealogical distance between them, but such marriages
are to be regarded as exceptions rather than the rule.[4]

*Procedure in Mate Selection.* Marriage in the traditional Indian
family system puts great emphasis on alliance of two families. Therefore, the bride and the bridegroom are expected to fit well into the
traditions of the families. In most of the marriages, initiative is taken
by the girl's parents since they are eager to get their daughters married at a reasonably young age. Men are not subjected to this upper
limit in terms of age. Since the girl has to spend her married life
with her husband's family, there is an added importance to the
suitability of the girl to adjust to the new family. A young lady
from Hyderabad, India, wrote:

> . . . it is considered a family project where the older and
> wiser members of the family are given the privilege of finding
> a healthy, industrious, intelligent and efficient girl who can
> be regarded as lovable by all members of the family and not
> just her husband. Likewise, a boy who cannot get along with
> his own family is looked upon with a little trepidation. Hence
> a marriage is not a selfish personal relationship that excludes
> consideration of generations to come.[5]

There is also an interest in arranging marriages to well-known
families. For this reason, "the family tree is carefully scrutinized
and approved before marriage takes place.[6]

The initial approach is made by close relatives and friends and
very seldom by the parents themselves. This is to avoid embarrassment by rejection. This precaution is taken by both girl's parents
as well as boy's parents. If the initial approach is favourable more
active steps are taken. The parents are eager to find out all available
details about the girl and the boy. The girls are subjected to these
enquiries more thoroughly than boys. When assessing the general
physical attractiveness of the girl considerable attention is given to
the complexion of the girl. In fact there is a premium for girls with
light complexion. This type of preference is clearly seen in discussions and also the matrimonial advertisements in newspapers. In
addition to physical features, age, character with some reliance on
candid comments from school and college mates, educational attain-
ments and ability to manage a home are carefully scrutinized. In
the families were members had some modern education, they are
aware of the advantages of education for prospective spouses. How-

ever, these conditions are not so important for the villagers where practical consideration with regard to ability to work hard is given particular attention.

Among all classes female chastity is most highly valued and the close-knit family system tries to protect the girls in this respect with the additional guarantee of little opportunity for heterosexual premarital interaction. In the traditional family system in India, there is also a high value attached to premarital chastity of men which is a contrast to open or overt double standards existing in some other cultures.

In the study made by the author among 240 families in Kerala State in summer, 1968, the following qualities were considered important in a wife, in order of importance: good character, obedience, ability to manage home, good cook, should take active part in social and political affairs, educated, religious, depending entirely on husband for major decisions, fair complexion, good companion with similar intellectual interests, and beauty. There is an emphasis on practical considerations in the choice of a wife when the above list is used as a guide.

As regards the boy, the girl's parents are interested in the social and economic status of the family, his education and the demand goes up depending on his future job prospects, especially if he has a foreign education which is considered of some significance by the middle and upper-middle-class families. In the rural areas, the ownership of land is a consideration since education as such is not a great asset if the bridegroom is planning to stay as a farmer. Ownership of land is also an added insurance if there is unemployment.

Within India, until recently, there was very little opportunity for the boys and girls to meet each other before a final decision on marriage was taken. The idea is that parents and close relatives will strive their best to find the most suitable match. However, now there are modifications in arranged marriages, especially in large urban areas like Bombay and New Delhi among people who have received modern education. Whenever modern education is available such changes are visible, even in the less urbanized areas. At present, it is quite normal to arrange a formal meeting of the boy and girl, or to be more precise, an opportunity for the boy to meet the girl soon after both families are satisfied about the wisdom of going ahead with the proposal. On a prearranged day, the boy will visit the girl's family accompanied by one or two married male relatives. During this visit, the girl appears on the scene with tea or coffee and refreshments for the visitors. This gives them a chance to assess the girl. At present, it has become increasingly possible for the boy and girl to have a brief conversation by themselves which is the only form of courting that is allowed. In a few families in large urban centres, they are allowed to see each other after the formal engagement. However, unchaperoned courtship is very rarely approved.

The traditional channels of communication have changed to some extent in the urban areas where one can find that the advertising is used on a very large scale by the families or individuals, both men and women, who are looking for prospective spouses. In large urban areas this has become an established method of finding out a suitable partner. All newspapers in India have a long column devoted to matrimonial advertisements. Interestingly enough, matrimonial advertisements have also appeared outside India; for example in Canada, in the issues of *The Canadian Times of India* a bimonthly publication printed in Ottawa, Canada.

Advertisements from *The Times of India*, Bombay, India:

(1) Respectable Hindu Gujarati parents, of graduate foreign-returned, good-looking, talented girl, 22 years, employed as Junior executive in foreign company, invites matrimonial correspondence from respectable, well-placed boys around 25 years earning at least Rs.1500/—vegetarians preferred. Box 34994, *The Times of India*, Bombay 1, India.

(2) Wanted beautiful, post-graduate Kanyakubja girl from U.P. below 25 years, above 160 cms., for 33 years, M.A., 180 cms., handsome Army Service Corps Captain, permanent commission. Apply Box 35728, *The Times of India*, (daily) Bombay 1, April 28, 1969.

(3) Correspondence invited, view matrimony from a beautiful, well-educated girl with post-graduate qualifications, hailing from a respected Gujarati Jain family, from well-settled graduates age 28 years or more. Jains or Banias preferred. *The Times of India*, Bombay 1, India, April 30, 1969.

Advertisements from *The Canadian India Times*, Ottawa, Canada:

(1) Tall, handsome Jat Sikh, 31, with Masters degree (Canadian) holding very good position, invites correspondence from Punjabi girl (preferably Jat Sikh), 20 to 30, well-educated and good-looking, *The Canadian India Times*, 19 Walford Way, Ottawa 5, Vol. 2, No. 6, April 17, 1969, p. 8.

(2) A Punjabi Sikh University professor in Canada wishes to

marry a suitable Indian girl. Send detailed replies to Box No. 25, *The Canadian India Times*, Vol. 2, No. 5, April 3, 1969.

(3) Match for a tall, beautiful Jat Sikh (Gill) girl, 21, of respectable family, M.A. student in India. Only Jat Sikh need apply, preferably graduate of a Canadian or American University. Please write to Box No. 30, *The Canadian India Times*, Vol. 2, No. 4, March 20, 1969.

The above advertisements are fairly similar in their emphasis on caste and physical appearance. However, there is an additional emphasis about caste in the advertisements in India. In Canada, the exposure to people from other parts of India has broadened the view about caste and regional differences.

*The Role of Dowry Payments.* When discussing the significance of arranged marriage in India, it is most important to consider the role of dowry payments. Dowry is usually paid by the girl's father which becomes almost an obligation even to the poorest father. There are some variations to the custom.

> Among Sanskritized castes there are certain further rules requiring payment of a dowry by the bride's father and prohibiting divorce and widow remarriage. Among the lower castes (generally the less Sanskritized groups), dowry was not uncommonly replaced by a system of bride-prize and there was no taboo against either divorce or remarriage.[7]

According to a law passed by the Parliament of India on May 9, 1961, to, take or demand dowry is an offence, but the penalty is relatively mild which is only six months in jail and fines up to Rs.5,000 ($700). However, it is difficult to eradicate an age-old custom by legislation since dowry has a definite role to play in the average Indian family. Dowry is paid in lieu of inheritance rights of daughters. The amount varies depending on the financial status of the family and also on the qualifications of the prospective bridegroom. In case a girl is not particularly attractive, a larger amount in dowry can be a compensating factor in clinching a marriage decision.

The custom of dowry payments has become so rigid that families with a number of daughters with only modest financial resources ruin themselves. In some cases, if the girl has a high school or university education she takes up a profession like nursing or teaching, until she is able to save sufficient money to pay for the dowry. An interesting example is Kerala State in south India where literacy is about sixty per cent, which is the highest in India. The predominant majority of nurses in India are from Kerala State which may be a good testimony to the problem faced by girls with education whose parents cannot afford a substantial amount as dowry.

*Adjustment after Marriage.* A question which is often asked by people who have accepted self-choice as the normal manner of mate selection is how it is possible for a couple in India to adjust themselves after an arranged marriage since they are, in a sense, strangers. The assumption is that if a young man and woman know each other in a dating situation for at least one year, the adjustment is easy. However, in actual practice in mate selection, when the two meet each other for several hours a day they are primarily concerned with close emotional ties. Once they get married and live in the same house life becomes different from the romantic situation. One has to face the numerous responsibilities of married life which include, among other things, reasonable efficiency of household management and planning of the limited financial resources, especially in the first years of marriage.

*Too-Great Expectations.* The difference between self-choice marriages and arranged marriages is the relative emphasis on expectations in marriage. In a self-choice marriage a couple falls in love and gets married. However much one might claim that love that precedes marriage in modern urban industrial society is not abstract love, but is also influenced by practical considerations of compatibility, the young man and woman do tend to idealize each other to a great extent. This is very important for maintaining their emotional ties. Therefore, when they get married they have very high expectations of each other. But when they start living together facing the many issues of daily life in a family, problems might arise. These problems can precipitate some amount of disillusionment in each other. This experience of disillusionment is inevitable since both have the maximum of expectations of each other, which is unlikely to be realized in daily life. The majority of the couples are able to overcome this transition from ideal to the practical without much strain because they have adequate, mature personalities enabling them to make adjustments in the early stages of married life. On the other hand, there are many who are not able to make proper adjustments. This is the beginning of serious strain in their relationships. At times the strain which builds up reaches a point where it is impossible to make adequate adjustments.

*Problems of Adjustment.* During these periods of strain, the young couple is primarily responsible for making adjustments without seeking advice from parents, kin, and friends. By the very nature of self-choice where individuality is much valued, and where relationship between parents, siblings and friends is one of mutual respect for each other's individuality, it is not easy to accept advice at the first sign of trouble and also it is difficult for others to initiate help without being accused of some kind of interference. In addition to these problems, survival of self-choice marriages depends to a most significant degree on the continuation of love and common interests. Once these conditions are weakened, the couple will seriously consider the possibility of separation or divorce.

The problems of adjustment in marriage in modern urban families are emphasized in the following comments:

> Consistent with the structural and geographical isolation of the conjugal family unit, parents are not expected to play a significant role in mate selection. In societies having large family systems, parents do typically participate in the selection of mates of their offspring because the new spouse will become a member of another household and kinship units; the parents and other family members have a large stake in the person selected. In our case, however, adjustment between the spouses is paramount, and relationships with other kin are largely irrelevant.[8]

> In the same vein, the fact that the conjugal unit is both structurally and geographically isolated from other kin groups encourages an emphasis on romantic love as the basis for marriage and as the primary reason for staying married. Large kin groups typically discourage the flowering of romantic love because the development of intense attraction between spouses would threaten the priority of their loyalties to parents and the group. Where the large kin group is absent, however, romantic love serves as a kind of substitute for a network of detailed role prescriptions.[9]

> When a husband and wife in our society come into conflict, there is no omnipresent group of kin urging them to moderate their differences and solve their disagreements. The emotional attraction between them is the functionally equivalent substitute therefor.[10]

Divorce in modern urban-industrial society is accepted as an alternative to unhappy marriages where marriage is more a civil contract than a sacrament; therefore the social stigma against divorce is less and less relevant, especially in view of the tendency toward liberalizing divorce laws in most countries. Religion in Western society is fighting a losing battle against the liberalization of divorce laws. The most notable example is the struggle between the Italian government and the Roman Catholic church.

With regard to adjustment in arranged marriages, the young man and woman are married only after the parents and close relatives have made adequate enquiries about their compatibility to each other and also in relation to the two families. In the absence of emotional commitments, it is possible for the elder people to make an objective appraisal of the qualities of the young man and woman. In all the cultures in the world where marriages are arranged these appraisals are made, and the young man and woman are informed of each other's qualities prior to the marriage. As regards the possibility of development of close emotional ties, in addition to each other's qualities they expect only the minimum, but it is no exaggeration to claim that in arranged marriages most of the couples get much more than the minimum from the marriage. One also has to consider the fact that these young people did not meet a number of people before getting married, so much so that they become less critical of each other. In modern self-choice marriages the fact that young people had opportunity to meet many of the opposite sex has not necessarily contributed to the greater success of these marriages.

In modern Western urban families,

> Often, marriage dissolution starts with the early disenchantment that results when a partner first discovers that his mate is incapable of meeting his expectations. [Peter Pireo has pointed out that] Men often suffer disenchantment earlier in marriage than women, perhaps because their expectations are more unrealistic in the first place. But which is the first to be disillusioned is unimportant. Sooner or later one partner's disillusionment will affect the other, and the entire relationship will suffer.[11]

On the other hand, even in Western society, the average girl seems to be realistic about expectations in marriage while the more glamorous girls are more prone to disillusionment. Some years ago, Sidonie Gruenberg and Hilda Kretch suggested that, as far as the reality of expectations was concerned, the less advantaged girls were often luckier than those brought up in luxury. Having had less pampered childhoods, the less advantaged were likely to be much more aware of the realities of the modern marriage relationship, including the long hours of routine involved in actual homemaking and the limitations on one's social life when small children must be cared for.[12]

A further comment with regard to expectation and adjustment in marriage by Professor Richard H. Klemer is most significant:

> In this general vein, I recall that while I was walking through the waiting room of a large marriage counselling clinic, I was struck with the overrepresentation of beautiful women waiting for help with marriage problems. In later discussion with other colleagues, the hypothesis was developed that the plain or average-looking women might have possessed more realistic expectations of what the marriage relationship would provide them in terms of attention from one husband, because before marriage they had not been accustomed to a great deal of attention from large numbers of males.[13]

The saying that in self-choice marriages you fall in love and then get married while in arranged marriages you get married and then fall in love, seems most significant. In arranged marriages the strengthening of the relationships between the couples with love in addition to the objective criteria of compatibility contributes to maximum possible adjustments.

In addition, the sacramental nature of marriage is still dominant in cultures where arranged marriage continues to exist. This means that marriage is viewed as a permanent tie and very little consideration is given to the possibility of separation. Therefore the couple develops a greater sense of tolerance with give-and-take. After all, no two people can be ideally compatible and therefore the greater your willingness to see the other person's point of view the more chances there will be of continued success of such marriages. If there are serious problems in a marriage, other family members will do all they can to help solve such problems. This is not considered as a case of interference since the good relationship between the two families is most important and therefore those people who have taken an interest in arranging the marriage are willing to help the couple in their emotional and financial difficulties. This discussion about the adjustment in arranged marriages is not an attempt to claim that all such marriages are successful. In the past, when family interests were more important than those of the individuals who were getting married, it was difficult to assess the success of such marriages. However, in modern arranged marriages the increasing possibility of expressing individual wishes has weakened the extreme authoritarianism of the families. On the other hand, the role of the family members to provide advice and help continues to be highly valued. This type of modified arranged marriage has definitely a lot to contribute to marital happiness and stability.

## Notes

1. Taya Zinkin, *India Changes* (London, 1958), p. 500.
2. D. A. Chekki, "Mate Selection, Age at Marriage and Propinquity among the Lingayats of India," *Journal of Marriage and Family*, Vol. 30, No. 4, November 1968, p. 709.
3. *Ibid.*, p. 711.
4. S. C. Dube, "Men's and Women's Role in India, a Sociological View." Paper published in *Women of Asia* (U.N.E.S.C.O. 1960), p. 181.
5. Sabeeha Hameduddin, "Arranged Marriages," *Chatelaine*, Toronto, July, 1965, p. 58.
6. *Ibid.*, p. 58.
7. M. S. Gore, "The Traditional Indian Family," *Comparative Family System*, M. F. Nimkoff (Boston: Houghton, Mifflin Co., 1965), p. 219.
8. Gerald R. Leslie, *The Family in Social Context* (Oxford: Oxford Press, 1967), p. 242.
9. *Ibid.*, p. 243. Ref. Talcott Parsons, "Social Structure of the Family," in Ruth N. Anschen, ed. *The Family—Its Function and Destiny* (New York: Harper & Brothers, 1959), pp. 241–274.
10. *Ibid.*, p. 243.
11. Richard H. Klemer, *Marriage and Family Relations* (New York: Harper & Row, 1970), pp. 32–33. Ref. Peter C. Pireo, "Disenchantment in the Later Years of Marriage," *Marriage and Family Living*, 23 (Feb. 1961), 3–11.
12. *Ibid.*, Richard H. Klemer, p. 331. Ref. Sidonie M. Gruenberg and Hilda S. Kretch, *The Many Lives of Modern Women* (Garden City, N.Y.: Doubleday, 1952, pp. 36–50.
13. *Ibid.*, Richard H. Klemer, p. 33.

# Family Stability in Non-European Cultures

*George Peter Murdock*

This paper presents the conclusions of a special study of the stability of marriage in forty selected non-European societies undertaken in an attempt to place the family situation in the contemporary United States in cross-cultural perspective. Eight societies were chosen from each of the world's major ethnographic regions—Asia, Africa, Oceania, and native North and South America. Within each region the samples were carefully selected from widely scattered geographical locations, from different culture areas, and from levels of civilization ranging from the simplest to the most complex. The data were obtained from the collections in the Human Relations Area Files, formerly the Cross-Cultural Survey. The selection was made in as random a manner as possible except that it was confined to cultures for which the descriptive literature is full and reliable. Once chosen, a particular society was rejected and another substituted only in a few instances where the sources failed to provide (1) information on the relative rights of the two sexes in divorce, or (2) evidence permitting a solid judgment as to the degree of family stability relative to that in our own society.

The method, it is believed, comes as close to that of purely random sampling as is feasible today in comparative social science. The results, it must be admitted, contain a number of surprises—even to the writer, who has been steeped for years in the literature of world ethnography. The forty selected societies are listed and located below.

From *The Annals* of the American Academy of Political and Social Science, 1950, 272, pp. 195–201. Reprinted by permission of the author and the American Academy of Political and Social Science.

1. *Asia:* the Chukchi of northeastern Siberia, the Japanese, the Kazak of Turkestan, the Kurd of Iraq, the Lakher of Assam, the Mongols of Outer Mongolia, the Semang Negritos of Malaya, and the Toda of southern India.

2. *Africa:* the Dahomeans of coastal West Africa, the Ganda of Uganda, the Hottentot of South-West Africa, the Jukun of Northern Nigeria, the Lamba of Northern Rhodesia, the Lango of Kenya, the Siwans of the oasis of Siwa in Egypt, and the Wolof of Senegal.

3. *Oceania:* the Atayal aborigines of interior Formosa, the Balinese of Indonesia, the Kalinga of the Northern Philippines, the Kurtatchi of the Solomon Islands in Melanesia, the Kwoma of New Guinea, the Murngin of northern Australia, the Samoans of Polynesia, and the Trukese of Micronesia.

4. *North America:* the Aztecs of ancient Mexico, the Creek of Alabama, the Crow of the high plains in Montana, the Haida of northern British Columbia and southern Alaska, the Hopi pueblo dwellers of Arizona, the Iroquois of northern New York, the Klamath of interior Oregon, and the Yurok of coastal California.

5. *South America:* the Cuna of southern Panama, the Guaycuru of Mbaya of the Gran Chaco, the Incas of ancient Peru, the Kaingang of southern Brazil, the Macusi of Guiana, the Ona of Tierra del Fuego, the Siroino of lowland Bolivia, and the Witoto of the northwest Amazonian jungle.

From these cases it emerges, as a first conclusion, that practically all societies make some cultural provision for the termination of marriage through divorce. The Incas stand isolated as the solitary exception; among them a marriage, once contracted in the presence of a high official representing the emperor, could not subsequently be dissolved for any reason. None of the other thirty-nine societies in our sample compels a couple to maintain their matrimonial relationship where there are reasons for separation that would impress most contemporary Americans as genuinely cogent.

Perhaps the most striking conclusion from the study is the extraordinary extent to which human societies accord to both sexes an approximately equal right to initiate divorce. In thirty of the forty cultures surveyed it was impossible to detect any substantial difference in the rights of men and women to terminate an unsatisfactory alliance. The stereotype of the oppressed aboriginal woman proved to be a complete myth.

The author expected, in line with general thought on the subject, that males would be found to enjoy superior, though perhaps not exclusive, rights in a substantial minority of the cultures surveyed, if not in a majority. They were discovered to possess such prerogatives, however, in only six societies—a bare 15 per cent of the total. In two of the Moslem societies, the Kurd and the Siwans, a husband can dismiss his wife with the greatest of ease, even for a momentary whim. He needs only to pick up three stones and drop them, uttering to his spouse a routine formula of divorce. She has no comparable right; she can only run away and hope that her male relatives will support her. Among the Japanese, divorce is very easy for the husband or by mutual consent, but can be obtained by a woman against the will of her spouse only for serious cause and with considerable legal difficulty. A Ganda man, too, is free to dismiss his wife for any cause, whereas she has no right to initiate a permanent separation. If severely mistreated she can only run away to her male relatives, to whom the husband must justify himself and make amends in order to get her back. For the Siriono it is reported that only men, never women, initiate divorce. A Guaycuru man who wants to terminate his marriage for any reason merely removes for a few days to another hut in the same village, until his wife takes the hint and returns to her family. Women rarely seek a divorce directly, but not infrequently they deliberately act in such a manner as to provoke their husbands into leaving them.

In four societies, or 10 per cent of the total sample, women actually possess superior privileges as regards divorce. Among the Kwoma a wife is relatively free to abandon her husband, but he has no right to dismiss her. His only recourse is to make life so miserable for her that she will leave of her own accord. In the stable form of Dahomean marriage, i.e., that characterized by patrilocal residence and the payment of a bride price, a woman can readily desert her husband for cause, but he cannot initiate divorce proceedings directly; he can only neglect his wife, insult her relatives, and subject her to petty annoyances until she takes matters into her own hands and departs. A Yurok marriage can be terminated at the initiative of either partner, but it involves the return of a substantial bride price. A wife is in a much better position to persuade her male relatives of the justice of her cause than is her husband. His claims are scrutinized with great skepticism, and are often rejected. While in theory he could still agree to an uncompensated separation, no male in his right mind in this highly pecuniary culture would think of incurring voluntarily such a financial loss. A Witoto woman can secure divorce by merely running away. In such a case the husband is always blamed, because people assume that no woman would leave her male protector unless cruelly mistreated. A man can dismiss his wife for cause, but this makes him a target of damaging ridicule and gossip, and unless he is able to justify his action to the complete satisfaction of the local council of adult men, he becomes a virtual social outcast.

Analysis of the relative frequency of divorce reveals that, in addition to the Incas, the stability of marital unions is noticeably greater than in our society among Atayal, Aztecs, Creek, Dahomeans, Ganda, Hopi, Hottentot, Jukun, Kazak, Lakher, Lango, Murngin, Ona, Siriono, and Witoto. In the remaining twenty-four societies, constituting 60 per cent of the total, the divorce rate manifestly exceeds that among ourselves. Despite the widespread alarm about increasing "family disorganization" in our own society, the comparative evidence makes it clear that we still remain well within the limits which human experience has shown that societies can tolerate with safety.

In most of the societies with relative infrequent divorce, the stability is achieved through the mores and the pressure of public opinion rather than through legal enactments and judicial obstacles. The Atayal, Aztecs, and Hottentot constitute partial exceptions. In the first of these tribes divorce is freely allowed for childlessness, but petitions on any other grounds must receive a hearing before the chief. He may refuse or grant the divorce, but in the latter case he usually sentences the guilty party to punishment and may even forbid him or her to remarry. Any other separation is likely to precipitate a feud between the families of the estranged spouses. Among the Aztecs, divorce cases were heard before a special court, and the party adjudged guilty forfeited half of his property to the other. Among the Hottentot, adequate grounds for divorce have to be proved to the satisfaction of a council consisting of all the adult men of the clan, which may order a runaway wife to return to her husband, or award the property of a deserting husband to his wife.

In only two of the societies with frequent divorce is separation effected by the action of constituted authorities—by village officials among the Balinese and by the courts in an action brought by a Japanese woman. Except in these five societies and the Incas, divorce is everywhere exclusively a private matter, and such restraints as are exercised are imposed by informal social pressures rather than by legal restrictions.

The cases reveal clearly some of the devices whereby different peoples have attempted to make marital unions more stable. One of the most common is the payment of a bride price, which comparative studies have shown to be customary among approximately half of the societies of the earth. Contrary to the popular impression, the bride price is almost never conceived as a payment for a purchased chattel. Its primary function nearly everywhere is that of providing an additional economic incentive to reinforce the stability of marriage. In our sample, the sources on Dahomeans, Klamath, Lango, Mongols, Wolof, and Yurok reveal particularly clear evidence of the stabilizing effect of the bride price.

An even more frequent device is to take the choice of a marital partner largely out of the hands of young men and women and vest it in their parents. Most cultures reflect a marked distrust of sexual attraction as a primary motive in marriage, as it is likely to be in the minds of young people, and it seems to be widely recognized that parents, with their greater worldly experience, are more likely to arrange matches on the basis of factors better calculated to produce a durable union. Having been responsible for a marriage, parents tend to feel humiliated when it shows signs of breaking up, and are likely to exert themselves to restore harmony and settle differences. This is attested very specifically for the Haida and the Iroquois, and the evidence shows that the influence of relatives is also a prominent stabilizing factor among Creek, Hopi, Jukun, Kalinga, Murngin, and Ona.

The lengths to which this precaution can be carried in cases of infidelity is well illustrated by the Jukun. A wife first attempts to persuade her husband to give up an adulterous relationship about which she has learned, whereas the husband in a similar situation merely requests a relative or friend to remonstrate with his wife. If the relationship still continues, the innocent spouse reports the matter to the father, uncle, or elder brother of the other, who exerts all the pressure in his power to bring the delinquency to an end. Only after these steps prove fruitless, and the infidelity continues, is a separation effected.

Occasionally, of course, relatives break up a union that is satisfactory to both the parties primarily concerned. Among the Chukchi, for example, the parents of the groom can send the bride home if they become dissatisfied with her at any time within a year or eighteen months after the wedding, and a woman's relatives attempt to break up her marriage if they become estranged from her husband's family at any time, even going to the extreme of carrying off the unwilling wife by force.

In one of the societies of the sample—the Crow Indians—public opinion, instead of exerting its usual stabilizing influence, actually tends to undermine the marital relationship. Divorce is exceedingly frequent, and a man subjects himself to ridicule if he lives too long with one woman. Rivalrous military societies make a sport of stealing wives from one another, and any husband feels ashamed to take back a wife thus abducted from him, however much against her will and his own.

The sources rarely give precise statistics on the incidence of divorce in societies where it occurs most frequently. All we have is fragmentary statements, for instance, that one-third of all adult Chukchi women have been divorced, or that the ethnographer encountered Cuna of both sexes who had lived through from seven to nine successive marriages, or that it is not uncommon to meet a Siwan woman of forty who has been married and divorced more than ten times.

It is nevertheless possible to segregate one group of societies in which the excessive frequency of divorce is confined to recently contracted marriages and dwindles to a rarity after a union has endured for a year or more, especially after children have been born. This is attested, for example, among the Japanese, the Kaingang, the Kalinga, and the Macusi. Among the Trukese, marriages are very brittle and shifting with people in their twenties, but by the end of this early period of trial and error the majority have found spouses with whom they are content to live in reasonable harmony for the rest of their lives.

In other societies, like the Semang, while the rate of divorce subsides markedly after the birth of children, it still remains high as compared with our own. All in all, the sample reveals nineteen societies, or nearly half of the total, in which permanent separations appear substantially to exceed the present rate in the United States throughout the lifetime of the individual. Among them, either spouse can terminate the union with little difficulty and for slight or even trivial reasons among Balinese, Chukchi, Crow, Cuna, Haida, Iroquois, Klamath, Kurtatchi, Lamba, Mongols, Samoans, Semang, Toda, and Wolof. In matrilocal communities like the Cuna or the Iroquois, the husband simply walks out, or the wife unceremoniously dumps his effects outside her door. It is more surprising to encounter an equal facility in divorce among patrilocal and even patriarchal peoples like the Mongols, who see no reason for moral censure in divorce and say in perfectly matter-of-fact manner that two individuals who cannot get along harmoniously together had better live apart.

The societies which condone separation for a mere whim are few. The great majority recognize only certain grounds as adequate. The

Lamba, for whom the information is particularly full, consider a man justified in seeking a divorce if he has been continually harassed by his parents-in-law, if his wife commits adultery or theft, if she has contracted a loathsome disease, if she is quarrelsome or disrespectful, or if she refuses to remain at his home after he has taken a second wife. For a woman the recognized grounds are impotence or loathsome disease in her spouse, his failure to prepare a garden or provide her with adequate clothing, persistent wife-beating, or mere cessation of her affection for him. If the marriage produces no issue, husband and wife argue as to who is responsible, and usually agree to separate. If the woman then bears a child to her new husband whereas the man fails to produce offspring by his next wife, the former husband is so overcome with shame that he usually either commits suicide or leaves the community.

Particular societies recognize interesting special grounds as adequate. Thus the Aztecs, who strongly disapproved of divorce and required proof of substantial cause before a special court, readily granted separation to a woman if she showed that her husband had done less than his share in attending to the education of their children. In general, however, a few basic reasons recur repeatedly as those considered justifiable in a wide range of societies. These are incompatibility, adultery, barrenness or sterility, impotence or frigidity, economic incapacity or nonsupport, cruelty, and quarrelsomeness or nagging. Desertion rarely appears, because it is, of course, not usually a reason for divorce, but the actual means by which a permanent separation is effected. The degree to which the more widespread grounds are recognized as valid in the forty sample societies is shown in Table 1. In order to provide comparability, an entry is made under each heading for every society. Judgments that are merely inferred as probable from the general context, however, are distinguished from evidence specifically reported or unmistakably implied in the sources.

The data in Table 1 reinforce the earlier comment concerning the extraordinary equality of the sexes in rights of divorce revealed by the present study. Where the table shows notable differences, these have relatively obvious explanations. That cruelty is recognized as an adequate ground for women far more often than for men merely reflects their comparative physical strength. The aggression of women toward their spouses is thus perforce directed more often into verbal channels, with the result that quarrelsomeness and nagging become an adequate justification for divorce much more commonly for the male sex.

TABLE 1

Reasons for Divorce
(Forty Sample Societies)

| Reasons | Permitted | | | | Forbidden | | | |
|---|---|---|---|---|---|---|---|---|
| | Definitely | | Inferen-tially | | Definitely | | Inferen-tially | |
| | To Man | To Wife | To Man | To Wife | To Man | To Wife | To Man | To Wife |
| Any grounds, even trivial | 9 | 6 | 5 | 6 | 14 | 13 | 12 | 15 |
| Incompatibility, without more specific grounds | 17 | 17 | 10 | 10 | 6 | 7 | 7 | 6 |
| Common adultery or infidelity | 19 | 11 | 8 | 12 | 8 | 10 | 5 | 7 |
| Repeated or exaggerated infidelity | 27 | 23 | 8 | 10 | 5 | 5 | 0 | 2 |
| Childlessness or sterility | 12 | 4 | 15 | 18 | 7 | 7 | 6 | 11 |
| Sexual impotence or unwillingness | 9 | 12 | 24 | 21 | 3 | 4 | 4 | 3 |
| Laziness, non-support, economic incapacity | 23 | 22 | 11 | 9 | 4 | 5 | 2 | 4 |
| Quarrelsomeness or nagging | 20 | 7 | 7 | 12 | 6 | 11 | 7 | 10 |
| Mistreatment or cruelty | 7 | 25 | 19 | 9 | 3 | 4 | 11 | 2 |

The demonstration that divorce tends to be easier and more prevalent in other societies than in our own does not warrant the conclusion that most peoples are indifferent to the stability of the marriage relationship and the family institution. In our sample, such a charge might be leveled with some justification at the Crow, the Kaingang, and the Toda, but for most of the rest of the data explicitly reveal a genuine concern with the problem. The devices of the bride price and the arrangement of marriages by parents, already alluded to, represent only two of the most common attempts to reach a satisfactory cultural solution. Others, demonstrated by the author in a previous study (*Social Structure*), may be briefly summarized here.

One such device is the taboo on primary incest, which is absolutely universal. There is not a single society known to history or ethnography which does not prohibit and penalize, among the general run of its members, both sexual intercourse and marriage between father and daughter, mother and son, and brother and sister. These universal prohibitions are understandable only as an adaptive provision, arrived at everywhere by a process of mass trial and error, by which sexual rivalry is inhibited within the nuclear family so that the unity and integrity of this basic institution are preserved for the performance of its crucial societal services—economic cooperation, sexual reproduction, and the rearing and education of children.

Nearly as universal are prohibitions of adultery. A very large majority of all known societies permit relatively free sexual experimentation before marriage in their youth of both sexes, but this license is withdrawn when they enter into matrimony. In a worldwide sample of 250 societies, only five—a mere 2 per cent of the total —were found to condone adulterous extramarital liaisons. In many of the remaining 98 per cent, to be sure, the ideal of marital fidelity is more honored in the breach than in the observance. Its very existence, nevertheless, can only reflect a genuine and widespread concern with the stability of marriage and the family, which are inevitably threatened by the jealousy and discord generated by infidelity.

It is clear that approximately as many peoples disapprove in theory of divorce as of adultery. They have learned through experience, however, that the reasons are commonly much more urgent for the former than for the latter, and they consequently allow it wider latitude. The vital functions of the family are not likely to be well performed where husband and wife have become genuinely incompatible. Children raised by stepparents, grandparents, or adoptive parents may frequently find their new social environment more conducive to healthy personality development than a home torn by bitter internal conflict. Even though less desirable than an ideal parental home, since this is unattainable divorce may represent for them, as for their parents, the lesser of two evils.

No society in our sample, with the possible exception of the Crow, places any positive value on divorce. The general attitude is clearly that it is regrettable, but often necessary. It represents merely a practical concession to the frailty of mankind, caught in a web of social relationships and cultural expectations that often impose intolerable pressure on the individual personality. That most social systems work as well as they do, despite concessions to the individual that appear excessive to us, is a tribute to human ingenuity and resiliency.

The cross-cultural evidence makes it abundantly clear that the modern American family is unstable in only a relative and not an absolute sense. From an absolute, that is, comparative, point of view, our family institution still leans quite definitely toward the stable end of the ethnographic spectrum. Current trends could continue without reversal for a considerable period before the fear of social disorganization would acquire genuine justification. Long before such a point is reached, however, automatic correctives, some of them already apparent, will have wrought their effect, and a state of relative equilibrium will be attained that will represent a satisfactory social adjustment under the changed conditions of the times.

APPENDIX.  A DATING SCALE and A FAMILISM SCALE

# A Dating Scale

*Panos D. Bardis*

Below is a list of issues concerning dating. Please read *all* statements very *carefully* and respond to *all* of them on the basis of *your own true* beliefs *without* consulting any other persons. Do this by reading each statement and then writing, in the space provided at its left, *only one* of the following numbers: 0, 1, 2, 3, 4. The meaning of each of these figures is:

0: Strongly disagree.
1: Disagree.
2: Undecided.
3: Agree.
4: Strongly agree.

(For research purposes, you must consider *all* statements *as they are*, without modifying any of them in any way.)

_____ 1. Every person should be allowed to choose his or her dating partner freely and independently.
_____ 2. Girls should be allowed to ask boys for dates.
_____ 3. Boys and girls between 14 and 16 should be allowed to date without any adult supervision.
_____ 4. It is all right to kiss on the first date.
_____ 5. Boys of 12 should be allowed to date.
_____ 6. Boys of 14 should be allowed to date.
_____ 7. Girls of 12 should be allowed to date.
_____ 8. Going on blind dates is all right.
_____ 9. It is all right for dating partners to talk about sex.

From *Social Science*, January, 1962. Reprinted by permission.

_____10. Adult supervision for first dates between 12 and 14 is unnecessary.

_____11. Even when a girl is below 18, it is unnecessary for her parents to meet her boy friend before she first goes out with him.

_____12. Boys of 14 should be allowed to go steady if they wish.

_____13. Boys of 16 should be allowed to go steady if they wish.

_____14. Girls of 12 should be allowed to go steady if they wish.

_____15. Girls of 14 should be allowed to go steady if they wish.

_____16. Young people should make as much love on a date as they wish.

_____17. It is not important for a person to remain pure until marriage.

_____18. It is all right for a young dating couple to park on a lonely road.

_____19. It is all right for a dating couple to kiss in public.

_____20. Persons between 15 and 18 do not have to inform their parents where they will be while dating.

_____21. It is all right for a boy to invite a girl to his home when no one is there.

_____22. It is all right for a girl to invite a boy to her home when no one is there.

_____23. When two young people are serious about each other, it is all right for them to make any kind of love.

_____24. It is all right for a girl to wait for her date in a public place.

_____25. Dating couples between 18 and 20 should be allowed to stay out as late as they wish.

(Score equals sum total of 25 numerical responses. Theoretical range: 0, least liberal, to 100, most liberal.)

# A Familism Scale

*Panos D. Bardis*

(Note: Familism score equals sum total of 16 numerical responses. Theoretical range of scores: 0 (least familistic) to 64 (most familistic). Separate scores may be obtained for "Nuclear Family Integration" and "Extended Family Integration." See PANOS D. BARDIS, "A Familism Scale," *Marriage and Family Living*. November 1959.)

Below is a list of issues concerning the family *in general, not your own*. Please read *all* statements very *carefully* and respond to *all* of them on the basis of *your own true* beliefs *without* consulting *any* other persons. Do this by reading each statement and then writing in the space provided at its left, *only one* of the following numbers: 0, 1, 2, 3, 4. The meaning of each of these figures is:

> 0: Strongly disagree.
> 1: Disagree.
> 2: Undecided.
> 3: Agree.
> 4: Strongly agree.

(A) *Nuclear Family Integration*

_____ 1. Children below 18 should give almost all their earnings to their parents.

_____ 2. Children below 18 should almost always obey their older brothers and sisters.

_____ 3. A person should always consider the needs of his family as a whole more important than his own.

---

From *Marriage and Family Living*, November, 1959. Reprinted by permission of Dr. P. D. Bardis.

_____ 4. A person should always be expected to defend his family against outsiders even at the expense of his own personal safety.

_____ 5. The family should have the right to control the behavior of each of its members completely.

_____ 6. A person should always avoid every action of which his family disapproves.

_____ 7. A person should always be completely loyal to his family.

_____ 8. The members of a family should be expected to hold the same political, ethical, and religious beliefs.

_____ 9. Children below 18 should always obey their parents.

_____10. A person should always help his parents with the support of his younger brothers and sisters if necessary.

(B) *Extended Family Integration*

_____11. A person should always support his uncles or aunts if they are in need.

_____12. The family should consult close relatives (uncles, aunts, first cousins) concerning its important decisions.

_____13. At least one married child should be expected to live in the parental home.

_____14. A person should always support his parents-in-law if they are in need.

_____15. A person should always share his home with his uncles, aunts or first cousins if they are in need.

_____16. A person should always share his home with his parents-in-law if they are in need.